Introduction To Verilog With Vivado

By: Emilio Martinez III

Introduction To Verilog

Contents

Introduction

This book is meant for undergraduate students who are currently enrolled in their very first FPGA course programming with Verilog. This book requires little to no prior knowledge. Ideally you would be an undergraduate student who has already taken logic design or who is enrolled in it concurrently with your FPGA course. The first half of this book will be devoted to nothing but reviewing logic design. The logic design review rivals or even surpasses what could be gained from a reading dedicated logic design book off amazon, due to all the key concepts being covered with intuitive tactics not usually thought. The remainder of the book will consist of many complete Verilog projects all being discussed in detail.

In this book, there will be QR codes to scan. These codes allow you to download the code from the book and simulate the exact circuits discussed! When scanning the QR codes for simulations, you will need to send yourself the link so you can access it on a computer. Every step, every line of code, everything will be shown. You are pretty much getting two undergraduate courses worth of content, since both the logic design and Verilog portion cover all the topics typically taught in a respective undergraduate course. In the Verilog portion of the book, most chapters will correspond to a lab typically assigned in a university course. In each of those chapters, a lab assignment will be provided and then a similar example will be solved step by step. Using the demonstration, you are expected to attempt the provided assignment yourself. It is highly recommended to attempt the assignments yourself since they are all based on what is typically assigned in a university FPGA course. In math when you must solve a problem, it's always a life saver when you find a similar solved example with different numbers right? Well, as powerful as that is in math, this book will be for Verilog.

Verilog is a very important specialization in electrical and computer engineering, so there is usually a greater demand for FPGA programmers. At the companies I've worked at, FPGA programming has consistently been one of the fields in great demand. Few engineers specialize in this field, which is why there is such huge a demand. Becoming skilled in FPGA's will put you on a great track to getting yourself a good career path in something that is in high demand, highly compensated, and in a job where replacing you will be very difficult for engineering firms.

Logic Design Review

Section 1 - Overview & Logic Gates

In the past, digital design would be done with logic design and hand drawn circuits. As time went on, engineers wanted a faster way of making circuits, so they invented Verilog, a high-level description language, which allowed them to describe any circuit. A computer would then take the lines of code written in Verilog and build the physical circuit on the FPGA board for the engineer. In other programming courses, you will write code to generate software, but in this course, we are writing code to generate hardware. What this means is that in order to have a better understanding of the Verilog code you write, you need to first understand the hardware you are wanting to create. This is why a review of logic design is necessary. If you are a student and want an even more comprehensive review of logic design, then you should consider purchasing a dedicated book. Even if you have a dedicated book on logic design, reading this review would still be recommended, since I am going to review only the most important concepts. Also, this chapter is going to highlight some extremely important tricks that you might not know.

To start off, we shall go over the building blocks of logic design. All digital circuits are created through logical gates. Logical gates are devices that use 1's and 0's as inputs to calculate an output that will be either a 1 or 0. Every logic gate will have its 2-terminal version shown below with a description showing the input and output relation. Next are the truth tables.

Logic Gate	Symbol	Description	Boolean
AND	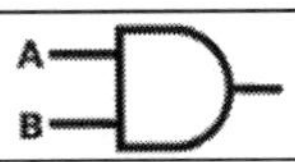	Output is 1 only when all its inputs are 1, otherwise the output is 0.	$X = AB$
OR		Output is 1 whenever one or more inputs are 1. Output will be 0 only when all inputs are 0.	$X = A + B$
NAND	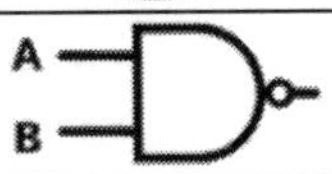	Output is 0 only when all its inputs are at 1, otherwise the output is at 1. This is the opposite of the AND gate.	$X = \overline{A \cdot B}$
NOR	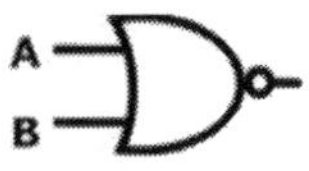	Output is 0 whenever one or more inputs are 1. Output will be 1 only when all inputs are 0. This is the opposite of the OR gate.	$X = \overline{A + B}$
XOR		Output is 1 only when a single input is 1. If multiple inputs are one, or if all the inputs are 0, then the output is 0.	$X = A \oplus B$
XNOR		Output is 1 only when a single input is 1. If multiple inputs are one, or if all the inputs are 0, then the output is 0. This is the opposite of the XOR gate.	$X = \overline{A \oplus B}$
NOT	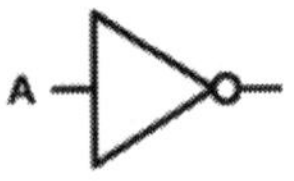	The output is equal to the opposite of the input. If the input is 1, the output is 0. If the input is 0, the output is 1. Unlike other gates, the NOT gate always has a single input and output.	$X = \sim A$

Logic Gate Truth Tables

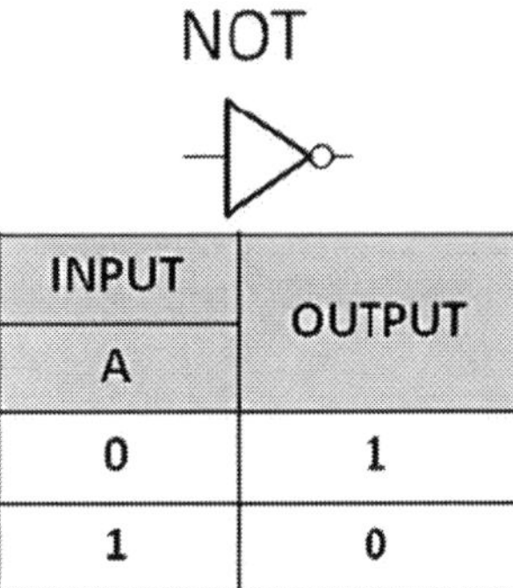

INPUT	OUTPUT
A	
0	1
1	0

AND

INPUT		OUTPUT
A	B	
0	0	0
1	0	0
0	1	0
1	1	1

OR

INPUT		OUTPUT
A	B	
0	0	0
1	0	1
0	1	1
1	1	1

XOR

INPUT		OUTPUT
A	B	
0	0	0
1	0	1
0	1	1
1	1	0

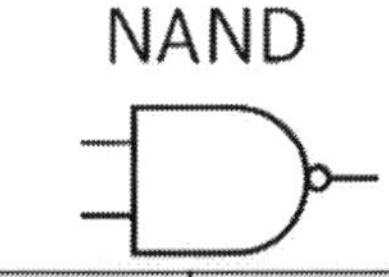

INPUT		OUTPUT
A	B	
0	0	1
1	0	1
0	1	1
1	1	0

INPUT		OUTPUT
A	B	
0	0	1
1	0	0
0	1	0
1	1	0

XNOR

INPUT		OUTPUT
A	B	
0	0	1
1	0	0
0	1	0
1	1	1

Fortunately, these seven gates are all that there is to know for fundamental components. There is nothing else that exists in digital circuits other than these seven gates. Now that you know what the seven building blocks of digital system design are, it's time to start building circuits with them. In digital design, there are only two types of circuits that exist, combinational circuits and sequential circuits.

Section 2 - Combinational Logic Review

To start, we will discuss combinational circuits, since those are much simpler. A combinational circuit is simply just a circuit that takes in inputs and then instantly changes the outputs to reflect those inputs. A combinational circuit is simple since its entire behavior can ALWAYS be modeled by a table, commonly referred to as a truth table. This is great since an algorithm exists for converting any table describing a circuit into its equation form. What this means is that if we want to create a piece of combinational hardware, we write its behavior in a table, use the algorithm to get the equations, and then build the hardware based off the equations.

2.1 Designing with Different Truth Table Sizes

In this section, we will review how to convert 2-variable, 3-variable, and 4-variable truth tables into hardware. At the end of this section, some other tips will be presented. One of the guiding philosophies of this book is that in order to effectively teach, many examples need to be demonstrated before having knowledge tested. For this reason, multiple examples will be shown from start to finish.

Before diving right in with an example, it is important to review the design process steps. Each step is different so stating them is a good way to understand the process.

Combinational Design Process Steps
1) Obtain truth table modeling the behavior. Place inputs on the left and outputs on the right.
2) Map the table to the corresponding K-Map. You will need one K-Map for each output.
3) Circle the 1's and generate the equations from the K-Map.
4) Convert the equations into hardware.

To begin, we will start with a 2-variable table. A 2-variable truth table will always have two inputs, hence the name 2-variable. In general, we shall refer to these inputs as "IN1" and "IN0". These inputs are always placed on the left of the table. There can be any number of outputs and the outputs are always placed on the right. A 2-variable truth table will always have the corresponding K-Map as shown in Figure 2.1.1.

Index	IN1	IN0	Outputs ...
0	0	0	...
1	0	1	...
2	1	0	...
3	1	1	...

IN1 \ IN0	0	1
0	0	1
1	2	3

Figure 2.1.1 2-variable truth table and K-Map

Now that the general format of a 2-variable truth table and K-Map have been introduced, it is time to dive right into an example. The example below shows the process of how a 2-variable table can be converted into hardware using the combinational design process steps.

Example 1

Convert the following truth table into hardware:

Index	A	B	OUT1	OUT2
0	0	0	1	1
1	0	1	1	0
2	1	0	0	0
3	1	1	0	1

Step 1: Table Was Provided

Step 2: Mapping Ones To K-Map

Referring to the general 2-variable table and K-map from Figure 2.1.1, since A is in the position of IN1 on the table, it goes to the location of IN1 on the general K-Map. Since B is in the position of IN0 on the table, it goes to the location of IN0 on the general K-Map. The K-Map with the names substituted is shown below.

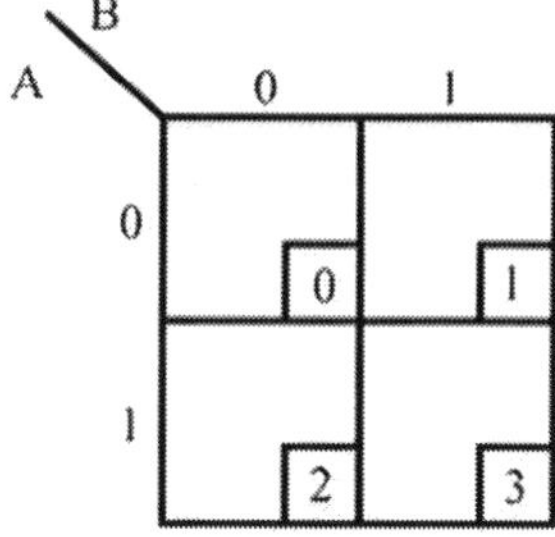

Since there are two outputs, we will need two K-Maps, one for "OUT1" and one for "OUT2". This is because the number of K-Maps is always equal to the number of outputs. In these K-Maps, the little number in the box shows the corresponding row index. Using this, we will copy the output value from each row in the table to the corresponding index in the K-MAP.

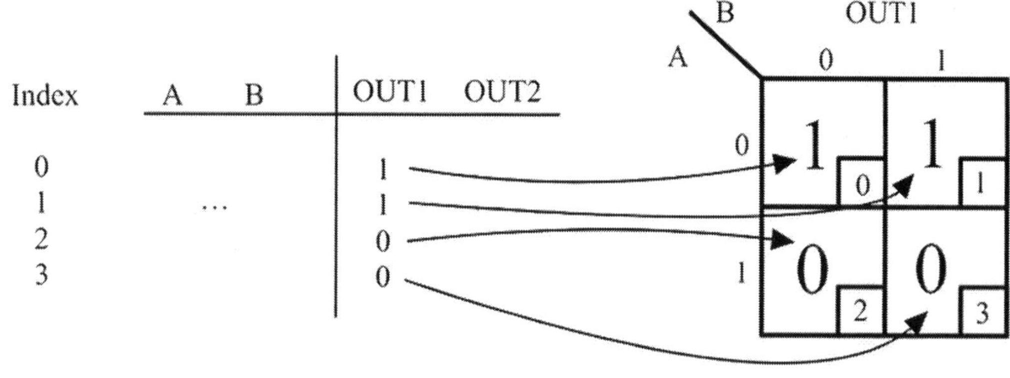

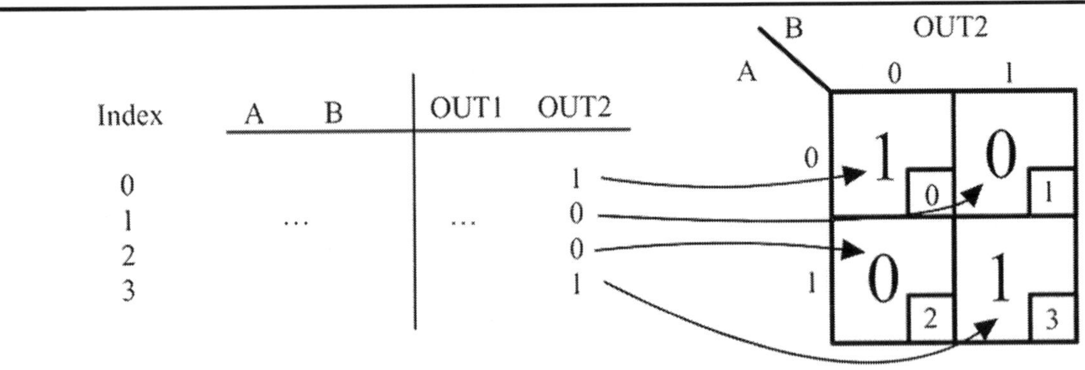

Step 3: Circling Ones & Extracting Equations

Next, we circle ones either individually, or though multiples of 2. For the "OUT2" K-Map, we had no choice but to circle them individually, **since it is forbidden to circle diagonally**.

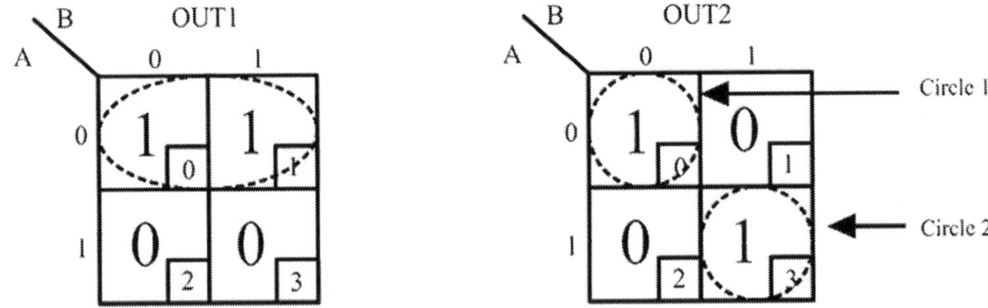

To obtain the equation from a K-Map, one algorithmic approach is to make a table for each circle and extract the terms. Once the table is made, if an input was 1 for all rows, it is included in the term. If an input was 0 for all rows, its inverse is included in the term. If its value alternated between 0 and 1, no variation of that input is included. For the "OUT1" K-Map, we can make the table below. Since only boxes 0 and 1 were circled, the table only has rows corresponding to those boxes. Applying the three rules results in "~A" being the term. Note that "~" is the symbol for the inverse.

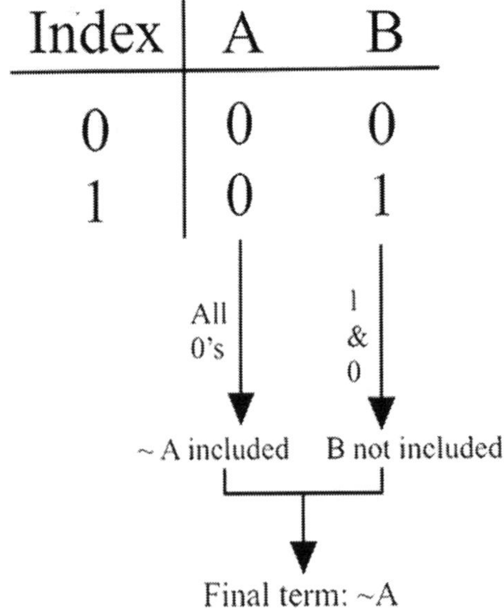

The final expression for "OUT1" will be all the circle terms OR-ed together. Since there is only one circle term, the final expression is the final term of the one circle: OUT1 = ~A

To obtain the equation from the K-Map for "OUT2", we need to make a table for all circled boxes. Since there are two circles, we must make a table for each and apply the algorithm. Since there is only a single 1 in each circle, the tables only have a single row.

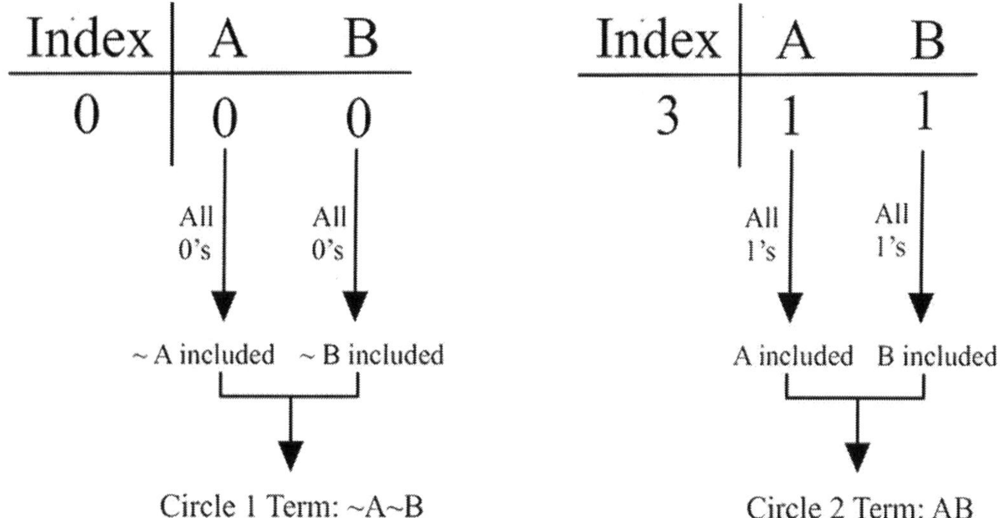

The final expression for OUT2 will be all the circle terms OR-ed together: OUT2 = ~A~B + AB

Step 4: Convert Boolean Expression into Hardware

For OUT1: OUT1 = ~A

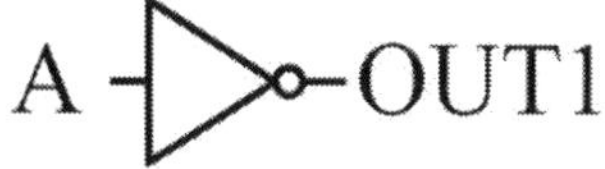

For OUT2: OUT2 = ~A~B + AB

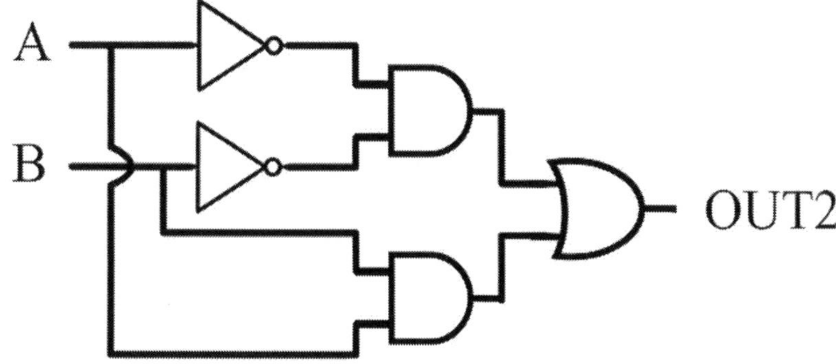

This concludes the example of how to convert a 2-variable table into hardware. If you would like to simulate the results, scan the QR code, and access the link on a computer. If you do simulate it, you will find that the hardware behaves exactly how the table describes.

To continue, we will move on to a 3-variable table. A 3-variable truth table will always have three inputs, hence the name 3-variable. In general, we shall refer to these inputs as "IN2", "IN1", and "IN0". These inputs are always placed on the left of the table. There can be any number of outputs and the outputs are always placed on the right. A 3-variable truth table will always have the corresponding K-Map shown in Figure 2.1.2. Below is a concise example demonstrating how to convert a 3-variable truth table into hardware.

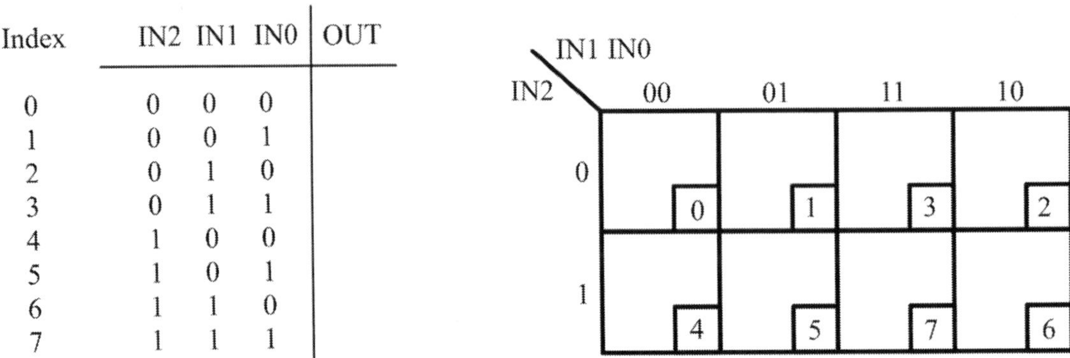

Figure 2.1.2 3-variable truth table and K-Map

Example 2

Convert the following truth table into hardware:

Index	A	B	C	D
0	0	0	0	1
1	0	0	1	0
2	0	1	0	1
3	0	1	1	1
4	1	0	0	0
5	1	0	1	1
6	1	1	0	0
7	1	1	1	1

Step 1: Table Was Provided

Step 2: Mapping Ones To K-Map

For the two numbers on the side, A will simply be 0 and 1. For the numbers on the top, BC will be 00,01,11,10. The reason why it increments like this instead of 00,01,10,11 is because at no time can more than one bit change. The pattern 00,01,11,10 and 0,1 both meet this requirement while simultaneously covering all combinations, which is why they work.

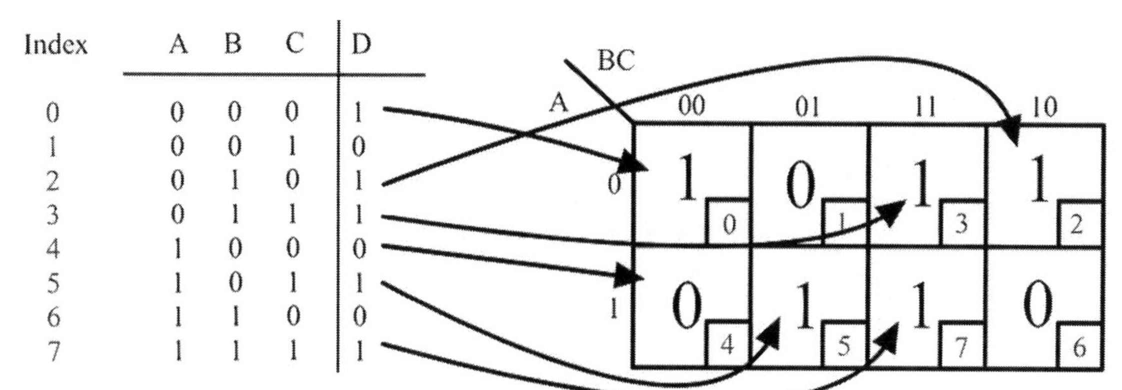

Index	A	B	C	D
0	0	0	0	1
1	0	0	1	0
2	0	1	0	1
3	0	1	1	1
4	1	0	0	0
5	1	0	1	1
6	1	1	0	0
7	1	1	1	1

Step 3: Circling Ones & Extracting Equations

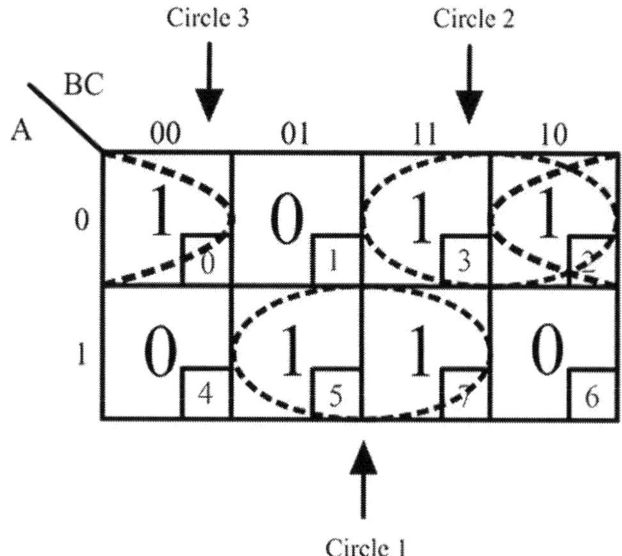

Index	A	B	C
5	1	0	1
7	1	1	1
	A		C

Circle 1 Term: AC

Index	A	B	C
3	0	1	1
2	0	1	0
	~A	B	

Circle 2 Term: ~AB

Index	A	B	C
0	0	0	0
2	0	1	0
	~A		~C

Circle 3 Term: AC

The final expression for D will be all the circle terms OR-ed together: D = ~A~B + ~AB + AC

Step 4: Convert Boolean Expression into Hardware

D = ~A~B + ~AB + AC

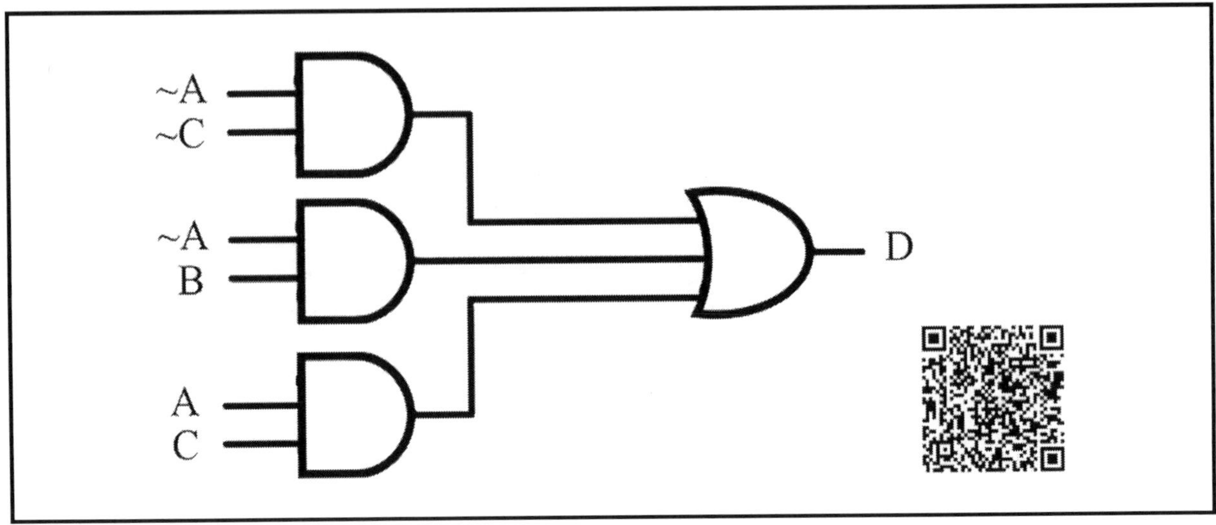

To continue, we will move on to a 4-variable table. A 4-variable truth table will always have four inputs, hence the name 4-variable. In general, we shall refer to these inputs as "IN3", "IN2", "IN1", and "IN0". These inputs are always placed on the left of the table. There can be any number of outputs and the outputs are always placed on the right. A 4-variable truth table will always have the corresponding K-Map shown in Figure 2.1.3. Below is a concise example demonstrating how to convert a 4-variable truth table into hardware.

Index	IN3	IN2	IN1	IN0	Outputs ...
0	0	0	0	0	...
1	0	0	0	1	...
2	0	0	1	0	...
3	0	0	1	1	...
4	0	1	0	0	
5	0	1	0	1	
6	0	1	1	0	
7	0	1	1	1	
8	1	0	0	0	
9	1	0	0	1	
10	1	0	1	0	
11	1	0	1	1	
12	1	1	0	0	
13	1	1	0	1	
14	1	1	1	0	
15	1	1	1	1	

IN3IN2 \ IN1IN0	00	01	11	10
00	0	1	3	2
01	4	5	7	6
11	12	13	15	14
10	8	9	11	10

Figure 2.1.3 4-variable truth table and K-Map

Example 3

Convert the following 4-variable truth table into hardware:

Index	A	B	C	D	Z
0	0	0	0	0	1
1	0	0	0	1	1
2	0	0	1	0	1
3	0	0	1	1	0
4	0	1	0	0	1
5	0	1	0	1	1
6	0	1	1	0	0
7	0	1	1	1	0
8	1	0	0	0	0
9	1	0	0	1	0
10	1	0	1	0	1
11	1	0	1	1	0
12	1	1	0	0	0
13	1	1	0	1	0
14	1	1	1	0	0
15	1	1	1	1	1

Step 1: Table Was Provided

Step 2: Mapping Ones To K-Map

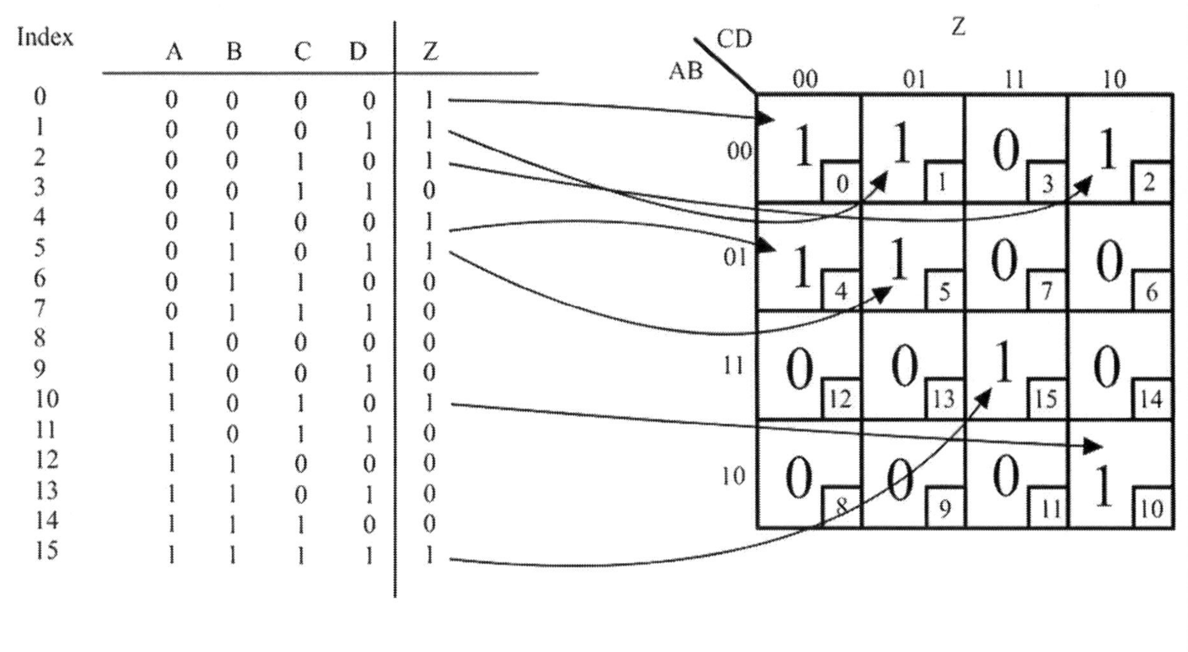

Step 3: Circling Ones & Extracting Equations

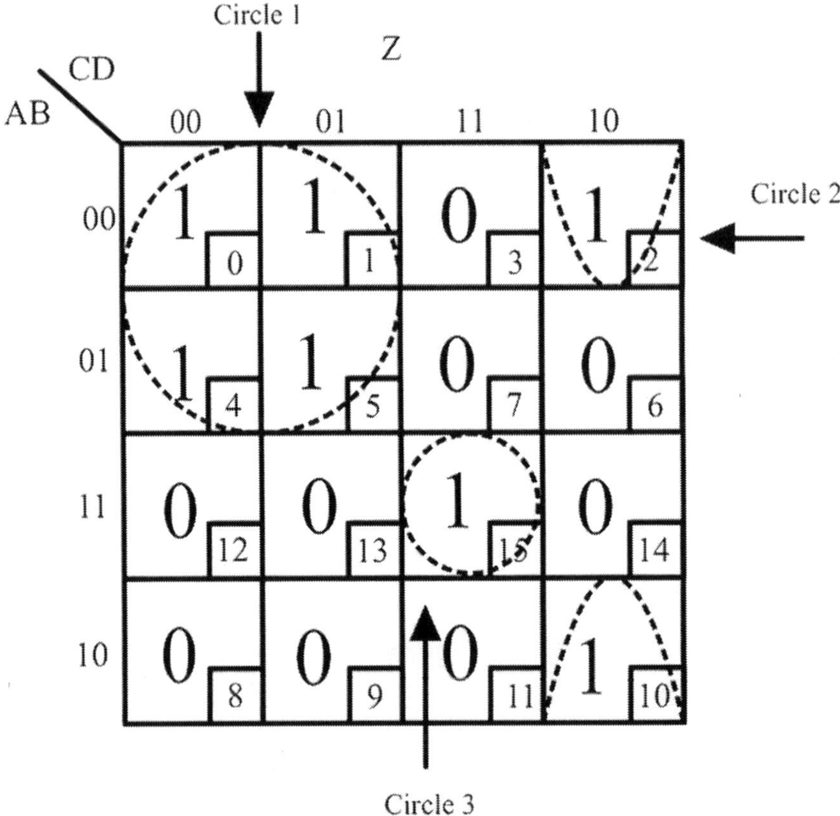

Index	A	B	C	D
0	0	0	0	0
1	0	0	0	1
4	0	1	0	0
5	0	1	0	1
	↓	↓	↓	↓
	~A		~C	

Index	A	B	C	D
2	0	0	1	0
10	1	0	1	0
	↓	↓	↓	↓
		~B	C	~D

Index	A	B	C	D
15	1	1	1	1
	↓	↓	↓	↓
	A	B	C	D

Circle 1 Term: ~A~C

Circle 2 Term: ~BC~D

Circle 3 Term: ABCD

To obtain the final expression for the output, Z, we must OR together the terms from all three circles. When we do this, we get: Z = ~A~C + ~BC~D + ABCD

Step 4: Convert Boolean Expression into Hardware

Z = ~A~C + ~BC~D + ABCD

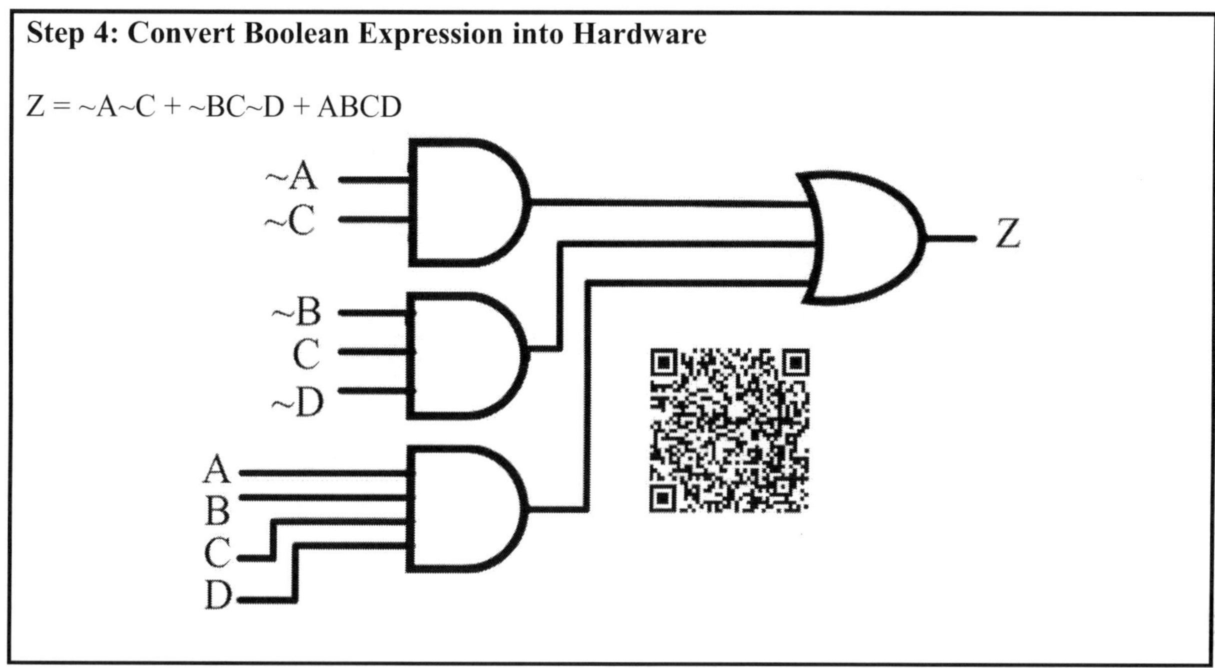

Now that you understand how to solve a K-Map, the next piece of information that needs to be discussed is how to solve a truth table that has don't cares. A don't care is a value in a truth table that is not defined, since it does not matter. It is always marked with an X symbol. Fortunately, taking care of this is extremely simple. The default course of action is to always assign the don't cares a value that leads to the smallest number of large circles. After doing that, you will solve the K-Map normally using the methodology previously discussed. For completeness's sake, a simple example of solving a 2-variable K-Map with don't cares will be shown.

Example 3

Convert the following truth table into hardware:

Index	A	B	OUT1
0	0	0	1
1	0	1	X
2	1	0	0
3	1	1	X

Step 1: Table Was Provided

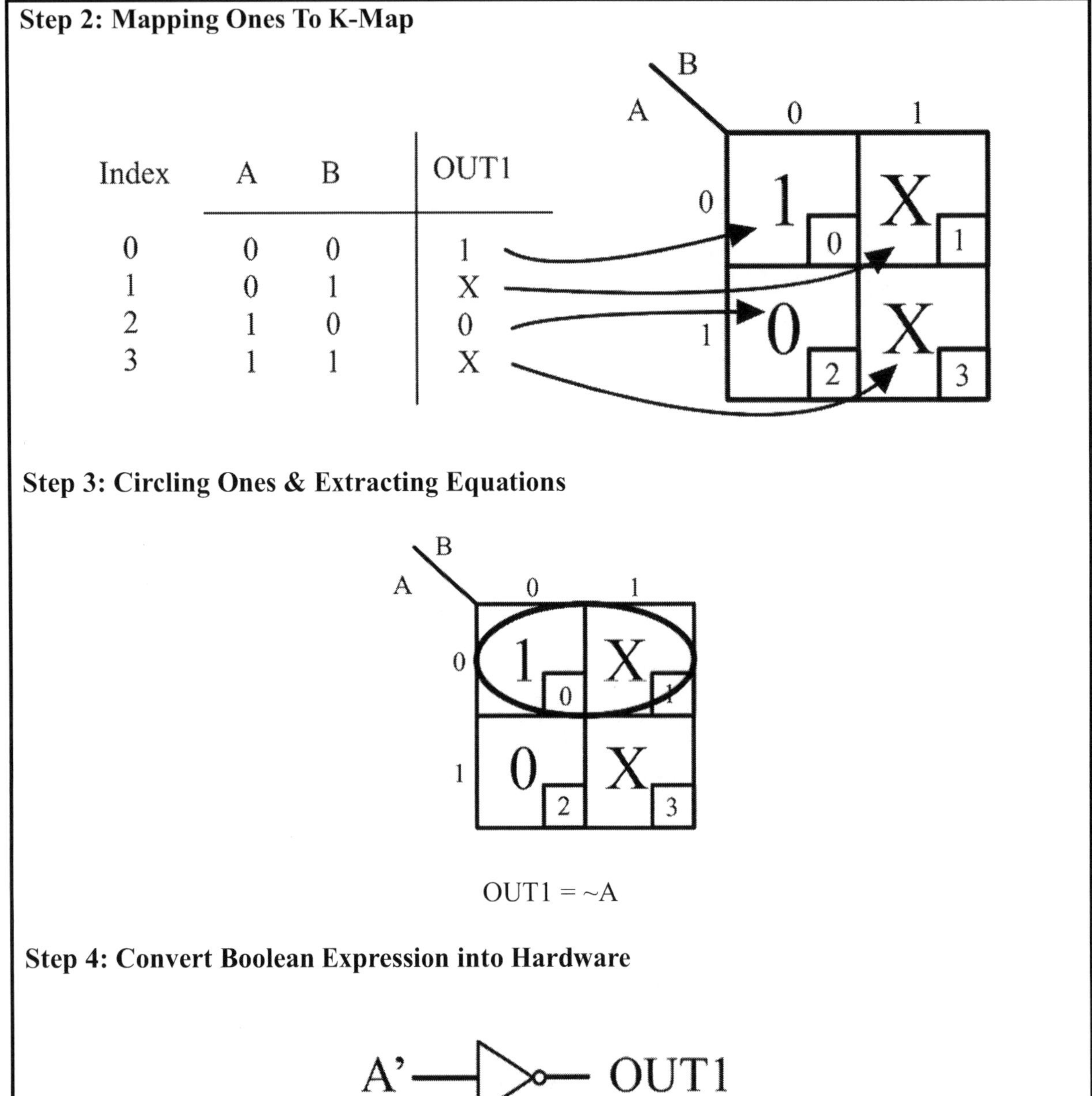

Another important situation to discuss is when you are given a truth table that does not match the template I provided. The template I provided for 2-variable, 3-variable, and 4-variable K-Maps will work 100% of the time, however it can be done differently. In your test, you will often be given a blank K-Map to fill in. This K-Map often may be different than what you are use too. In theory, you could just ignore whatever template is given to you and always use the one from this book to always get the correct answer, however understanding how to do it multiple ways will give you valuable insights as to what's going on. The example that follows shows the conversion of a 3-variable truth table using two different K-Map variations. Both of which were different than the template given in Figure 2.1.2.

Example 4

Convert the following truth table into hardware using the following blank K-Maps. Determine the indices yourself.

IN1	IN2	IN3	OUT
0	0	0	0
0	0	1	0
0	1	0	1
0	1	1	0
1	0	0	0
1	0	1	1
1	1	0	1
1	1	1	1

The first step is to assign numbers to the K-Map. For the top two numbers, it will simply be 0 and 1. The left numbers will be 00,01,11,10. The reason why it increments like this instead of 00,01,10,11 is because at no time can more than one bit change. The pattern 00,01,11,10 and 0,1 both meet this requirement while simultaneously covering all combinations, which is why they work. Next shows this step completed.

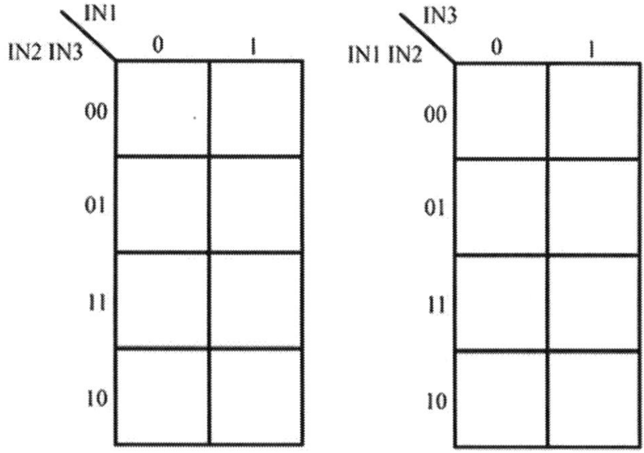

The next step is to fill in the indices. In the table, each row is assigned an index that is equal to the binary value formed by the row's inputs. For the K maps, the binary value was formed by "IN1", "IN2", and "IN3". In case it is unclear, the identification of index 1 of both K-Maps will be shown. The process was identical for the remaining indices.

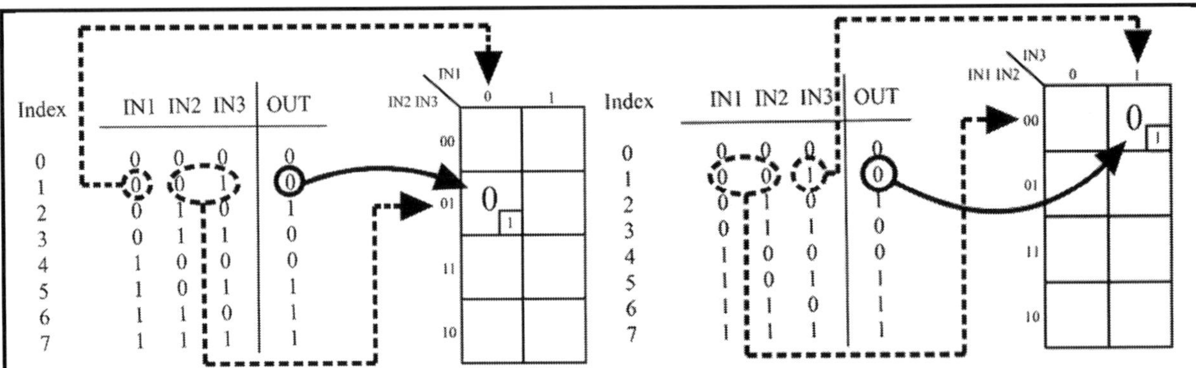

The result of identifying the index for the remaining boxes is the following for both K-Maps.

Index	IN1	IN2	IN3	OUT
0	0	0	0	0
1	0	0	1	0
2	0	1	0	1
3	0	1	1	0
4	1	0	0	0
5	1	0	1	1
6	1	1	0	1
7	1	1	1	1

IN2 IN3 \ IN1	0	1
00	0	4
01	1	5
11	3	7
10	2	6

IN1 IN2 \ IN3	0	1
00	0	1
01	2	3
11	6	7
10	4	5

After filling in the K-Maps, the following is obtained. Both K-Maps yield the same answer, which is to be expected, since both K-Maps were made to solve for the output, OUT.

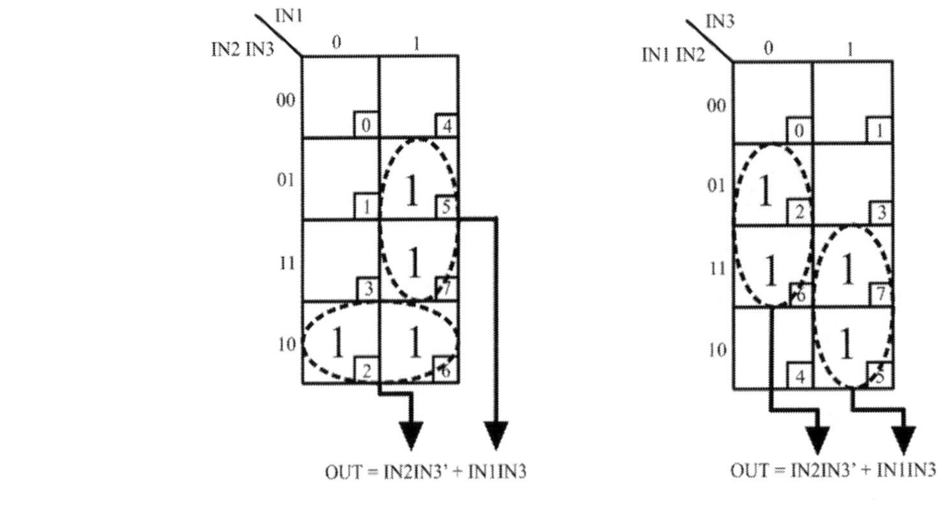

To give you even more preparation, one last example will be provided showing how to deal with a 4-variable K-Map with don't cares and two outputs.

Example 5

Convert the following 4-variable truth table into equations:

Index	A	B	I0	I2	Z1	Z2
0	0	0	0	0	1	1
1	0	0	0	1	0	X
2	0	0	1	0	1	X
3	0	0	1	1	0	0
4	0	1	0	0	0	1
5	0	1	0	1	X	1
6	0	1	1	0	0	0
7	0	1	1	1	X	0
8	1	0	0	0	1	0
9	1	0	0	1	0	X
10	1	0	1	0	1	1
11	1	0	1	1	0	X
12	1	1	0	0	0	0
13	1	1	0	1	X	0
14	1	1	1	0	0	0
15	1	1	1	1	1	1

Step 1: Table Was Provided

Step 2: Mapping Ones To K-Map

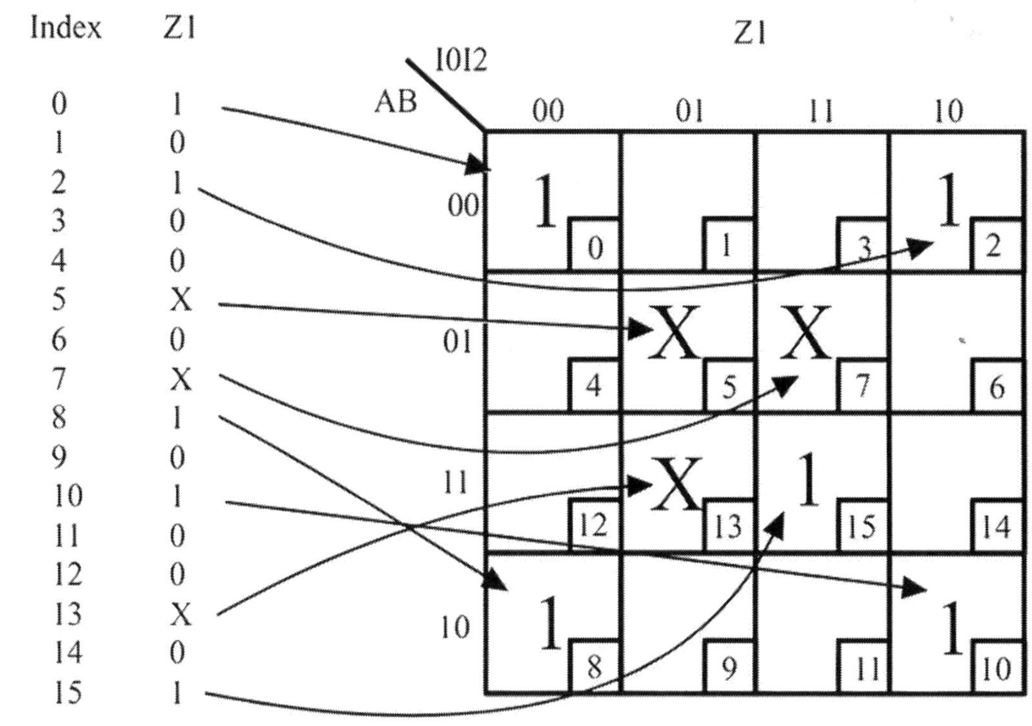

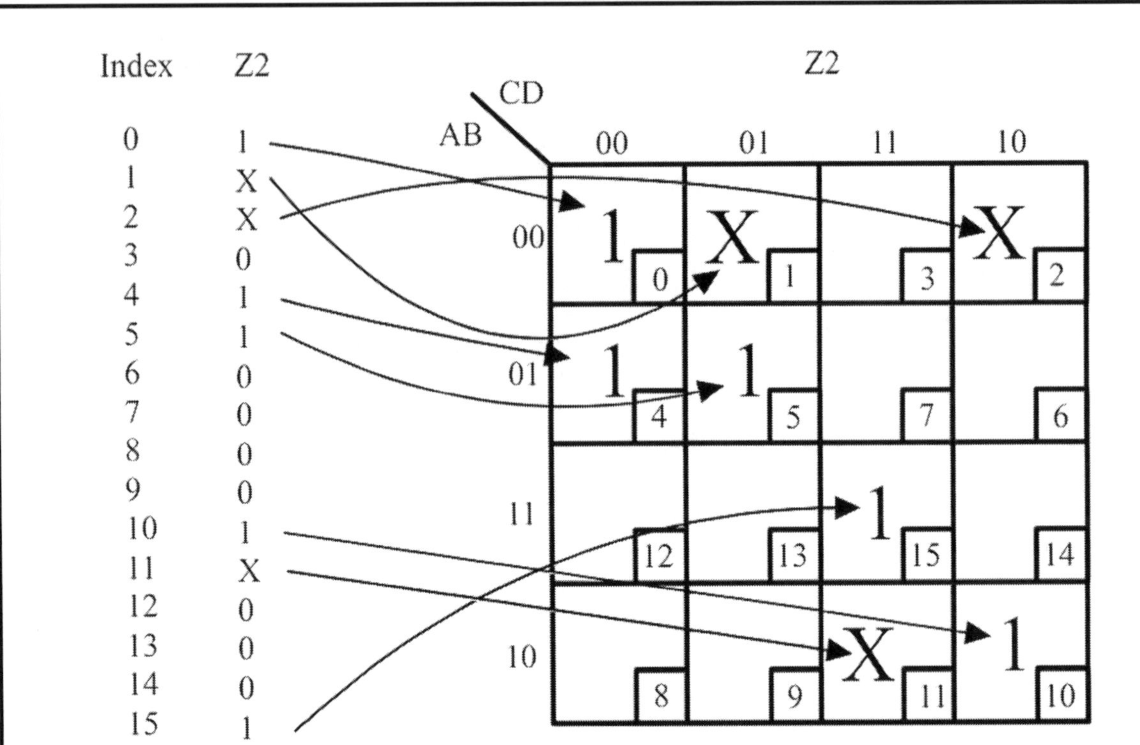

Step 3: Circling Ones & Extracting Equations

Below is the K-Map for Z1. Circle 1 is a wrap around type of circle and is valid. The wrap around technically does not violate the rule of no diagonals, since the parts of circle 1 are connected by going up and to the side, not diagonally. Circle 2 had all the don't cares assigned a value of 1 so that way circle 2 could be as large as possible. The larger the circle, the better. The fewer the circles the better too.

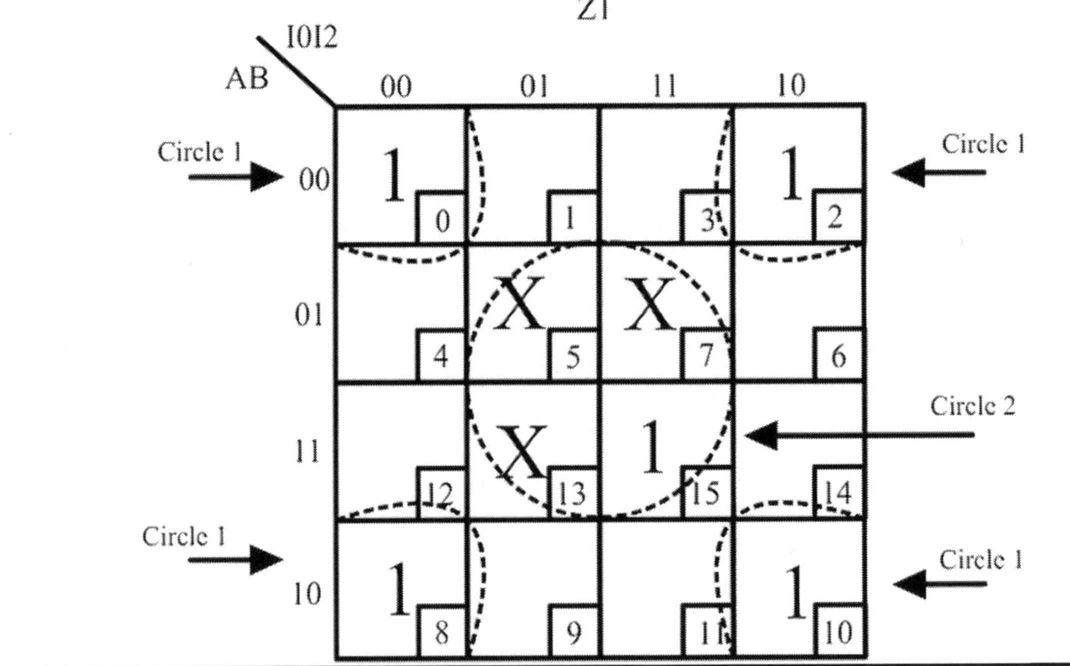

Index	A	B	I0	I2
0	0	0	0	0
2	0	0	1	0
8	1	0	0	0
10	1	0	1	0
	↓	↓ ~B	↓	↓ ~I2

Circle 1 Term: ~B~I2

Index	A	B	I0	I2
5	0	1	0	1
7	0	1	1	1
13	1	1	0	1
15	1	1	1	1
	↓	↓ B	↓	↓ I2

Circle 2 Term: BI2

To obtain the final expression for the output, Z2, we must OR together the terms from the circles. When we do this, we get: Z1 = ~B~I2 + BI2

Below is the K-Map for Z2. The don't care in box 1 was assigned a value of 1 so that way circle 1 could be made to encompass all three 1's in boxes 0, 4, and 5. The don't care in box 11 was also assigned a value of 1 so that was circle 2 and 3 would be larger. If 0 was assigned to the don't care in box 11, then circle 2 and 3 would have been smaller, leading to a solution that though still correct, is less simplified. The don't care in box 2 was assigned a value of 0. Assigning it a value of 1 would have created an extra circle that was not needed to encompass the original 1's in boxes 0, 4, 5, 15, and 10, leading to a solution that though still correct, is less simplified.

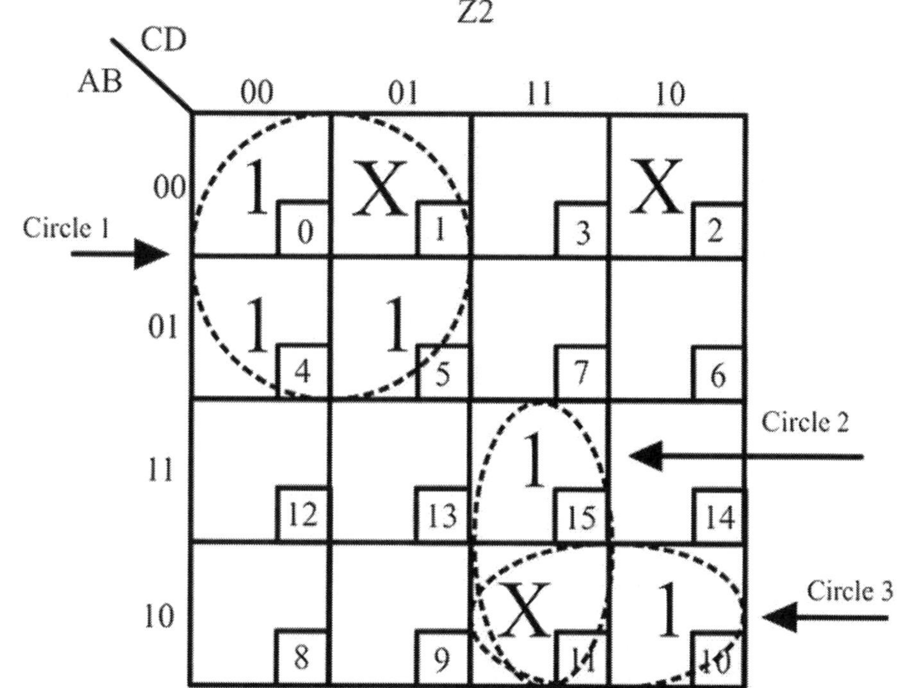

Index	A	B	I0	I2
0	0	0	0	0
1	0	0	0	1
4	0	1	0	0
5	0	1	0	1
	↓ ~A	↓	↓ ~I0	↓

Index	A	B	I0	I2
15	1	1	1	1
11	1	0	1	1
	↓ A	↓	↓ I0	↓ I2

Index	A	B	I0	I2
10	1	0	1	0
11	1	0	1	1
	↓ A	↓ B	↓ I0	↓

Circle 1 Term: ~A~I0

Circle 2 Term: AI0I2

Circle 2 Term: ABI0

To obtain the final expression for the output, Z2, we must OR together the terms from all three circles. When we do this, we get: Z2 = ~A~I0 + AI0I2 + ABI0

Z1 = ~B~I2 + BI2

Z2 = ~A~I0 + AI0I2 + ABI0

2.2 Building a 2:1 Mux with Combinational Logic

In this chapter, we will go over how to create a 2:1 multiplexer. A 2:1 multiplexer is a very important combinational piece of hardware that you should be very familiar with. In case you are not, do not worry, it will be reviewed.

To start, a 2:1 multiplexer acts like an electrical switch. In the figure below, its two signal inputs are labeled "I0" and "I1," and the control input that chooses which signal connects to the output, "out" is called "sel." For instance, if "sel" is set to 1, then the "I1" signal connects to the output. If "sel" is set to 0, then the "I0" signal is connected instead, as illustrated in the figure below. To physically simulate a 2:1 multiplexer, scan the QR code and follow the link on a computer for it to function correctly. Note that the simulation also includes a 4:1 multiplexer to give an idea of what a larger multiplexer looks like.

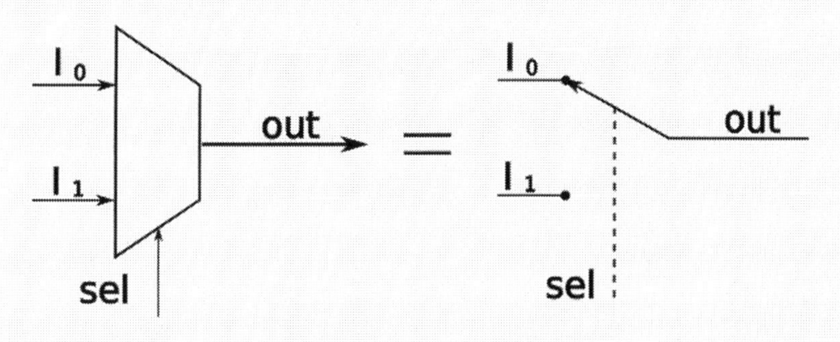

Figure 2.2.1 2:1 Multiplexer

Before we can think about how to build a 2:1 multiplexer, let's analyze the behavior. Imagine that inputs {I1, I0, sel} are equal to {0,0,0}. Since "sel" is zero, that means "out" will obtain the value of "I0", which is 0. Using this we can write {0,0,0,0} in the 1st row, at index 0, of the table. What if inputs {I1, I0, sel} are equal to {0,0,1}? Since "sel" is 1, that means "out" will obtain the value of "I1", which is 0. Using this we can write {0,0,1,0} in the 2nd row, at index 1, of the table. Again, imagine that inputs {I1 ,I0, sel} are equal to {0,1,0}. Since "sel" is zero, that means "out" will obtain the value of "I0", which is 1. Using this we can write {0,1,0,1} in the 3rd row, at index 2, of the table. Repeating this by testing what the output will be for the remaining 5 possibilities results in the truth table below.

Index	I1	I0	sel	out
0	0	0	0	0
1	0	0	1	0
2	0	1	0	1
3	0	1	1	0
4	1	0	0	0
5	1	0	1	1
6	1	1	0	1
7	1	1	1	1

Figure 2.2.2 Truth table for 2:1 multiplexer

Now that we have the behavior of the circuit modeled in a truth table, we can finally re-introduce the algorithm that is used to convert the table into equations. The example below demonstrates the algorithm being used.

Example 1

Convert the following truth table into hardware:

Index	I1	I0	sel	out
0	0	0	0	0
1	0	0	1	0
2	0	1	0	1
3	0	1	1	0
4	1	0	0	0
5	1	0	1	1
6	1	1	0	1
7	1	1	1	1

Step 1: Table Was Generated

Step 2: Mapping Ones To K-Map

The truth table we are using here is a 3-variable truth table, so we will be mapping it to the K-Map that corresponds to a 3-variable truth table.

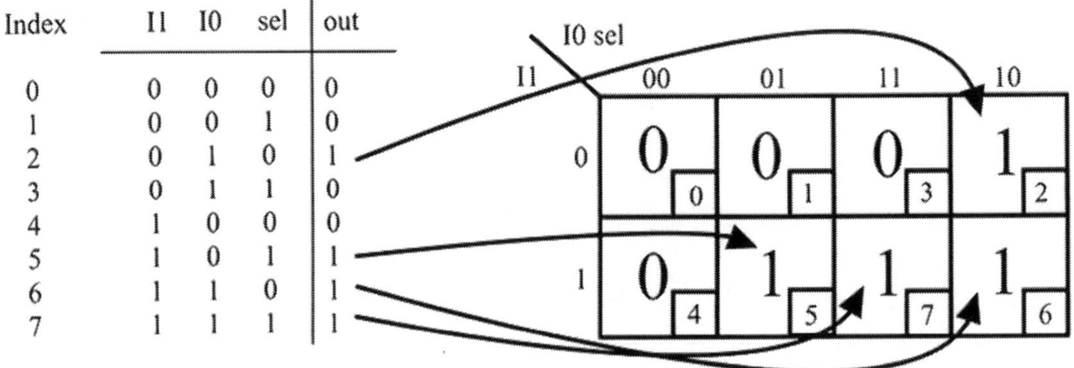

Step 3: Circling Ones & Extracting Equations

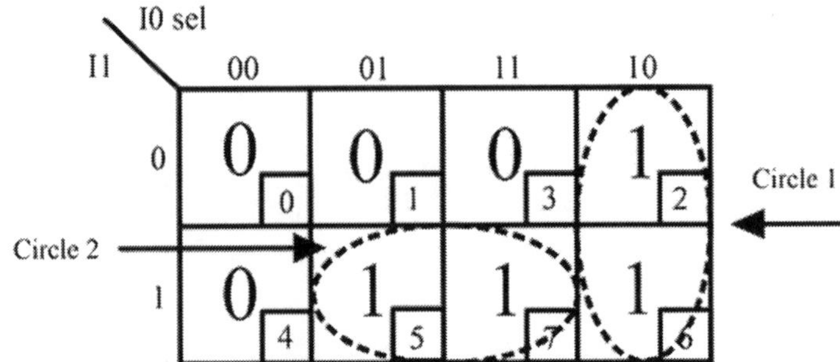

Index	I1	I0	sel
2	0	1	0
6	1	1	0
	↓	↓	↓
		I0	~sel

Index	I1	I0	sel
5	1	0	1
7	1	1	1
	↓	↓	↓
	I1		sel

Circle 1 Term: I0~sel

Circle 2 Term: I1sel

To obtain the final expression for the output, "out", we must OR together the terms from both circle 1 and circle 2. When we do this, we get the following: out = I0~sel + I1sel

Step 4: Convert Boolean Expression into Hardware

Since we now know the equation, the final step to build our circuit is to build it using gates. Since we have the first term, "I1sel", we know that we will need an AND gate AND-ing both "I1" and "sel" together. Since we have "I0~sel", we know that we will need an AND gate AND-ing both "I0" and the "~sel". Since "~sel" is inverted, there will need to be an inverter gate in front of "sel". Lastly, since both terms are being OR-ed together, we will need an OR gate. Below shows the result. You may access the QR code to simulate it to verify that this is correct.

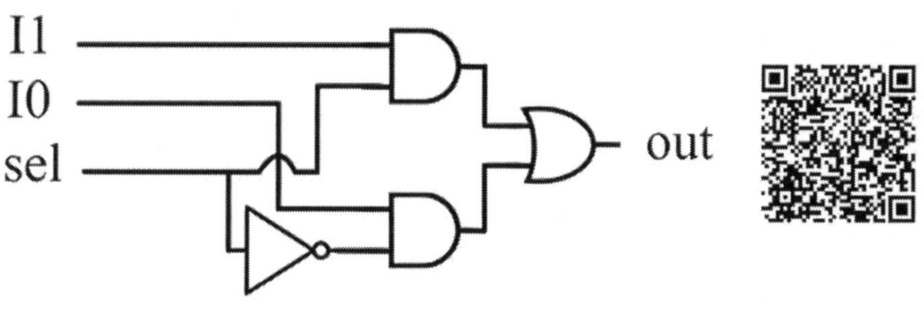

Now that you know how to create a 2:1 multiplexer from scratch, you may be wondering, 'Could I use the same approach to create a 4:1 multiplexer, an 8:1 multiplexer, or even a 32:1 multiplexer?' Technically, you could; however, in practice, this would be nearly impossible. The reason is that the truth tables would become too large to process with K-Maps. For example, in an 8:1 multiplexer, there would be eight data inputs and three selection inputs. This would mean that the truth table for an 8:1 mux would have 11 inputs. Since the formula for determining the rows of a truth table is #Rows = 2 , there would be $2^{11} = 2048$ rows! Solving a K-Map with that many rows is impossible without a super computer. You may be wondering how large multiplexers are made knowing that you cannot use K-Maps. The answer is through modularization. Modularization is an extremely important tool in digital design. Your very first lab writing code will be to implement a 4:1 mux by using modularization. This will be discussed more in depth in the chapter devoted to lab two.

2.3 Minterm & Maxterm representation

In logic design, truth tables may not be represented using a table or K-Map. Sometimes to represent a truth table, we represent it in what is called the minterm or maxterm representation. The minterm representation is just the summation of all the rows that are one. The maxterm representation is just the summation of all the rows that are zero. For example, if we have the following truth table:

Index	A	B	C	F
0	0	0	0	0
1	0	0	1	0
2	0	1	0	1
3	0	1	1	0
4	1	0	0	0
5	1	0	1	1
6	1	1	0	1
7	1	1	1	1

Figure 2.3.1 3-variable truth table and K-Map

Then we can say that the minterm representation will be $F(A, B, C) = \sum(2,5,6,7)$, since rows indices 2, 5, 6, and 7 have the output F, equal to one. The maxterm representation is $F(A, B, C) = \prod(0,1,3,4)$, since rows indices 0, 1, 3, and 4 have the output F, equal to zero. Often you will only be given the minterm or maxterm representation of a system and you will have to generate the truth table for it yourself.

2.4 Sum of Products (SOP)

Sum of products, or SOP for short, refers to the format of a Boolean equation where the literals are AND-ed together to form terms and then these terms are then OR-ed together to get the full expression. The definition of both a literal and a term are shown next. Examples of SOP expressions are also shown.

Terminology
Literal: A literal is a single Variable. It can be inverted or not. For example, "A" and "~A" are both literals. Term: A term is a bunch of literals AND-ed together. For example, in the expression Z =ABC + CD, "ABC" and "AC" would be considered terms. It is also possible for a literal to be a term. For example, in the expression F = AB + C, both "AB" and "C" would be considered terms.

Example 1

The following expressions are all in SOP format, since they consist of terms being OR-ed together:

$F = AB + C'$
$F = A'B + CD + AC + A'$
$F = ABC$

One great thing about minterm notation is that you can directly obtain an unsimplified SOP expression from it. Using the previous example, $F(A, B, C) = \sum(2,5,6,7)$, this will be shown. Remember that the truth table represented by this minterm notation can be found on page 30.

Example 2

Extract the SOP Equation from $F(A, B, C) = \sum(2,5,6,7)$.

2 = 0 1 0 → A' B C'
5 = 1 0 1 → A B' C
6 = 1 1 0 → A B C'
7 = 1 1 1 → A B C

$F = A'BC' + AB'C + ABC' + ABC$

As you can see, you first begin by changing the minterm from decimal to binary, then for each row, you replace the leftmost digit with A (if 1) or A′ (if 0). You replace the middle digit with B (if 1) or B′ (if 0). You replace the rightmost digit with C (if 1) or C′ (if 0). This simple algorithm will always work for converting the truth table into a SOP equation. If you want to obtain the simplified SOP expression, then you must use a K-Map.

2.5 Product of Sums (POS)

Product of Sums, or POS for short, refers to the format of a Boolean equation where the literals are OR-ed together to form addition terms and then these terms are then AND-ed together to get the full expression. The definition of both a literal and an addition term are shown next. Examples of POS expressions are also shown.

Terminology

Literal: A literal is a single Variable. It can be inverted or not. For example, "A" and "~A" are both literals.

Addition Term: An Addition term is a bunch of literals OR-ed together. For example, in the expression Z = (A+B+C)(C+D), "(A+B+C)" and "(C+D)" would be considered addition terms. It is also possible for a literal to be an addition term. For example, in the expression F = (A+B)C, both "(A+B)" and "C" would be considered addition terms.

Example 1

The following expressions are all in POS format, since they consist of addition terms being AND-ed together:

F = (A+B)C′
F = (A′+B)(C+D)(A+C)A′
F = (A+B+C)

One great thing about maxterm notation is that you can directly obtain an unsimplified POS expression from it. Using the previous example, $F(A,B,C) = \prod(0,1,3,4)$, this will be shown. Remember that the truth table represented by this maxterm notation can be found on page 30.

Example 2

Extract the POS Equation from $F(A,B,C) = \prod(0,1,3,4)$

0 = 0 0 0 → 1 1 1 → (A+B+C)
1 = 0 0 1 → 1 1 0 → (A+B+C')
3 = 0 1 1 → 1 0 0 → (A+B'+C')
4 = 1 0 0 → 0 1 1 → (A'+B+C)

F = (A+B+C)(A+B+C')(A+B'+C')(A'+B+C)

As you can see, you first begin by changing the minterm from decimal to binary, then we invert it. Next, you replace the leftmost digit with A (if 1) or A′ (if 0). You replace the middle digit with B (if 1) or B′ (if 0). You replace the rightmost digit with C (if 1) or C′ (if 0). You insert a plus sign between each literal this time since these are addition terms. Once you have created all the addition terms, they are all AND-ed together to get the final expression for F. This simple algorithm will always work for converting the truth table into a POS equation. If you want to obtain the simplified SOP expression, then you must use a K-Map.

2.6 Converting an SOP expression to POS

Now that you are familiar with how to convert a truth table into SOP or POS by using the minterm or maxterm notation, it is time to go over how to convert between the two types. Also, we will go over how to obtain the minimal SOP or POS expression given an equation or truth table.

Say we have the following minimized SOP expression: F = AB + C. This expression is already simplified, so how could we obtain its original K-Map? Well, from the expression, we know that it is a 3-variable K-Map, since there are only three inputs A, B, and C. So, we can already draw the following.

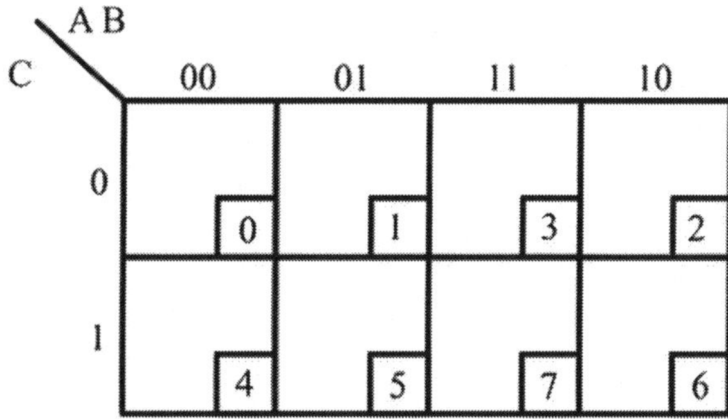

Figure 2.6.1 3-Variable K-Map

We know that the AB term comes from a circle with two boxes where both boxes have A and B as one and C different. The only possible circle that represents this would be below.

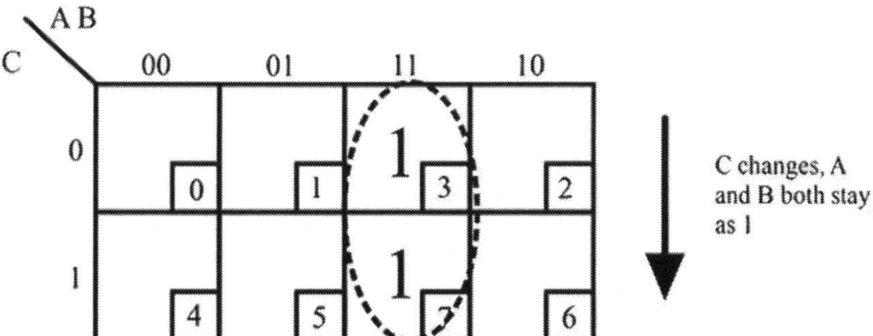

Figure 2.6.2 3-Variable K-Map with AB term

We know that the C term has a circle with four boxes, where all four boxes have C as one. Both A and B change though these boxes, so they are eliminated. The only possible circle that represents this behavior is shown next.

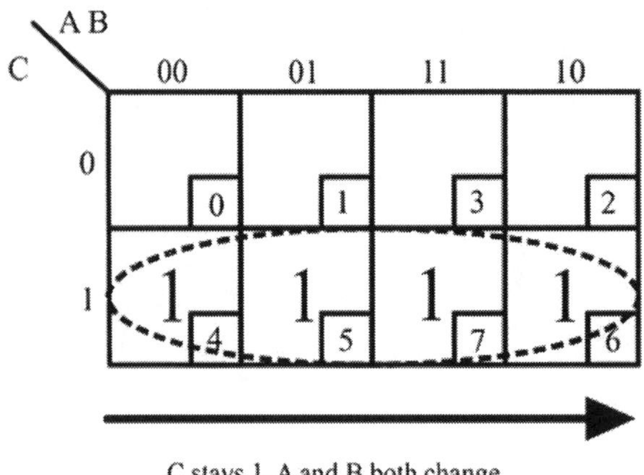

Figure 2.6.3 3-Variable K-Map with C term

Now putting it all together, we can conclude that the original K-Map must be the following:

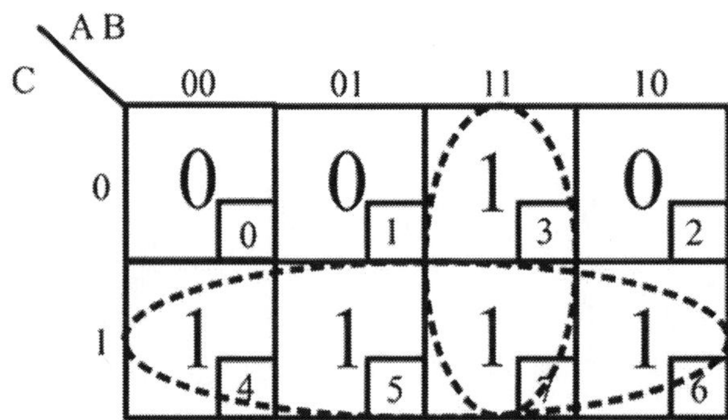

Figure 2.6.4 3-Variable K-Map with AB & C term

Now that we have the K-Map, the only step that remains is to extract the POS expression from it. Now we could easily note that the minterm expression of the table is $F(A, B, C) = \prod(0,1,2)$ and use this minterm notation to directly obtain an unsimplified POS expression. But how would we obtain a simplified POS expression? Well just like how there was an algorithm to circle ones to generate the simplified SOP expression with a K-MAP, a similar algorithm exists for SOP. The steps to execute this algorithm will be shown in the example below using the K-Map we reverse engineered.

Example 1

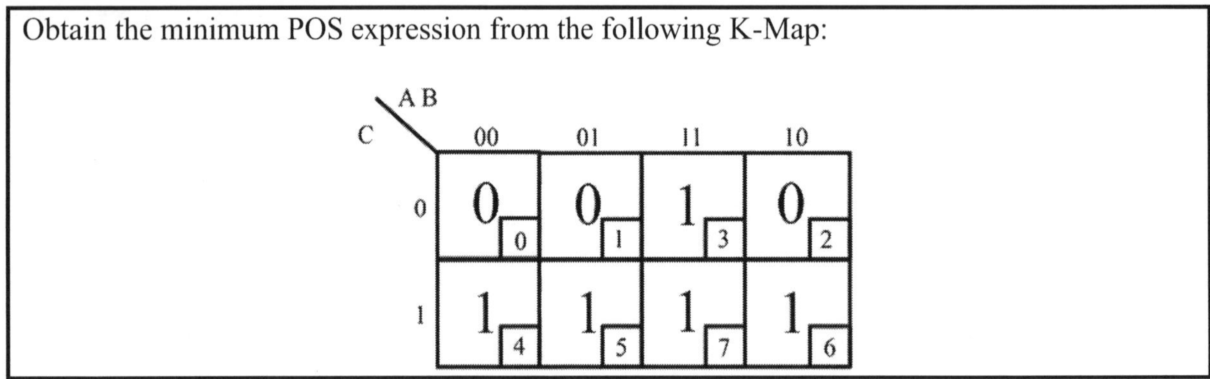
Obtain the minimum POS expression from the following K-Map:

Step 1: Circle The Zeros, Instead Of Ones.

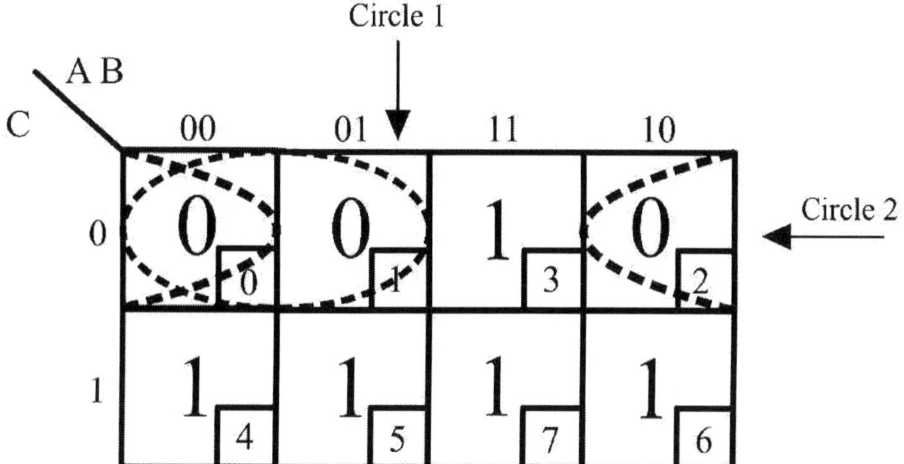

Step 2: Generate The Corresponding Equations For Each Circle As If They Were Ones.

Circle 1 Table:

Index	A	B	C
0	0	0	0
1	0	0	1

~A ~B

Circle 2 Table:

Index	A	B	C
0	0	0	0
2	0	1	0

~A ~C

F = ~A~B + ~A~C

Step 3: Invert Each Literal.

F = AB + AC

Step 4: Change The AND Operators To OR Operators & The OR Operators To AND Operators.

F = (A+B)(A+C)

So, there you have it! We have successfully converted the expression from a minimized SOP expression, F = AB + C, into its minimized POS expression, F = (A+B)(A+C). This simple algorithm can always be used to convert an SOP expression to a POS expression. All you do is reverse engineer the K-Map, then apply the previous steps after circling the zeros.

2.7 Converting a POS expression to SOP

If you have a minimized POS expression and would like to obtain the minimized SOP expression, all you need to do is reverse engineer the K-Map, then solve it by circling the ones and finding the equations. Here is a quick example of how to reverse engineer a K-MAP from a POS expression to get the minimal SOP expression.

Example 1

Given the POS expression Z = (A+B)(C+D+A)B, find the minimal SOP expression.

To start off, we know that the given equation, Z = (A+B)(C+D+A)B, has three addition terms, (A+B), (C+D+A), and B. We can apply step 4 from the previous example in reverse by changing the OR operators to AND operators & the AND operators to OR operators:

Z = (A+B)(C+D+A)B ⟶ Z = AB + CDA + B

If we apply step 3 of the previous example in reverse and invert the literals, we get the following:

Z = AB + CDA + B ⟶ Z = ~A~B + ~C~D~A + ~B

Now we just need to find out what circles correspond to each of the terms. We know it's a 4-variable K-Map, since there are four variables "A", "B", "C" and "D". We know that the ~A~B term comes from a circle with four boxes where both boxes have A and B as zero with C and D changing. We know it must be a circle with four boxes, since this is a 4-variable K-MAP, and only a circle with 4 boxes will reduce the term from 4 to 2 literals. The only possible circle that represents this would be below. Remember that there are zeros in the circle, not ones, because we are applying step 2 of the previous example in reverse.

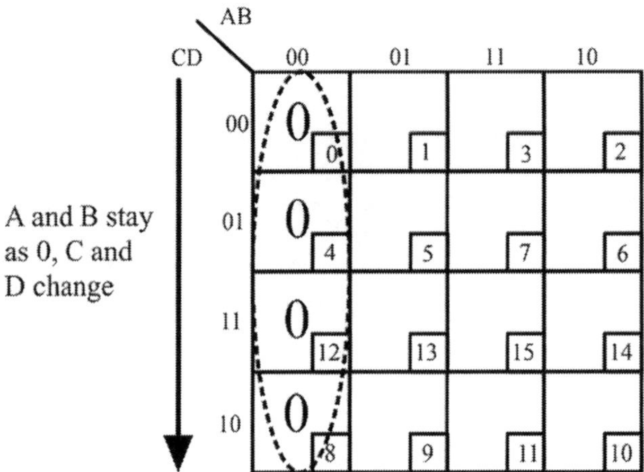

We know that the ~C~D~A term comes from a circle with two boxes where both boxes have C, D, and A as zero and B changing. We know it must be a circle with two boxes, since this is a 4-variable K-MAP, and only a circle with 2 boxes will reduce the term from 4 to 3 literals. The only possible circle that represents this is shown next.

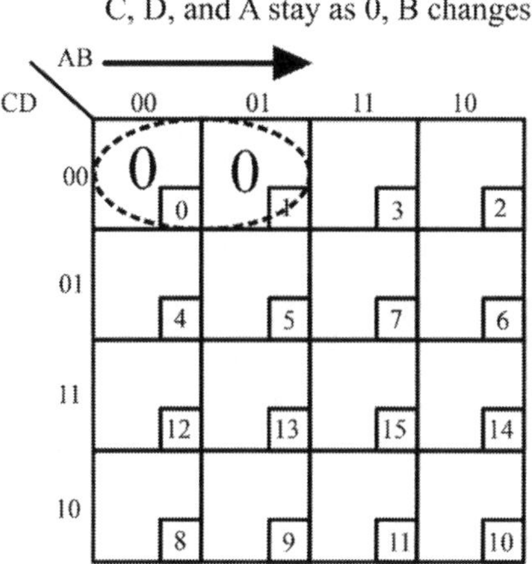

The last term is ~B. Since the last term has only one literal, it means that the circle has 8 boxes. The only possible circle that represents this would be below.

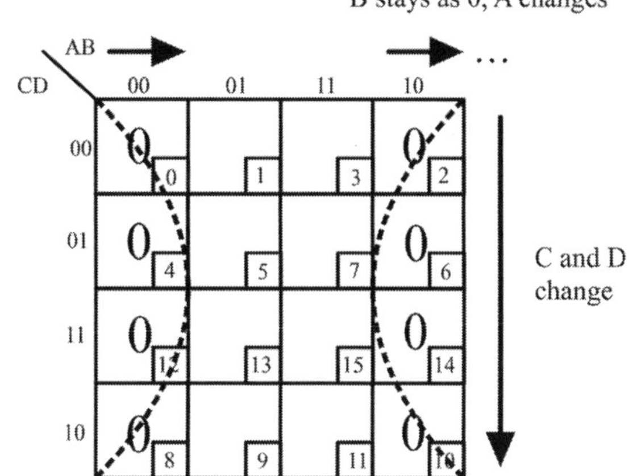

Putting it all together yields the following K-Map. Using this K-Map, we can obtain the simplified SOP expression after circling the ones: Z = AB + BD + BC

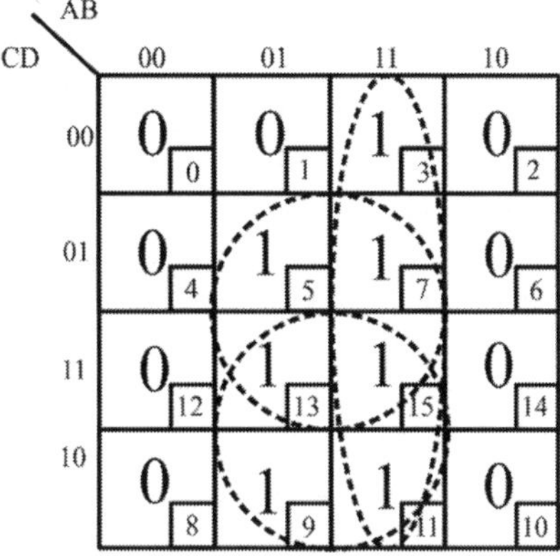

There you have it! We have successfully converted the POS expression, Z = (A+B)(C+D+A)B, into the minimized POS expression, Z = AB + BD + BC. This algorithm can be used to convert any POS expression into a simplified SOP expression.

If you were unsure why I was able to know how many boxes would be in each circle just by looking at the number of literals in each term, the following table should clarify. The trick is to know that $\#\text{Boxes} = \frac{\text{Total Squares}}{2^{\#\text{ Literals}}}$. For example, since there are 16 total squares in a 4 variable K-Map, a term with 3 literals would have $\frac{16}{2^3} = 2$ boxes circled.

# Literals In a term	# Circled Boxes
1	8
2	4
3	2
4	1

Figure 2.7.1 Table to determine number of boxes

2.8 Implicant Types

Now the next topic to discuss is the types of implicants that exist. This is something that universities love to test, so it will be covered. In summary, there are only three kinds of implicants. They are prime implicants, essential implicants, and nonessential implicants. There are no others that you need to know about for this course. The definitions of each are provided below. There are also a few examples.

Terminology
Prime Implicant: The smallest implicant that can form from adjacent ones. Essential Implicant: An implicant that must be included in the final expression. Nonessential Implicant: An implicant that is not required.

Example 1

Given the following K-Map, determine the number of each kind of implicant:

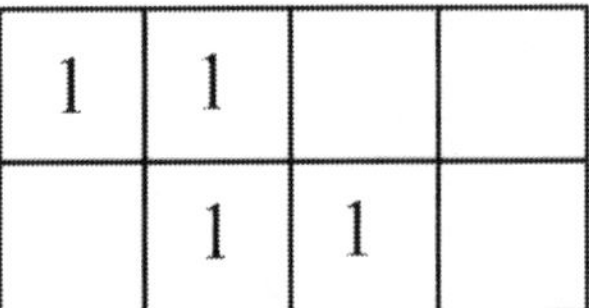

There are three total prime implicants as shown:

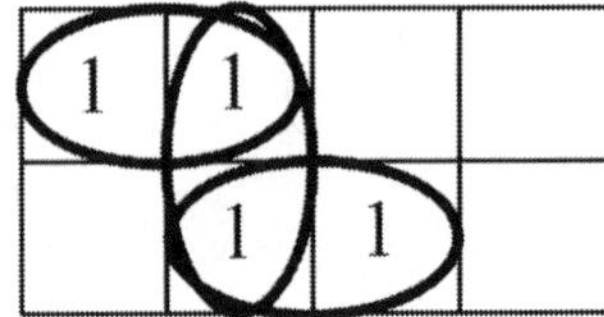

There are two essential prime implicants, shown in a solid line, and one nonessential implicant, shown in a dotted line:

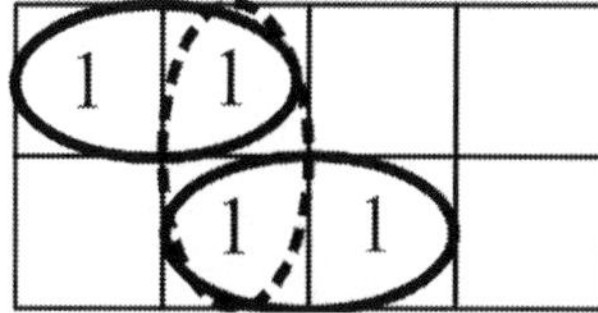

Example 2

Given the following K-Map, determine the number of each kind of implicant:

	1		
	1	1	1
1	1	1	
		1	

There are five total prime implicants as shown:

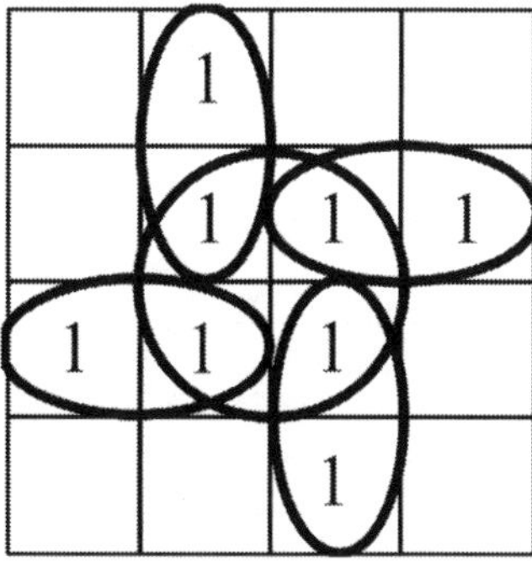

There are four essential prime implicants, shown in a solid line, and one nonessential implicant, shown in a dotted line:

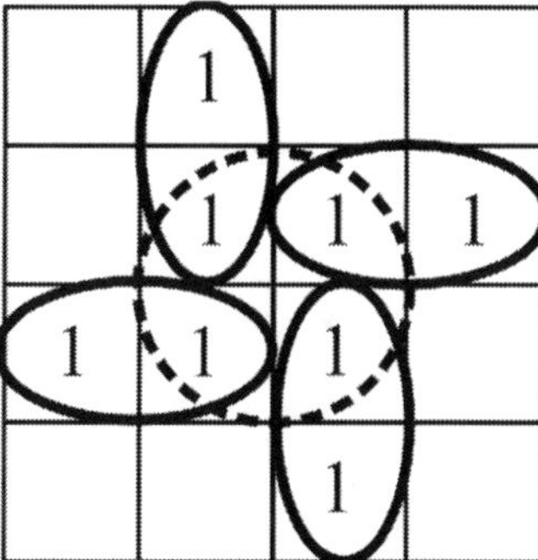

2.9 Unsigned Binary Numbers

The next topic to cover in the review of combinational logic design is the use of binary numbers. There are different levels of depth that a decimal number can be expressed using ones and zeros. In general, there are signed and unsigned representations. Then within these representations, there can be integer and floating-point representations. Fortunately for the scope of this course, mainly unsigned integers will be discussed, since that is usually all that is needed. In the future when you take courses such as "Computer Organization and Architecture", you will need to know more about number systems.

To start off, there exists a specific simple algorithm for converting decimal numbers to the equivalent unsigned binary number, consisting of 1's and 0's. All it is, is to divide the number by 2, record the remainder and answer, then repeat. Once the answer is zero, you write the remainder from the most recent one to the first one up, which will be the final answer. Next are some examples showing the execution of this algorithm.

Example 1

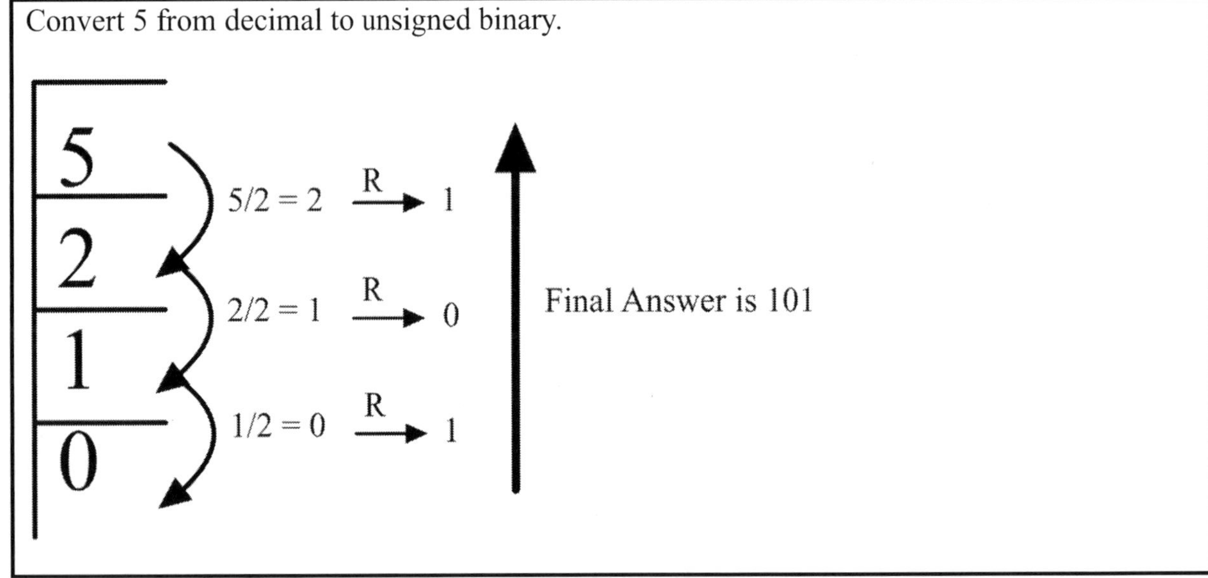

Example 2

Convert 127 from decimal to unsigned binary.

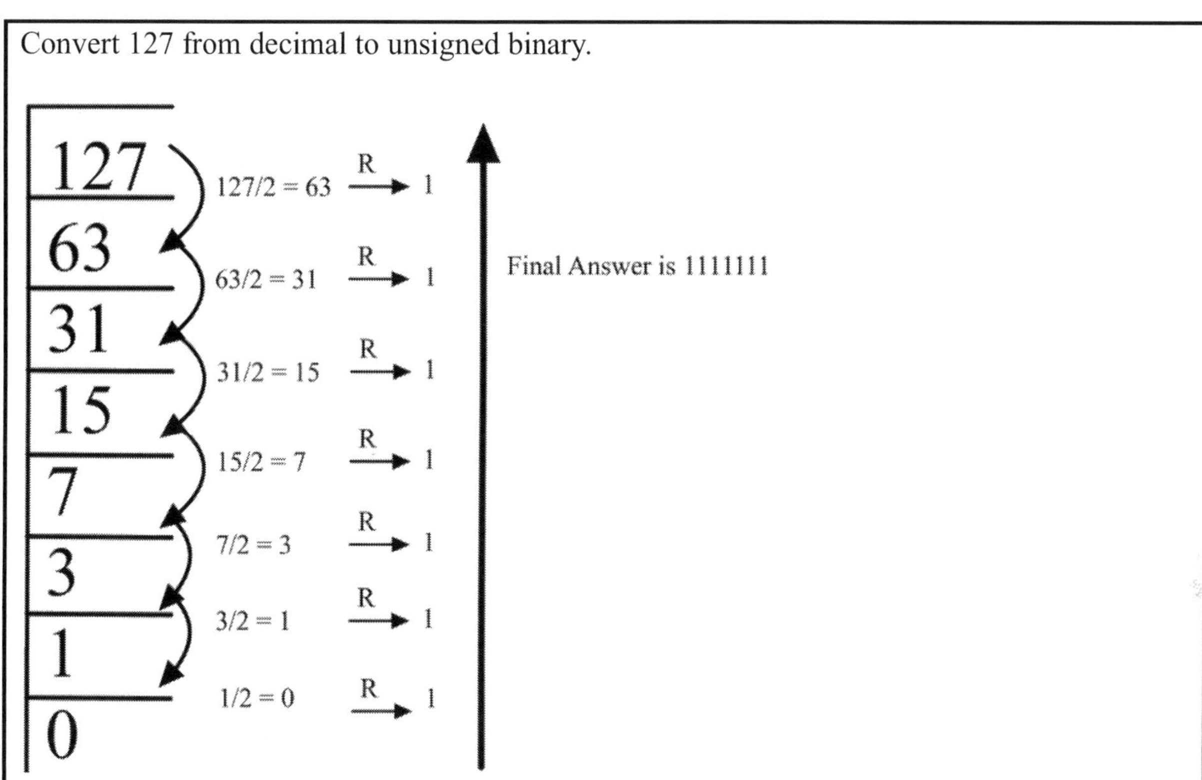

After these two examples, you may be asking yourself how to check if the answer is correct. Fortunately, we can check with the equation below. Below are examples too.

Equation to convert from unsigned binary to decimal

$\sum \text{nth digit} * 2^{n}$, where n is the index of each digit, starting from 0 at the rightmost digit.

Example 3

Verify that 101 in unsigned binary is equal to 5 in decimal.

To start, let us write down the index under each digit:

Nth digit: 1 0 1
Index n: 2 1 0

Now let's apply the summation:

$$\sum_{n=0}^{2} \text{nth digit} * 2^{n} = 1 * 2^{2} + 0 * 2^{1} + 1 * 2^{0} = 5$$

Example 4

Verify that 1111111 in unsigned binary is equal to 127 in decimal.

To start, let us write down the index under each digit:

Nth digit: 1 1 1 1 1 1 1
Index n: 6 5 4 3 2 1 0

Now let's apply the summation:

$$\sum_{n=0}^{6} \text{nth digit} * 2^n = 1 * 2^6 + 1 * 2^5 + 1 * 2^4 + 1 * 2^3 + 1 * 2^2 + 1 * 2^1 + 1 * 2^0 = 127$$

The next topic that you need to know about is hexadecimal notation. All hexadecimal is, is just a more compact way of representing 1's and 0's. For example, if we have the binary number 100011110001, we can represent it in hexadecimal as 8F1, which is much more compact. Next is the table that is used to convert from hexadecimal to binary.

Decimal	Binary	Hexadecimal
0	0000	0
1	0001	1
2	0010	2
3	0011	3
4	0100	4
5	0101	5
6	0110	6
7	0111	7
8	1000	8
9	1001	9
10	1010	A
11	1011	B
12	1100	C
13	1101	D
14	1110	E
15	1111	F

Figure 2.9.1 Conversion Table

If you can't tell from the table how 100011110001 can be converted to 8F1, don't worry. I will explain it here. For the first four bits of the binary number 100011110001 are 0001, which according to the table, is 1 in hex. The next group of four bits in the binary number 100011110001 are 1111, which according to the table is F in hex. The last group of bits is 1000, which is 8 in hex. Putting it all together gives 8F1.

2.10 Signed Floating Point Binary Numbers

In the previous section, only unsigned binary numbers were discussed, so the signed floating-point format will be briefly introduced here. Although most labs won't require the use of signed floating-point values, it will occasionally come up, which is why this chapter is necessary. Suppose we have a binary number 0101, which is 5 in decimal. The way we know that it is positive 5 is through using the following formula.

Equation to convert from signed binary to decimal

$$\text{Sum} = \sum_{\text{Min n}}^{\text{Max n}} \pm(\text{value at index n}) * 2^{\text{n}}$$

Where n is the index of each digit, starting from 0 at the digit left of the decimal.

In the equation, n is the index starting at zero at the bit left of the decimal. For example, in "0101", there is no decimal, but it is implied to be "010<u>1</u>.0". The underlined number is the bit with index zero. The index of all the bits to the left of the index zero bit increases by one the farther you go. The index would decrease by one should you go right. Sum is the value that when evaluated, should be equal to the decimal equivalent.

It is important to note that in the above equation, the most significant bit is **always** a sign bit. This is where this equation is different than the one in the last section. For example, if the most significant digit is a 1, then the number expressed is negative. If it is a zero, it means a positive number being expressed. This is because the highest magnitude term in the sum is set negative. By doing this, if the most significant bit is a zero, then when its corresponding term is evaluated, it will be zero multiplied by $-2^{\text{Max n}}$, leading to only the remaining positive terms contributing to the sum. If the most significant bit was a one, then its term will be $-2^{\text{Max n}}$, which will result in the overall sum being negative due to this term being the greatest in magnitude.

The example below shows how this formula can be used to check why 0101 in signed binary is equal to 5. Notice how the most significant bit of 0101 is zero. This is to be expected, since it is +5 that we are expressing. If the most significant bit was a one, then that would be a major red flag, since already we would know that the binary value could not possibly represent +5.

Example 1

Verify that our number, 0b0101, is equal to +5 in decimal.

$$Sum = \sum_{n=0}^{n=3} \pm(\text{value at index}) * 2^{n}$$

Index n	3	2	1	0
Value at index n	0	1	0	1
Term to be added	$0 * -2^3$	$1*2^2$	$0*2^1$	$1*2^0$

$\text{Sum} = -0 * 2^3 + 1 * 2^2 + 0*2^1 + 1*2^0 = 5$

After using the formula to convert 0101, back to decimal, we have verified that it is indeed equal to positive 5. The question remains, how would we obtain -5? Fortunately, there is a simple algorithm to convert a positive binary number into its negative and vice versa. This algorithm is to simply copy the original number starting from right to left and after copying the first one, you start copying the inverse. Performing this algorithm is called taking the two's compliment of a number. Below shows the two's compliment being taken of 5 to obtain -5. Since the very first digit was 1, we copy the 1 and then copy the inverse of the remaining 3 bits. Note that another way of performing a two's compliment is to invert all the bits and then add 1.

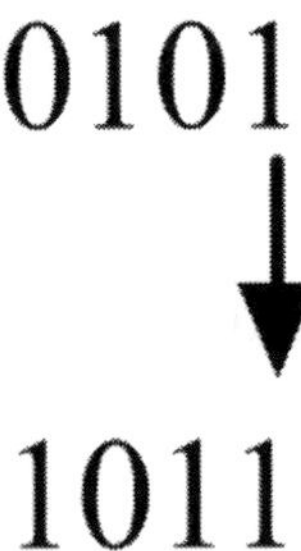

Figure 2.10.1 Two's Compliment of +5

Since the two's complement of 5 in binary was 1011, we must use the formula to verify that -5 in decimal is indeed equal to 1011 in binary.

Example 2

Verify that our number, 0b1011, is equal to -5 in decimal.

$$\text{Sum} = \sum_{n=0}^{n=3} \pm(\text{value at index n}) * 2^{n}$$

Index n	3	2	1	0
Value at index n	1	0	1	1
Term to be added	$1 * -2^3$	$0*2^2$	$1*2^1$	$1*2^0$

Sum = $-1 * 2^3 + 0 * 2^2 + 1*2^1 + 1*2^0 = -5$

Now this section mentioned at the start that floating point would be discussed. To start off, the steps to express any number in floating point 2's compliment notation is as follows.

Steps to represent a signed decimal number in binary
1) Obtain the expression of the positive integer portion. 2) Obtain the expression of the fractional portion and combine with the expression obtained in step 1. If there is no fractional component, proceed to step three. 3) If the number you are trying to express is positive you are done. If it is negative, take the two's compliment of the entire thing.

You should be familiar with step 1 since it was discussed in the last section, however step 2 is new. To obtain the expression of the fractional portion, all you do is multiply the decimal by 2, record the number in the 1's place and repeat. Once the product of the two fractions is 1.00, you combine the digits to obtain the result starting from the first product down. The examples below should clarify how the process works.

Example 3

Convert 0.75 into binary.

0 | .75 — 0.75 x 2 = 1.50

1 | .50 — 0.50 x 2 = 1.00

1 | .00

Final Answer is .11

From this, we can clearly see that 0.75 = 0.11

Example 4

Convert 0.6 into binary.

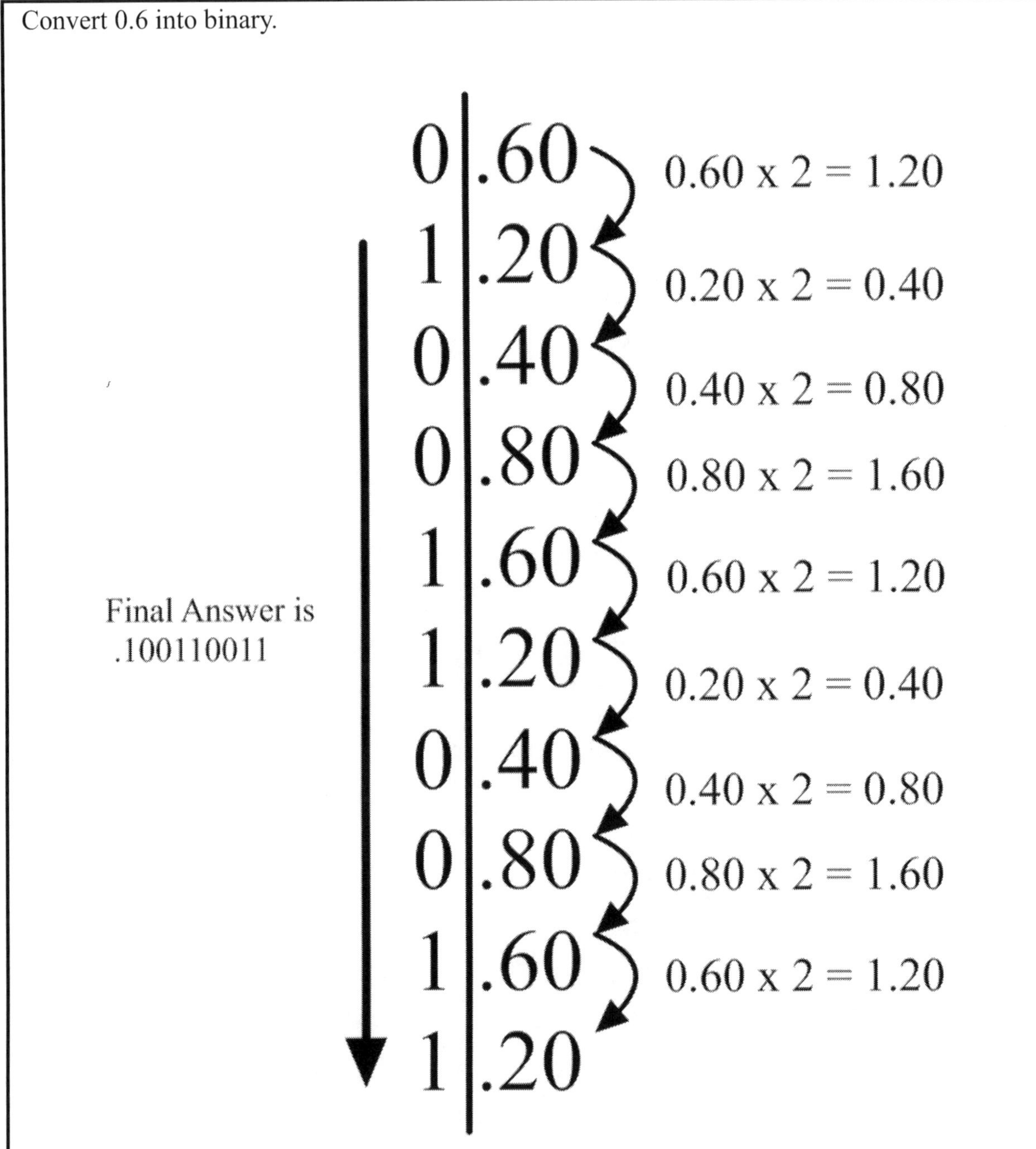

From this, we can clearly see that 0.60 = 0.100110011

Example 5

Convert .32465 into binary.

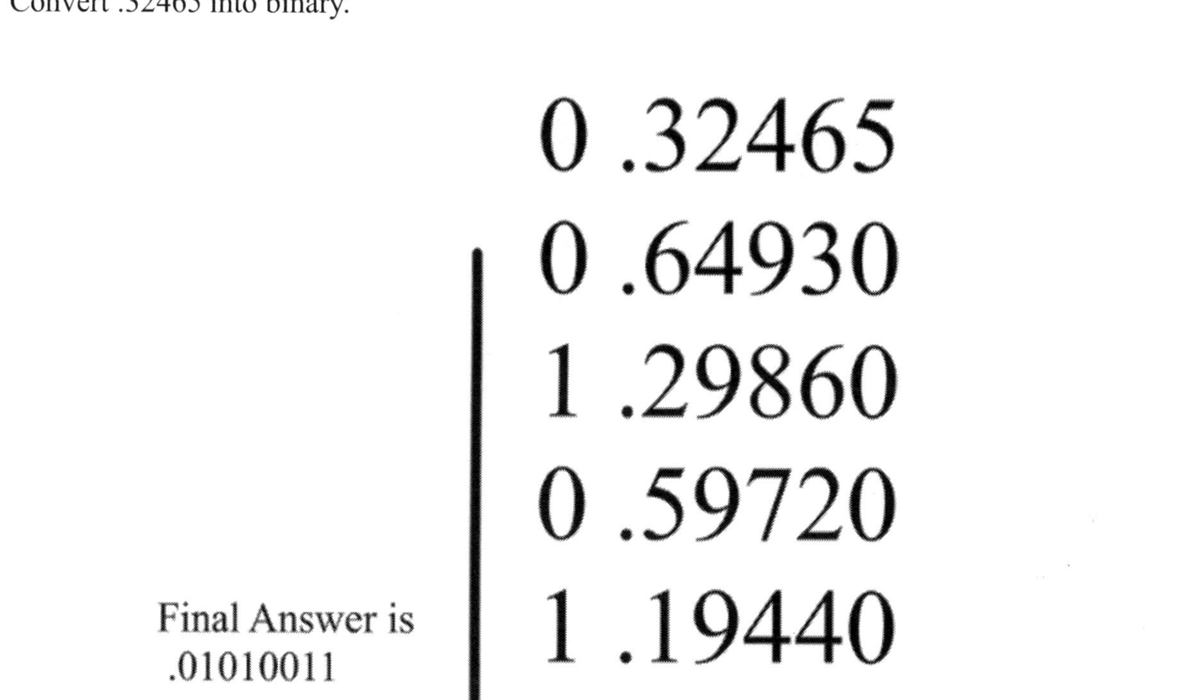

From this, we can clearly see that 0.32465 = 0.01010011

Now that step 2 has been clarified, more complex examples utilizing all three steps can be demonstrated. The examples that follow show how floating-point numbers can be expressed in binary.

Example 6

Convert 3.75 into binary.

Step 1: Find +3 in binary.

3	3/2 = 1	R →	1
1	1/2 = 0	R →	1
0		R →	0

Final Answer is 011

Step 2: Find 0.75 in binary.

0	.75
1	.50
1	.00

0.75 x 2 = 1.50

0.50 x 2 = 1.00

Final Answer is .11

Step 3: Combine them together to get 011.11. Since 3.75 is positive, no two's compliment is necessary, so 011.11 is the answer.

Example 7

Convert -10.45 into binary.

Step 1: Find +10 in binary.

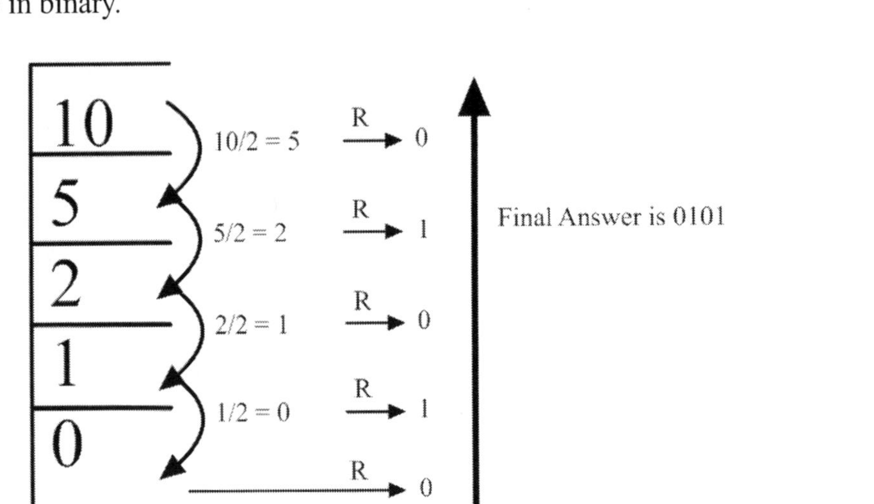

Step 2: Find 0.45 in binary.

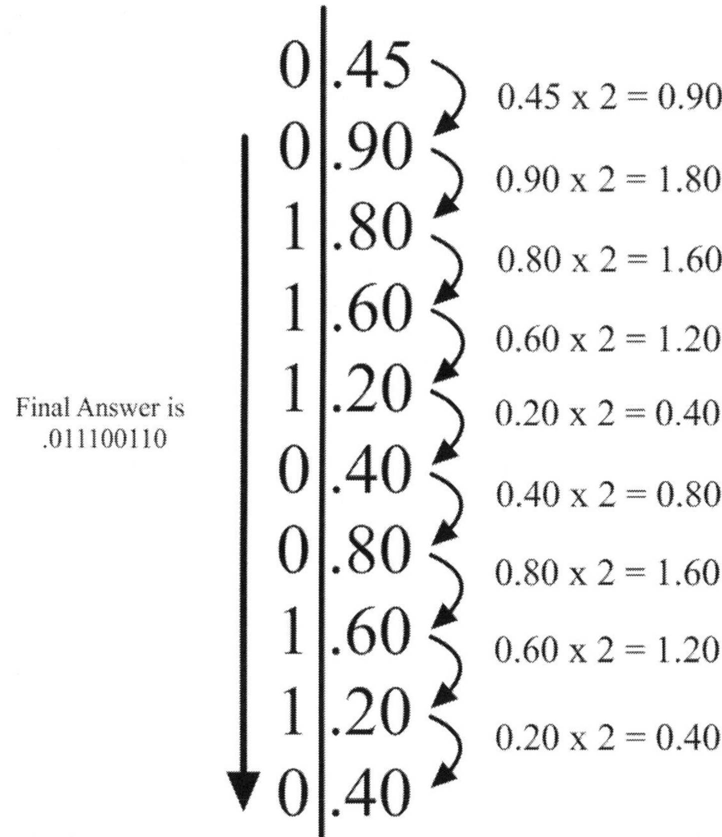

Step 3: Combine and take two's compliment if necessary.

+10.45 = 0101.011100110

↓

-10.45 = 1010.100011010

Since -10.45 is negative, we need to take the two's compliment of +10.45. Doing thing gives us our final answer of 1010.100011010 for the binary equivalent of -10.45.

2.11 Boolean Algebra

In section 2.6 and 2.7 we covered how to obtain a simplified SOP or POS expression by reverse engineering the truth table. This section aims to introduce a much more formal way of doing the exact same thing. Since Boolean algebra can become extremely complex, and will seldom be used in any designs, only a few theorems and examples will be covered. To start off, the theorems shall be listed below. Note that the tick symbol is used to invert. For example, A′ and ~A both mean the same thing.

Boolean Theorems		
Name	AND Form	OR form
Identity law	1A = A	0 + A = A
Null law	0A = 0	1 + A = 1
Idempotent law	AA = A	A + A = A
Inverse law	AA′ = 0	A + A′ = 1
Commutative law	AB = BA	A + B = B + A
Associative law	(AB)C = A(BC)	(A+B) + C = A + (B + C)
Distributive law	A + BC = (A+B)(A+C)	A(B+C) =AB+AC
Absorption law	A(A+B) = A	A +AB = A
De Morgans law	(AB)′ = A′ + B′	(A+B)′ = A′B′
Consensus Law	AB + A′C + BC = AB + A′C Note that BC is the consensus term, so it is deleted	(A+B)(A′+C)(B+C) = (A+B)(A′+C) Note that B+C is the consensus term, so it is deleted

Example 1

Convert (A+B′+C)(A′+C′) to minimal SOP.

Apply distributive law: (A+B′+C)(A′+C′) = AA′ + AC′ + B′A′ + B′C′ + CA′ + C′C′
Apply inverse Law: AC′ + B′A′ + B′C′ + CA′
Apply consensus law on region in parentheses (B′A′ was the consensus term): AC′ + (B′A′ + B′C′ + CA′)

Final Answer: AC′ + B′C′ + CA′

Example 2

Convert AC+AB′+A′C to minimal POS.

Rewrite: AC+A′C+AB′
Rewrite: C(A+A′) + AB′
Apply inverse law: C+AB′
Apply distributive law: (C+A)(C+B′)

2.12 Combinational Logic Problems

Now that we have gone over everything, it is finally time to give you some problems for combinational logic. It is highly recommended to attempt all these problems, since they are intended to serve as great practice. At the end of this section, you'll find step-by-step solutions to each problem, something typically not done in university-mandated textbooks. You spent money for this textbook, so you're getting the very best service, nothing less.

2.1 - 2.2 Problems

Problem 1) For the following truth table, map it onto the template for a 4-variable K-Map and solve for the equation for Z.

Index	A	B	C	D	Z
0	0	0	0	0	0
1	0	0	0	1	0
2	0	0	1	0	1
3	0	0	1	1	X
4	0	1	0	0	X
5	0	1	0	1	0
6	0	1	1	0	1
7	0	1	1	1	0
8	1	0	0	0	0
9	1	0	0	1	0
10	1	0	1	0	0
11	1	0	1	1	X
12	1	1	0	0	0
13	1	1	0	1	0
14	1	1	1	0	1
15	1	1	1	1	1

Problem 2) For the following K-Maps, find the Boolean expression.

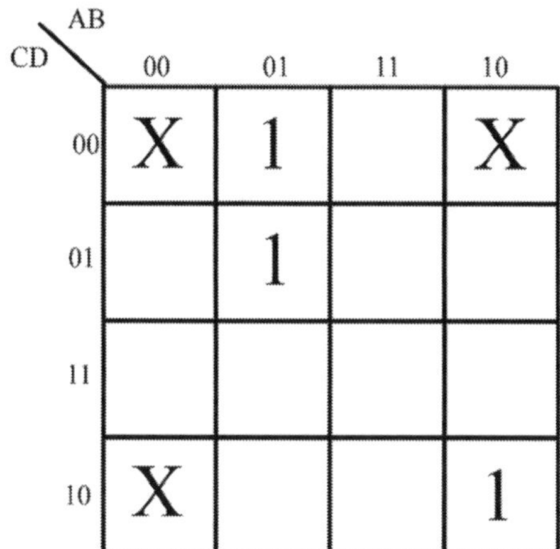

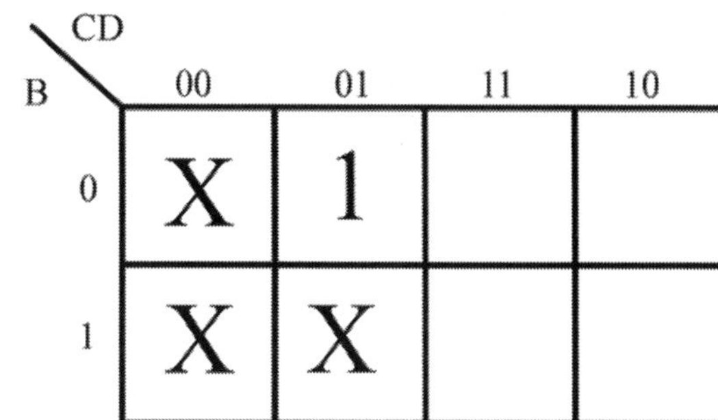

Problem 3) Convert the following expressions into hardware.

A = WE + G

F = (A+Q+W)(W+D)

2.3 Problems

Problem 1) Write the minterm and maxterm equivalent for the following truth table.

Index	A	B	C	D	Z
0	0	0	0	0	0
1	0	0	0	1	0
2	0	0	1	0	1
3	0	0	1	1	0
4	0	1	0	0	0
5	0	1	0	1	0
6	0	1	1	0	1
7	0	1	1	1	0
8	1	0	0	0	0
9	1	0	0	1	0
10	1	0	1	0	0
11	1	0	1	1	1
12	1	1	0	0	0
13	1	1	0	1	0
14	1	1	1	0	1
15	1	1	1	1	1

2.4 - 2.5 Problems

Problem 1) Using the Truth table in the previous question, find the minimized SOP expression. Also find the unsimplified (also known as canonical) SOP expression.

Problem 2) Using the Truth table in the previous question, find the minimized POS expression. Also find the unsimplified (also known as canonical) POS expression.

2.6 – 2.7 Problems

Problem 1) Find the minimized SOP expression of the POS expression, (A+B+C′)(B+C+D′)(C′+B), by reverse engineering the K-Map.

2.8 Problems

Problem 1) How many essential, prime, and nonessential implicants are in the following K-Map

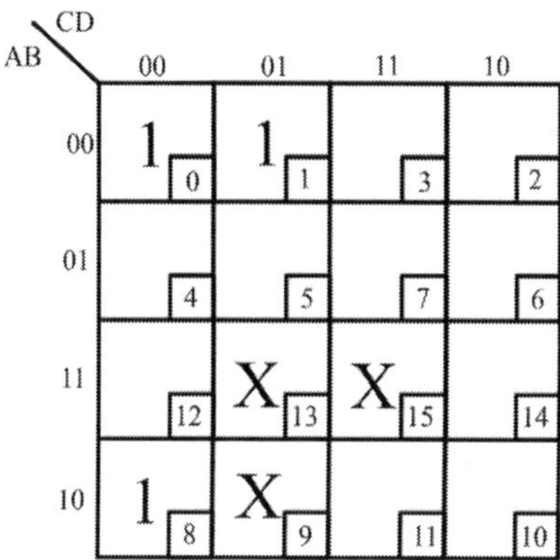

2.9 Problems

Problem 1) What is 37 in binary?

Problem 2) What is 000011110101 in hexadecimal?

2.10 Problems

Problem 1) What is +3 and -3 in binary? Use 3-bits and verify both using the formula.

Problem 2) What is +1 and -1 in binary? Use 3-bits and verify both using the formula.

Problem 3) What is 50.575 in binary?

Problem 4) What is -100.675 in binary?

2.11 Problems

Problem 1) Find the minimized SOP expression of the POS expression, (A+B+C′)(B+C+D′)(C′+B), by using Boolean equations.

Problem 2) Find the minimized POS expression of the SOP expression, BCD+C′D+B′C′D+CD, by using Boolean equations.

Solutions

Section 2.1-2.2 Problem 1

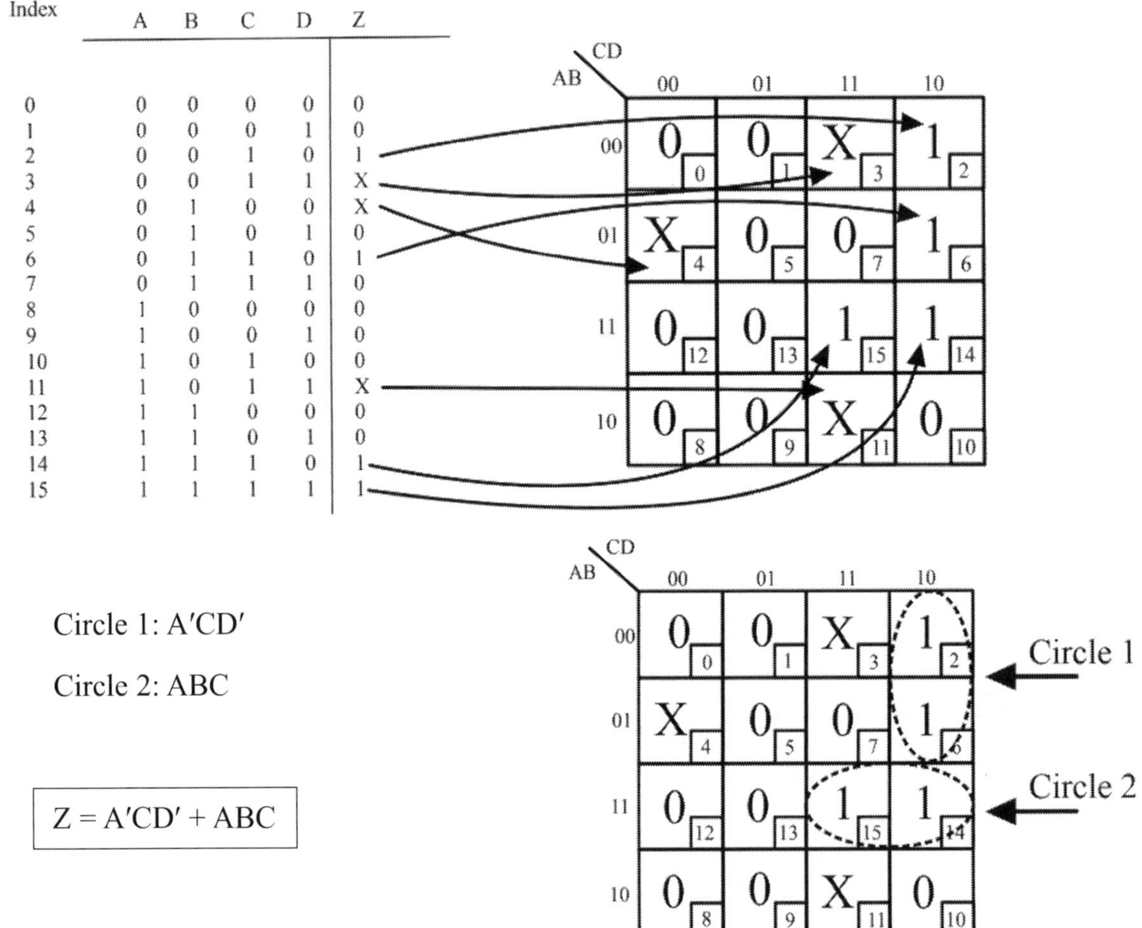

Index	A	B	C	D	Z
0	0	0	0	0	0
1	0	0	0	1	0
2	0	0	1	0	1
3	0	0	1	1	X
4	0	1	0	0	X
5	0	1	0	1	0
6	0	1	1	0	1
7	0	1	1	1	0
8	1	0	0	0	0
9	1	0	0	1	0
10	1	0	1	0	0
11	1	0	1	1	X
12	1	1	0	0	0
13	1	1	0	1	0
14	1	1	1	0	1
15	1	1	1	1	1

Circle 1: A′CD′

Circle 2: ABC

Z = A′CD′ + ABC

Section 2.1-2.2 Problem 2

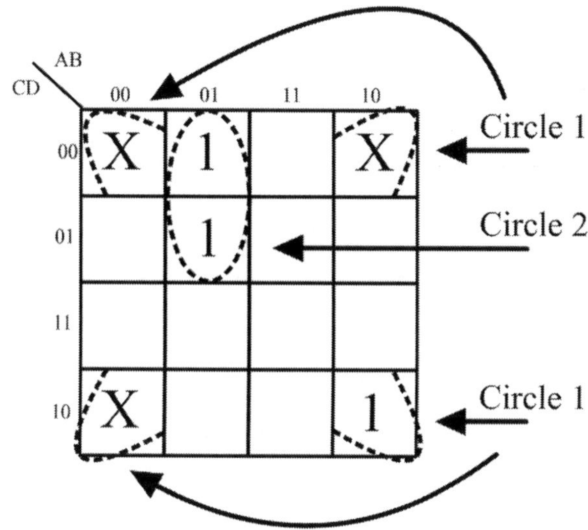

Circle 1: B′D′

Circle 2: A′B C′

Output = B′D′+ A′B C′

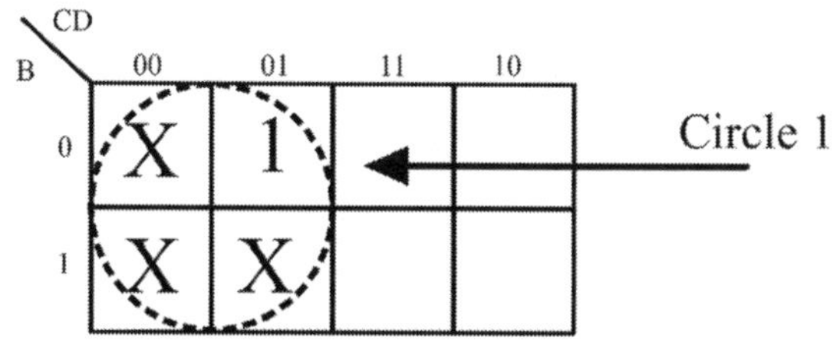

Circle 1: C′

Output = C′

Section 2.1-2.2 Problem 3

A = WE + G

F = (A+Q+W)(W+D)

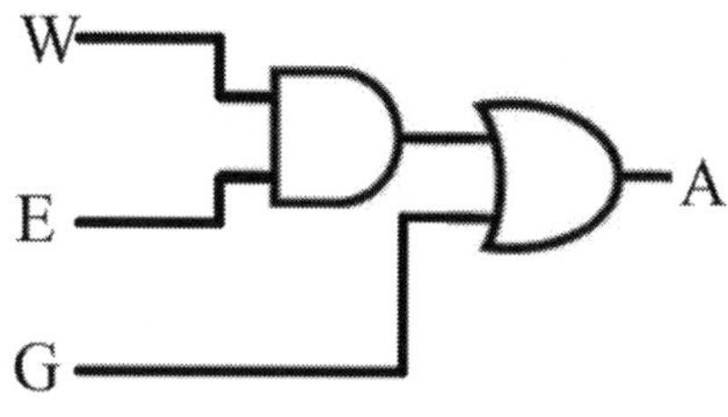

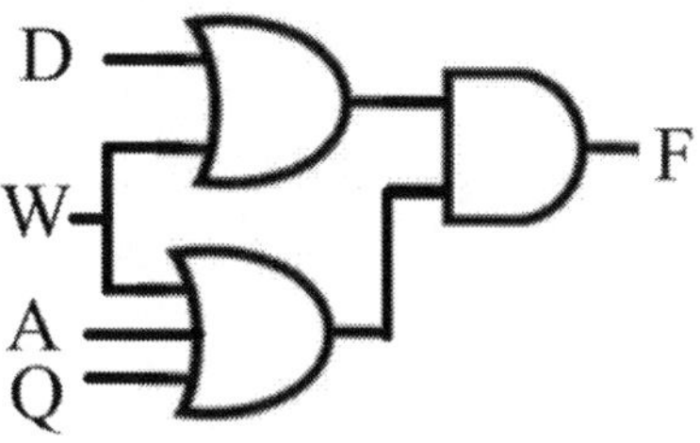

Section 2.3 Problem 1

$$F(A, B, C, D) = \sum(2,6,11,14,15)$$

$$F(A, B, C, D) = \prod(0,1,3,4,5,7,8,9,10,12,13)$$

Section 2.4-2.5 Problem 1

Finding Minimum SOP

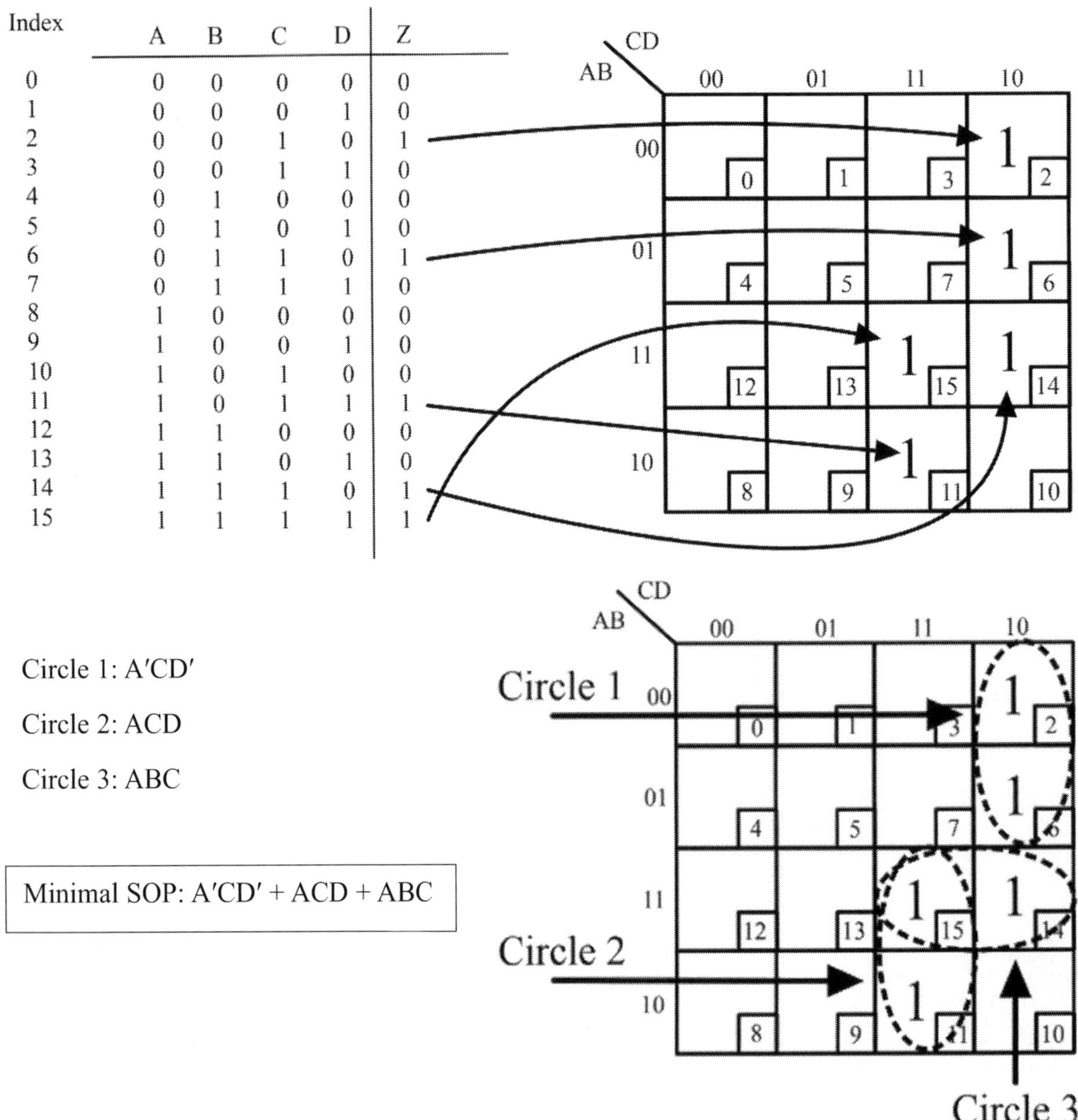

Index	A	B	C	D	Z
0	0	0	0	0	0
1	0	0	0	1	0
2	0	0	1	0	1
3	0	0	1	1	0
4	0	1	0	0	0
5	0	1	0	1	0
6	0	1	1	0	1
7	0	1	1	1	0
8	1	0	0	0	0
9	1	0	0	1	0
10	1	0	1	0	0
11	1	0	1	1	1
12	1	1	0	0	0
13	1	1	0	1	0
14	1	1	1	0	1
15	1	1	1	1	1

Circle 1: A′CD′

Circle 2: ACD

Circle 3: ABC

Minimal SOP: A′CD′ + ACD + ABC

Finding Canonical SOP

$$F(A, B, C, D) = \sum(2,6,11,14,15) = \underset{2}{0010} + \underset{6}{0110} + \underset{11}{1011} + \underset{14}{1110} + \underset{15}{1111}$$

$$= A'B'CD' + A'BCD' + AB'CD + ABCD' + ABCD$$

Canonical SOP: A′B′CD′ + A′BCD′ + AB′CD + ABCD′ + ABCD

Section 2.4-2.5 Problem 2

Finding Minimum POS

Index	A	B	C	D	Z
0	0	0	0	0	0
1	0	0	0	1	0
2	0	0	1	0	1
3	0	0	1	1	0
4	0	1	0	0	0
5	0	1	0	1	0
6	0	1	1	0	1
7	0	1	1	1	0
8	1	0	0	0	0
9	1	0	0	1	0
10	1	0	1	0	0
11	1	0	1	1	1
12	1	1	0	0	0
13	1	1	0	1	0
14	1	1	1	0	1
15	1	1	1	1	1

AB \ CD	00	01	11	10
00	0	1	3	1 (2)
01	4	5	7	1 (6)
11	12	13	1 (15)	1 (14)
10	8	9	1 (11)	10

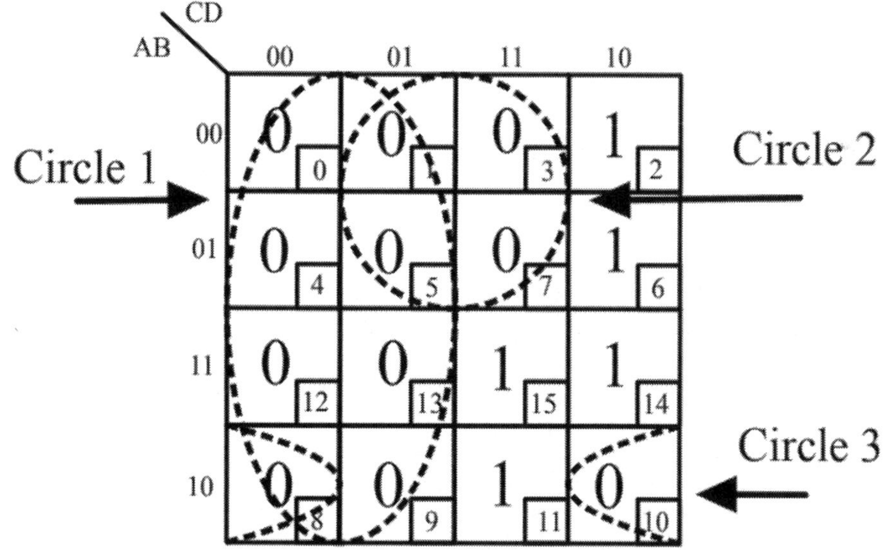

Circle 1: C′ Circle 2: A′D Circle 3: AB′D′

Expression as if the circled zeros were ones: C′ + A′D + AB′D′

Expression with inverted literals: C + AD′ + A′BD

Expression with OR operators switching with AND operators: C(A+D′)(A′+B+D)

Minimal POS: C(A+D′)(A′+B+D)

Finding Canonical POS

$F(A, B, C, D) = \prod(0,1,3,4,5,7,8,9,10,12,13)$

$= (A + B + C + D)(A + B + C + D')(A + B + C' + D')(A + B' + C + D)(A + B' + C + D')$
$(A + B' + C' + D')(A' + B + C + D)(A' + B + C + D')(A' + B + C' + D)(A' + B' + C + D)$
$(A' + B' + C + D')$

Table Summarizing Steps:

Maxterm	Binary	Literal Term	Inverted Literal	Inverted Operators
0	0000	A′B′C′D′	ABCD	(A + B + C + D)
1	0001	A′B′C′D	ABCD′	(A + B + C + D′)
3	0011	A′B′CD	ABC′D′	(A + B + C′ + D′)
4	0100	A′BC′D′	AB′CD	(A + B′ + C + D)
5	0101	A′BC′D	AB′CD′	(A + B′ + C + D′)
7	0111	A′BCD	AB′C′D′	(A + B′ + C′ + D′)
8	1000	AB′C′D′	A′BCD	(A′ + B + C + D)
9	1001	AB′C′D	A′BCD′	(A′ + B + C + D′)
10	1010	AB′CD′	A′BC′D	(A′ + B + C′ + D)
12	1100	ABC′D′	A′B′CD	(A′ + B′ + C + D)
13	1101	ABC′D	A′B′CD′	(A′ + B′ + C + D′)

Section 2.6-2.7 Problem 1)

Original Expression: (A+B+C′)(B+C+D′)(C′+B)

Reverse Operators: (ABC′)+(BCD′)+(C′B)

Reverse Literals: (A′B′C)+(B′C′D)+(CB′)

K-Map of Terms: Using K-Map To Obtain SOP Expression:

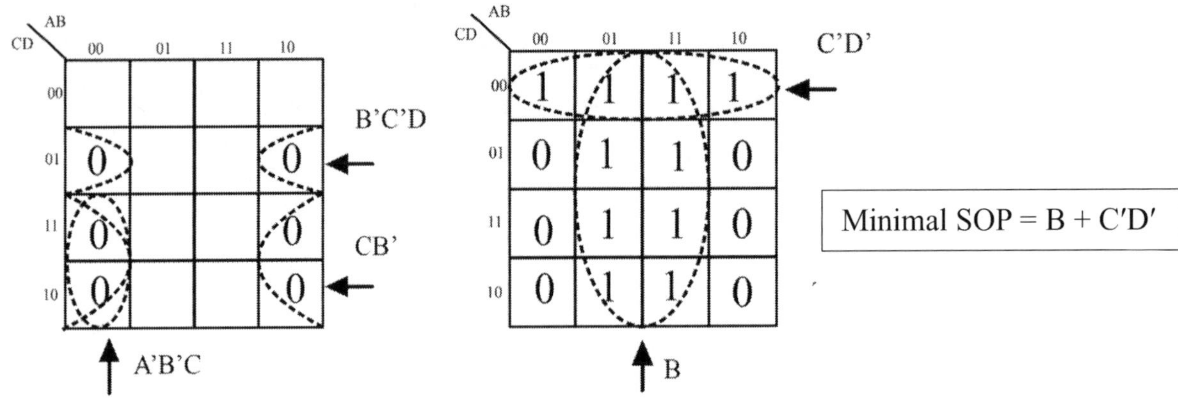

Section 2.8 Problem 1)

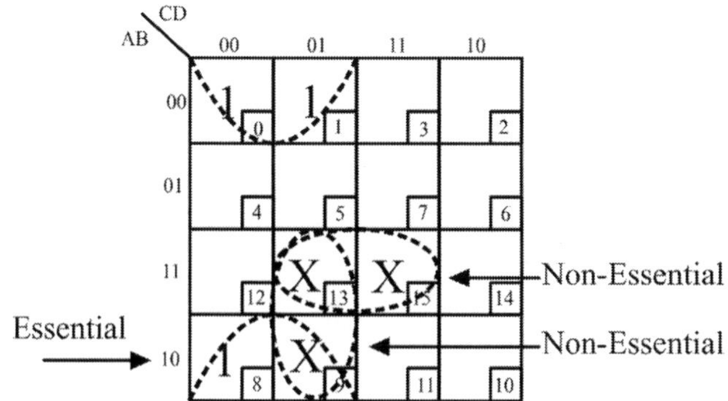

Essential: 1
Non-Essential: 2
Total Prime Implicants: 3

Section 2.9 Problem 1)

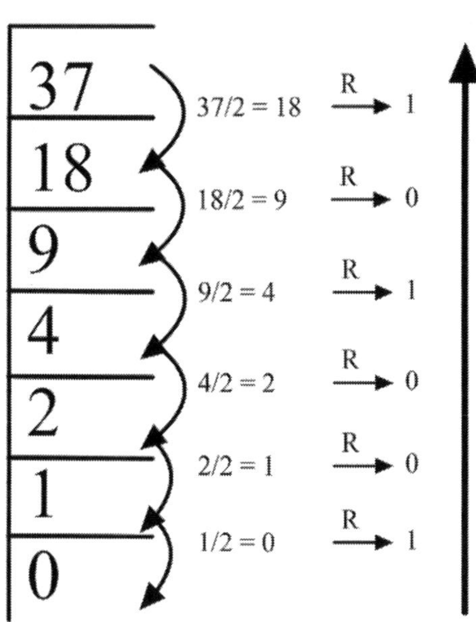

Final Answer is: 100101

Section 2.9 Problem 2)

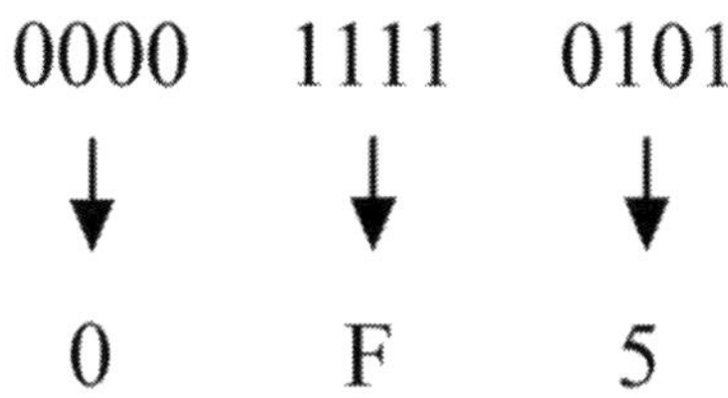

Final Answer is: 0F5

Section 2.10 Problem 1)

+3 = 011

-3 = 101

Section 2.10 Problem 2)

+1 = 001

-1 = 111

Section 2.10 Problem 3) 50.575 = 0110010.1001001100110011

Section 2.10 Problem 4) -100.675 = 10011011.01010011001101

Section 2.11 Problem 1)

Original Expression: (A+B+C′)(B+C+D′)(C′+B)

Rewrite: (A+B+C′)(B+C′)(B+C+D′)

Apply Absorption Law: (B+C′)(B+C+D′)

Apply Distributive Law: BB+BC+BD′+BC′+CC′+C′D′

Apply Inverse Law: BB+BC+BD′+BC′+C′D′

Apply Idempotent Law: B+BC+BD′+BC′+C′D′

Apply Absorption Law: B+C′D′

Final SOP expression: B+C′D′

Section 2.11 Problem 2)

Original Expression: BCD+C′D+B′C′D+CD

Rewrite: CD+BCD+C′D+B′C′D

Apply Absorption Law: CD+C′D+B′C′D

Apply Absorption Law: CD+C′D

Apply Distributive Law: D(C+C′)

Apply Inverse Law: D

Final POS expression: D

Section 3 - Sequential Logic Review

Now that we have finally finished covering combinational logic, it is time to review sequential logic. There is only one real difference between sequential logic and combinational logic. That difference is essentially that a circuit made from combinational logic will update the output instantly whenever the inputs change, were as a sequential circuit will not be able to update until a pulse is received. This pulse will be called a clock. Since we can control when the values update in a sequential circuit by choosing when to apply the pulse, we can use this to our advantage by storing information whenever we choose not to send a pulse. Now the first logical place to start in all of this would be the building blocks of a sequential circuit. We know that in combinational circuits, there were only seven pieces of hardware that needed to be understood. For sequential circuits, the building blocks consist of those same seven gates but also consist of a component called a register. A register is also commonly called a flip-flop. Fortunately, are only four registers in existence that you need to know about and understand. They are the D flip-flop, the JK flip-flop, the SR flip-flop, and the T flip-flop. Once you understand these, then you will understand every single fundamental building block that exists in a sequential digital circuit, since all other major components are created using these building blocks, nothing else.

3.1 D flip-flop

The first component we will discuss will be the D flip-flop. This is because this flip-flop is by far going to be the most important one in your undergraduate career. In most design problems you will encounter in this course, and in other courses such as computer organization, you will primarily be expected to solve your problems using D flip-flops. The second most important one will be the JK flip-flop, which will be covered later. So, to start off, before going over the internals of a D flip-flop, it's best to describe its overall behavior. We will focus much more on the overall behavior of the D flip-flop and study how multiple D flip-flops can then be assembled to form a larger circuit that has a desired behavior. In the review of combinational logic design, we took this same approach, since we learned how to model digital circuits with the inputs and outputs in a table, and how to apply an algorithm to convert that table to a physical piece of hardware that consisted of the seven building blocks. We never once in that chapter cared to discuss what the internals of the logic gates were, since it was not relevant. For that same reason, the internals of the D flip-flop will not be emphasized. At the end of this section, the D flip-flop internals will be discussed, but note it is not the focus.

So, to start off, the simplest D flip-flop variation can be written using the symbol shown in the following figure. It has two inputs and one output, so it will be a simple thing to understand. There is an input called "D" and an input called "Clock". There is one output called "Q."

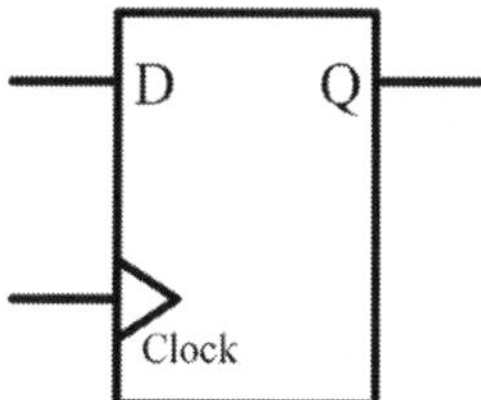

Figure 3.1.1 Basic D flip-flop

So, the voltage at input D will be either 1 or 0. Then, when a pulse is applied into the Clock input, the output Q will change to whatever value was present at D. If there is no pulse present, then Q will always stay the same regardless of if D changes or not. That's essentially everything you need to know about how a D flip-flop works. Just like how the table describing each logic gate was provided, the table describing the D flip-flop will be provided.

Clock	D	Q
⎍	0	Change to 0
⎍	1	Change to 1
⎍	0	No Change
⎍	1	No Change
⎍	0	No Change
⎍	1	No Change

Figure 3.1.2 D flip-flop Table

In the table, Clock and D are on the left since they are inputs and Q is on the right since it is an output. From the first and second row on the table, it is shown that Q will change to the value of D whenever the rising edge of the pulse coming into the clock input is detected. On the third and fourth row of the table, it is shown that whenever the pulse is ending, there is no change. On the fifth and sixth row of the table, it is shown that no change will occur at the middle of the pulse either. In case it is not clear, the beginning of the pulse is referred to as the rising edge and the ending of the pulse is referred to as the falling edge. The following figure shows this in case it's still not clear. The rising edge is the instant the voltage changes from zero to one and the falling edge is when the voltage changes from one to zero.

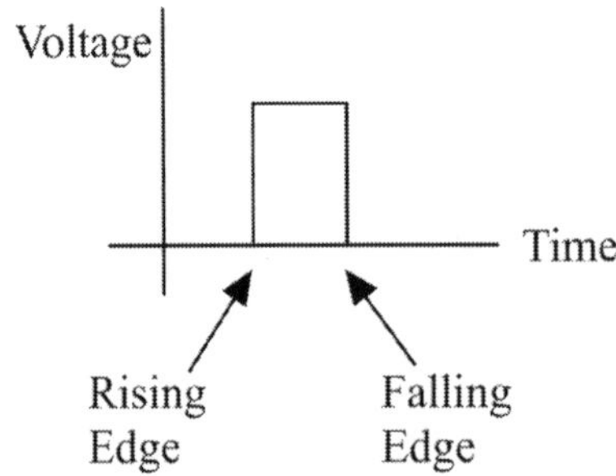

Figure 3.1.3 Clock Pulse

If you are still having trouble understanding how a D flip-flop behaves, there is a timing diagram for an ideal D flip-flop in Figure 3.1.4 that should help. From the diagram, you can clearly see that Q updates to reflect D only on the rising edge of the pulse that is applied into the clock input. The rising edge is marked with an arrow and has a dotted line going down. Times t1, t2, t3, t4, and t5 all correspond to the rising edges of the clock. Originally, Q is zero and D is one. At t1, the first rising edge occurs, which causes the output Q to be updated to the input D, which was one, resulting in Q changing to one. At time t2, D is equal to one when the rising edge of the pulse occurs, so Q remains one. At time t3, D is one, so Q remains one. At time t4, D is zero, so Q becomes zero. At time t5, D is one, so Q is updated to one. It is important to reiterate that the output Q is updated to D only on the rising edge of each pulse. It is also important to note that between times t2 and t3, D changed to zero, however this was not reflected in Q, due to the next rising edge at time t3 not occurring during the time D was zero.

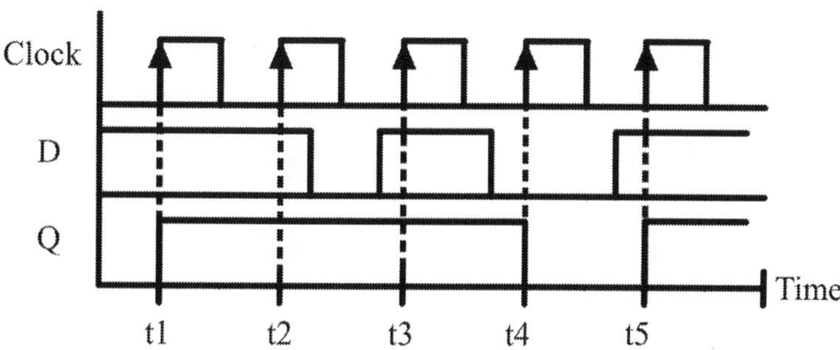

Figure 3.1.4 Timing diagram of ideal D flip-flop behavior

If you are still having trouble understanding the behavior of the D flip-flop, then scan the QR code to access a simulation where you can physically see the behavior of a D flip-flop by controlling the input D and pulse going into the clock input. You will notice that the value of Q only updates on the rising edge, i.e. when the clock changes from 0 to 1.

So hopefully you now completely understand how a D flip-flop should behave when subjected to different inputs. It is important to note that the D flip-flop discussed this far is the simplest of all the D flip-flop variations and has been assumed to be ideal. Before moving onto the next section, it is important to discuss the remaining variations of D flip-flops and how a non-ideal flip-flop will behave.

In the D flip-flop we just discussed, all changes occurred on the rising edge of the clock pulse, meaning at the instant the voltage changed from zero to one. There is a variation of the D flip-flop that is identical to this expect in that it updates on the falling edge of the clock pulse, meaning it updates at the instant the clock changes from one to zero. The schematic for a falling edge flip-flop is identical to the last one, except that there is a bubble on the clock input as shown in Figure 3.1.5. Figure 3.1.6 shows the timing diagram for an ideal falling edge flip-flop using the exact same input signals as from Figure 3.1.4. From Figure 3.1.6, you can clearly see that it behaves the same as the previous except that it updates on the falling edge.

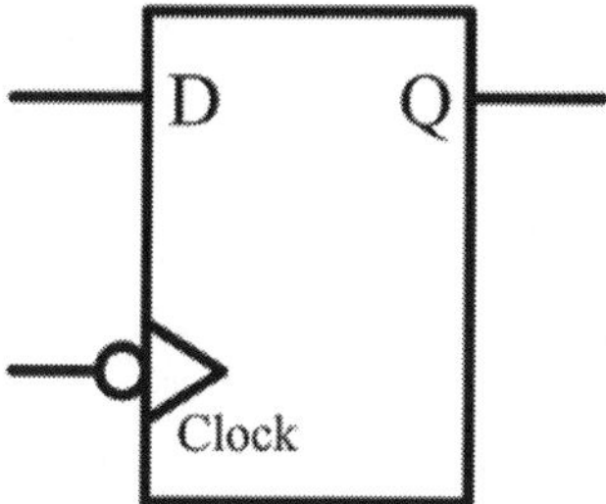

Figure 3.1.5 D flip-flop variation that updates on falling edge.

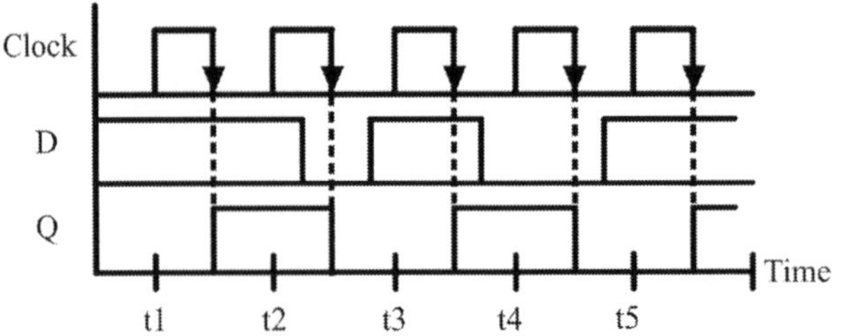

Figure 3.1.6 Timing diagram of ideal D flip-flop that is triggered on the falling edge.

In the two kinds of D flip-flops discussed so far, there have only been two inputs and a single output. Well, in truth, there are actually two outputs always present in any D flip-flop. Seldom is the second output used, which is why it is commonly left out of the D flip-flop symbol. The first output is Q and the second output, which was previously not shown, is simply Q′. Figure 3.1.7 shows the two previously discussed flip-flops with both outputs labeled. Figure 3.1.8 shows the two previous time diagrams from Figures 3.1.4 and 3.1.6 with Q′ included. Remember that all Q′ is, is the inverse of Q.

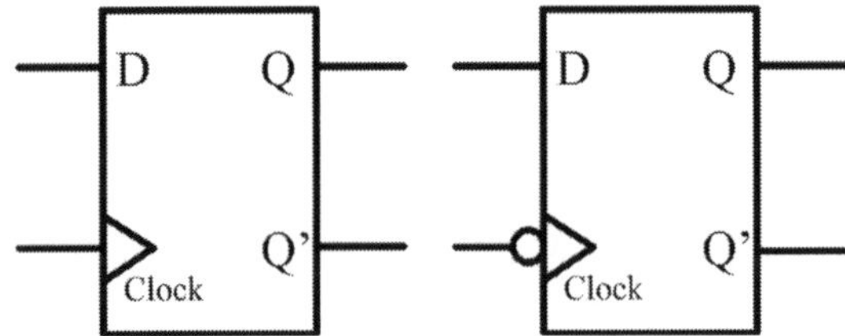

Figure 3.1.7 Rising edge triggered flip-flop (left) and falling edge triggered flip-flop (right) with both outputs shown.

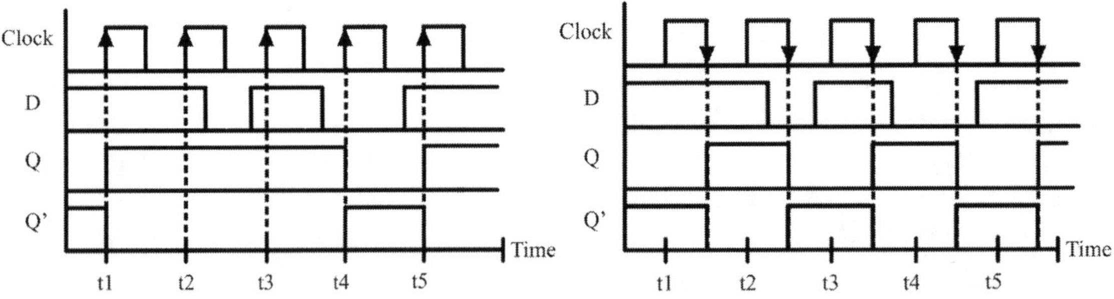

Figure 3.1.8 Timming diagram for rising edge triggered flip-flop (left) and falling edge triggered flip-flop (right). Both diagrams include outputs Q and Q′.

As you can clearly see, the timing diagram for both flip-flops are identical to the past diagrams, except that the output Q′ is present and is always the opposite of Q at any given moment. For both diagrams, whenever Q was one, Q′ was zero and vice versa.

Now that we have discussed how a flip-flop can be triggered on either the rising or falling edge, let's discuss the variations that incorporate a reset function, also referred to interchangeably as a clear function. There are two types of resets a flip-flop can employ: asynchronous resets and synchronous resets. An asynchronous reset is an input that, when set to one, immediately forces the output Q to zero. On the other hand, a synchronous reset, when set to one, causes the output Q to transition to zero on the subsequent clock pulse. Additionally, a reset can be configured to set Q to zero whenever the reset input is zero, rather than one. This configuration can be determined by the presence or absence of a bubble at the reset or clear input. When no bubble is present, indicating an active-high reset, the output Q is reset to zero only when the reset pin is high. Conversely, when a bubble is present, indicating an active-low reset, the output Q is reset to zero only when the reset pin is low. For example, the following figure shows a D flip-flop triggered on the rising edge of the clock and equipped with an asynchronous active-low reset. The corresponding timing diagram is provided below.

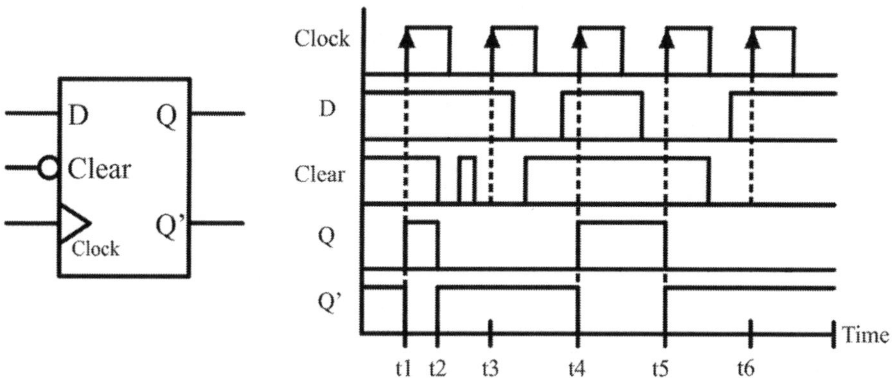

Figure 3.1.9 D flip-flop with rising edge triggered clock and active low asynchronous reset. Corresponding timing diagram included.

From the timing diagram, at t2, we can see that the instant the clear input becomes zero, Q becomes zero. At time t2, we say that the clear input is asserted, since at that time, the output Q, is reset to zero because of the clear input being zero. If the clear input was one at time t2, then the clear would not be asserted and Q would not be reset. Once the clear is asserted, even if it is changed back to one immediately after, as seen between times t2 and t3, Q and Q′ will not change since a new rising edge would be needed to do that. The dotted lines going down from the rising clock edges show which times the clear input allows for an update. At times t3 and t6, the rising clock edge has no effect, since the clear input is asserted, meaning that no matter what, Q and Q′ will be zero and one respectively.

If the D flip-flop shown in Figure 3.1.9 had a synchronous clear the timing diagram would be the following in Figure 3.1.10. The only difference is that the clear no longer can set Q to zero instantly. For this reason, instead of setting it to zero at t2, it must wait for the next active clock edge, at t3, to set it to zero. For both the timing diagrams in Figure 3.1.9 and Figure 3.1.10, at time t5, Q was already set to zero due to input D being zero, so both the asynchronous and synchronous clear timing diagrams had no difference.

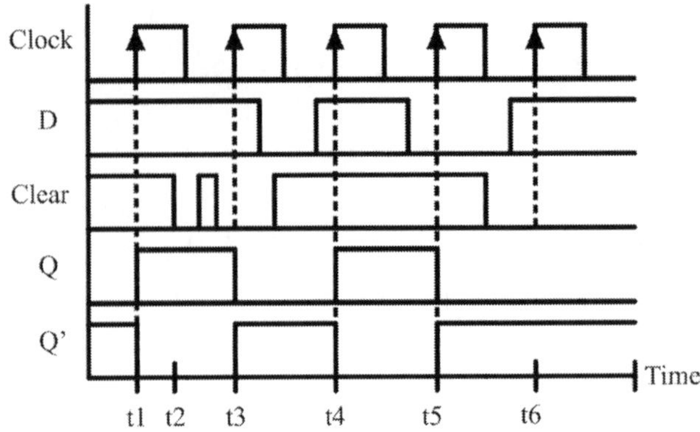

Figure 3.1.10 Timming diagram for D flip-flop with rising edge triggered clock and active low asynchronous clear.

The next variation to be discussed is the use of a set function. A set, like its name implies, does the exact opposite of reset. It sets the output Q to one when it is asserted. There can also be synchronous and asynchronous resets. The schematics for a D flip-flop with an active high and low set are shown below. It is important to note that at no time will there be a D flip-flop that contains both a set and reset/clear function. This is because such a flip-flop will be unpredictable should both the set and reset function be asserted at the same time. In some unconventional cases, a custom D flip-flop might have both, however that is not something that need be discussed in this course.

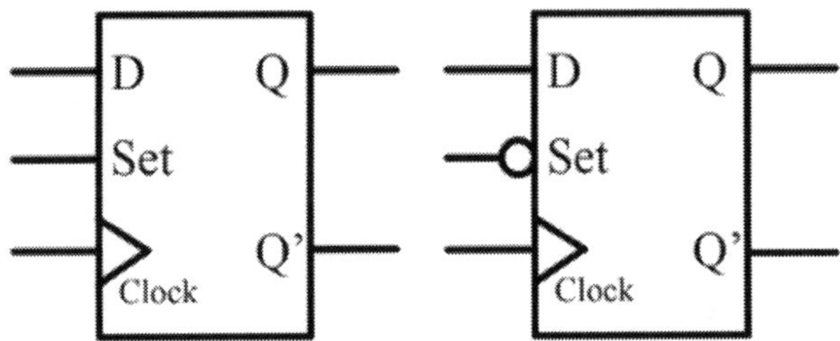

Figure 3.1.11 D flip-flop with active high (left) and active low (right) set function.

To briefly summarize the behavior of the synchronous and asynchronous set function, some examples will be provided. The process for understanding the set function is extremely similar to that of a reset function.

Example 1

For an ideal D flip-flop that is triggered on the rising clock edge and has a synchronous active high set, draw the flip-flop symbol, and complete the following timing diagram.

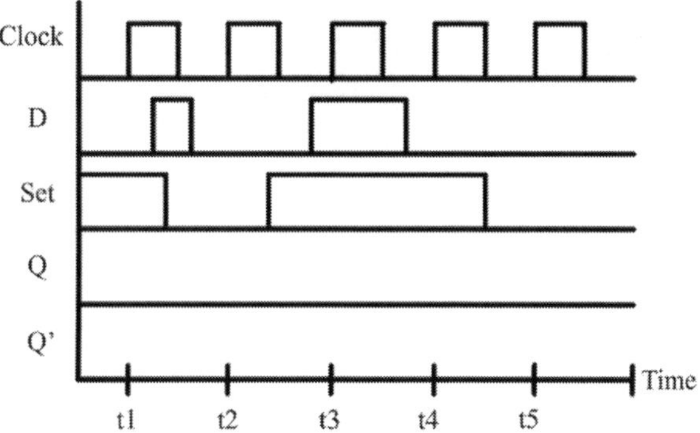

Since this is an active high set, there will be no bubble present at the set input. Since the D flip-flop is triggered on the rising edge, there will be no bubble present at the clock input. From this, we can deduce that the schematic will be the following.

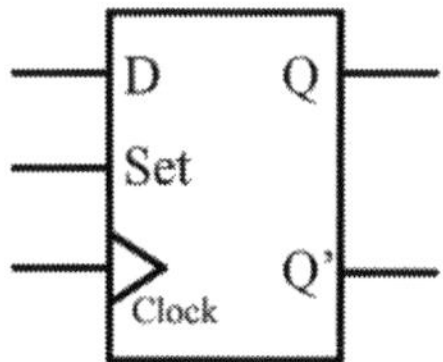

Since this is a flip-flop that is triggered on the rising clock edge, we can draw the following lines to signify the times a change may occur.

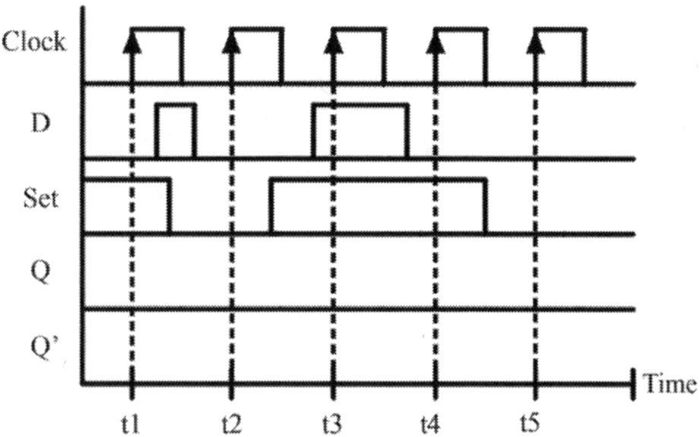

Since this set is synchronous, at each rising edge, whenever set is one, Q will be set to one regardless of the input at D. Whenever set is zero at the times of a rising edge, Q will be updated to whatever value is present at D. Applying these basic rules yields the following.

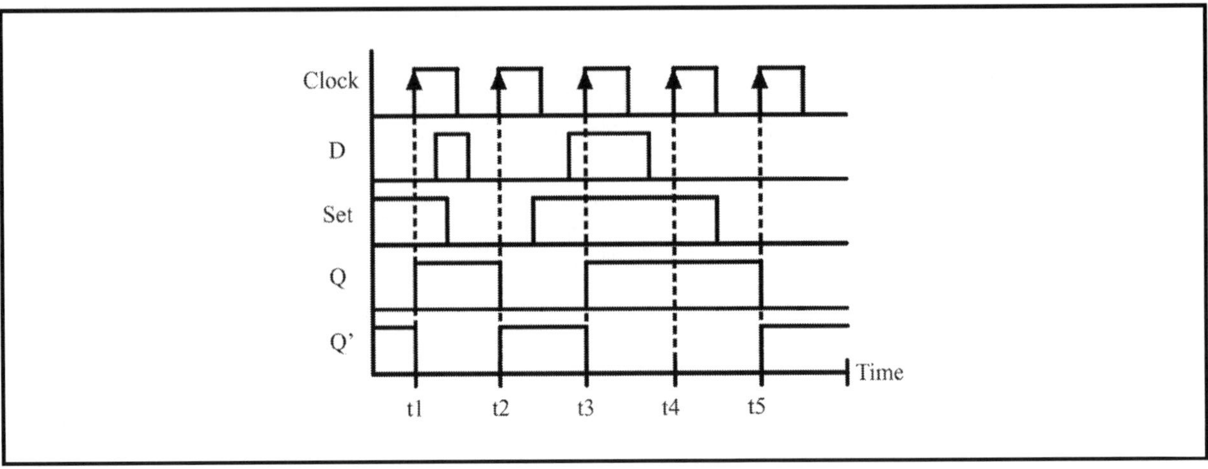

Example 2

For an ideal D flip-flop that is triggered on the falling clock edge and has an asynchronous active low set, draw the flip-flop symbol, and complete the following timing diagram.

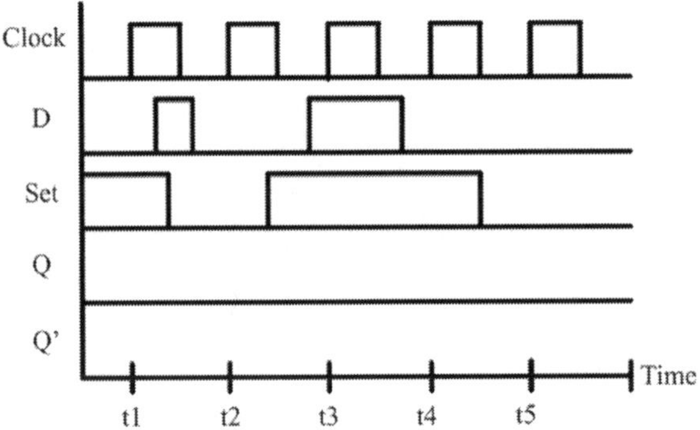

Since this is an active low set, there will be a bubble present at the set input. Since it is triggered on the falling edge, there will be a bubble present at the clock input. From this, we can deduce that the schematic will be the following.

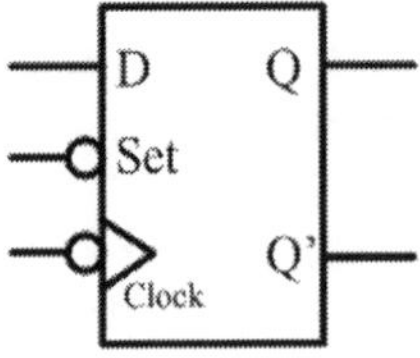

Since this is a flip-flop that is triggered on the falling clock edge, we can draw the following lines to signify the times a change may occur.

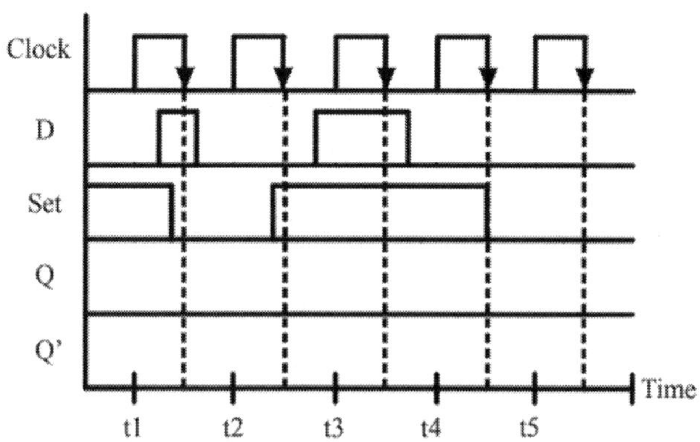

Since this set is an asynchronous and active low, whenever set is zero, Q will be set to one regardless of the input at D or clock pulse. Whenever set is one, then at the times of a rising edge, Q will be updated to whatever value is present at D. Applying these basic rules yields the following.

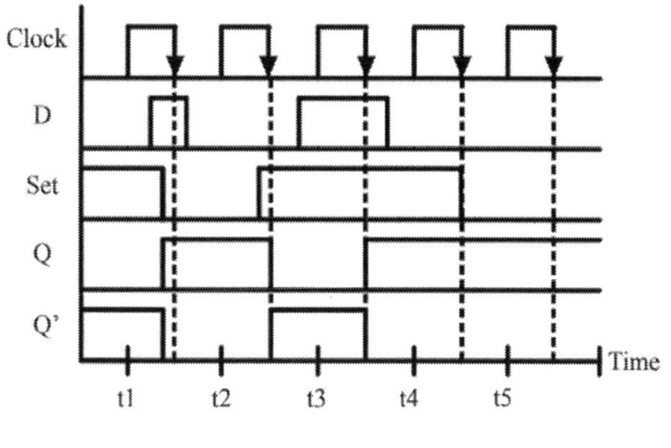

The last remaining flip-flop variations to discuss are D flip-flops that have enable signals. An enable signal essentially controls when a D flip-flop can update on each clock edge. One great way to implement an enable signal is to connect the output of a two input AND gate into the clock input of a D flip-flop. The AND gate will have both its inputs be the clock and enable signal. When the enable signal is zero, then no matter what the clock input is, the output of the AND gate will be zero, meaning no rising edge will be detected by the clock input of the D flip-flop, resulting in no updates to Q. When the enable signal is one, then the clock signal will be passed through the AND gate, enabling the flip-flop to function normally. The following figure shows how this works. In the figure, the circuit just now described is located on the left and has its equivalent simplified symbol on the right. It is important to note that an enable signal, just like the set and reset, may be active high or low. Figure 3.1.12 shows an active high enable, due the absence of a bubble. Had the figure been for an active low enable, then the circuit on the left would be modified to have an inverter between the enable signal and the top input of the AND gate. The symbol to the right would have been modified to have a bubble at the enable input.

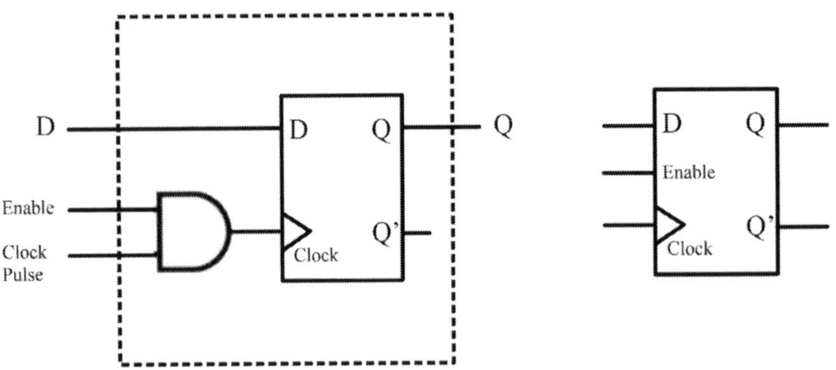

Figure 3.1.12 D flip-flop with active high enable. The internal view is on the left and overall symbol on the right.

To effectively demonstrate how an enable signal works, a complete example will be shown below.

Example 3

For an ideal D flip-flop that is triggered on the rising edge and has an active high enable, complete the following timing diagram. Also draw the schematic.

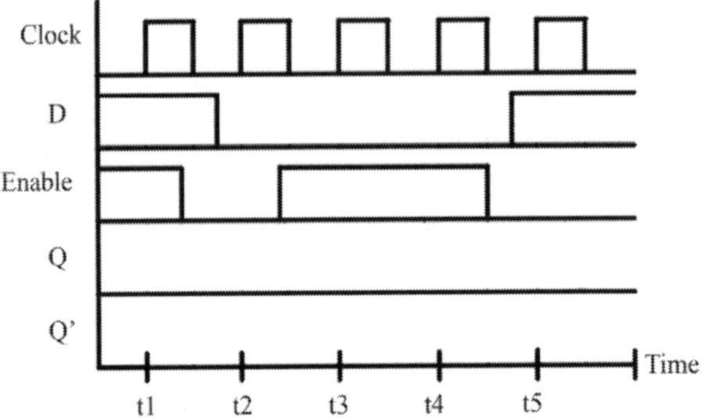

Since the enable signal is active high, there will be no bubble at the enable input. Since the flip-flop is rising edge, there will be no bubble at the clock input. Using this information, we can deduce that the schematic will be the following.

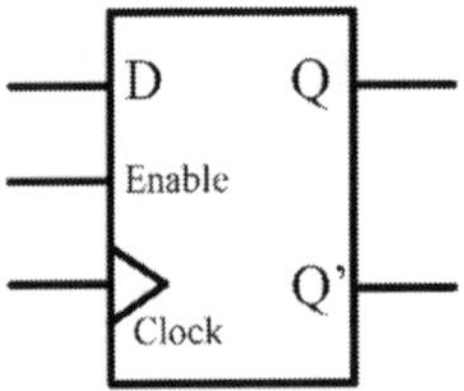

Since the flip-flop is triggered on the rising edge, we can modify the template to be the following.

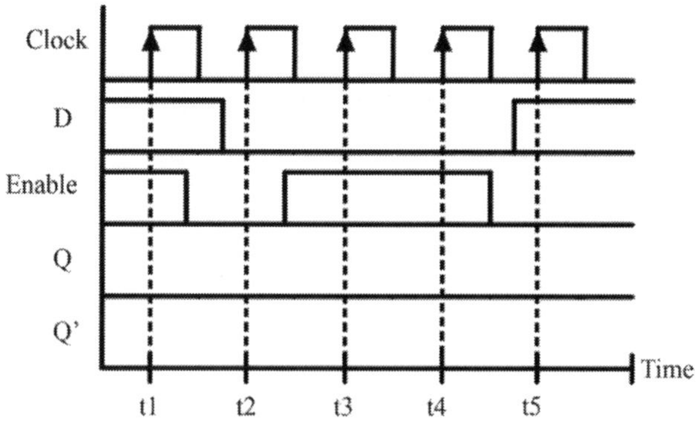

Since the enable is active high, this means that it will only enable the flip-flop to function normally whenever the enable input is one. When the enable signal is zero, then the rising clock edge will not update as if there were no clock edge in the first place. Using this information, we can modify the diagram to be the following.

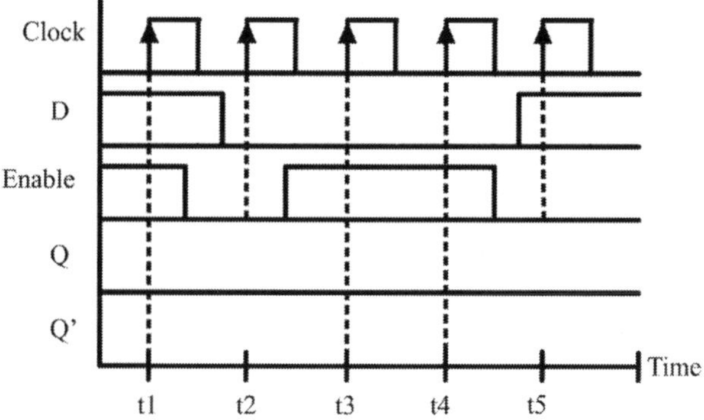

Now from this modified diagram, it is apparent that the enable signal only allows Q to update to the value present at D at times t1, t3, and t4. Using this we can obtain the final timing diagram.

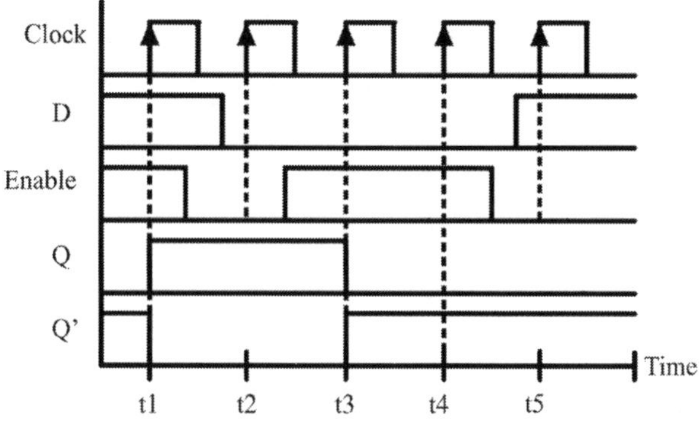

Now that the set, reset, enable, and different edge triggered variations of flip-flops have all been discussed, there is nothing more to be covered regarding D flip-flop types. The last remaining detail to discuss is the modeling of unideal flip-flops. So far, every flip-flop discussed was ideal since the updates to Q and Q′ were instant. In reality, these updates take time due to the flip-flops being non ideal. The time delay a flip-flop has when updating its output is commonly called the propagation delay. Before going into a complex example, it is best to see how the propagation delay affects the timing diagram of a standard flip-flop, i.e. one with no set, reset, or enable and is rising edge. The figure below shows the timing diagram for a standard D flip for both the ideal and unideal case, when subjected to the same input.

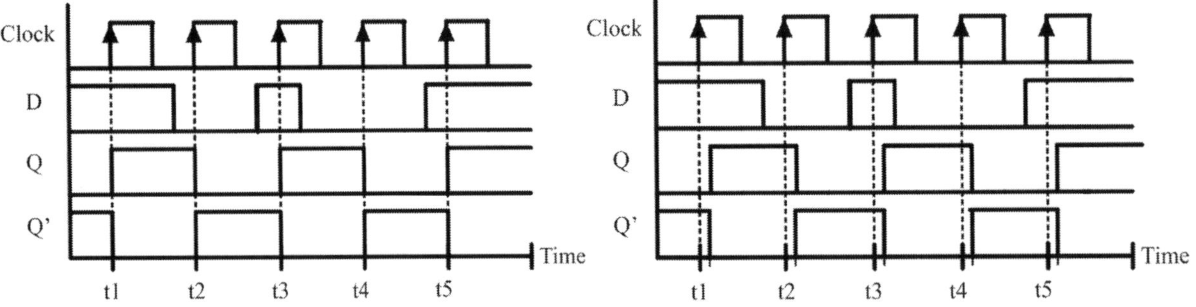

Figure 3.1.13 Ideal timing diagram (left) and non-ideal (right).

So, from the figure, you can see the timing diagram for the ideal flip-flop is on the left and the timing diagram for the non-ideal flip-flop is on the right. In the ideal diagram, the outputs Q instantly change on the rising edge. In the non-ideal diagram, there is a small propagation delay after each rising edge, meaning the transition for each rising edge happens slightly later. Fortunately for us, having the transition occur slightly after the clock edge is all that is needed to model the propagation delay. So now that we have completely gone over all the D flip-flop variations and discussed propagation delays, it's time to summarize everything with some comprehensive examples that incorporate everything.

Example 4

Using the D flip-flop pictured, complete the following timing diagram. Assume that the time for the output to change after the active edge of the clock is 10ns. The flip-flop has an asynchronous clear. Determine if this flip-flop is a rising or falling edge triggered one. Note that each division on the time axis is 5ns.

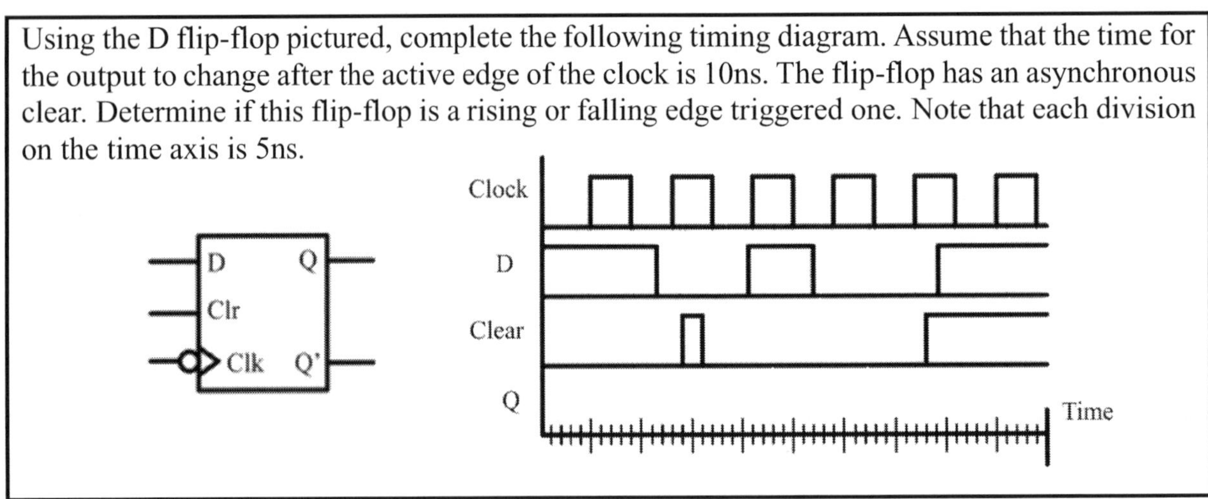

From the flip-flop symbol, the bubble on the clock input, abbreviated here as clk, means that the flip-flop is falling edge. As a result, we can update the timing diagram to the following.

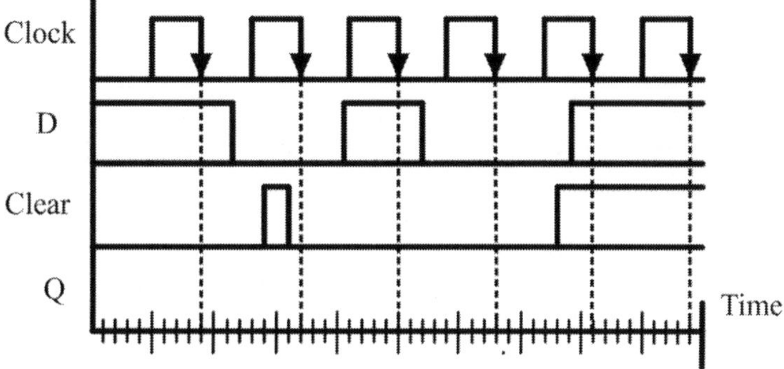

To start, we can follow the two following rules when creating the timing diagram. The first is that whenever Clr is high, Q is immediately reset to zero due to the clear being asynchronous. The second is that at each falling edge of the clock, after a 10 ns delay, Q is updated to match the value of D that was sampled at the falling clock edge, provided Clr has not been activated. When we apply these two rules, we are left with the final waveform below.

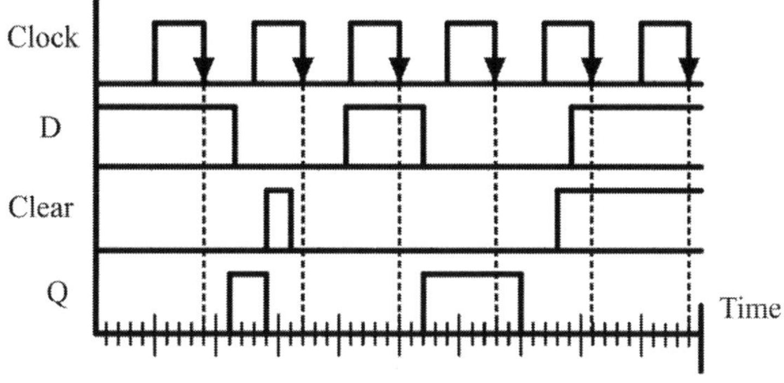

Example 5

Using the D flip-flop pictured, complete the following timing diagram. Assume that the time for the output to change after the active edge of the clock is 10ns. The flip-flop has a synchronous set. Determine if this flip-flop is a rising or falling edge triggered one. Note that each division on the time axis is 5ns.

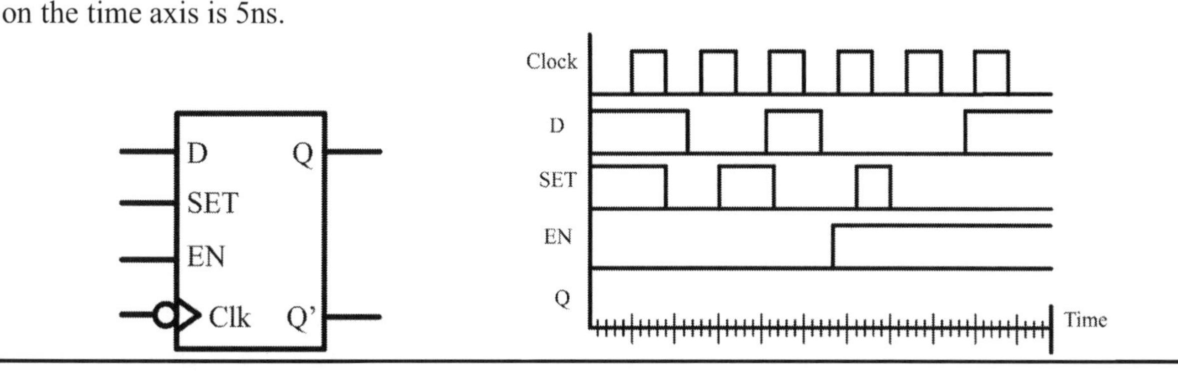

To start off, due to there being a bubble present at the clock, we know that this is a falling edge flip-flop. Also, the enable signal has no bubble, we know it is active high. These two things mean that the flip-flop will only update on its falling edge when EN is one. The timing diagram below shows how EN disables the first three falling edges but enables the remaining three.

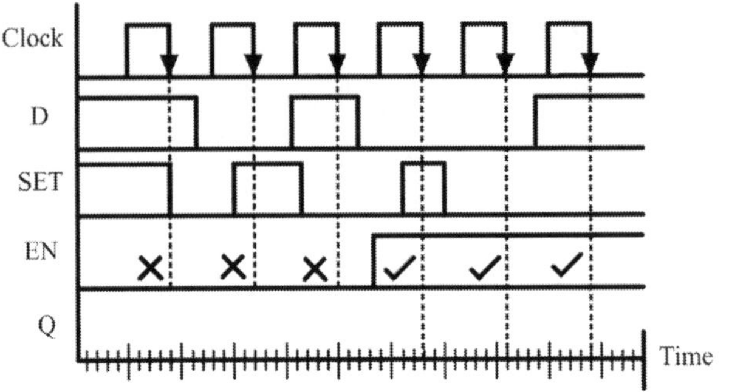

Next, due to there being no bubble present at the set input, we know it is active high. Since it is synchronous, we know that Q will update to be one 10 ns after SET is determined to be high. If SET is low, then Q it will update to D 10 ns later. Applying these rules results in the final diagram.

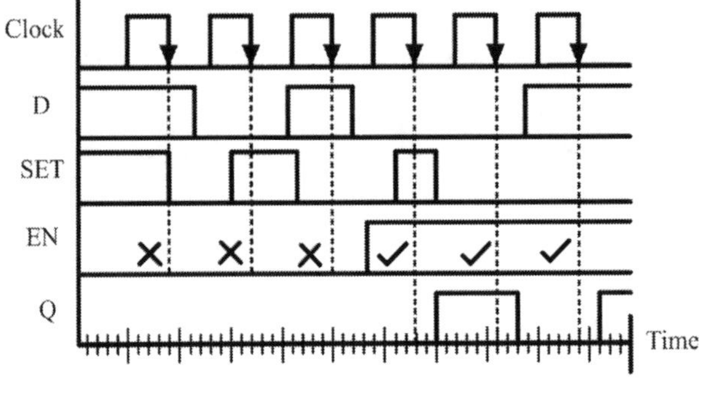

Now before discussing the next flip-flop, I will reveal the internals of the standard D flip-flop. All it is, is just a bunch of logical gates arranged in the configuration shown in the figure below. This arrangement of gates allows for the D flip-flop to have all its properties.

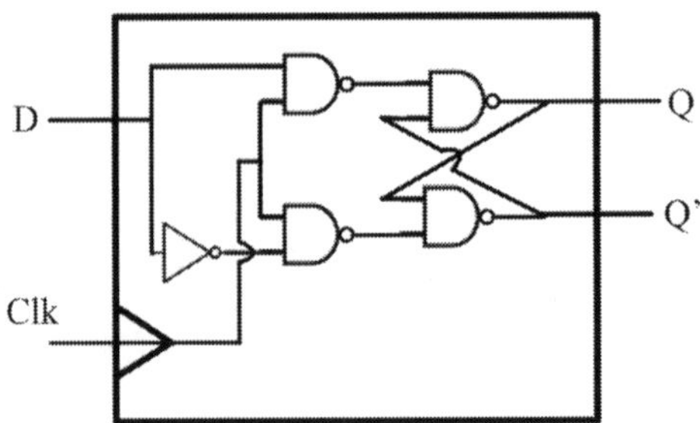

Figure 3.1.14 Internal view of generic D flip-flop.

3.2 JK Flip-Flop

Now that we have finally discussed all the nuances that you will need to know about the D flip-flop, it is time to discuss the second most important flip-flop, which is the JK flip-flop. The JK flip-flop is often chosen to be used in designs over the D flip-flop, since although choosing JK flip-flops over D flip-flops means performing more design work, it will result in a more hardware efficient solution than what would have been possible with D flip-flops. Fortunately, the variations of the JK flip-flop are done in the exact same way as for a D flip-flop. For example, a bubble on a clear input of a JK flip-flop would mean the JK flip-flop would clear the output to zero whenever the clear input is zero. Just like in the D flip-flop, the clear input may be synchronous or asynchronous. This chapter will, as a result, go much faster, due to there being very little new stuff to cover. So, to start, the only logical place to begin is in discussing the physical behavior of a standard JK flip-flop.

To begin, a standard JK flip-flop has three inputs, J, K, and Clock, with two outputs, Q and Q′. Fortunately, the JK flip-flops behavior is very simple. Whenever J and K are one, then the output Q will toggle on the next active clock edge. When J and K are both zero, then Q will not change on the next active clock edge. Whenever J is zero and K is one, then Q will become zero on the next active clock edge. Whenever J is one and K is zero, then Q will become one on the next active clock edge. The following figure shows both the symbol for a standard JK flip-flop and the associated truth table.

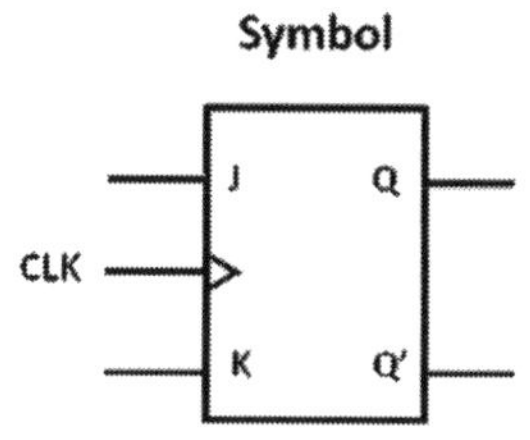

Truth Table

CLK	J	K	Q
↑	0	0	No Change
↑	0	1	0
↑	1	0	1
↑	1	1	Toggle

Figure 3.2.1 JK flip-flop symbol and truth table.

Now that the basic behavior of the JK flip-flop has been described, it is time to go over some examples of variations. The only new variations of a JK flip-flop are those that may have an enable vs no enable, be rising vs falling edge, and lastly have a synchronous vs asynchronous set or reset. Since every one of these terms has been described in the previous section on D flip-flops, only a table summarizing each term will be provided for your reference before jumping straight into the examples. In this section, no paragraphs will be written describing or using each term, due to that having already happened in the previous section.

Terminology	
Asserted	If an input is asserted, it means that the input received the value required to influence the output, Q. For example, if a one is present at an active-high set input, then the set will be asserted and set the output, Q, to one. If a zero was present at the same active-high set input, then the set would be de-asserted and have no effect on the output.

Enable	An enable when asserted, will allow the output of the flip-flop to update in accordance with its truth table. For example, is a zero is present at an active-low enable input, then the flip-flop will update its output, Q, on the rising edge.
Synchronous Reset	A synchronous reset means that if the reset pin is asserted on the next clock edge, the output of the flip-flop, Q will be set to zero.
Asynchronous Reset	An asynchronous reset means that if the reset pin is asserted, the output of the flip-flop, Q, will be set to zero instantly.
Synchronous Set	A synchronous set means that if the set pin is asserted on the next clock edge, the output of the flip-flop, Q will be set to one.
Asynchronous Set	An asynchronous set means that if the set pin is asserted, the output of the flip-flop, Q, will be set to one instantly.
Rising Edge Flip-Flop	A rising edge flip-flop is one that updates its output Q on the rising edge of a pulse coming into the clock input. A rising edge flip-flop will have no bubble present at the clock input.
Falling Edge Flip-Flop	A falling edge flip-flop is one that updates its output Q on the falling edge of a pulse coming into the clock input. A falling edge flip-flop will have a bubble present at the clock input.
Active High	An active high input is one that requires one to be asserted. An active high input has no bubble.
Active Low	An active low input is one that requires zero to be asserted. An active low input has a bubble.

Example 1

Using the JK flip-flop pictured, complete the following timing diagram. Assume that the time for the output to change after the active edge of the clock is 10ns. The flip-flop has an active-low enable. Determine if this flip-flop is a rising or falling edge triggered one. Note that each division on the time axis is 5ns.

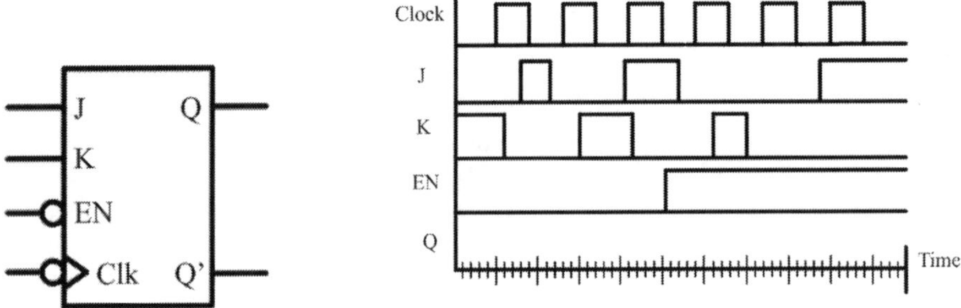

We should first note that the flip-flop is falling edge due to the bubble present at the clock input. It also has an active low enable due to the bubble present at the enable input. Using these two pieces of information we can modify the timing diagram to be the following. The check marks at times t1, t2, and t3, indicate that since the enable pin is low, the flip-flop will update Q with each falling edge. The X marks at times t4, t5, and t6, indicate that since the enable pin is high, no updates will be permitted.

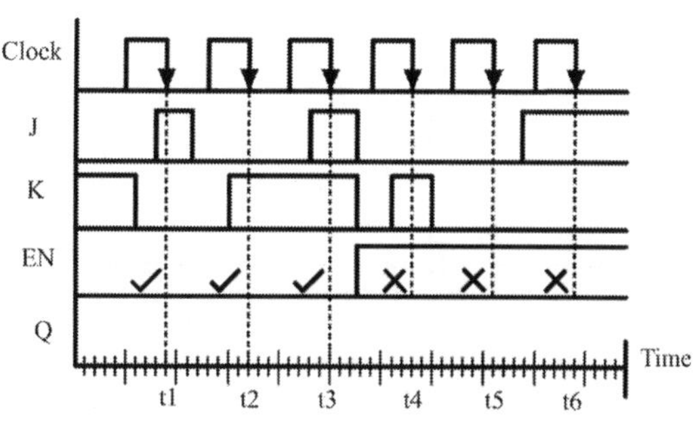

At time t1, since J was one and K was zero, the output according to the truth table and delay, will change to one at t1+10ns. At time t2, since J was zero and K was one, the output will change to zero at t2+10ns. At time t3, since J was one and K was one, the output will toggle from its current value, resulting in Q changing to one at t3+10ns. Since the enable was de-asserted for the remining three clock edges, no change occurs again. Below shows the result.

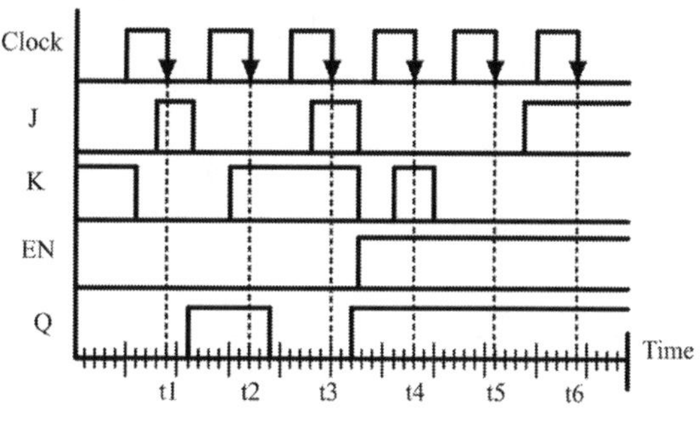

Example 2

Using the JK flip-flop pictured, complete the following timing diagram. Assume that the time for the output to change after the active edge of the clock is 10ns. The flip-flop has an asynchronous set. Determine if this flip-flop is a rising or falling edge triggered one. Note that each division on the time axis is 5ns.

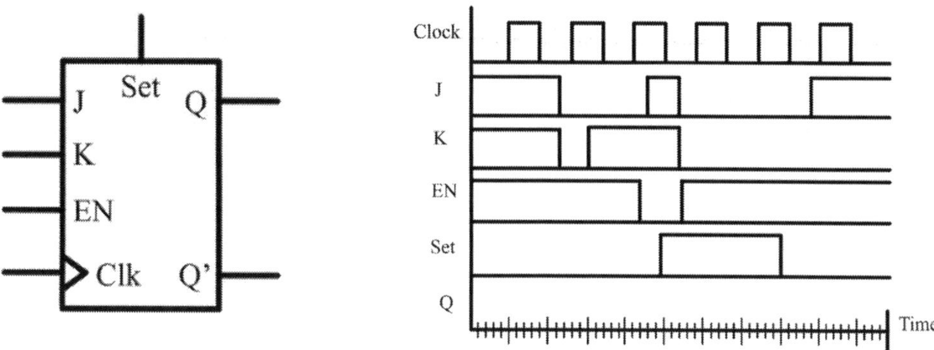

From the flip-flop symbol not having a bubble on the clock input, it should be evident that this flip-flop is rising edge. Since the enable sinal does not have a bubble, we know it is active high. From these two facts, we can redraw the diagram to be the following.

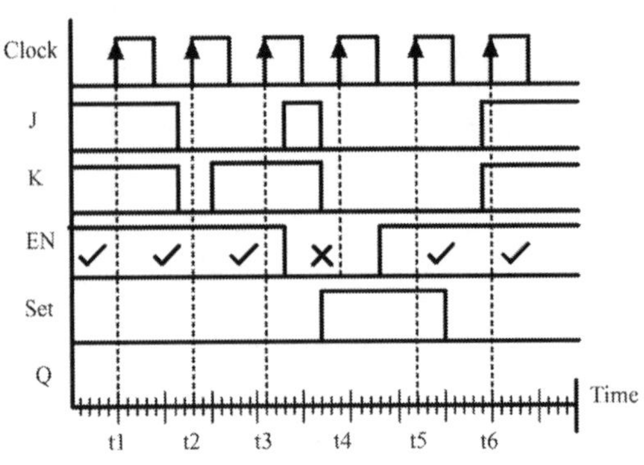

At time t1, both J and K are one, meaning Q will toggle after the propogation delay, at t1+10ns. At time t2, both J and K are zero, meaning Q will not change. At time t3, J is zero and K is one, meaning that Q will become zero after the propogation delay, at t3+10ns. At time t4-15ns to t5+15ns, the set input is asserted, meaning that Q will be one during this time. At time t6, both J and K are one, meaning Q will toggle after the propogation delay, at t6+10ns. The resultant diagram is below.

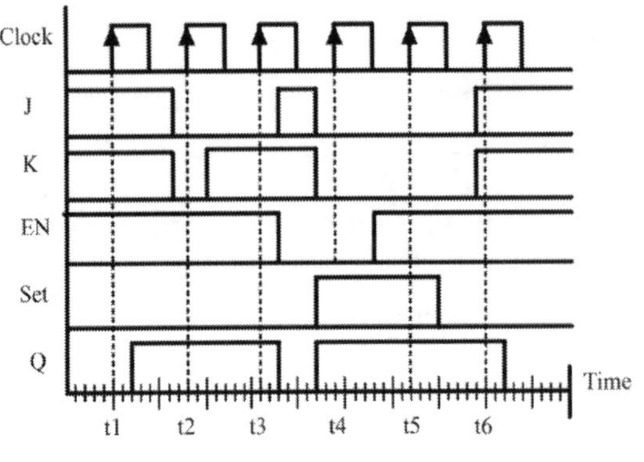

Example 3

Using the JK flip-flop pictured, complete the following timing diagram. Assume that the time for the output to change after the active edge of the clock is 10ns. The flip-flop has a synchronous set. Determine if this flip-flop is a rising or falling edge triggered one. Note that each division on the time axis is 5ns. Note that this problem is identical to example 2 except in that the set is now synchronous.

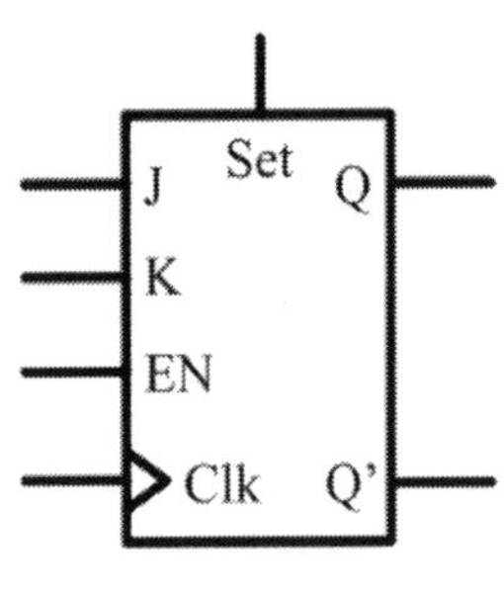

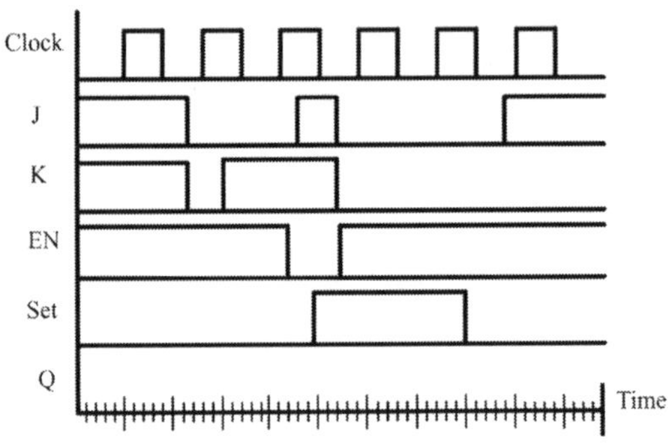

As in example 2, it should be evident that this flip-flop is rising edge and that it is active high. From these two facts, we can redraw the diagram to be the following.

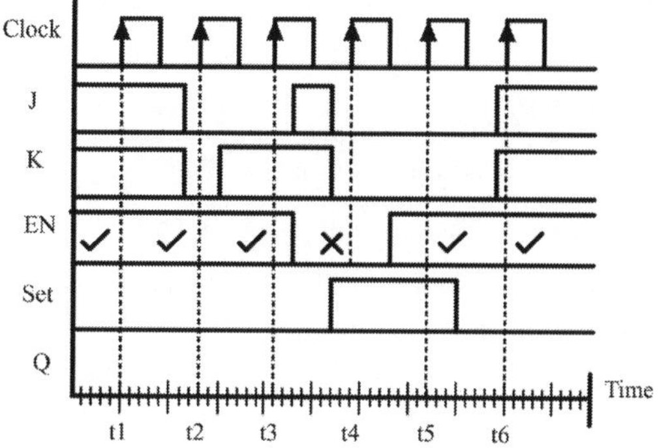

Now that it is a synconouse set, instead of Q instantly changing to one at t4-15ns, the flip-flop must wait for the next enabled rising clock edge. The clock edge at time t4 was disabled due to the enable signal being low, so the set was not able to occur at t4+10ns. The clock edge at time t5 was enabled due to the enable signal being high, so the set was able to occur at t5+10ns. The final diagram is below.

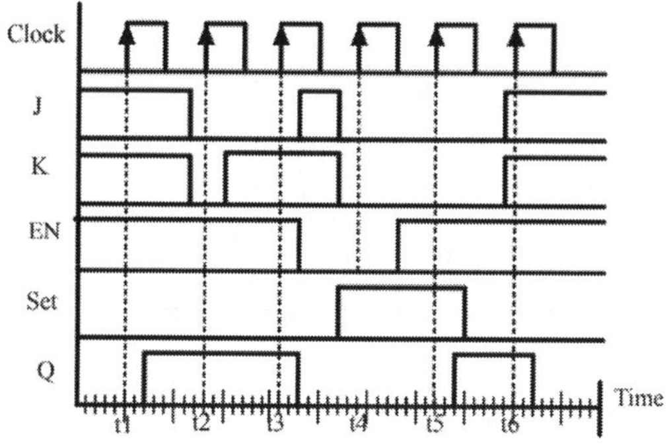

3.3 T Flip-Flop and SR Flip-Flop

Now that we have discussed the two main flip-flops, the D and JK flip-flop, it is time to cover the remaining two, which are the T and SR flip-flop. These two flip-flops are usually not used much, so the different variations of each will not be covered. All that will be discussed in this section is the behavior of these flip-flops.

To start off, I will go over the T flip-flop. The T flip-flop is by far the simplest flip-flop due to it only having a single input, T, with the two outputs Q and Q′. When the input to the T flip-flop is zero, the output Q will remain unchanged on the next clock edge. When the input is one, the output Q will toggle on the next clock edge. For this reason, the T flip-flip is short for Toggle flip-flop. Below shows the symbol and truth table. One interesting fact is that a T flip-flop can be made from a JK flip-flip by connecting the J and K inputs together.

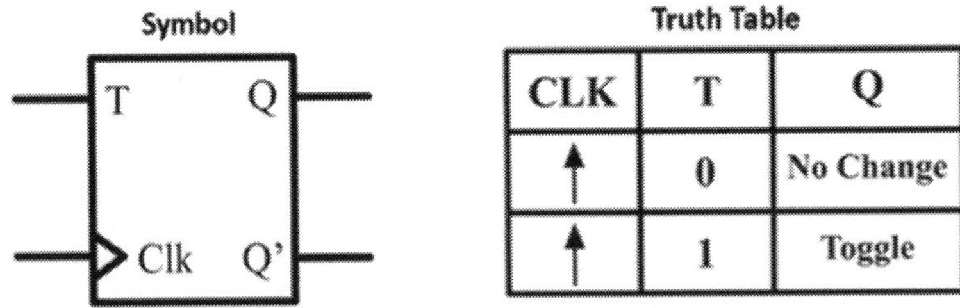

Truth Table

CLK	T	Q
↑	0	No Change
↑	1	Toggle

Figure 3.3.1 T flip-flop symbol and truth table.

Now that the T flip-flop has been discussed, it is time to go over the behavior of the SR flip-flop. The SR flip-flop, short for Set-Reset flip-flop has two inputs S and R. The outputs for the SR flip-flop are still Q and Q′, just as in the other three flip-flops. The flip-flip is very simple because its first input, S, is used to set the output, Q, to one on the next clock edge. The second input, R, is used to reset the output, Q, to zero on the next clock edge. It makes a ton of sense that this is the case since S stands for set and R for reset. When both S and R are zero, there is no change, when both S and R are one, the output, Q, is unknown. For this reason, S and R should never be one at the same time. The symbol and truth table are shown below for the SR flip-flop.

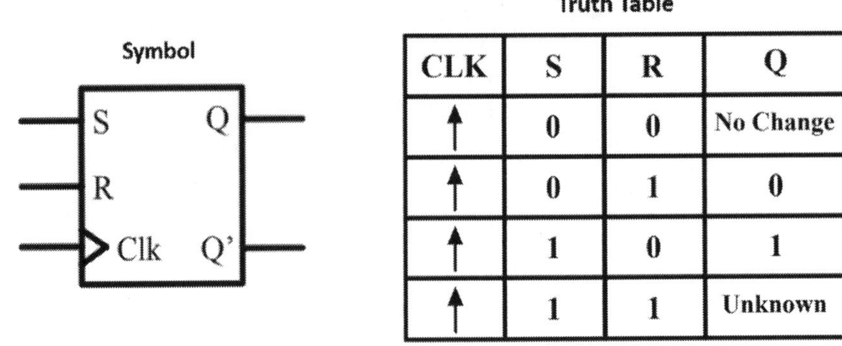

Truth Table

CLK	S	R	Q
↑	0	0	No Change
↑	0	1	0
↑	1	0	1
↑	1	1	Unknown

Figure 3.3.2 T flip-flop symbol and truth table.

3.4 Building a Traffic Light with sequential logic

Now that we have gone over the basic building blocks of a sequential circuit, we can finally begin to move on to using them to build a digital circuit. Just like how in the combinational logic section, we started with a simple example showing how to create a multiplexer from scratch using combinational logic, we will start with a simple example showing how to make a traffic light from scratch using sequential logic. Going through the entire design process for the traffic light example will be a great way to introduce you to all the steps involved in a sequential design. The sections that follow will then go into the specifics of each phase in the design process.

So, when making a traffic light, we will need to consider what the inputs and outputs are. Assuming we are making a traffic light system for the figure below, we will have a total of six outputs. They are G1, G2, G3, R1, R2, and R3. Note that G stands for green and R stands for red. This means for example, that G1 stands for green light one and the R2 stands for red light two. In this example there are no yellow lights to keep it simple.

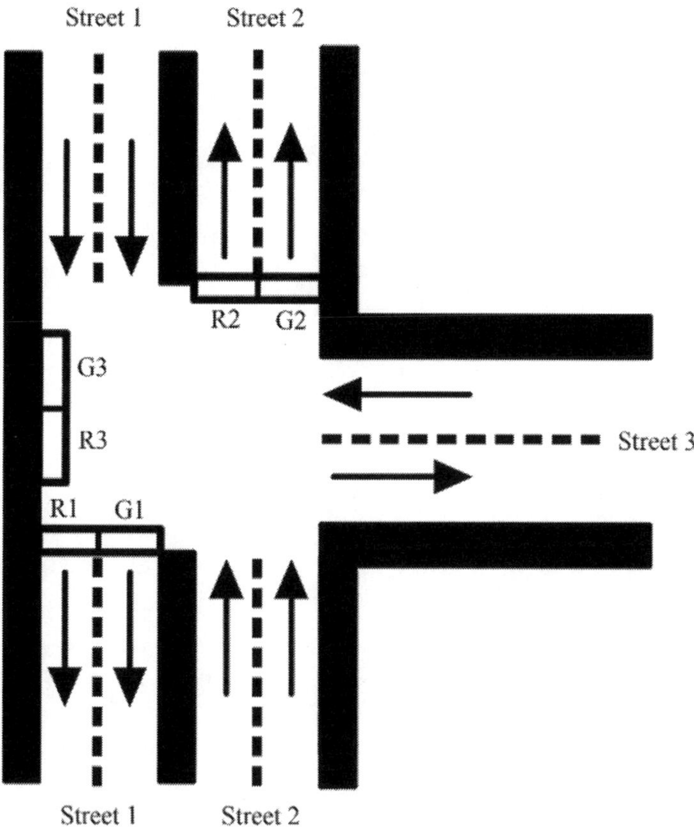

Figure 3.4.1 Simple Street with three green lights and three red lights.

For a simple traffic light, there will be no inputs, since the light will alternate between states giving the cars in each street time to pass. This means that for a simple traffic light design there will be a total of three states. One where G1, R2, and R3 are 1, with the rest zero. One where G2, R1, and R3 are 1, with the rest zero. And lastly, one where G3, R1, and R2 are 1, with the rest zero. Now we must make a state table to show what states correspond to this fixed output sequence. The following table shows this.

State	G1	G2	G3	R1	R2	R3
0	1	0	0	0	1	1
1	0	1	0	1	0	1
2	0	0	1	1	1	0

Figure 3.4.2 State table for simple street with three green lights and three red lights.

Now that we have the state table describing the behavior of the circuit, we must convert the state into two binary digits that two D flip-flops can use to store the state. When we do the conversion, we get the following table in Figure 3.4.3 One D flip-flop will store the digit S1, and another D flip-flop will store the digit S0. Note that in place of state 0, came {S1, S0} = {0, 0}. This is because 00 in binary is equal to 0 in decimal. For state 1, in its place came {S1, S0} = {0, 1} because 01 in binary is equal to 1 in decimal. The same thing occurred for state 2. Now you may be wondering why an additional state 3 was added. This state was added because when doing the 2-variable K-Maps for this table, we will need to know what value was present when S1 and S0 are both one. Since we never really needed this state, we put don't cares in the outputs. Another thing you may notice is the addition of S1+ and S0+ as outputs. What these outputs mean is the next state the circuit will go to. For example, when we are in state 0, G1, R2, and R3 will be on with the rest zero, allowing the cars in street 1 to pass. Next, upon exiting state 0, we will go to state 1, signified by {S1+, S0+} = {0, 1}. In state 1, the outputs will allow for the cars in street two to pass. Next, upon exiting state 1, we will go to state 2, signified by {S1+, S0+} = {1, 0}. In state 2, the outputs will allow for the cars in street 3 to pass. Next, upon existing state 2, we will go to state 0 again, signified by {S1+, S0+} = {0, 0}. By going in a loop of states, we can give each street a turn forever for an equal amount of time each. It is important to note that the state table made in Figure 3.4.3 was done with the assumption that D flip-flops were used. The procedure is different for JK flip-flops, which will be discussed later.

S1	S0	G1	G2	G3	R1	R2	R3	S1+	S0+
0	0	1	0	0	0	1	1	0	1
0	1	0	1	0	1	0	1	1	0
1	0	0	0	1	1	1	0	0	0
1	1	X	X	X	X	X	X	X	X

Figure 3.4.3 State table with binary states for D flip-flop design.

Now that we have the state table with the binary states, we simply create K-Maps and generate the equations for each output. The following figure shows the K-Maps for G1, S1+, and S0+. The equations for all are given next.

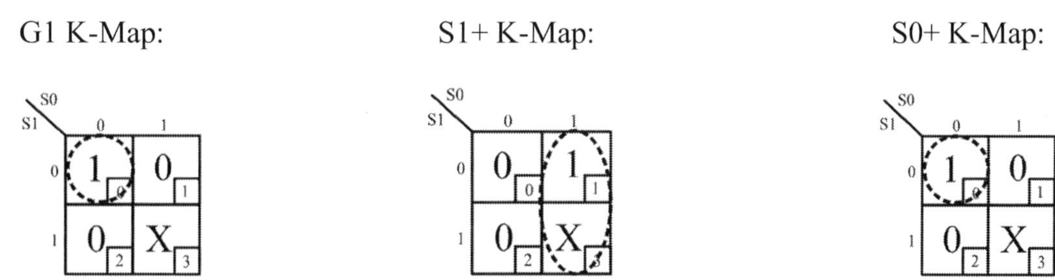

Figure 3.4.4 K-Maps for G1, S1+, and S0+

Equations for all outputs:

G1: S1'S0'
G2: S0
G3: S1
R1: S1 + S0
R2: S1 + S0'
R3: S1'
S1+: S0
S0+: S1'S0'

Now that we have the equations, all that remains is to convert them into hardware. The circuit below shows the entire circuit for the simple traffic light. If you really want to see this circuit in action, scan the QR code to simulate it.

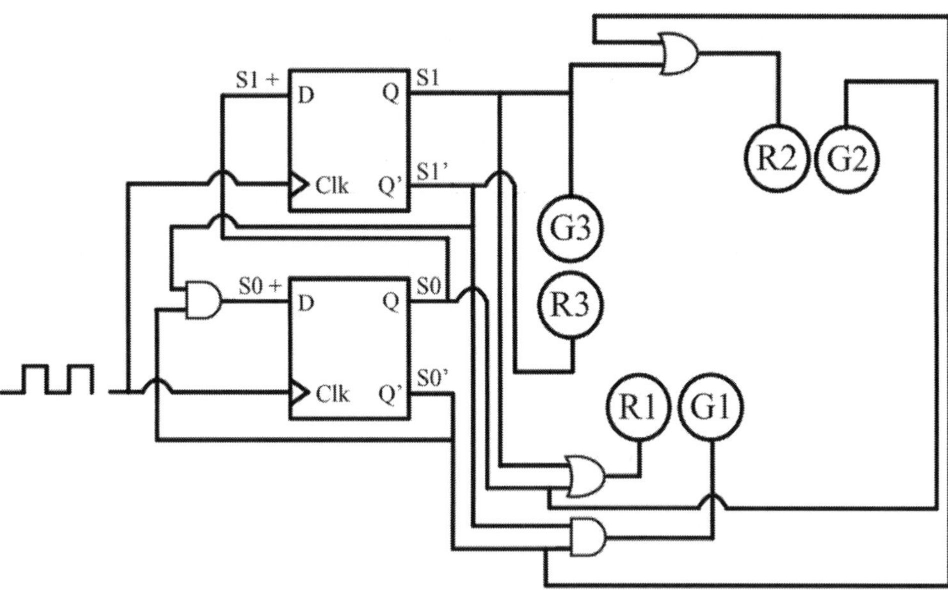

Figure 3.4.5 Sequential circuit for simple traffic light.

So, there you have it! We have completely gone through the sequential design process for a simple traffic light. Now although this was the design flow for this instance, we usually don't always start with a state table, since for more complicated designs it may not be as easy to make it from scratch using common sense like we did here. In general, we usually start with a state diagram, then generate our state table, replace the states with binary states, generate K-Maps, get equations from the K-Maps, then finally assemble the hardware. The next section will explain this initial state diagram step that was omitted in the traffic light example due to it just not being necessary at the time.

3.5 Mealy Vs Moore State Diagrams

To start off, there are two kinds of state diagrams, Mealy and Moore. Both can usually be used to get the job done, so it usually is up to you which one you want to use. In some instances, one type will be required, so it's good to know both.

We will first go over a Moore machine, due to it being much simpler. A Moore diagram, also referred to as a Moore machine, generates its outputs based solely on the current state. The inputs may determine the next state, but the outputs are fixed for any given state. A Moore state diagram will have a circle, also called a node, for each state and will have the format shown in the figure below. As you can see, the state is always on the top and the output will be on the bottom.

Figure 3.5.1 Node format for Moore diagram

When your sequential circuit has multiple states, which is always the case, the nodes for each will be connected as shown in the following figure. The figure below shows a random Moore state machine with four states, one input, I0, and two outputs, A and B.

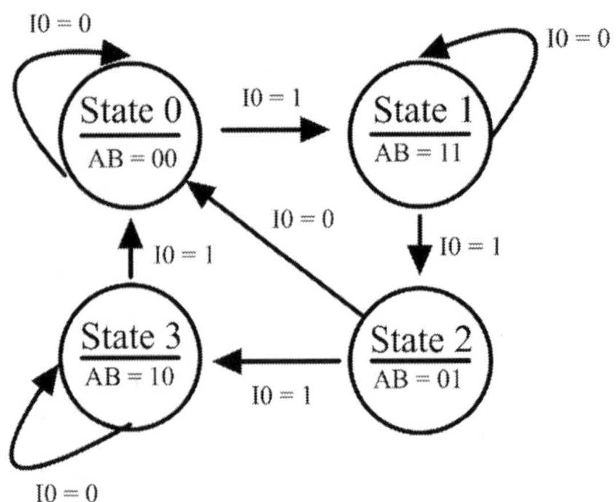

Figure 3.5.2 Moore diagram example

The input is what determines what the next state is, which is why each node has two arrows going out for every possible input combination, which in this case is just two. If we had two inputs, then the diagram would immediately become complex, since then each node would have not two, but four arrows going out. If there were three inputs, then there would be eight arrows going out. Now that you have a basic idea of what a Moore diagram is, it is time to use it in a few examples to demonstrate how practical a tool it is.

Example 1

A state machine detects a sequence of 3 ones in a row through its input, I0, and has its output, Z, turn to one when the third 1 is received. When the third one is received, the machine goes back to the state needed to repeat again on the next read input. The following shows the desired response of Z given an input sequence into I0. Make a Moore machine to model the system.

I0:	0	0	1	1	**1**	0	0	1	0	0	1	1	**1**	1	1	**1**
Z:	0	0	0	0	**1**	0	0	0	0	0	0	0	**1**	0	0	**1**

To start off, we need to decide how many states to have. It is logical to have state 0 correspond to when no one's have been received, state 1 correspond to when a single one was received, state 2 correspond to when two ones were received, and state three correspond to when all three ones have been received. This line of reasoning results in four total states. We know that the only state where the output will be one is in state 3, since only that state is when the target was reached. Using this information, we can write the following when starting the state diagram.

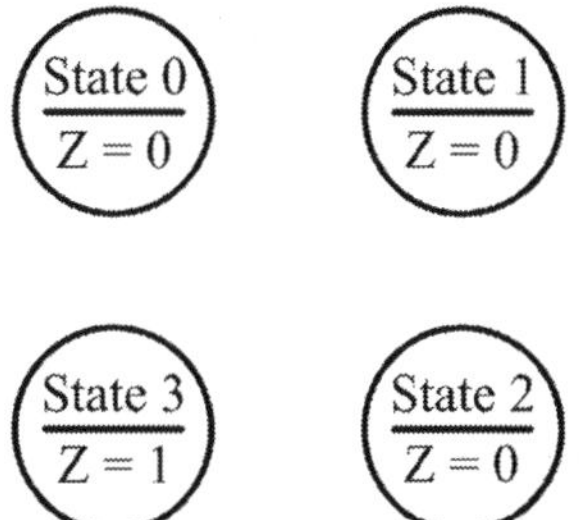

Now that we have the state nodes all written with the correct output, all that is needed now is to connect them with arrows for the input, I0. We know that when we are in state 0, if we get a zero, we don't have the first one yet, so we stay in state 0. We know that when we are in state 0, if we get a one, we have the first one, so we go to state 1. From this, we can write the arrows for state 0 to be the following.

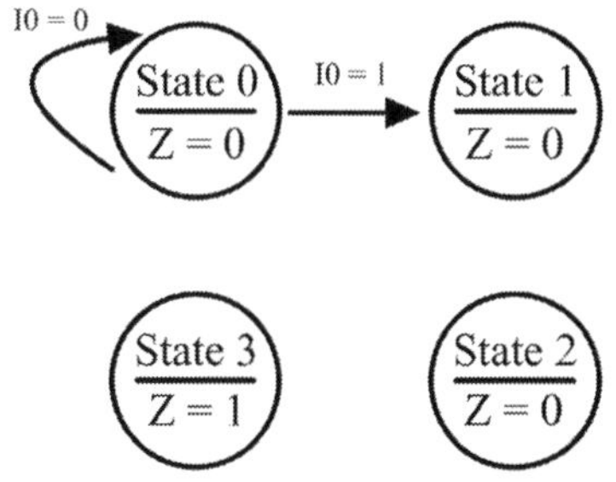

In state 1, when we get a one, we will have gotten the second one, meaning we will go to state two. In state 2, when we get a one, we will have gotten the third one, meaning we will go to state three. For both state 1 and 2 if we get a zero, we have no chance of getting three in a row anymore, so we go back to the first state, state 0. Below shows the arrows representing this behavior.

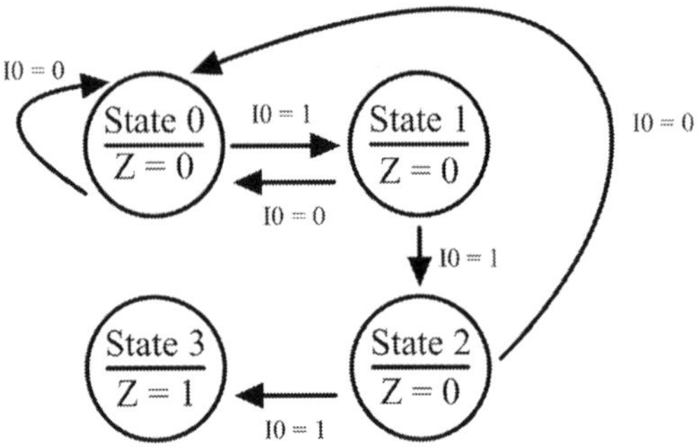

The only question that remains now is what to do when we are in state 3 and receive the next input. When in state three and a zero is received, obviously, we go to state zero. But what of when a one is received? Would we go to state 0 or state 1? Well, if a one is received, we will have gotten the first one needed for a new set of three, meaning we would need to go to state 1. For clarity the two sequence inputs show what would happen if we incorrectly went to state 0 when a 1 was received, since it would behave as if it were a zero that was received. The final diagram is also shown.

When state 3 correctly changes to state 1 upon receiving a one:

I0:	0	0	1	1	**1**	1	1	**1**
Z:	0	0	0	0	1	0	0	1
State:	0	0	1	2	3	1	2	3

When state 3 incorrectly changes to state 0 upon receiving a one:

I0:	0	0	1	1	**1**	1	1	**1**
Z:	0	0	0	0	1	0	0	0
Sate:	0	0	1	2	3	0	1	2

The final diagram:

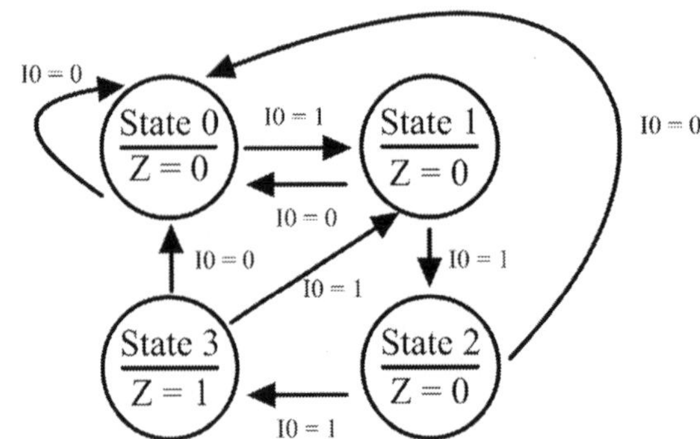

Example 2

A state machine counts in an arbitrary sequence of 4, 5, 9, 2, 3, 0 before repeating again. Make a Moore machine to model the system.

To make a counter, we take advantage of the fact that the state itself can be an output, due to it physically corresponding to 1s and 0s stored in flip-flops. Using this fact, there are no other needed outputs or inputs. The state machine will go to the next state upon each clock edge automatically as shown below.

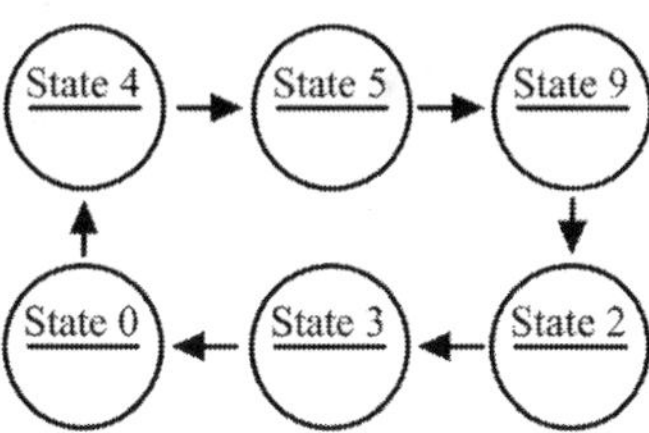

Example 3

A state machine has one input and one output that will produce an output of 0 whenever three 0's are input in a row and 1 otherwise. It resets as soon as a 1 is received, but overlapping targets are allowed. An example sequence is provided. Make a Moore machine to model the system.

IN:	0	0	**0**	1	1	0	0	1	0	0	**0**	**0**	0	1	0	0
OUT:	1	1	**0**	1	1	1	1	1	1	1	**0**	**0**	1	1	1	1

To start off, we need to decide how many states to have. It is logical to have the first state, state 0, correspond to when no zeros have been received, then to have the second state, state 1, correspond to when one zero has been received, then to have the third state, state 2, correspond to when two zeros have been received and the have the fourth state, state 3, correspond to when three zeros have been received. We know that the output is zero only in state 3 since that's when three zeros have been received. Using this information we can draw the following.

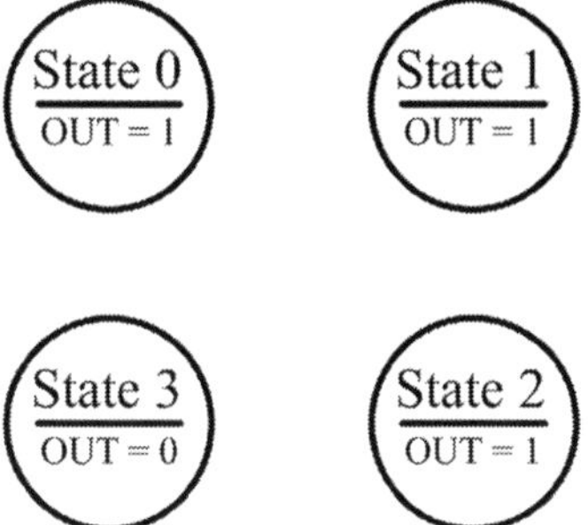

Now all that is needed to do is connect the nodes with arrows for the input. We know that anytime we get a one in any state, it resets back to state 0. We know that when in state 0, we go state 1 when receiving the first zero. We know that when in state 1, we go state 2 when receiving a second zero. We know that when in state 2, we go state 3 when receiving the third zero. When in state 3, since overlapping targets are allowed, we will stay in state 3 when a zero is received. Using this we can draw the following to obtain the final diagram.

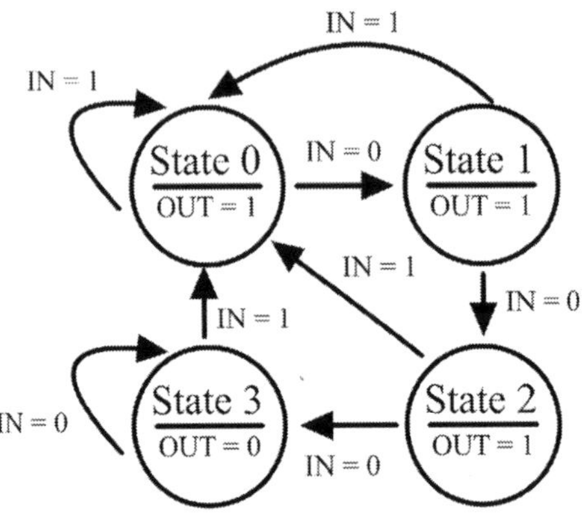

So now that you have been exposed to the Moore machine and seen the Moore machine model a variety of different situations, it is time to move on to the next type of state diagram, which is the Mealy machine. The outputs in a Mealy machine depend on the current state and the input, not just the current state as in a Moore machine. This means the output can change as the inputs change, even within the same state. This means a Mealy circuit will in a sense behave like a combinational circuit due to the output being able to instantly with the input. It must however wait for the edge signal to progress to the next state. A Mealy state diagram will have nodes like in the Moore diagrams, however there will only be the state inside the node. Below shows the format of a node in a Mealy machine.

Figure 3.5.3 Node format for Mealy diagram

Now that you know what the nodes look like, it is time to reveal what an entire Mealy diagram would look like. The figure that follows shows a random Mealy state machine with four states, one input, I0, and two outputs, A and B.

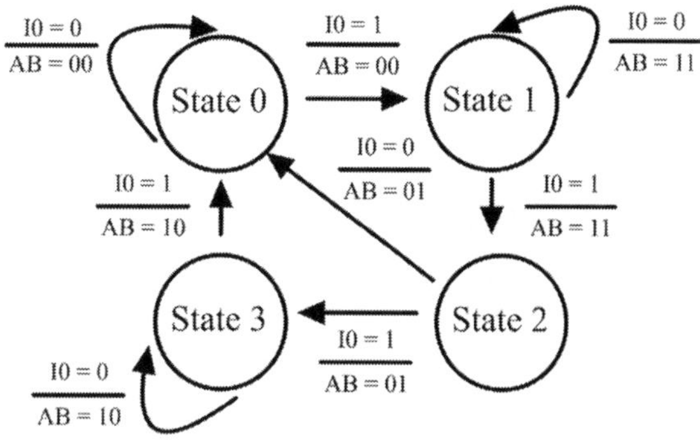

Figure 3.5.4 Mealy diagram example

The primary difference between a Moore machine and a Mealy machine is that a Mealy machine has the outputs associated with the links, whereas the Moore Machine had its output associated with the state. To convert a Moore machine to a Mealy machine, all you must simply do is move the output to be associated with the links rather than the state. In any Mealy machine, the links will always have the format shown in Figure 3.5.5 where the input is on top and the output on the bottom. It is also important to note that this random Mealy machine isn't entirely random, as it is the Mealy equivalent of the Moore machine from Figure 3.5.2. You are free to perform the conversion yourself if you want to see how that process works.

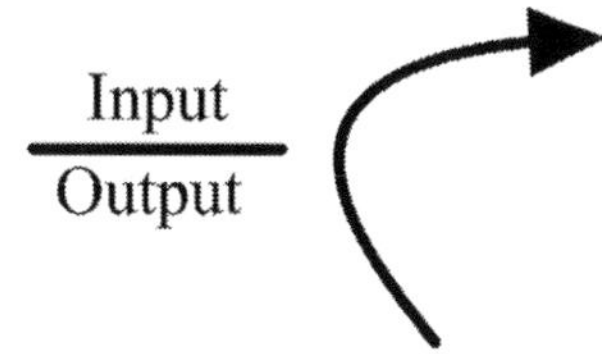

Figure 3.5.5 Mealy Link Format

Now that the Mealy diagram has been fully discussed, the next logical course of action is to show it being used in practice. The following examples will demonstrate the use of a Mealy diagram.

Example 4

A state machine detects a sequence of 2 ones in a row through its input, I0, and has its output, Z, turn to one when the second 1 is received. The following shows the desired response of Z given an input sequence into I0. Make a Mealy machine to model the system. The bold columns show when the target of two consecutive ones have been received.

I0:	0	0	0	1	**1**	0	0	1	0	0	1	**1**	**1**	1	**1**	**1**
Z:	0	0	0	0	**1**	0	0	0	0	0	0	**1**	**1**	0	**1**	**1**

The first step is to decide how many states to have. It is logical to have state 0 correspond to when no ones have been received, state 1 correspond to when the first one has been received, and lastly, state 3 correspond to when the second one has been received. This leaves us with a total of three states from 0-2. Using this line of reasoning, we can start with the following template for the Mealy diagram.

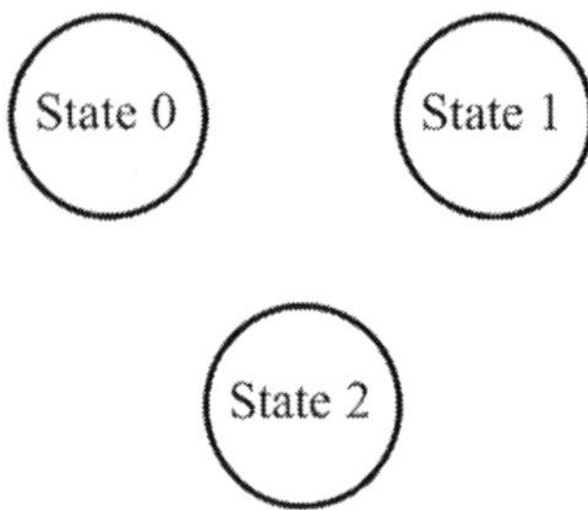

The next step is to write the links for when the target is reached, i.e. when many ones are received consecutively. When in state 0, upon receiving the first one, we go to state 1 with Z outputting a zero in the link. When in state 1, upon receiving the second one, we go to state 2 with Z outputting a one in the link, due to having reached the target. When in state 2, upon receiving a another one, to allow for overlapping targets as shown in the given response, we go to state 2 again with Z outputting a one in the link. The diagram below shows the template modified to represent this behavior.

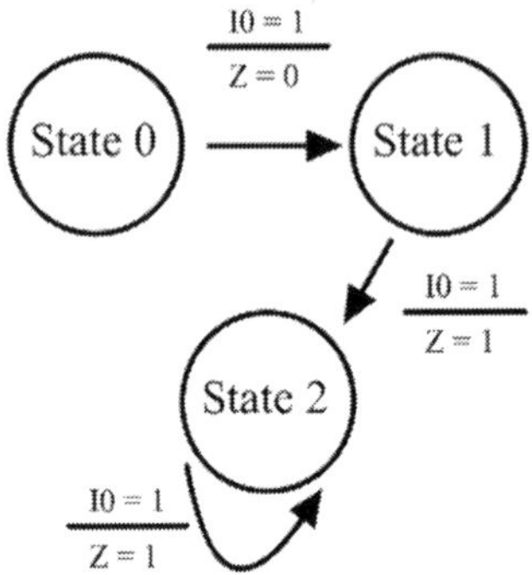

The final step is to consider what links would come for when an input of zero is received. Looking at the example sequence, it is evident that when a zero is obtained, the state machine resets because it now requires two ones to reach the target. Using this, the links for every state will go to state 0 with Z as zero when an input of zero is received. The diagram below shows the final diagram after adding the links needed to reflect when an input of zero was received.

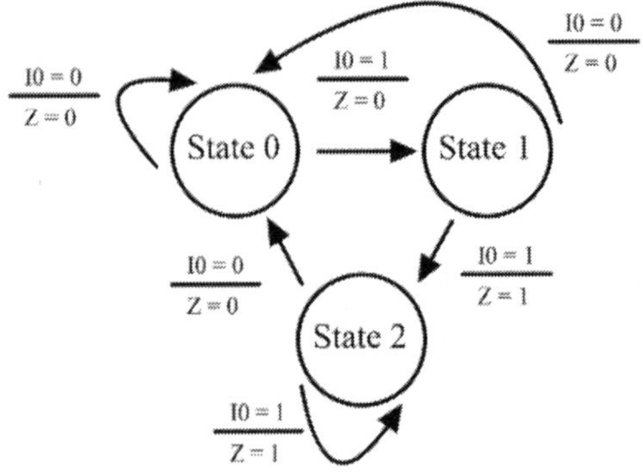

Example 5

A state machine detects a sequence through its input, I0, and has its output, Z, turn to one when the most recent three inputs were 010. The following shows the desired response of Z given an input sequence into I0. Make a Mealy machine to model the system. The bold columns show when the target of 010 has been received.

I0:	0	0	0	1	**0**	0	0	1	**0**	0	1	**0**	1	**0**	1	**0**
Z:	0	0	0	0	**1**	0	0	0	**1**	0	0	**1**	0	**1**	0	**1**

The first step is to decide how many states to have. It is logical to have state 0 correspond to when the first digit of the target, zero, has been received, state 1 correspond to when the second digit of the target, one, has been received, and lastly, state 2 correspond to when the final digit of the target, zero, has been received. This leaves us with a total of three states from 0-2. Using this line of reasoning, we can start with the following template for the Mealy diagram. The table summarizing the meaning of each state is included too.

Table of State Meaning:

State	Meaning
0	Has "0", so still need a "1" and "0" to obtain "010"
1	Has "01", so still need a single "0" to obtain "010"
2	"010" has been attained

Diagram Template:

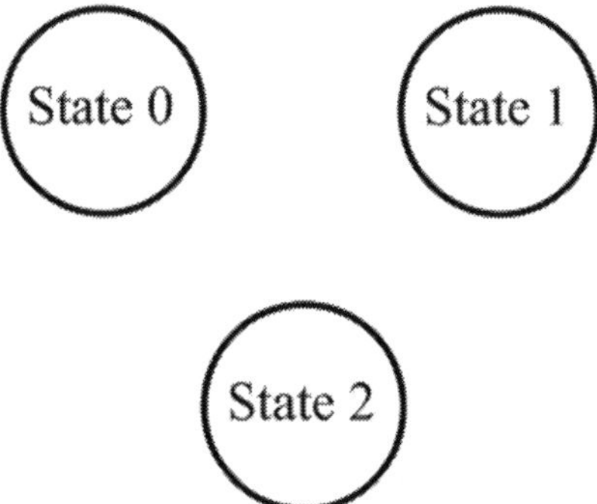

Let's consider the effect of when 010 is entered in starting from state 0. When in state 0 and a zero is received, we will remain in state 0 and output nothing, since we still need a 1 and 0. When in state 0 and we receive a one, we will have gotten the second digit of the target, resulting in the transition to state 1 with an output of zero in the link. When in state 1 and receiving a zero, we go to state 2 and output a one though Z in the link, due to having reached the target. The following diagram represents the behavior described.

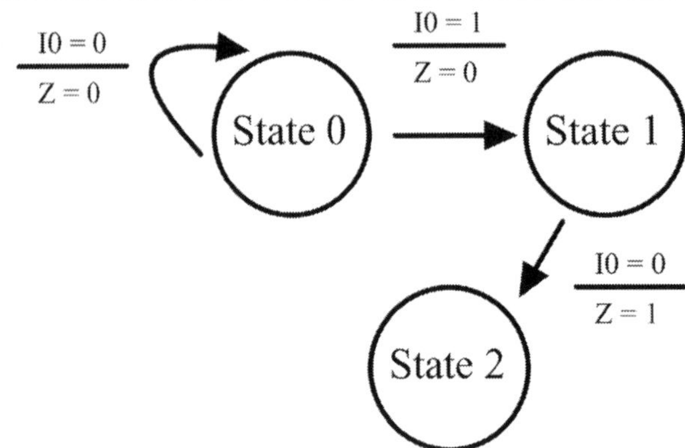

Now, there are still three links missing. The first link missing is the case of where to go from state 1 when I0 = 1. In state 1, it is implied that the previous two digits received were 01. When a one is received in state 1, we will have 011, meaning we must start over to have a chance of receiving the digits 010 consecutively. For this reason, state 1 when I0 = 1 will have its link go to state 0 to reset. The output in this link will be zero due to having not reached the target of 010. The diagram below shows this.

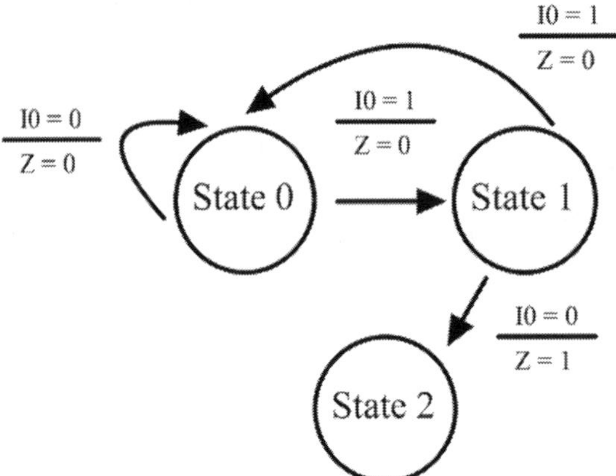

The only remaining two situations to discuss now are when I0 = 0 and I0 = 1 in state 2. When in state 2, it is implied the previous three digits received were 010, so when a zero is received, we would have 0100, meaning we still need a one and zero before having the three most recent digits received be 010 again. The only state that requires these two new digits to be received before reaching the target is state 0. For this reason, the link in state 2, when I0 = 0 will go to state zero. The output Z will be zero in this link. The diagram below shows this.

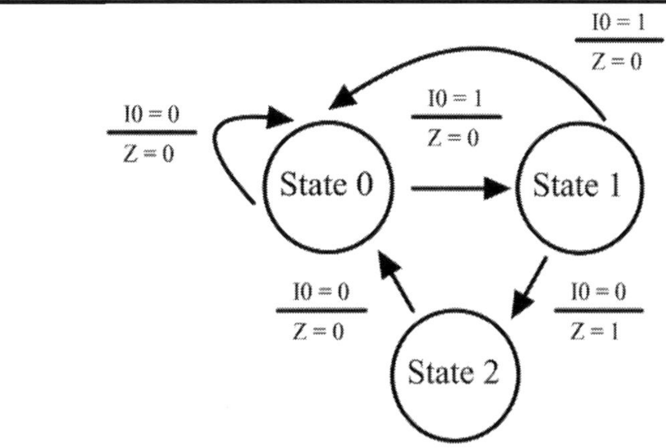

The only situation to consider now is when I0 is one in state 2. When in state 2, it is implied the previous three digits received were 010, so when a one is received, we would have 0101, meaning we still would need a single zero before reaching the target again. The only state that requires a single zero to be received before reaching the target is state 1. For this reason, the link in state 2, when I0 = 1 will go to state 1. The output Z will be zero in this link. The final Mealy diagram below shows this link added.

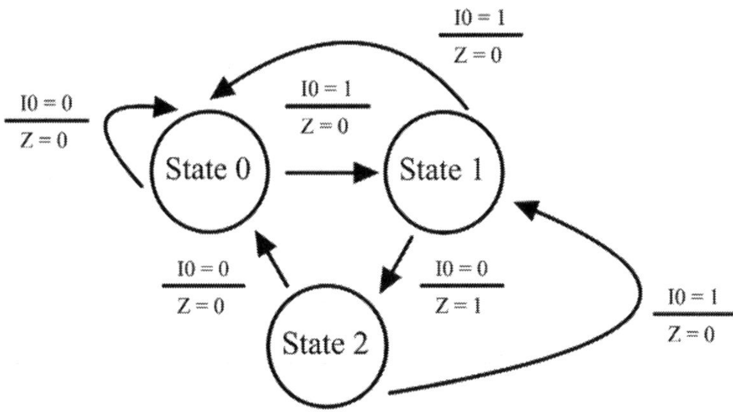

3.6 Converting State Diagrams to State Tables

Now that a variety of examples have been shown for both Mealy and Moore state diagrams, it is time to discuss the algorithmic procedure used to convert these diagrams into a state table. A state table is extremely useful because, when used in conjunction with K-Maps, allows for the straightforward derivation of the final equations required for constructing the circuit. I will first demonstrate how to convert a Moore diagram to an equivalent state table. The same thing will then be done for a Mealy diagram. Then at the end of this section, the general algorithm will be summarized for clarity.

We will start with how to convert a Moore machine due to it being simpler. For our discussion, assume we are converting the following Moore diagram to a state table. Note that this diagram was from example one of section 3.5.

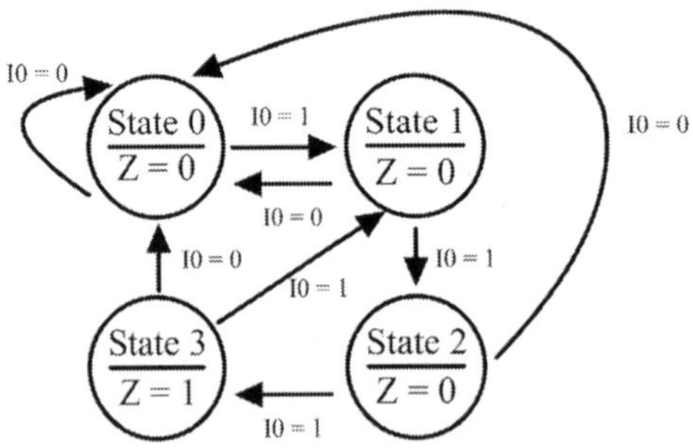

Figure 3.6.1 Moore Diagram

To construct a state table based on the state diagram depicted in Figure 3.6.1, the first step is to always identify the inputs and write them on the left side of the state table. The current state is always a required input, so it receives a column labeled "State." The current state is intrinsic to the design, as it is always present. The other input is "I0," which is non-intrinsic, and is unique to this specific diagram. We list each state—states 0 through 3—in ascending order, with each state repeated twice to account for the two possible conditions of the input "I0"—either 0 or 1. This method ensures that all potential state transitions are captured in the table. If there were two inputs, then each state would be listed four times to encompass all possible combinations. Notably, both the state and input "I0" are on the left side of the table, as they are inputs. Also, "State" is always placed to the left of "I0." The rationale for this ordering will be clarified later. Figure 3.6.2 illustrates the completion of this first step.

State	I0	
0	0	
0	1	
1	0	
1	1	
2	0	
2	1	
3	0	
3	1	

Figure 3.6.2 State Table with Inputs

The second step is to fill in the outputs on the right side of the table. "Next State" is always a required output, and "Z" is an output that is specific to this diagram. To determine the correct entries for the "Next State" column, each scenario must be analyzed individually. This process involves selecting a state, observing the transitions it makes based on different input combinations, and then recording these transitions in the "Next State" column of the corresponding row. For instance, when referencing Figure 3.6.1 to complete the first row of the table, we see that an input of 0 in state 0 results in a transition back to state 0; hence, the "Next State" for the first row is identified as 0. Similarly, when an input of 1 occurs in state 2, the transition leads to state 3; therefore, the "Next State" for the sixth row is identified as 3. Figure 3.6.3 demonstrates this for both the first and sixth rows, while Figure 3.6.4 will present the completed process for the remaining rows.

State	I0	Next State	Z
0	0	0	
0	1		
1	0		
1	1		
2	0		
2	1	3	
3	0		
3	1		

Figure 3.6.3 State Table with Next State column partially filled.

State	I0	Next State	Z
0	0	0	
0	1	1	
1	0	0	
1	1	2	
2	0	0	
2	1	3	
3	0	1	
3	1	0	

Figure 3.6.4. State Table with Next State column filled.

To complete the "Z" column, we look at each state's output from Figure 3.6.1 For example, "Z" is 0 in states 0, 1, and 2, but in state 3, "Z" is 1. This lets us easily complete the "Z" column by writing 0 in the rows where "State" is 0, 1, or 2 but writing 1 where "State" is 3, as shown in Figure 3.6.5.

State	I0	Next State	Z
0	0	0	0
0	1	1	0
1	0	0	0
1	1	2	0
2	0	0	0
2	1	3	0
3	0	1	1
3	1	0	1

Figure 3.6.5 State Table with inputs and outputs.

The last step involves translating the "State" and "Next State" columns into unsigned binary numbers. This conversion process assigns 0 to 00, 1 to 01, 2 to 10, and 3 to 11. To accommodate two digits, we replace the "State" with "Q1" and "Q0" and "Next State" with "Q1+" and "Q0+." For guidance on converting decimal numbers to binary, see section 2.9. Figure 3.6.6 displays the final state table after this conversion. Notice how, because "State" was written to the left of I0, when "Q1" and "Q0" replace "State," the concatenation of "Q1", "Q0", and "I0" forms a binary number from 0 to 7 as we go down the table. Had we written the state to the right of "I0", this convenient pattern would not have occurred.

Q1	Q0	I0	Q1+	Q0+	Z
0	0	0	0	0	0
0	0	1	0	1	0
0	1	0	0	0	0
0	1	1	1	0	0
1	0	0	0	0	0
1	0	1	1	1	0
1	1	0	0	1	1
1	1	1	0	0	1

Figure 3.6.6 Complete state table.

So, there you have it! The entire process of converting a Moore diagram into a state table has been completely demonstrated. The state table in Figure 3.6.6 can then be used in conjunction with K-Maps to generate the equations needed to build the state machine. This procedure can be applied to any Moore machine.

Now it is time to repeat the same process for a Mealy diagram. The process is nearly identical. For our discussion, assume we are converting the following Mealy diagram to a state table. Note that this diagram was from example five of section 3.5.

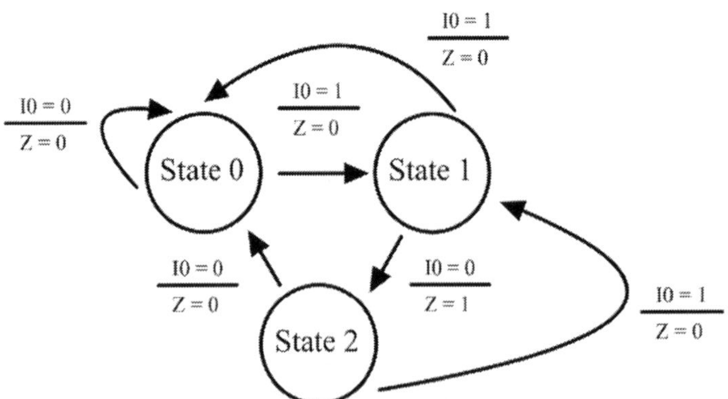

Figure 3.6.7 Mealy Diagram.

To construct a state table based on the state diagram depicted in Figure 3.6.7, the first step is to always identify the inputs of the state table. The current state is always a required input, and in this diagram, "I0" is the specific input. Each state is listed in the table as many times as there are different combinations of non-intrinsic input values. Since there is only one non-intrinsic input, "I0", and it can be either 0 or 1, there are two combinations. This means each state is represented twice: once for when "I0" is 0 and once for when "I0" is 1. Next, the completion of this first step is shown. There is no difference in this step for both a Moore and Mealy machine.

State	I0	
0	0	
0	1	
1	0	
1	1	
2	0	
2	1	

Figure 3.6.8 Step one of creating Mealy diagram.

The second step is to identify the outputs and record their values in the table. The next state is always a required output, so it gets a column labeled "Next State" on the right side of the table. There is one non-intrinsic output, "Z", which will get a column labeled "Z" in the table. To fill in the "Next State" and "Z" column, we use a similar procedure as in the Moore machine. The figure below demonstrates the process you would need to perform.

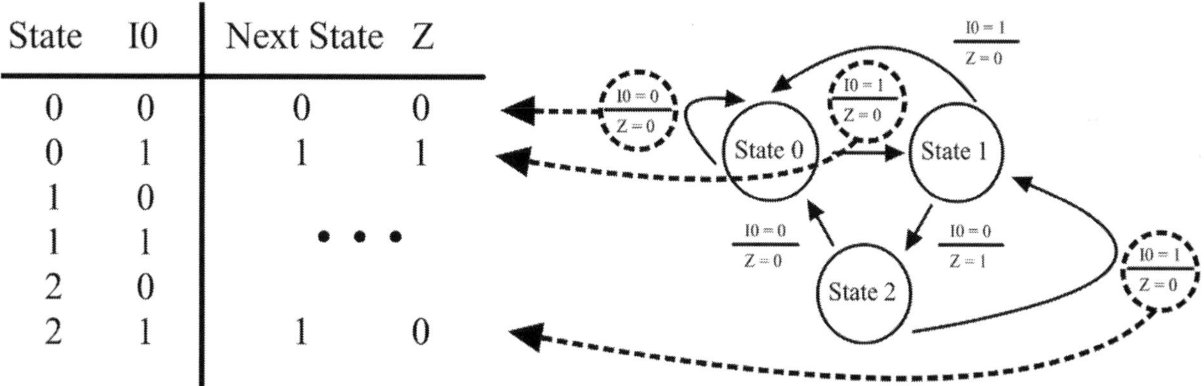

State	I0	Next State	Z
0	0	0	0
0	1	1	1
1	0		
1	1	• • •	
2	0		
2	1	1	0

Figure 3.6.9 Step two process of creating Mealy diagram.

To complete the first row of the table, we need to identify the link that is affiliated row one's inputs. This means when "State" is 0 and "I0" is 0. The link reflecting this is circled and has an arrow pointing to the first row of the table for your convenience. From this link, we see that it points to state 0, signaling us to put 0 under the "Next State" column of the first row. From this link, we also see that "Z" is 0, so under the "Z" column of the first row, we put 0. The procedure for rows two and six have been shown as well. The result of completing the table for the remaining rows is shown next.

State	I0	Next State	Z
0	0	0	0
0	1	1	1
1	0	2	1
1	1	0	0
2	0	0	0
2	1	1	0

Figure 3.6.10 Step two of creating Mealy diagram.

The last step involves translating the "State" and "Next State" columns into unsigned binary numbers. This conversion process assigns 0 to 00, 1 to 01, 2 to 10, and 3 to 11. To fit two-digit binary numbers, we replace "State" with "Q1" and "Q0" and "Next State" with "Q1+" and "Q0+." For guidance on converting decimal numbers to binary, refer to section 2.9. Figure 3.6.11 shows the state table after this conversion. Notice that because "State" was written to the left of "I0," the concatenation of "Q1," "Q0," and "I0" forms a binary number from 0 to 7 down the table. Had "State" been written to the right of "I0," this convenient pattern would not have emerged. It's also important to note that state 3, which is unused, is included with its output values marked as don't-cares. Including state 3 facilitates the process of solving K-Maps, as it indicates where to place don't-cares for the boxes where "State" equals 1 and "I0" equals 1.

Q1	Q0	I0	Q1+	Q0+	Z
0	0	0	0	0	0
0	0	1	0	1	1
0	1	0	1	0	1
0	1	1	0	0	0
1	0	0	0	0	0
1	0	1	0	1	0
1	1	0	X	X	X
1	1	1	X	X	X

Figure 3.6.11 State Table

Now that the methods have been discussed on how to methodically convert a Mealy or Moore machine into a state table, it is time to summarize the algorithm. Next shows the summarized procedure. Some terminology will be clarified again. One example will be provided showing how the steps in the summary can be directly applied. In time, you will be able to skip some steps and do it in your head, but in case you're not there yet, the provided example should give you a great place to start after having already read this section.

State Diagram to Table Algorithm

Step 1: Identify Inputs and Assign Values

1.1) Create an input column labeled "State" on the left-hand side. This column is intrinsic, due to it always being present. For non-intrinsic inputs, meaning those unique to the state diagram, assign a separate column for each. Ensure that the "State" column is positioned as the leftmost among all input columns.

1.2) Populate the table with "State" starting from 0 for the first group and increasing incrementally by one for subsequent groups. The number of times the state is repeated in a group is equal to the number of combinations the non-intrinsic inputs can be.

1.3) For each group, i.e. rows that have the same state in decimal, have the non-intrinsic inputs start from 0 in binary incrementing by one as you go down all the way until the end of the group.

Step 2: Determine Outputs and Document Values

2.1) Create an output column labeled "Next State" on the right-hand side. This column is intrinsic, due to it always being present. For non-intrinsic outputs, meaning those unique to the state diagram, assign a separate column for each.

2.2) From the "State" input, identify the corresponding node. Then, use non-intrinsic inputs like "I0" to find links for each combination of inputs.

2.3) Determine the next state by observing where each identified link points. For a Moore machine, document the non-intrinsic outputs based on the state. For a Mealy machine, document them from the transitions indicated by the links.

Step 3: Binary Conversion for States

3.1) Convert both the "State" and "Next State" columns into binary representation, maintaining the correct sequence of values.

The example that follows is going to be extremely detailed. Do not be intimidated by how long the explanation is. It is long because from an instructional design perspective, every single step is shown, a rare feat accomplished by any book. No other textbook on logic design is willing to try this hard to show the work for something like this. In time, you will be able to skip these steps or do them very quickly in your head, meaning your work when solving a similar problem should be very short in comparison. Once again, the explanation in the example below is long due to it being broken up into so many simple steps.

Example 1

Convert the following Mealy diagram into a state table:

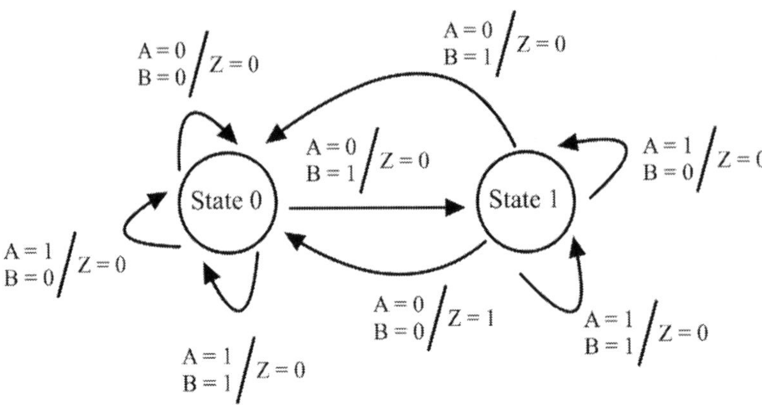

Step 1: Identify Inputs and Assign Values

1.1)

State A B	

1.2)

2 non-intrinsic inputs

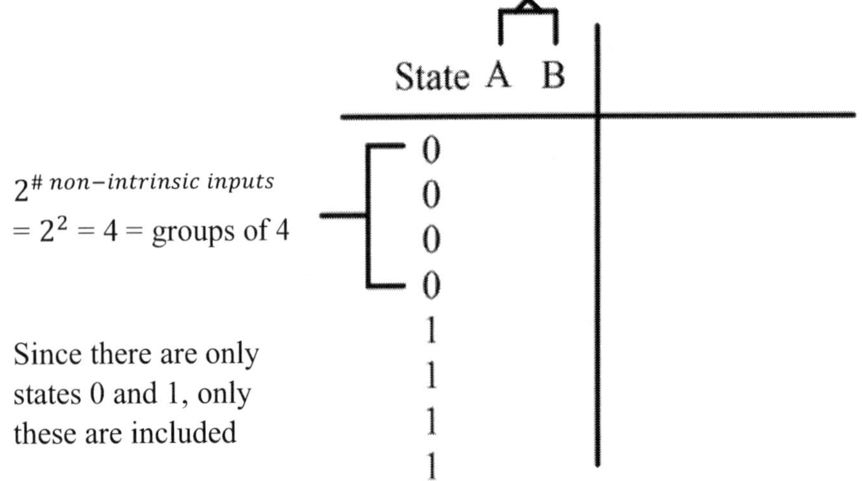

1.3)

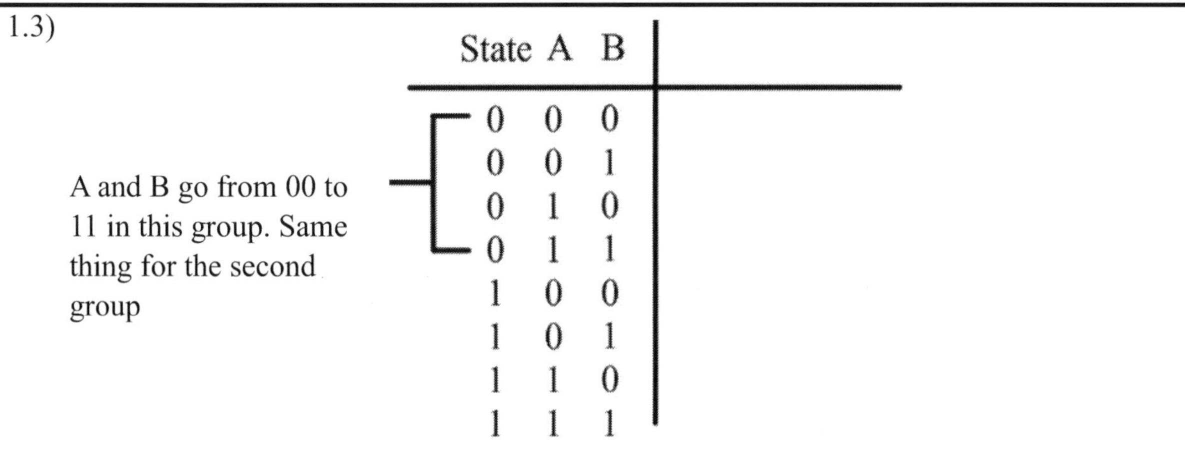

State	A	B	
0	0	0	
0	0	1	
0	1	0	
0	1	1	
1	0	0	
1	0	1	
1	1	0	
1	1	1	

Step 2: Determine Outputs and Document Values

2.1)

State	A	B	Next State	Z
0	0	0		
0	0	1		
0	1	0		
0	1	1		
1	0	0		
1	0	1		
1	1	0		
1	1	1		

2.2) For row 1, we know to look at the links around states zero from the input "State" being 0. We knew from both inputs "A" and "B" being 0, that it would be the link where "A = 0" and "B = 0". The identified link is circled. Although the process will not be shown for the remaining seven rows, the procedure is the same.

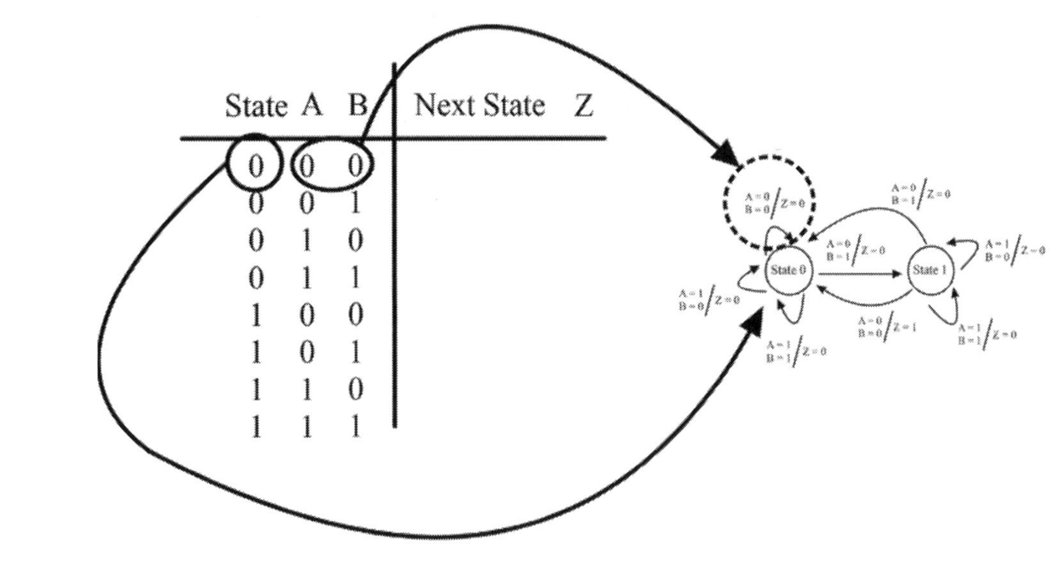

2.3) For row 1, we can observe that link circled in 2.2 points to state 0, so we write 0 under the "Next State" column. We can observe from the link that "Z = 0", so we write 0 under the "Z" column. Although the process will not be shown for the remaining seven rows, the procedure is the same.

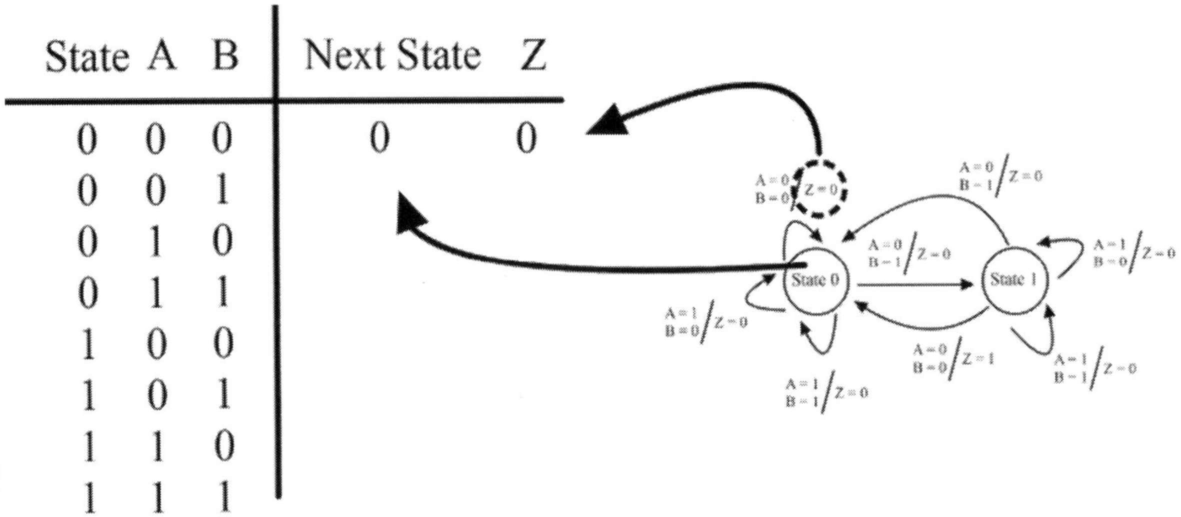

State	A	B	Next State	Z
0	0	0	0	0
0	0	1		
0	1	0		
0	1	1		
1	0	0		
1	0	1		
1	1	0		
1	1	1		

Step 3: Binary Conversion for States

3.1) For row one, the converted columns are shown. Since 0 and 1 are the same in binary as they are in decimal, nothing changed. Although the process will not be shown for the remaining seven rows, the procedure is the same.

Q0	A	B	Q0+	Z
0	0	0	0	0
0	0	1		
0	1	0		
0	1	1		
1	0	0		
1	0	1		
1	1	0		
1	1	1		

3.7 State Machine Charts

Now that we have concluded the long and arduous review of Mealy and Moore Machines, we can move on to the final major topic you will have to study for your test. This topic is that of state machine charts, or SM charts for short. An SM chart is used to model a sequential circuit just like a state diagram can. The reason why we use SM charts is because an SM chart can be directly converted into equations. Both a Mealy and Moore Machine can be represented by an SM chart. Fortunately, there are only three basic components of an SM chart, which are shown in the following figure.

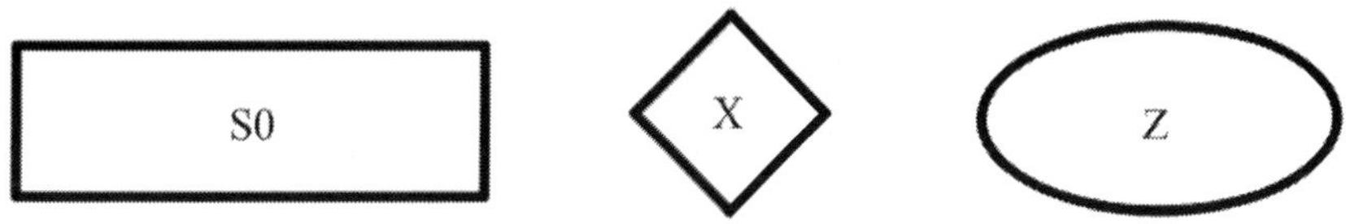

Figure 3.7.1 SM chart components

The rectangle is called the state box. The state box represents a state within the state machine, like a node did for state diagrams. "S0" is an example of how a particular state might be labeled. The state box is always required, since without it, there are no states and without states, there is no state machine. The diamond is called a decision box. The "X" term in the diamond represents a general input. The decision box will have arrows coming out of going towards the next state box depending on what the value received though the input was. The bubble is called an output box since it represents when an output is high. In a state chart, "Z", represents an output that is currently one. It is important to note that the bubble is used only in Mealy SM charts, since it will only be present in the links of the SM chart. In Moore SM charts, both the state and output will be stored in the state box of the SM chart. This is very similar to how in Moore diagrams, the state and output were in the node and how in Mealy diagrams, the state was in the node and the output in the link.

We will first start by going over a Moore SM chart. A Moore SM chart will only have a state box and an input box. Both the state and output will be contained in the state box. The decision box will still be in the links. To best continue the discussion, an example will be shown.

Example 1

For the following sequence, make a Moore SM chart:

IN	0	1	1	0	0	**0**	**0**	1	1	0	1	1	**1**	1	1	**1**	0	0	**0**
OUT	0	0	0	0	0	**1**	**1**	0	0	0	0	0	**1**	0	0	**1**	0	0	**1**

From the sequence, it is apparent that the target is reached whenever three consecutive zeros have been received or every 3rd time a one is received. The first step is to identify what states to have. Since there are two ways of reaching a target, there will be multiple paths. To keep things simple, let's first make an SM chart for the path taken when "000" is entered. We begin by writing the state box for state 0. State 0 will be the state for when no "0" has been received yet, or in other words, when a "1" was most recently received. State 1 will be when we receive the first "0". State 2 will be when we receive the second "0". State 3 will be when we receive the final "0" and reach the target of "000". Whenever a 1 is received, the next state will always be state 0 since we would need to start all over again to get "000" to be the most recent three inputs entered. When in state 3, if we receive a "0", we stay in state 3, since targets overlap. "Z" will only be 1 in state 3 since that's when the target was reached. The chart reflecting all this is shown below.

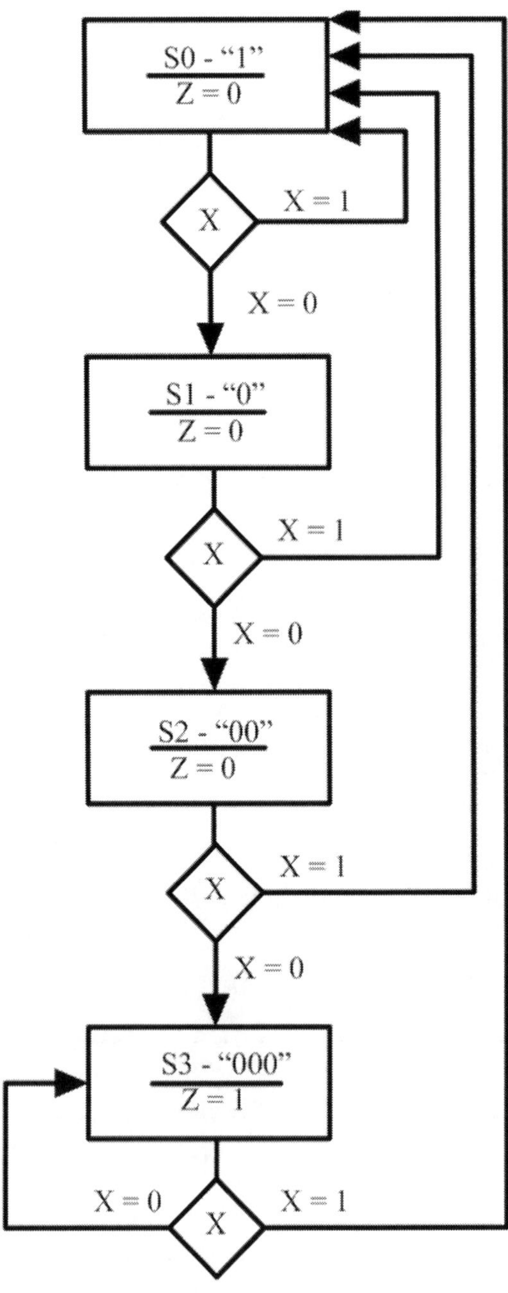

Now that we have completed the half of the state chart for the first target, we must do it again for the second one. We will start from state 0. We know that state zero is when the first "1" is received, so when we get a one in state 0, rather than going back to state 0, we go to a new state, state 4, signifying when "11" has been entered. In state 4, when a "1" is received, we go state 5, signifying when "111" has been reached. In both state 4 and state 5, when a zero is received, we must go to the state signifying that the first zero has been received, state 1. When in state 5 and a one is received, since the output comes every third time, we must go to state 0 to start again. State 5 has "Z" as 1 that's when the target of "111" was reached. The chart reflecting all this is shown below.

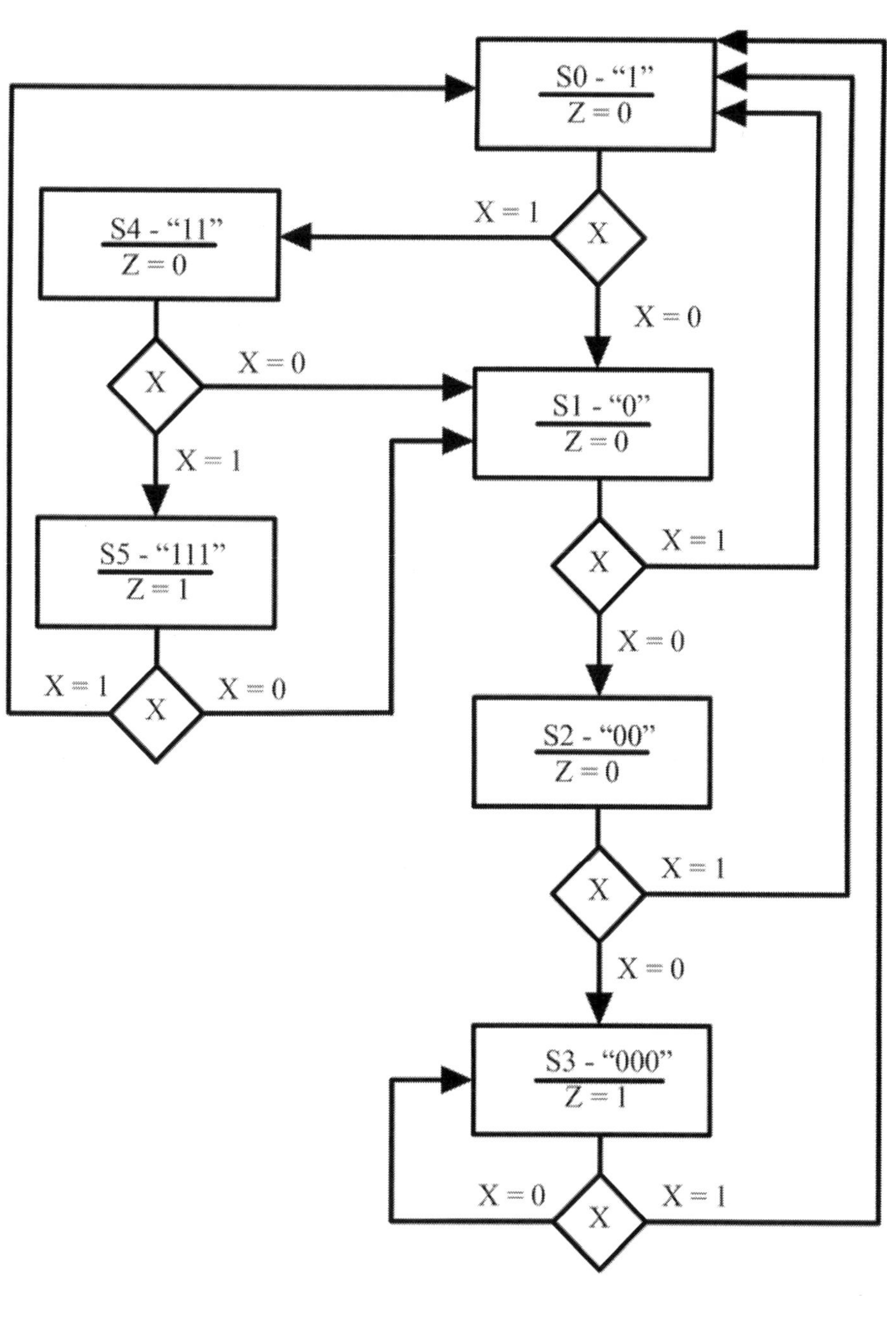

Now that the example for the Moore state chart has been finished, it is time to do the same for the Mealy state chart. The following example shows how to build a Mealy state chart.

Example 2

For the following sequence, make a Mealy SM chart:

IN	1	1	**1**	0	0	1	1	**1**	**1**	**1**	0	0
OUT	0	0	**1**	0	0	0	0	**1**	**1**	**1**	0	0

From the sequence, it is apparent that the target is reached when the most recent three values received are "111" at any given moment. Logic would lead us to assign state 0 to when no "1" was received, or when "0" is the most recent input. State 1 would be when the first "1" was received. State 2 would be when we receive another "1", making the two most recent inputs be "11". State 3 would be when we receive another "1", making the three most recent inputs be "111". When receiving a "1" in state 3, since targets overlap, we remain in state 3. For any state, when a "0" is received, we reset back to state zero. Using this logic, we can derive the following Mealy diagram.

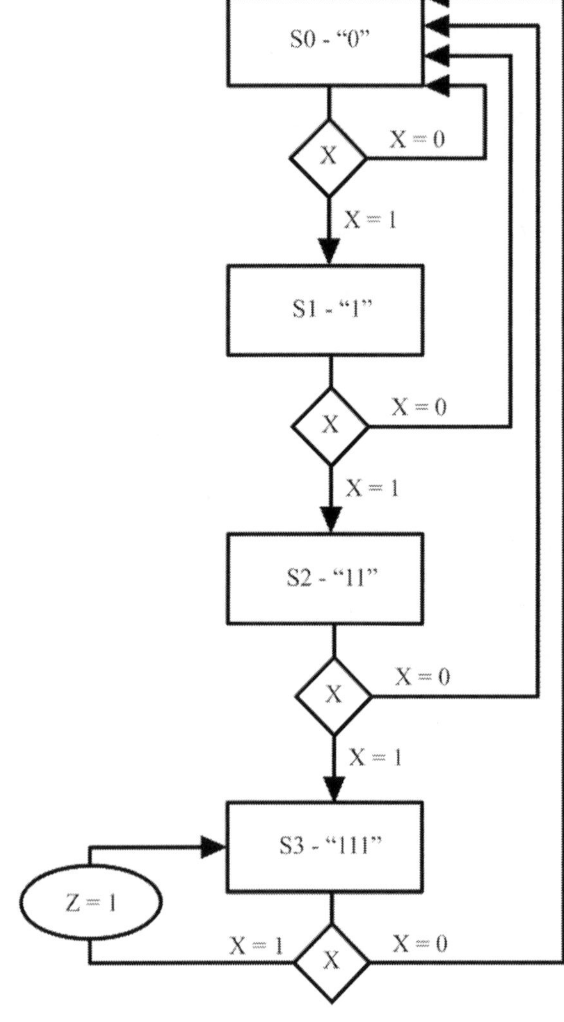

3.8 Equations from State Machine Charts

Now that SM charts have been discussed, it is time to go over how to convert them into equations. The algorithm is shown below. Examples demonstrating its application follow for a Moore machine, Mealy machine, and a machine that is a combination of both.

SM Chart to Equations Algorithm

Finding Next state Equations

1) Replace the states with $Q_n \ldots Q_1\ Q_0$ equivalent.

2) Start with Q_0 by finding all the states that have Q_0 as 1. Record them.

3) Find all the paths leading to those states and record them.

4) For each path, write the state and inputs involved concatenated with the binary value. If the value of an input was 1, it gets copied directly. If it was 0, the inversion gets copied into the final term. Once the term for each path is found, they are all OR-ed together go get the final expression.

5) Repeat step 2-4 for the other Q_n states.

Finding Output Equations

1) Identify all the paths and states that have the output as 1. Then write the term for each path and state. Lastly, you will AND-together the terms to get the expression for the output.

2) Repeat step 1 for the other outputs.

Example 1

Convert the following pure Moore SM chart into equations.

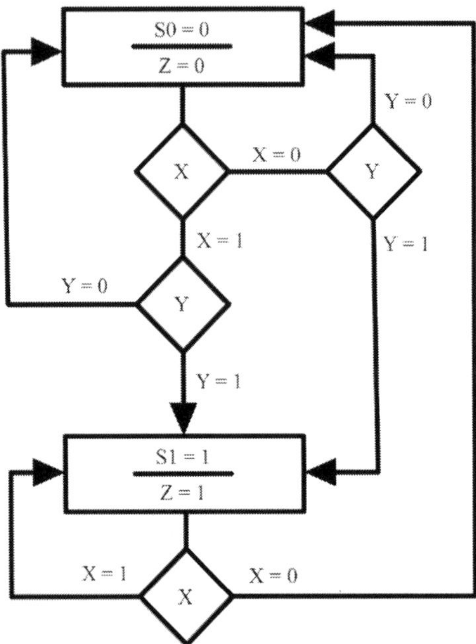

Finding Q0+

Step 1: Step 1 has already been completed, since each state has the binary equivalent shown in each state box. S0 was "0" and S1 was "1".

Step 2:

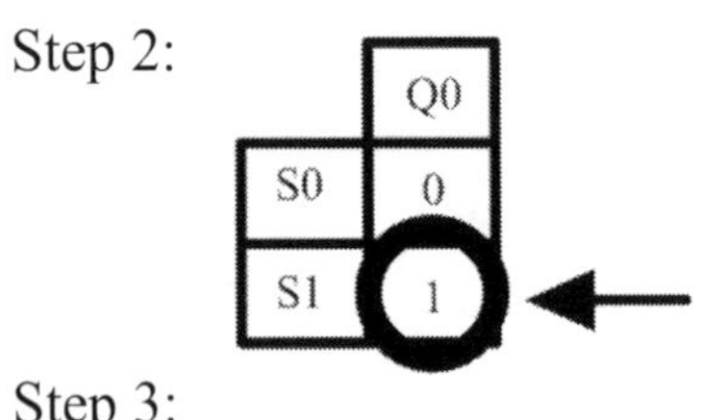

	Q0
S0	0
S1	1

Only state 1 has Q0 as 1, so only the paths leading into state 1 determine Q0+. Step 3 demonstrates these paths being identified.

Step 3:

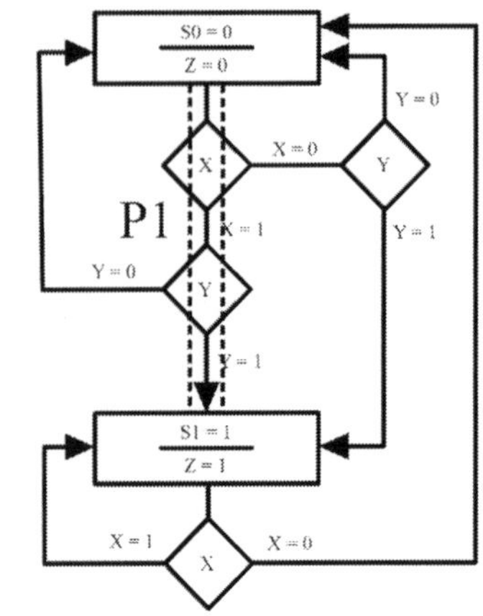

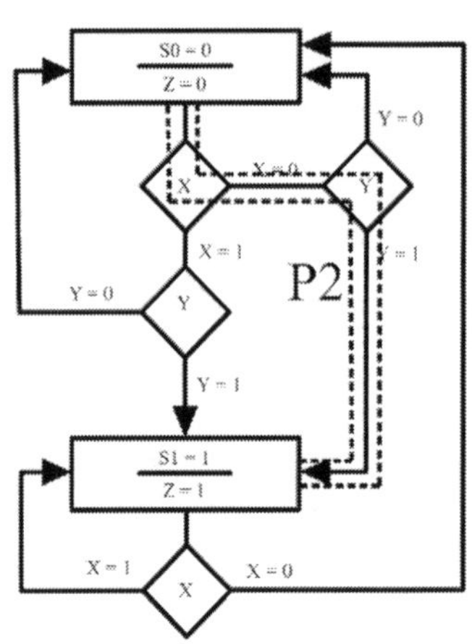

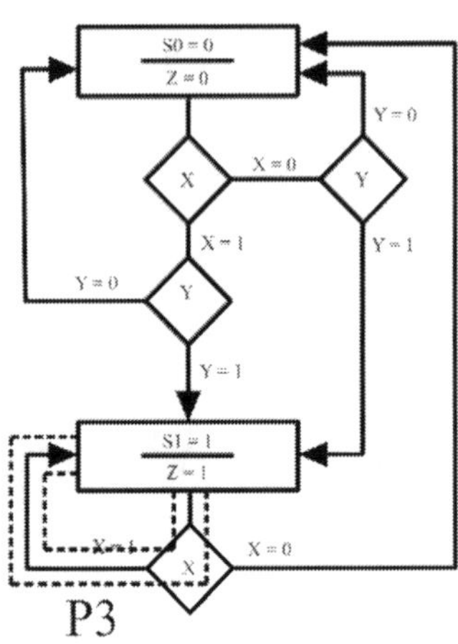

Step 4: The work for determining the term for each path is shown below. For P1, the path starts in state 0, which is why Q0 is 0. Path P1 also goes through X = 1 and Y = 1, so both X and Y get a value of 1. This results in the binary Concatenation of Q0XY being 011. Then after copying the terms based off the values, we get Q0'XY. The procedure is identical for P2 and P3.

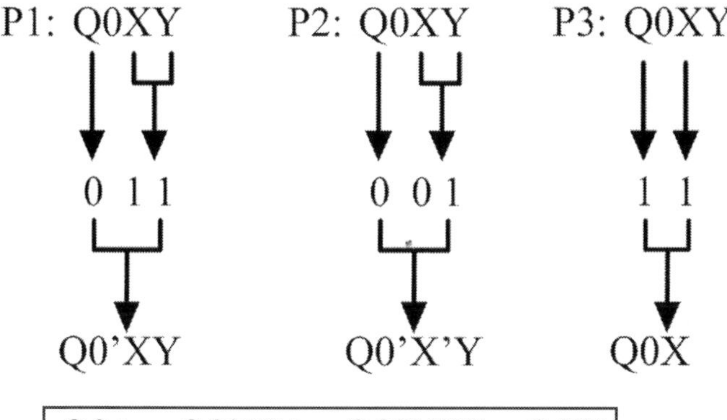

Q0+ = Q0'XY + Q0'X'Y + Q0X

Finding Z

Step 1: Only state 1 has Z equal to 1, so only the term for that state determines the equation.

Z = Q0

Example 2

Convert the following pure Mealy SM chart into equations.

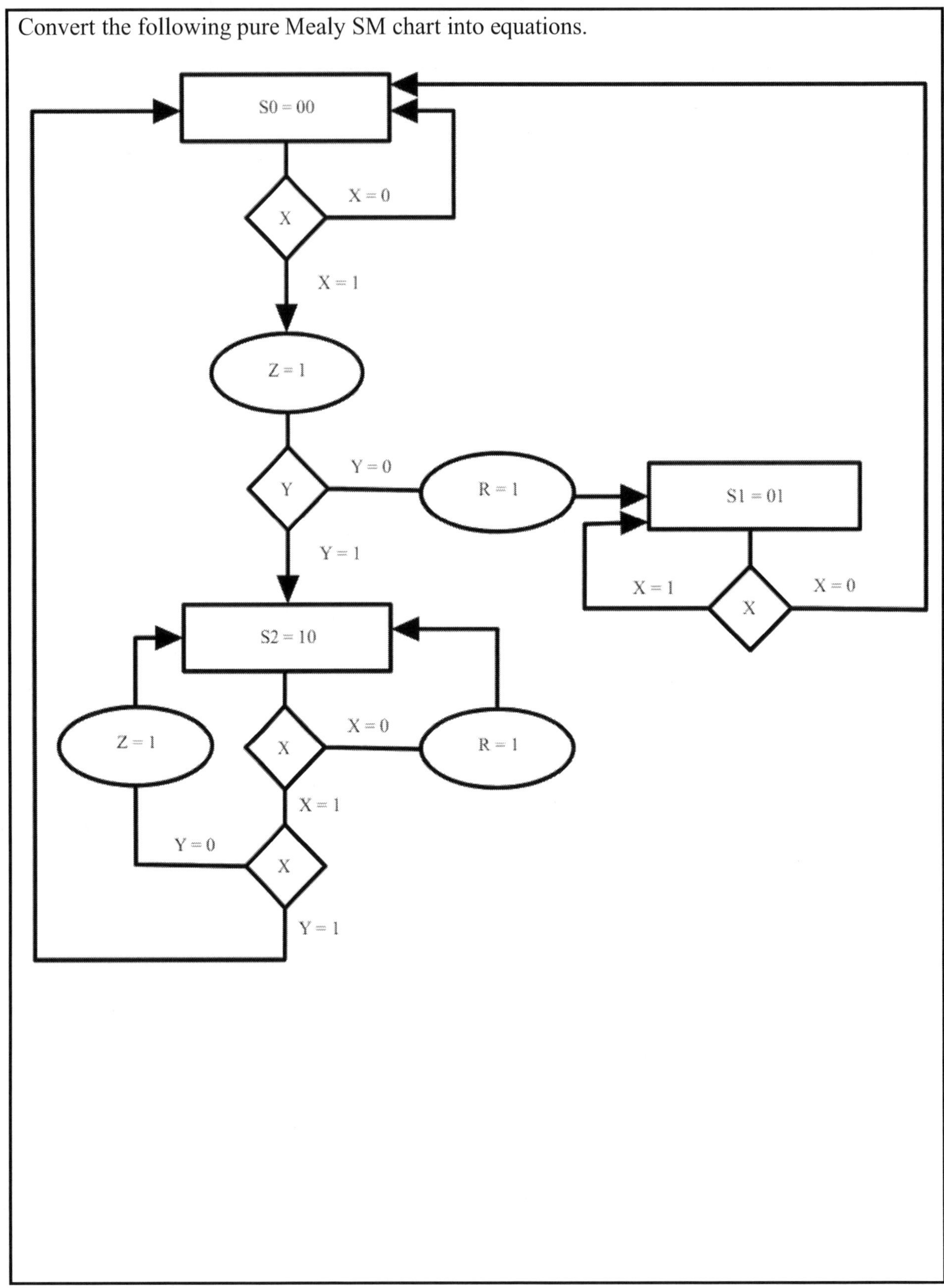

Finding Q0+

Step 1: Step 1 has already been completed, since each state has the binary equivalent shown in each state box. S0 was "00", S1 was "01", and S2 was "01".

Step 2:

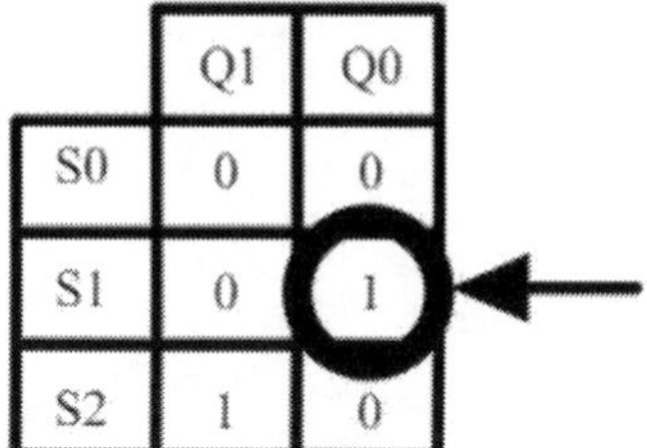

	Q1	Q0
S0	0	0
S1	0	1
S2	1	0

Only state 1 has Q0 as 1, so only the paths leading into state 1 determine Q0+. Step 3 demonstrates these paths being identified.

Step 3:

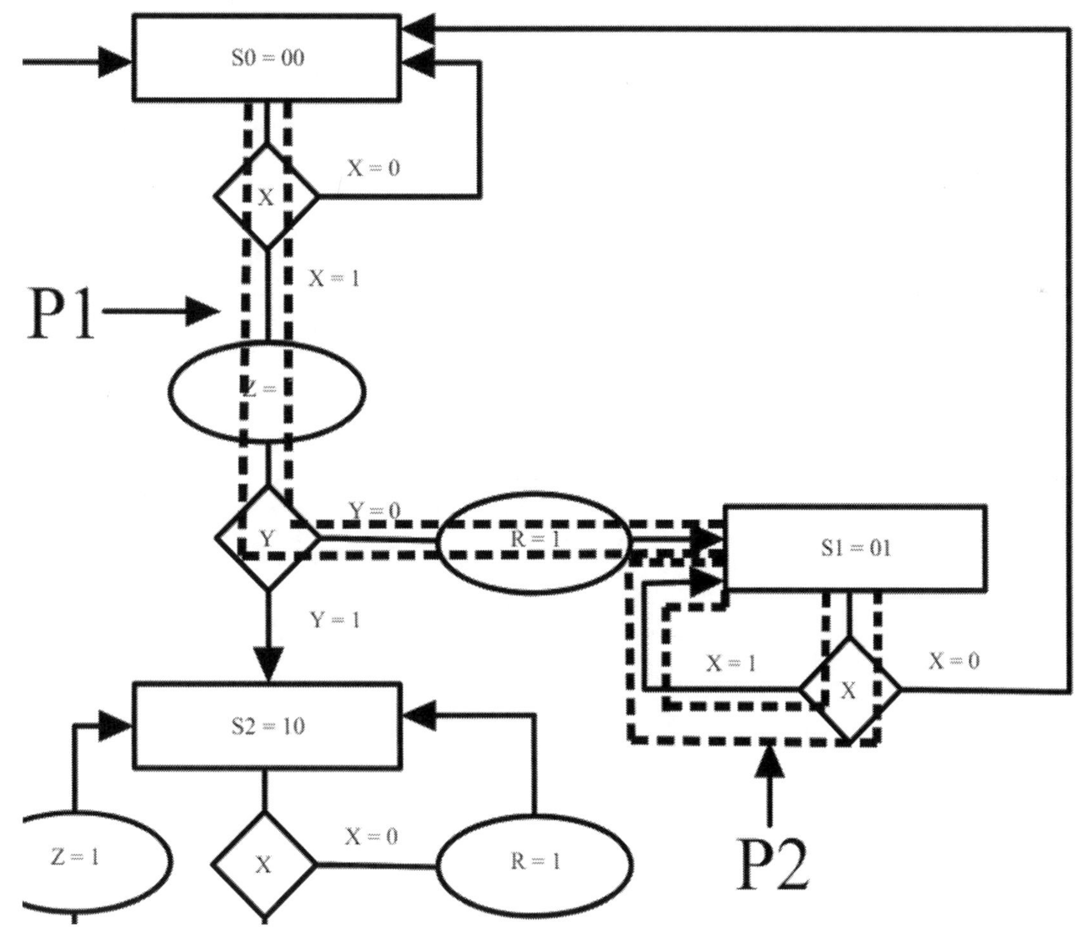

Step 4:

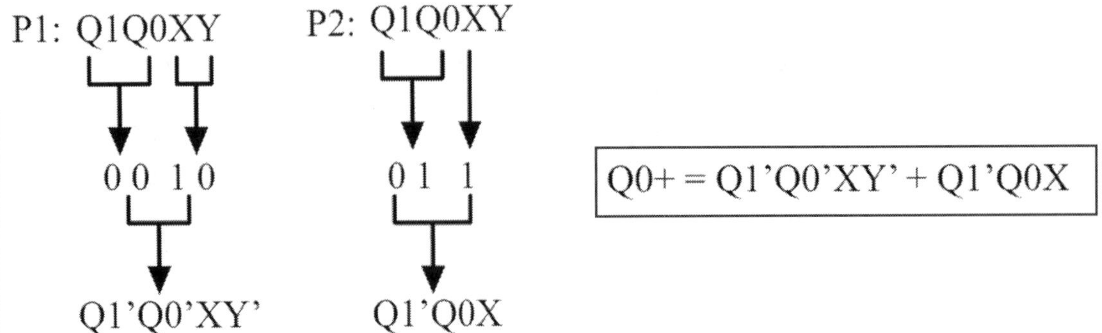

Finding Q1+

Step 2:

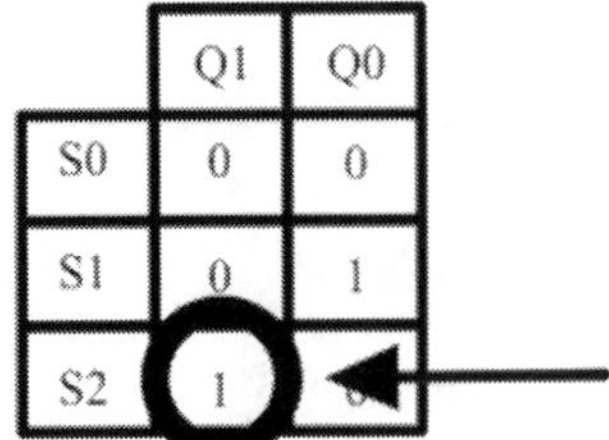

	Q1	Q0
S0	0	0
S1	0	1
S2	1	0

Only state 2 has Q1 as 1, so only the paths leading into state 2 determine Q1+. Step 3 demonstrated these paths being identified.

Step 3: The first and third paths will be shown on the following page, since the image was too large to display on this page. Path 2 is shown below.

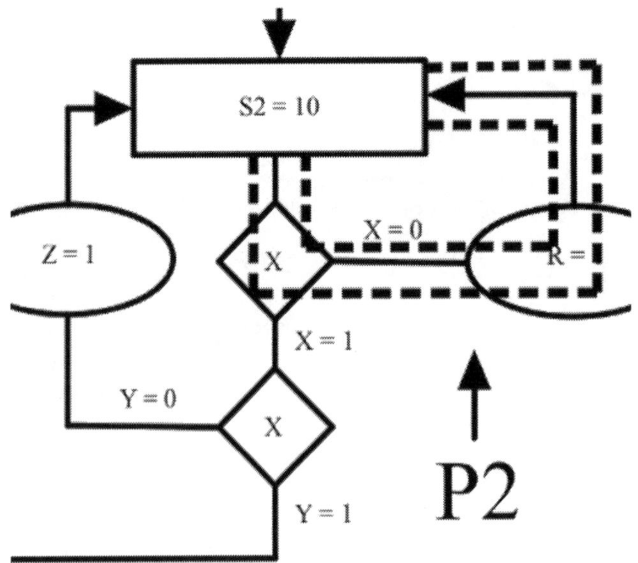

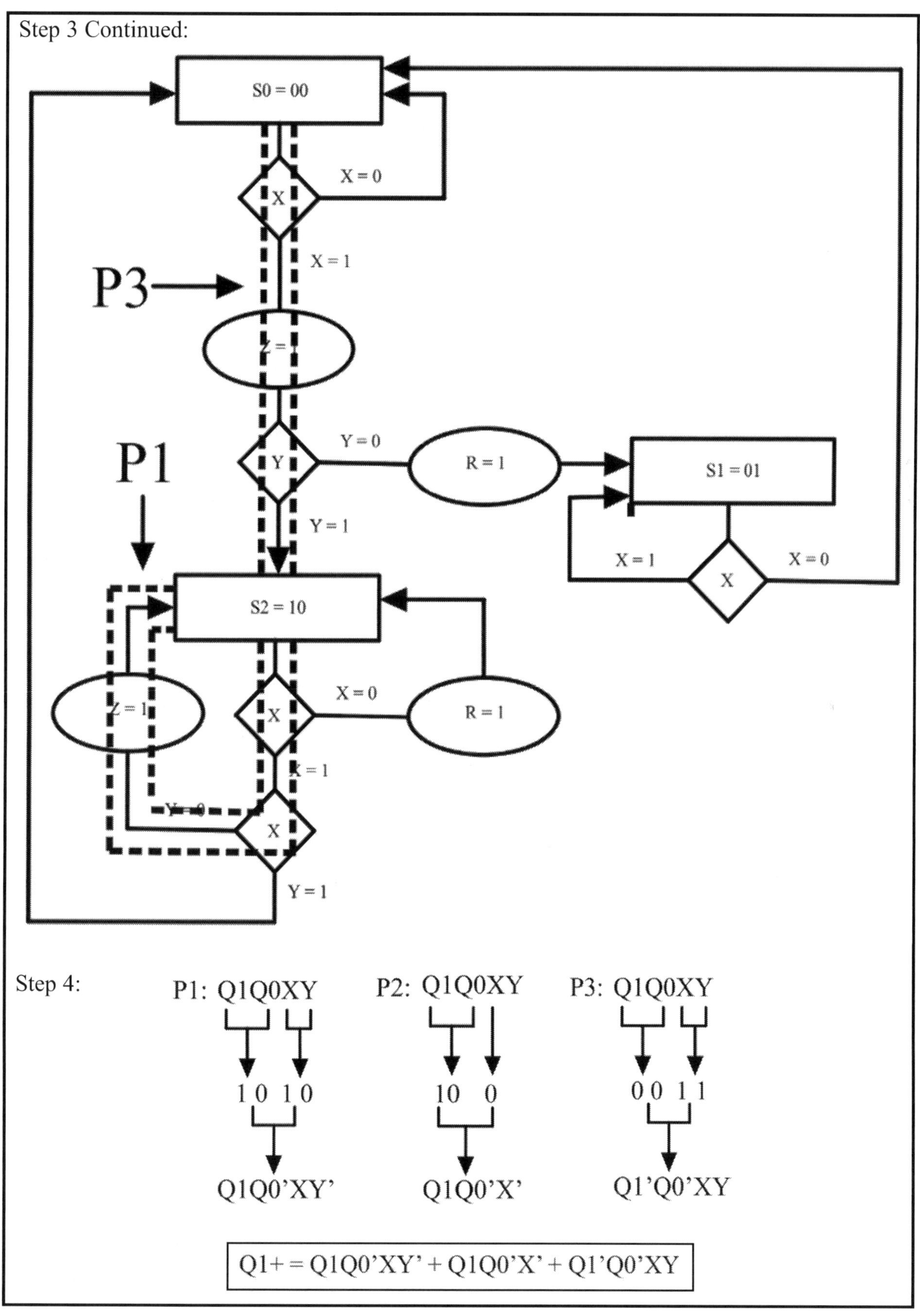

Step 3 Continued:
S0 = 00
X
X = 0
X = 1
P3
Y = 0
Y
R = 1
S1 = 01
P1
Y = 1
X = 1
X
X = 0
S2 = 10
Z = 1
X
X = 0
R = 1
X
Y = 1
Step 4:
P1: Q1Q0XY
1 0 1 0
Q1Q0'XY'
P2: Q1Q0XY
10 0
Q1Q0'X'
P3: Q1Q0XY
0 0 1 1
Q1'Q0'XY
Q1+ = Q1Q0'XY' + Q1Q0'X' + Q1'Q0'XY

Finding Z & R

Step 1: Identify the paths containing Z and generating equations.

P1: Q1Q0XY → 10 10 → Q1Q0'XY'

P2: Q1Q0XY → 00 11 → Q1'Q0'XY

Z = Q1Q0'XY' + Q1'Q0'XY

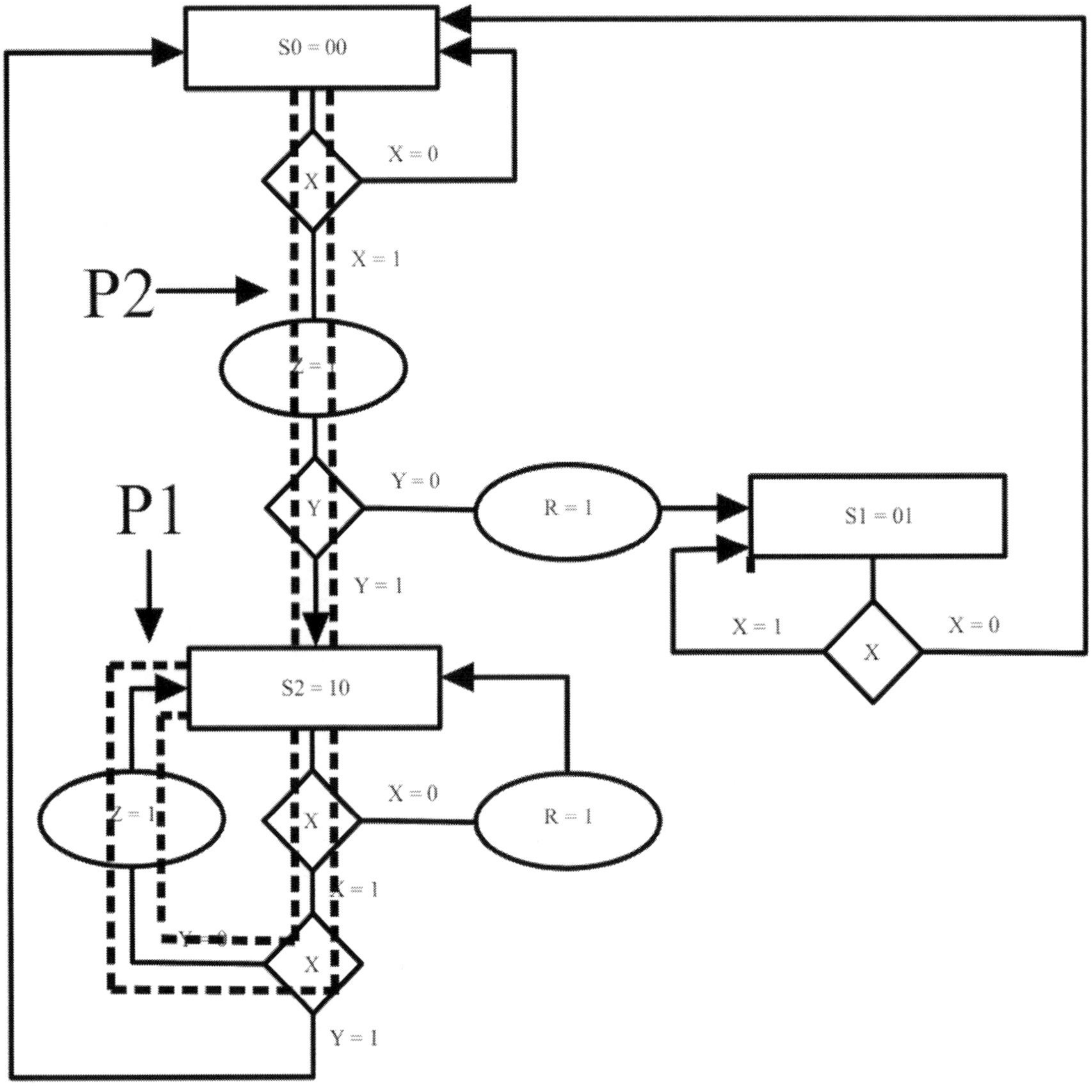

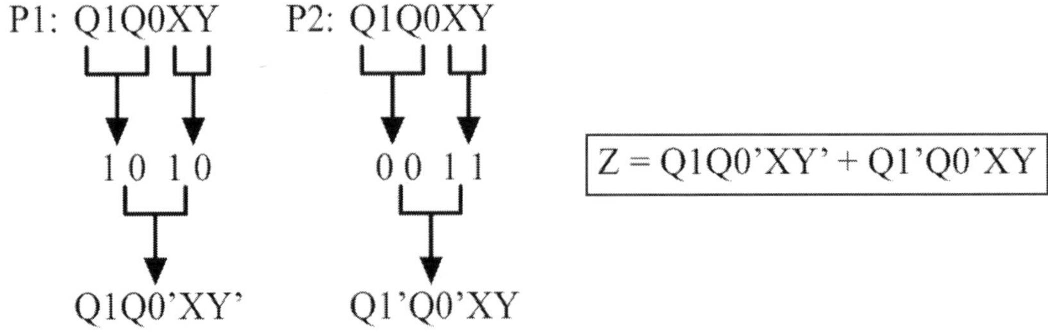

Step 2: Repeating the process for R yields the following.

R = Q1'Q0'XY' + Q1Q0'X'

Example 3

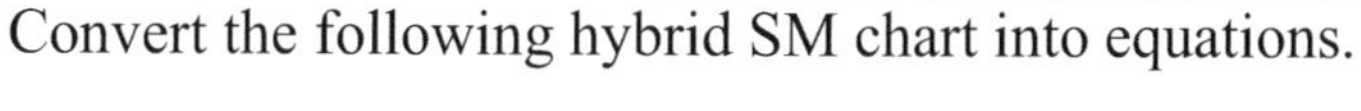
Convert the following hybrid SM chart into equations.

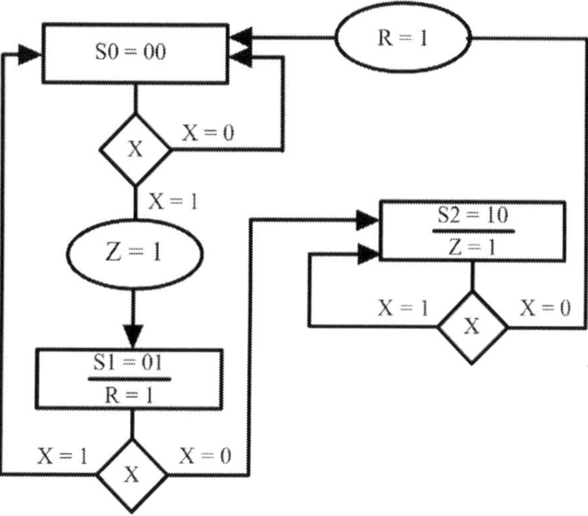

Finding Q0+

Step 1: Step 1 has already been completed, since each state has the binary equivalent shown in each state box. S0 was "00", S1 was "01", and S2 was "10".

Step 2:

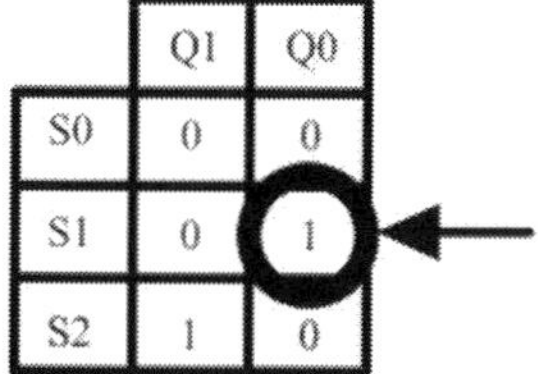

	Q1	Q0
S0	0	0
S1	0	1
S2	1	0

Only state 1 has Q0 as 1, so only the paths leading into state 1 determine Q0+. Step 3 demonstrates these paths being identified.

Step 3:

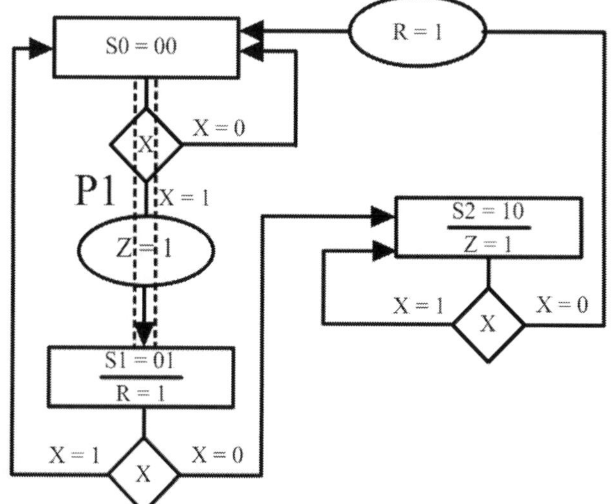

Step 4:

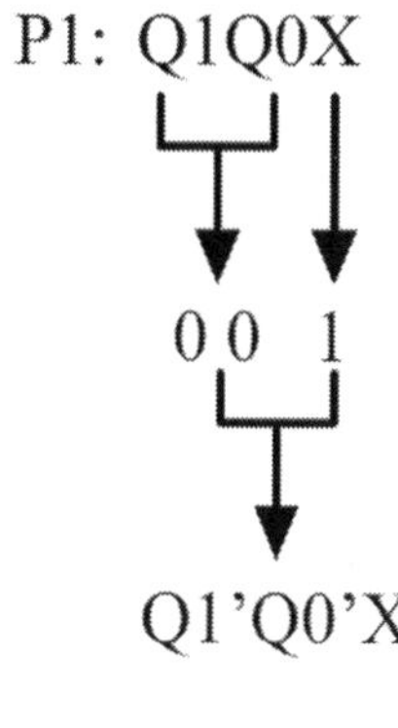

Q0+ = Q1'Q0'X

Finding Q1+

Step 2:

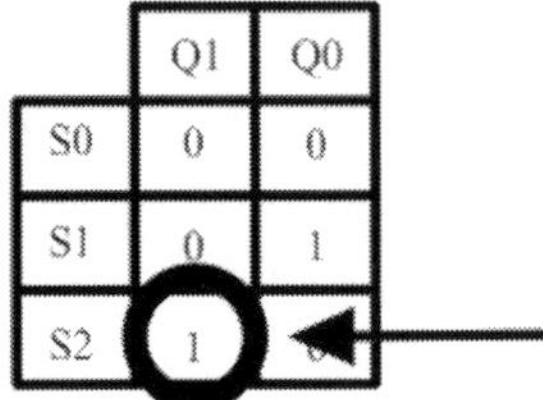

Only state 2 has Q1 as 1, so only the paths leading into state 2 determine Q1+. Step 3 demonstrated these paths being identified.

Step 3:

Step 4:

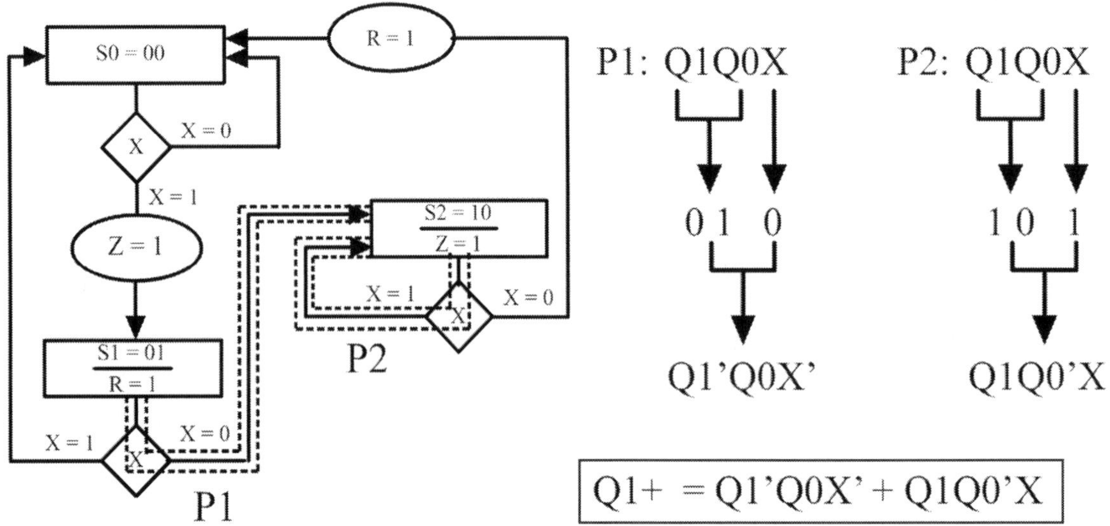

Finding Z & R

Step 1: Identify paths and states containing Z and generate the equation.

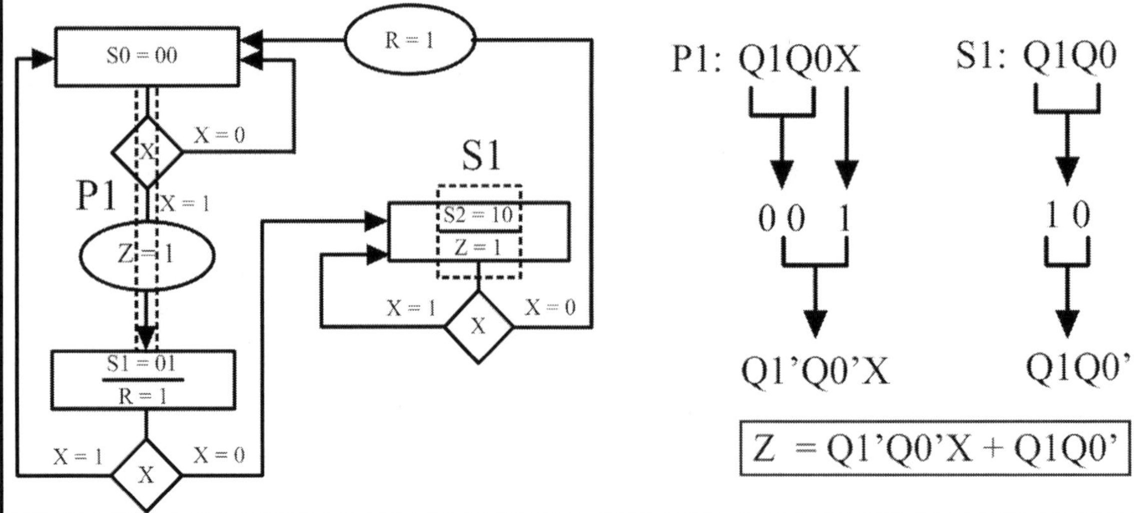

Finding R

Step 2) Repeating the process again yields the following.

R = Q1Q0'X' + Q1'Q0

3.9 JK-FF Design VS D-FF Design

The final topic to discuss before finally finishing the review of logic design is the difference between designing sequential circuits using D flip-flops vs using JK flip-flops. The procedure is very similar for both. In this section, the already familiar process will be re-done using D flip-flops, then the same thing will be done for JK flop-flops. This approach will be a good way of introducing how to do it with JK flip-flops while reinforcing how to already to it with D flip-flops. To begin, we will go over how to use D flip-flops to construct the circuit for the diagram in Figure 3.9.1.

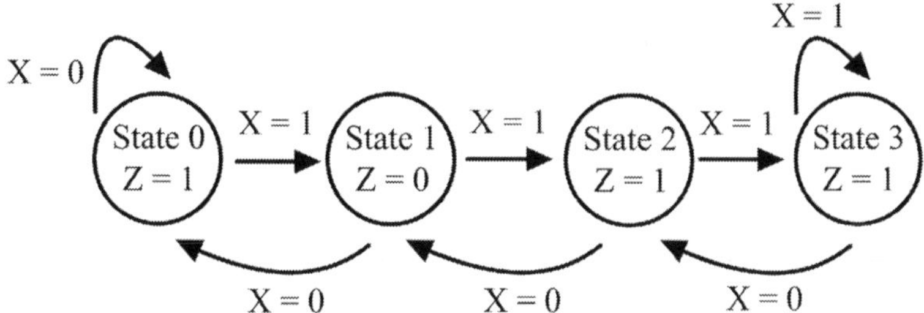

Figure 3.9.1 State Diagram

The first step will be to convert the state diagram into a state table, as shown in Figure 3.9.2. If you are not familiar with how to convert a state diagram to a state table, refer to section 3.6.

Q1	Q0	X	Q1+	Q0+	Z
0	0	0	0	0	1
0	0	1	0	1	1
0	1	0	0	0	0
0	1	1	1	0	0
1	0	0	0	1	1
1	0	1	1	1	1
1	1	0	1	0	1
1	1	1	1	1	1

Figure 3.9.2 State Table

Now that the state table has been obtained, the next step is to create the K-Maps and generate the equations for each as shown in Figure 3.9.3. Since there are three outputs, there will be three K-Maps. If you are unsure on how to convert a truth table into hardware, re-visit sections 2.1-2.2.

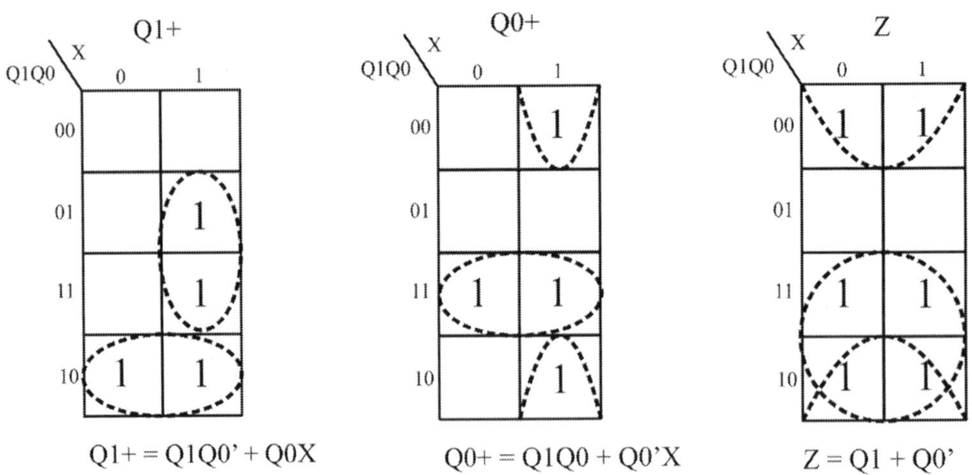

Figure 3.9.3 K-Maps and equations.

So then using the equations from each K-Map, we would be able to assemble logic gates and D flip-flops to acquire the sequential circuit. Now you might be asking yourself what the difference would be if we wanted to make the circuit with JK flip-flops. Well, the answer is that we first obtain the state table in Figure 3.9.2 but then perform a transformation on it to obtain a state table that is meant for JK flip-flops. Then using this transformed table, we can use K-Maps to obtain the equations needed to make the sequential circuit using logic gates and JK flip-flops. The first step of obtaining the derived table is to make two new output columns, Jn and Kn for each input Qn. The following figure shows this carried out for the state table in Figure 3.9.2.

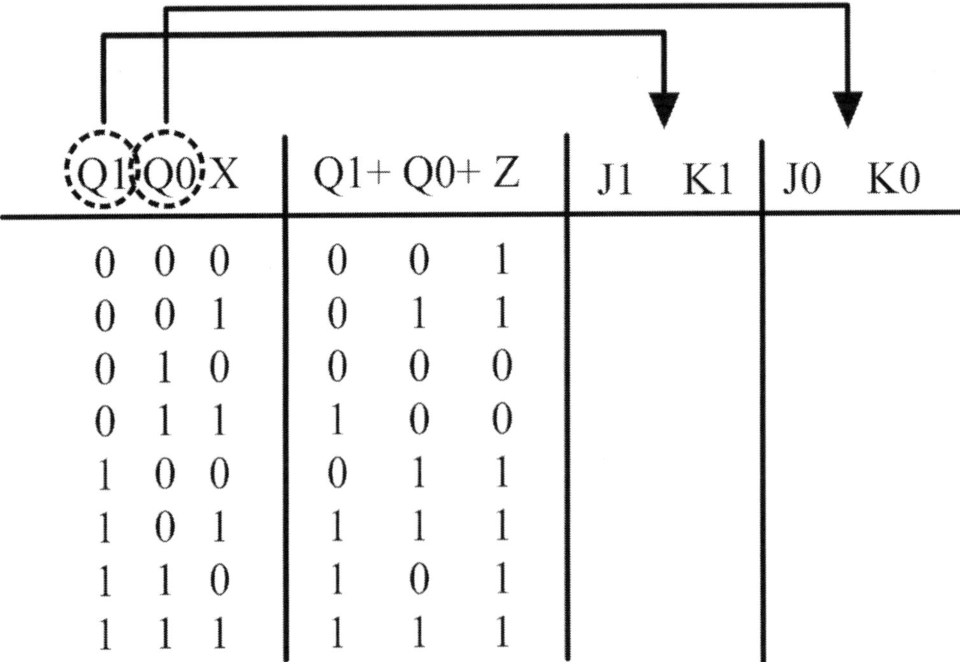

Q1	Q0	X	Q1+	Q0+	Z	J1	K1	J0	K0
0	0	0	0	0	1				
0	0	1	0	1	1				
0	1	0	0	0	0				
0	1	1	1	0	0				
1	0	0	0	1	1				
1	0	1	1	1	1				
1	1	0	1	0	1				
1	1	1	1	1	1				

Figure 3.9.4 New output columns from Q input columns

Now the next step is to fill in the rows for each of these newly added output columns. The way we will do this is by using the excitation table for JK flip-flops and looking at the Qn, and Qn+ values for each row. The excitation table will reveal what the J and K output should be for each row based on the Qn and Qn+ inputs for each row. The figure below shows the excitation table.

Qn	Qn+	Jn	Kn
0	0	0	X
0	1	1	X
1	0	X	1
1	1	X	0

Figure 3.9.5 JK flip-flop excitation table

The figure that follows shows the excitation table being used to obtain the values for J1 and K1 for rows one, two, and three. For each of these rows, "Q1 " and "Q1+ " are "00", so looking at the excitation table, we know that "J1 " and "K1 " should be "0X".

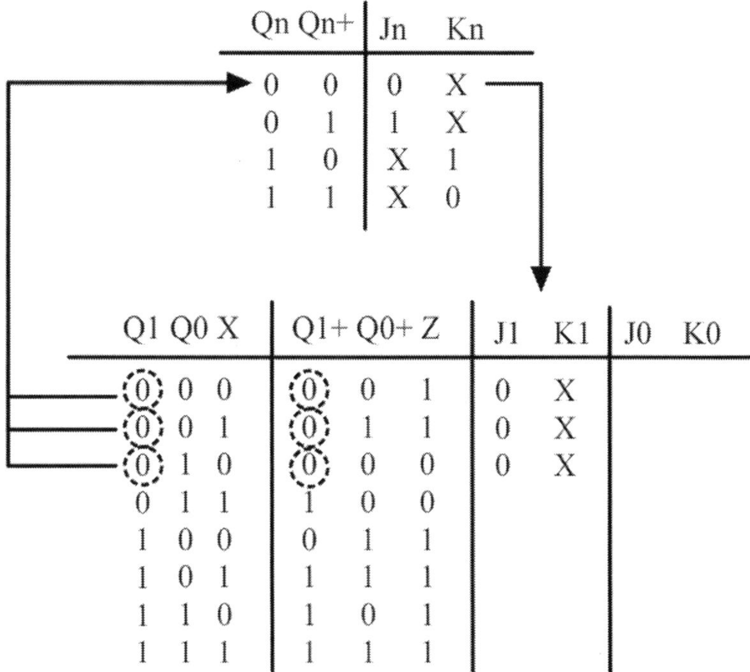

Qn	Qn+	Jn	Kn
0	0	0	X
0	1	1	X
1	0	X	1
1	1	X	0

Q1	Q0	X	Q1+	Q0+	Z	J1	K1	J0	K0
0	0	0	0	0	1	0	X		
0	0	1	0	1	1	0	X		
0	1	0	0	0	0	0	X		
0	1	1	1	0	0				
1	0	0	0	1	1				
1	0	1	1	1	1				
1	1	0	1	0	1				
1	1	1	1	1	1				

Figure 3.9.6 JK flip-flop state table being filled for rows 1-3 using Q1 and Q1+

The figure below shows the excitation table being used to obtain the values for J1 and K1 for row four. For this row, "Q1 " and "Q1+ " are "01", so looking at the excitation table, we know that "J1 " and "K1 " should be "1X".

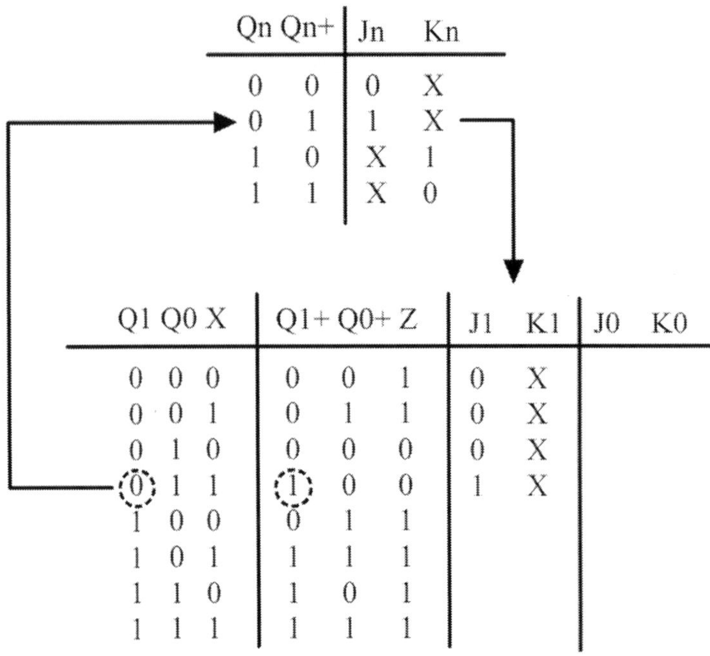

Figure 3.9.7 JK flip-flop state table being filled for row 4 using Q1 and Q1+

The figure below shows the excitation table being used to obtain the values for J1 and K1 for row five. For this row, "Q1 " and "Q1+ " are "10", so looking at the excitation table, we know that "J1 " and "K1 " should be "X1".

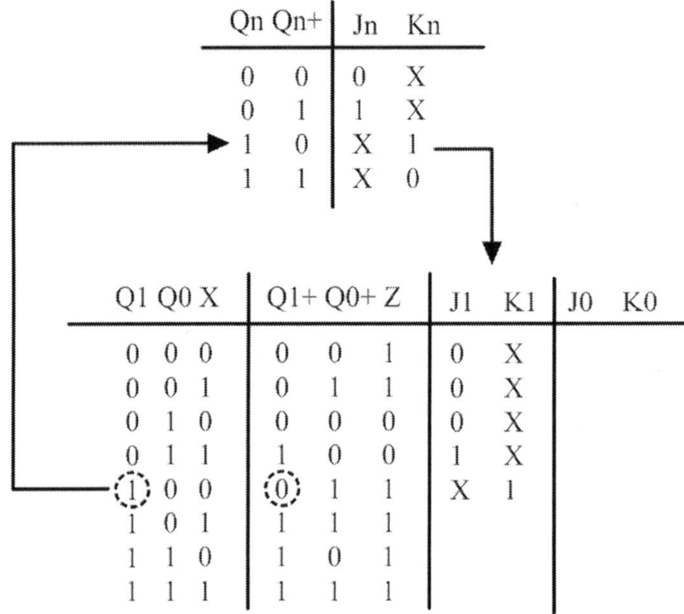

Figure 3.9.8 JK flip-flop state table being filled for row 5 using Q1 and Q1+

The figure below shows the excitation table being used to obtain the values for "J1" and "K1" for row six, seven, and eight. For these rows, "Q1" and "Q1+" are "11", so looking at the excitation table, we know that "J1" and "K1" should be "X0".

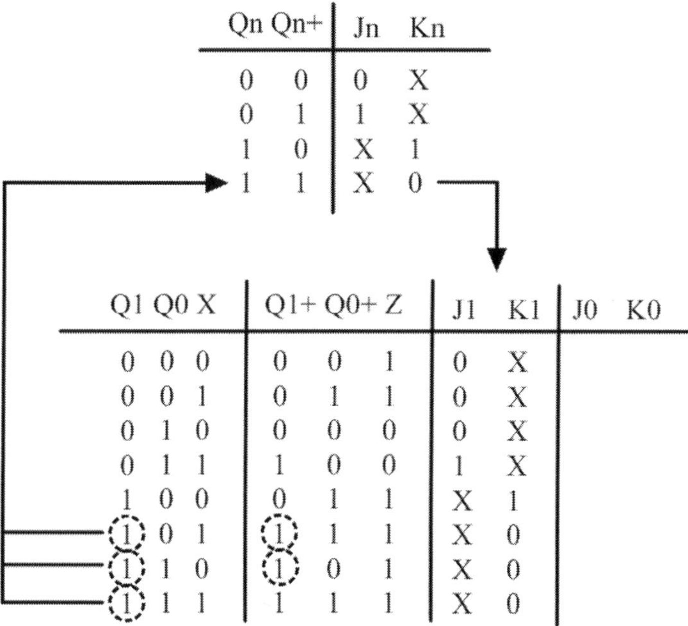

Qn	Qn+	Jn	Kn
0	0	0	X
0	1	1	X
1	0	X	1
1	1	X	0

Q1	Q0	X	Q1+	Q0+	Z	J1	K1	J0	K0
0	0	0	0	0	1	0	X		
0	0	1	0	1	1	0	X		
0	1	0	0	0	0	0	X		
0	1	1	1	0	0	1	X		
1	0	0	0	1	1	X	1		
1	0	1	1	1	1	X	0		
1	1	0	1	0	1	X	0		
1	1	1	1	1	1	X	0		

Figure 3.9.9 JK flip-flop state table being filled for rows 6-8 using Q1 and Q1+

Repeating the procedure for "Q0" and "Q0+" to obtain the columns for "J0" and "K0" yields the following.

Q1	Q0	X	Q1+	Q0+	Z	J1	K1	J0	K0
0	0	0	0	0	1	0	X	0	X
0	0	1	0	1	1	0	X	1	X
0	1	0	0	0	0	0	X	X	1
0	1	1	1	0	0	1	X	X	1
1	0	0	0	1	1	X	1	1	X
1	0	1	1	1	1	X	0	1	X
1	1	0	1	0	1	X	0	X	1
1	1	1	1	1	1	X	0	X	0

Figure 3.9.10 JK flip-flop state table being filled for rows 6-8 using Q1 and Q1+

Now that we have obtained the final state table for JK flip-flops, we can use K-Maps to obtain the final equations and be done. The only difference between this step and when we did it for D flip-flops is that we will make K-Maps for "J1", "K1", "J0", and "K0" instead of for "Q1+" and "Q0+".

Below shows the K-Maps and equations for the JK state table. We still do the K-Map for "Z" since it is an output.

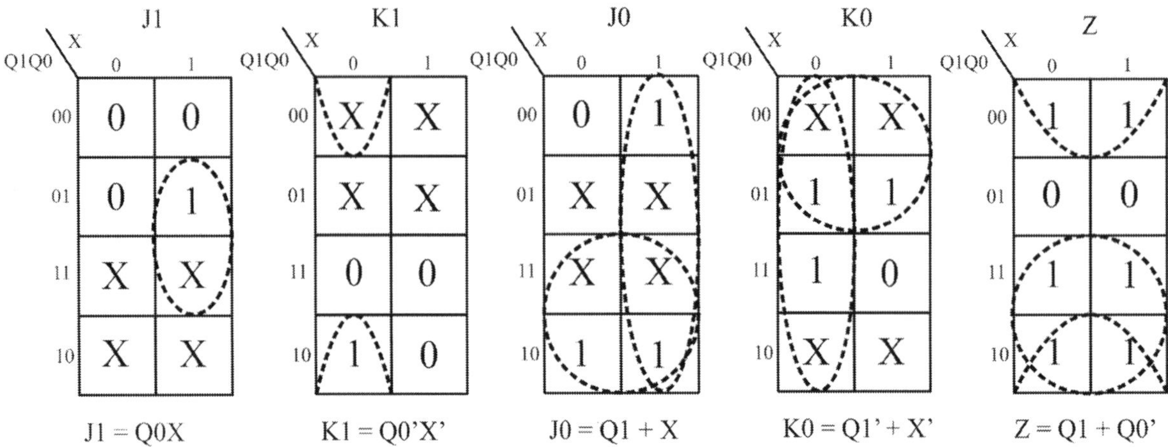

Figure 3.9.11 Equations for JK state table

These equations can then be used to build the following circuit. So, there you have it! That's how you design with a JK flip-flop. It's essentially the same as for a D flip-flop, expect you need to transform the table and use K-Maps on the new columns.

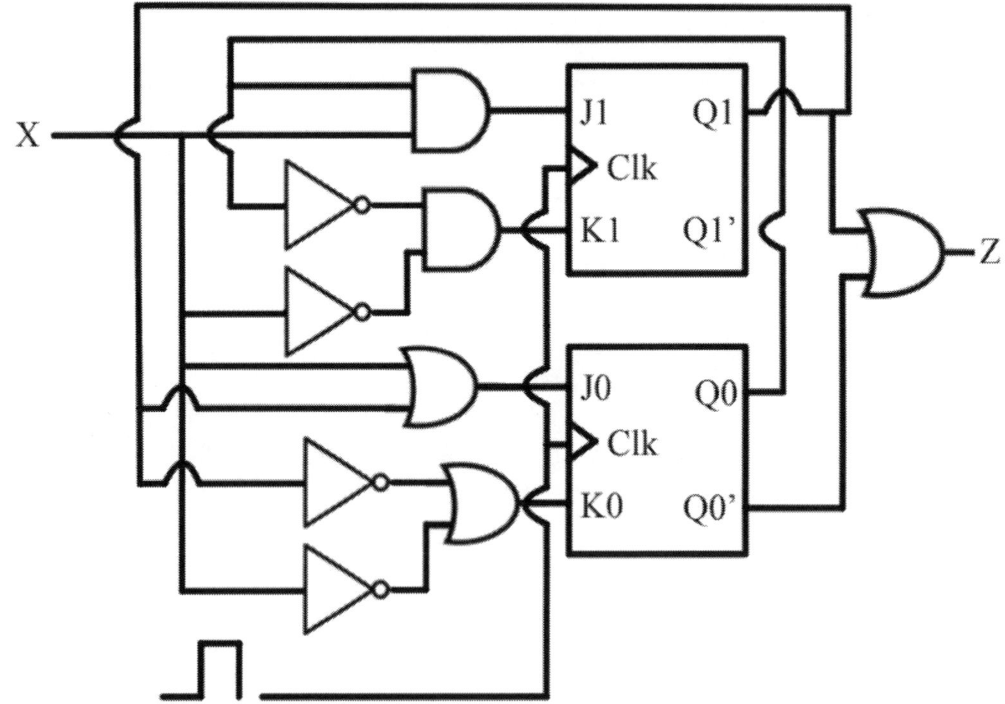

Figure 3.6.12 State machine using JK flip-flops

3.10 Sequential Logic Problems

Now that we have gone over everything, it is finally time to give you some problems for sequential logic. It is highly recommended to attempt all these problems, since they are intended to serve as great practice.

3.1 - 3.3 Problems

Problem 1) Complete the timing diagram for the following D flip-flop. Assume a propagation delay of three-time divisions. The flip-flop has a synchronous clear.

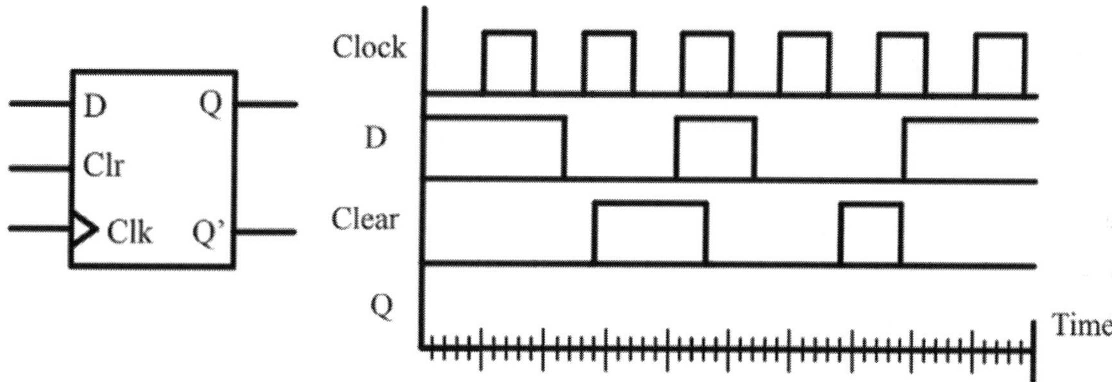

Problem 2) Complete the timing diagram for the following JK flip-flop. Assume a propagation delay of one-time division. The flip-flop has an asynchronous clear.

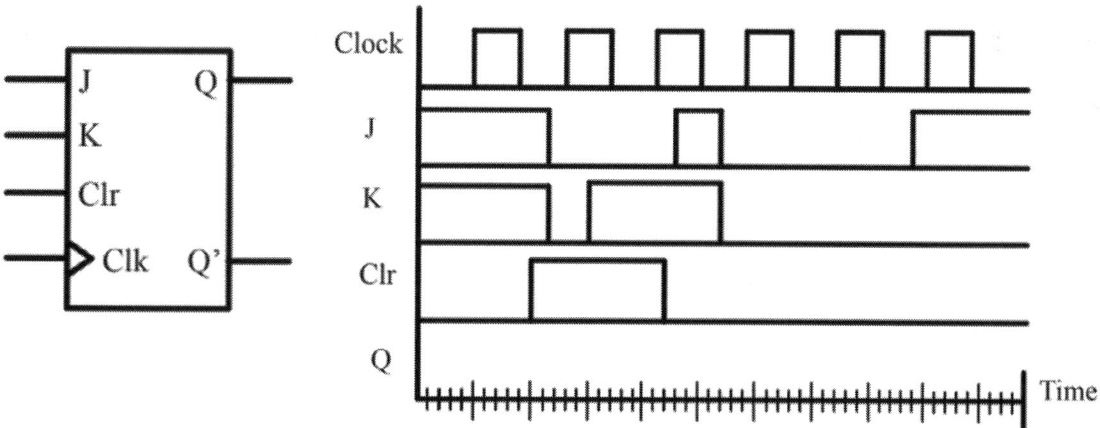

Problem 3) Repeat problem 2 but where the clear is synchronous.

3.4 - 3.6 Problems

Problem 1) A sequential circuit has an input X, and an output Z. It outputs Z=0 unless it sees sequence 1100 or 1110 where Z=1. The network resets to state 0 as soon as the target cannot be realized, regardless of the value just received. If the target is realized, then the next input causes it to reset at the state that causes the next possible target. Create a Moore diagram.

Problem 2) A sequential circuit has one input and one output that will produce an output of 1 whenever two 0's are input in a row and 0 otherwise. Resets as soon as a 1 is received, but overlapping targets are allowed. Create a Mealy diagram.

3.7- 3.8 Problems

Problem 1) From the following SM chart, derive the equations.

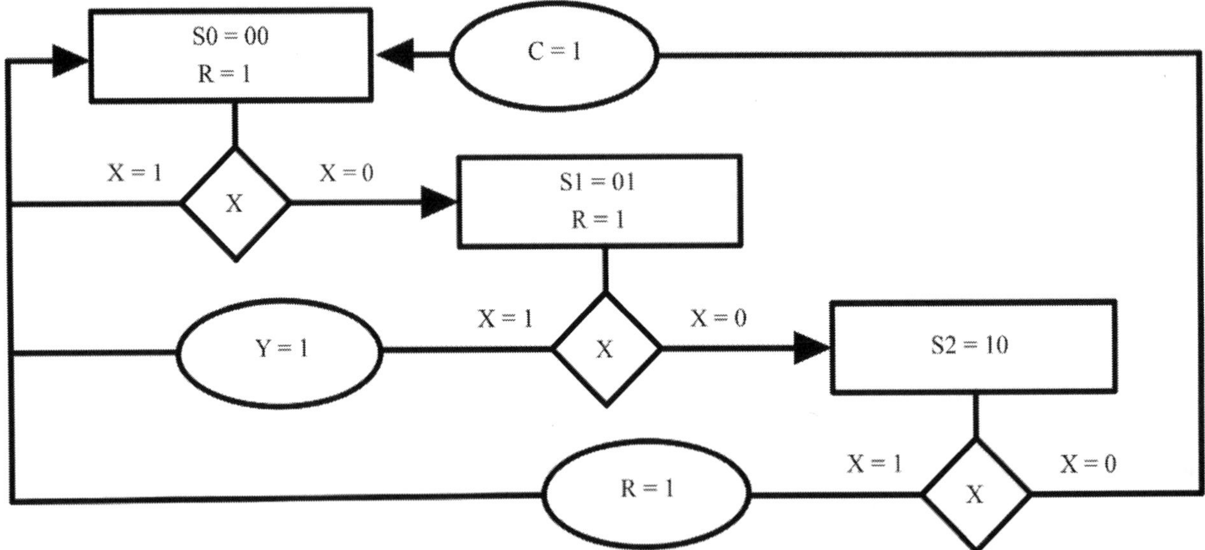

Problem 2) Make a Mealy SM chart to represent the following behavior. Also generate the equations from the SM chart. The input is X and the output is Z.

X	1	1	1	**0**	0	1	1	1	1	**0**	1	1	1	**0**	1	0	0	1
Z	0	0	0	**1**	0	0	0	0	0	**1**	0	0	0	**1**	0	0	0	0

3.9 Problems

Problem 1) Design an arbitrary counter to count 000,111,101,001 and repeat. Use D flip-flops first. Then use JK flip-flops.

Solutions

Section 3.1-3.3 Problem 1)

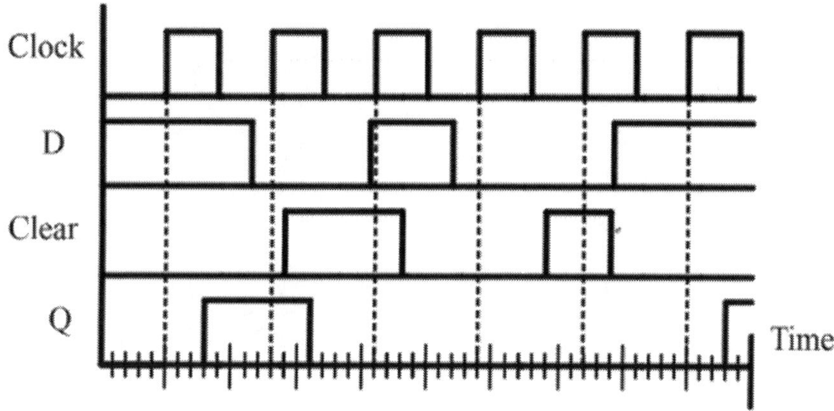

Section 3.1-3.3 Problem 2)

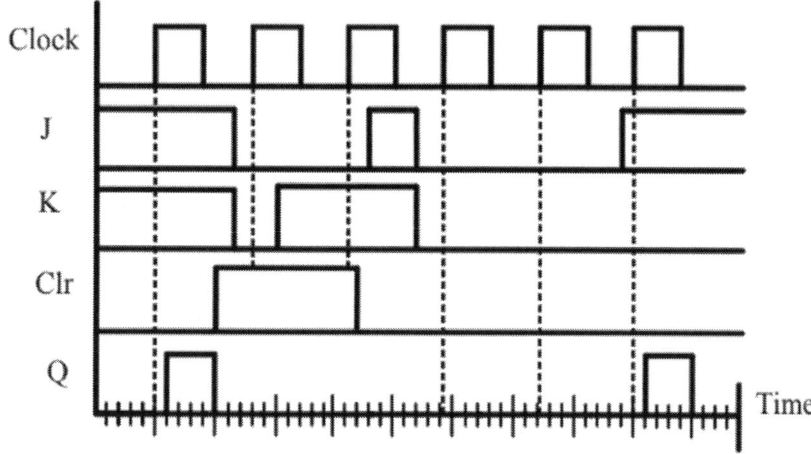

Section 3.1-3.3 Problem 3)

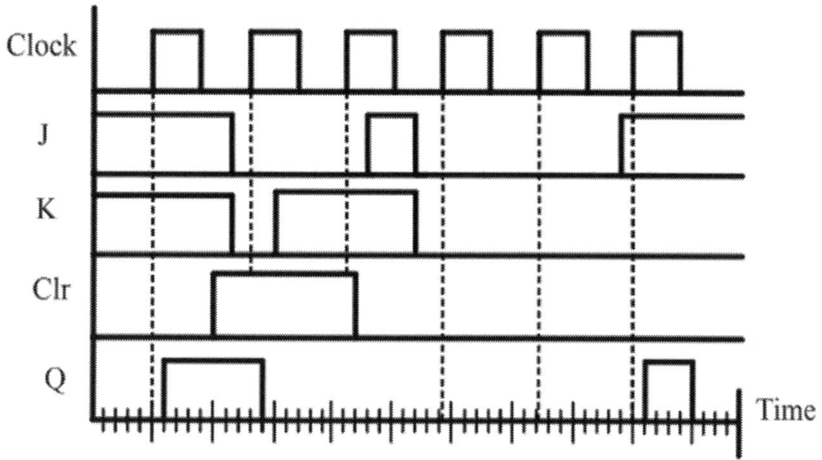

Section 3.4-3.6 Problem 1)

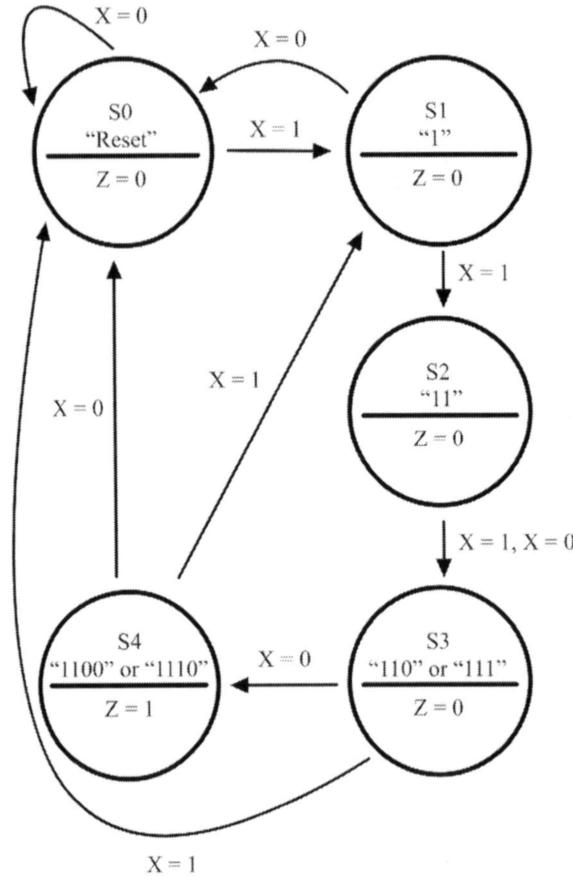

Section 3.4-3.6 Problem 2)

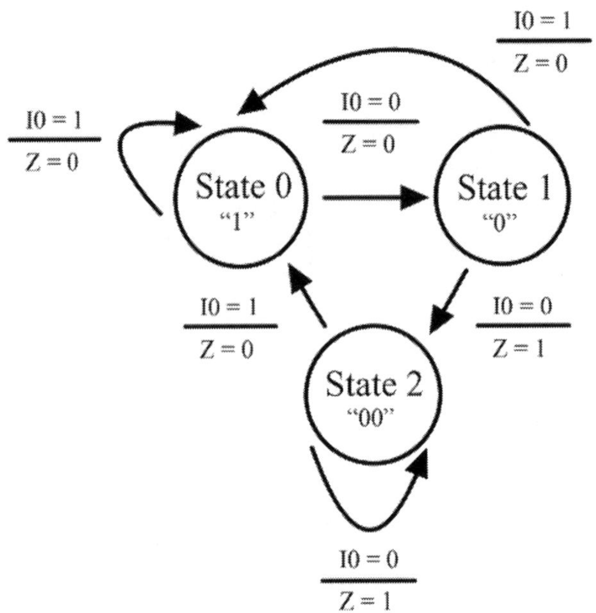

Section 3.7-3.8 Problem 1)

$$Q_{1+} = Q_1'Q_0X'$$

$$Q_{0+} = Q_1'Q_0'X'$$

$$Y = Q_1'Q_0X$$

$$R = Q_1'Q_0' + Q_1'Q_0 + Q_1Q_0'X$$

$$C = Q_1Q_0'X'$$

Section 3.7-3.8 Problem 2)

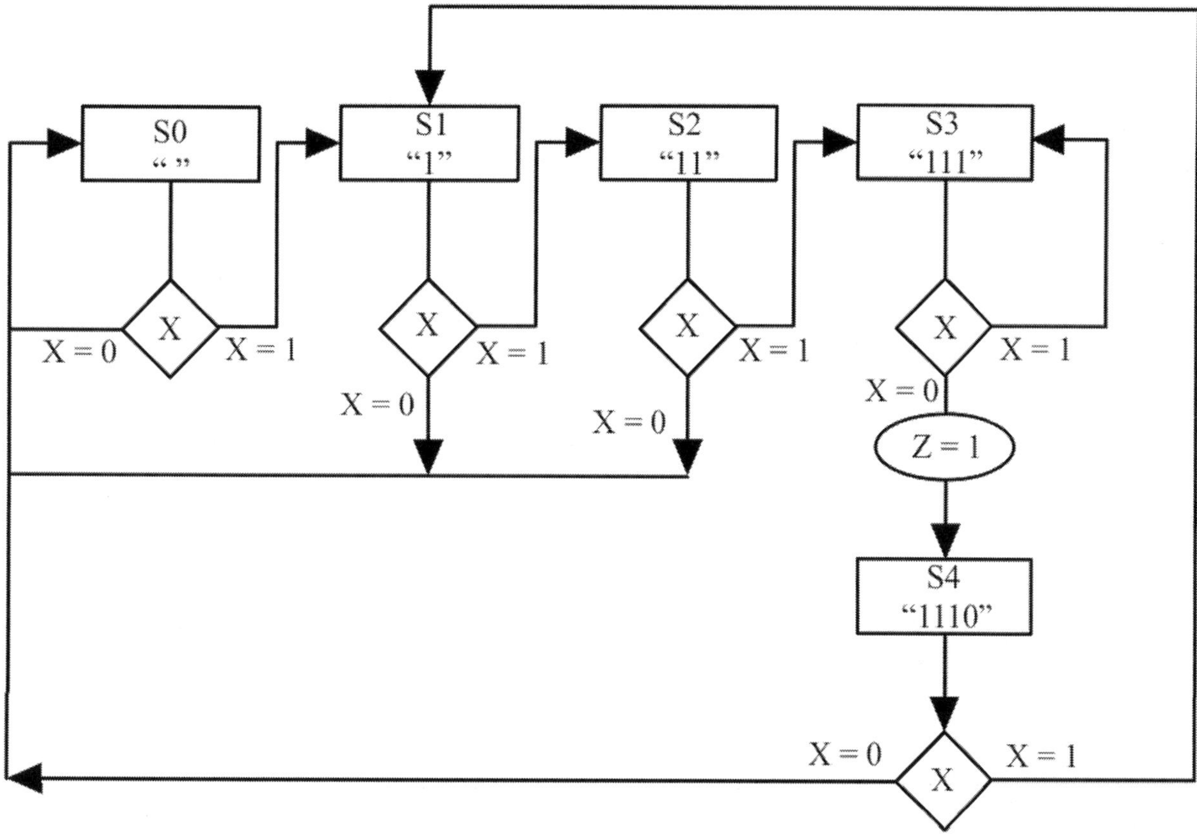

Section 3.9 Problem 1)

To make a truth table for the arbitrary counter, we note that the only inputs and outputs are the state and next state. Since the sequence was "000,111,101,001", when the state is 000, the next state must be 111. When the state is 111, the next state must be 101. When the state is 101, the next state must be 001. Since the counter repeats, when the state is 001, the next state must be 000. Using this logic, the truth table compatible for realizing the circuit using D flip-flops is below. The corresponding K-Maps are also provided.

D flip-flop truth table:

Q2	Q1	Q0	Q2+	Q1+	Q0+
0	0	0	1	1	1
0	0	1	0	0	0
0	1	0	X	X	X
0	1	1	X	X	X
1	0	0	X	X	X
1	0	1	0	0	1
1	1	0	X	X	X
1	1	1	1	0	1

K-Maps for circuit made with D flip-flops:

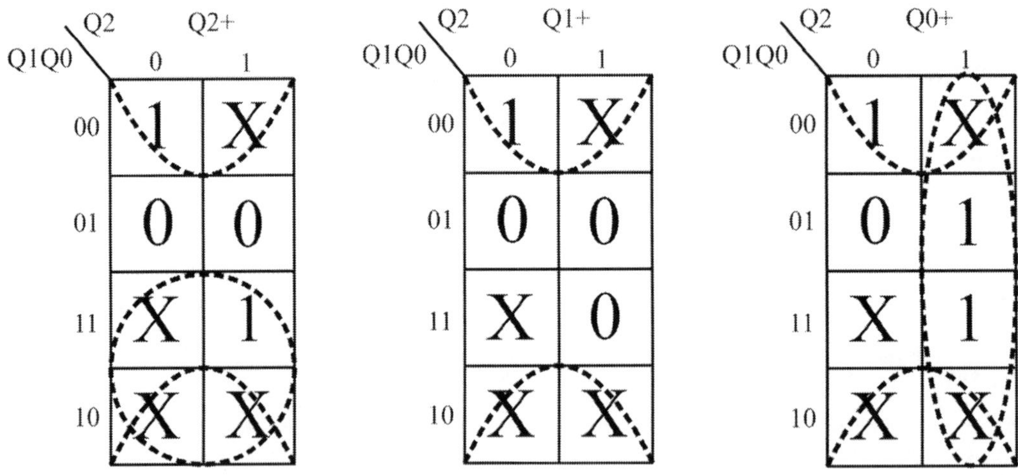

Equations for circuit made with D flip-flops:

$$Q_{2+} = Q_1Q_0'$$

$$Q_{1+} = Q_0'$$

$$Q_{0+} = Q_0'Q_2$$

To redo it again but with JK-flop flops, the truth table must be modified to be the following:

Q2	Q1	Q0	Q2+	Q1+	Q0+	J2	K2	J1	K1	J0	K0
0	0	0	1	1	1	1	X	1	X	1	X
0	0	1	0	0	0	0	X	0	X	X	1
0	1	0	X	X	X	X	X	X	X	X	X
0	1	1	X	X	X	X	X	X	X	X	X
1	0	0	X	X	X	X	X	X	X	X	X
1	0	1	0	0	1	X	1	0	X	X	0
1	1	0	X	X	X	X	X	X	X	X	X
1	1	1	1	0	1	X	0	X	1	X	0

Using the table to make and then solve the K-Maps will yield the following equations:

$$J_2 = Q_0'$$

$$K_2 = Q_1'$$

$$J_1 = Q_0'$$

$$K_1 = 1$$

$$J_0 = 1$$

$$K_0 = Q_2'$$

Digital Design with Verilog

In this half of the book, we will start programing an FPGA using Verilog. Each chapter will have a lab assignment where a similar problem is solved, and the theory is fully explained. There will also be additional chapters in this book covering foundational topics in more detail. If the title of a chapter starts with "Lab" then that means it is a required chapter to read, since it covers all the information relevant to the lab. If a chapter starts with "Lesson", then that means it is covering foundational knowledge. If you think you can skip the lessons, think again. These lessons will cover the knowledge needed to be proficient in your labs.

Before we begin, I do have a few more opening statements for my own students enrolled here at UTSA. If you're a student here at UTSA, then you likely already took Microcomputer Systems I, where you learned how to program the Pic16F microcontroller. I understand that many people may have felt like they had a hard time in that course and might think this course will be the same way. If you are one of those people, don't worry, learning Verilog is a completely different branch of knowledge, so think of this as a fresh start. In Microcomputer Systems I, you wrote code that resulted in a program being executed by the Pic16F microcontroller. In Verilog, we will be writing code that will result not in a program to be executed, but rather a physical piece of hardware to be built using the FPGA. What this means is that the FPGA is a lot more powerful, since the FPGA can be re-made into any physical piece of hardware, whereas the Pic16F microcontroller is always going to have the same set-in stone hardware. Anything a microcontroller can do; the FPGA can re-made do too. In fact, it is entirely possible to replicate an entire microcontroller on an FPGA. What this means is that every project performed in microcomputer systems I, could be done using the FPGA you will learn to program in this book. If you're in the camp of people who had a hard time in Microcomputer systems I, then think of this course as a second chance. You don't always get a second chance, but you do here, so make it count.

Lab 1 – Getting Started

In this first lab, you will be expected to create and run the given Verilog code. The procedure will be shown entirely in this chapter, so all you need to do is follow along. This is the only chapter of the entire book where the solution to the lab is here for you to just copy. What this means is that there's no excuse to not have this lab done on time. Sections 1.1 and 1.2 will show you how to run the provided code. If you prefer a video showing the lab, scan the QR code. The code from the video can be downloaded using the barcodes in section 1.2. Also note that if you follow the video instead of reading sections 1.1 and 1.2, remember to have your FPGA connected to your computer with the power switch on. Once you have completed the steps in the video, you should see behavior in an LED when you flip the three rightmost switches.

1.1 Creating a Project

After you have downloaded the programming IDE, Vivado, the first step is to create a project. If you have not downloaded Vivado yet, then do that first. Vivado does occupy around 30 GB of disk space, so it might require using a hard drive to store. Once installed, you should see the following Icon on your computer. Your version may be different but that is fine as long as it's 2020 or later.

Figure 1.1.1 Vivado IDE Icon

Double click the icon and you should see the screen shown in Figure 1.1.2. You will then click on "Create Project" under the "Quick Start" section.

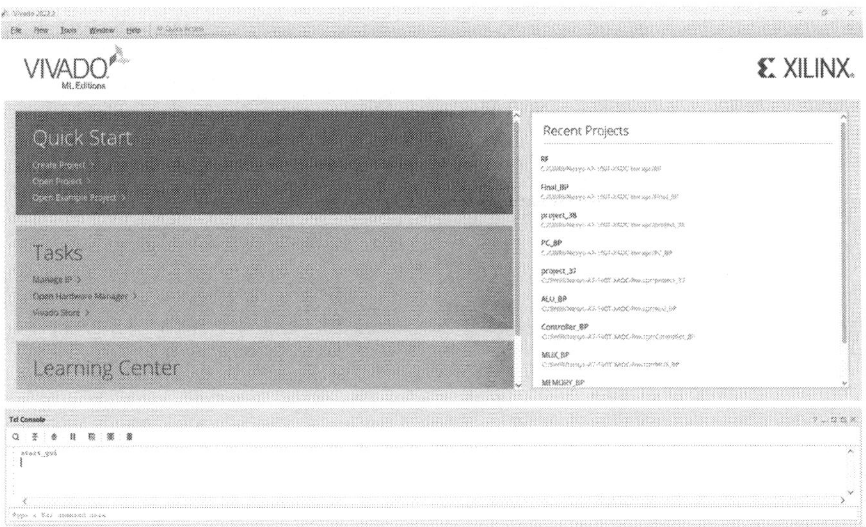

Figure 1.1.2 Vivado IDE starting screen

After clicking "Create Project", the screen shown in Figure 1.1.3 will appear, for which you will click "Next".

Figure 1.1.3 "Create a New Vivado Project" Icon

Then the screen shown in Figure 1.1.4 will appear. You will name the project whatever you want using the "Project name" field. The "Project location" field should automatically be filled, so you don't need to do anything there, unless you want to save it to a specific spot. Once you have entered a name, click "Next".

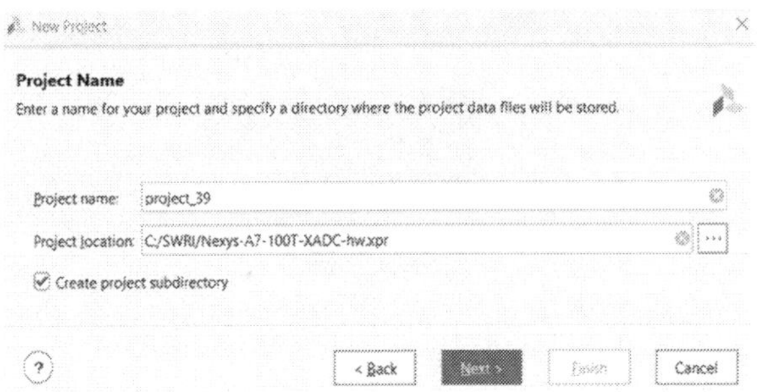

Figure 1.1.4 "Project Name" Icon

Then the screen shown in Figure 1.1.5 will appear. It should automatically only have RTL project selected, but if it doesn't change it to only have RTL selected as shown in Figure 1.1.5 and then click "Next".

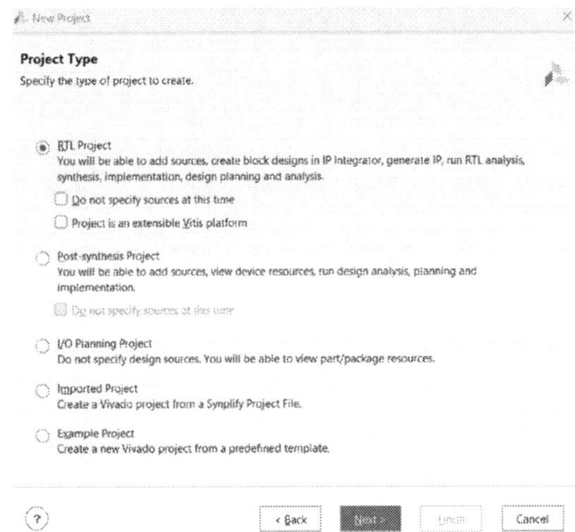

Figure 1.1.5 "Project Type" Icon

You will then see the screen shown in Figure 1.1.6. To create a source file, click "Create File". A source file is the file that will be used to write our code in Verilog.

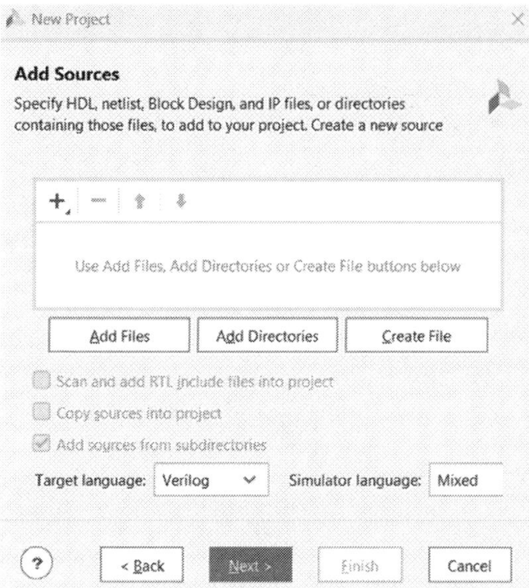

Figure 1.1.6 "Add Sources" screen

Then the following screen shown in Figure 1.1.7 should appear. The "File type" and "File location" field should automatically populate to be as shown in Figure 1.1.7. The "File name" field must be filled in by you to name your file. Since the source file is where we will normally write our code in, I named it "NF" for normal file. You may choose to follow this convention or name it something else. Once you have named it, click "OK" and the screen shown in Figure 1.1.7 should disappear.

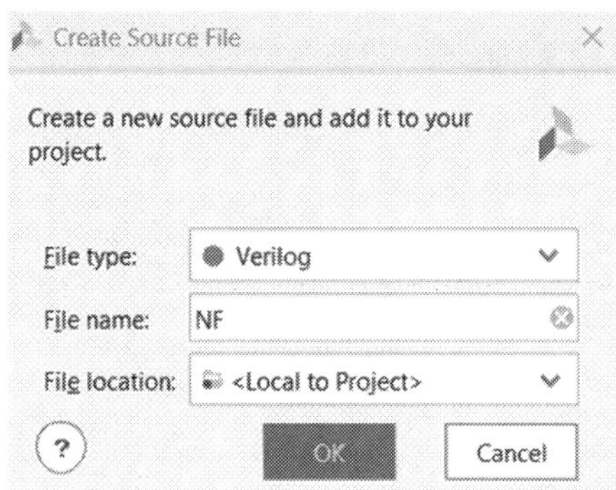

Figure 1.1.7 "Create Source File" screen

Once you have done this, the screen shown in Figure 1.1.6 should update to have contents in the box that previously said, "Use Add Files, Add Directories or Create File buttons below". Click "Next" once you see this happen.

You will then see the screen shown in Figure 1.1.8. To create a constraint file, click "Create File". A constraint file is the file that will be used to map the inputs and outputs that we will later declare in our code to physical pins on the board.

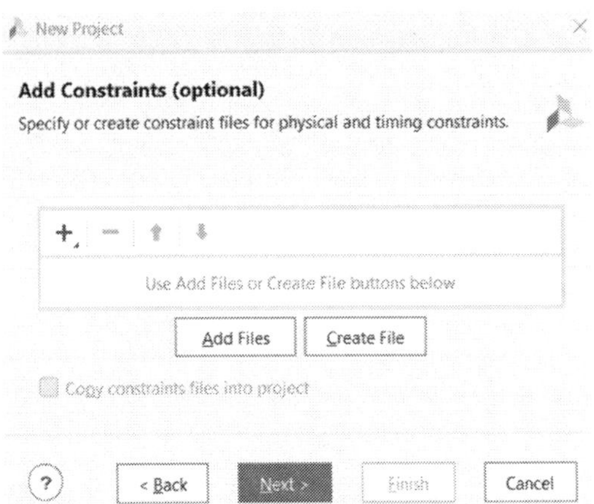

Figure 1.1.8 "Add Constraints" screen

Once you clicked "Create File" on the screen shown in Figure 1.1.8, the screen shown in Figure 1.1.9 should appear. The "File type" and "File location" field should automatically populate to be as shown in Figure 1.1.9. The "File name" field must be filled in by you to name your file. Since the constraint file is where we write code to constrain our inputs and outputs to physical pieces of hardware, I named it "CF" for constraint file. You may choose to follow this convention or name it something else. Once you have named it, click "OK" and the screen shown in Figure 1.1.9 should disappear.

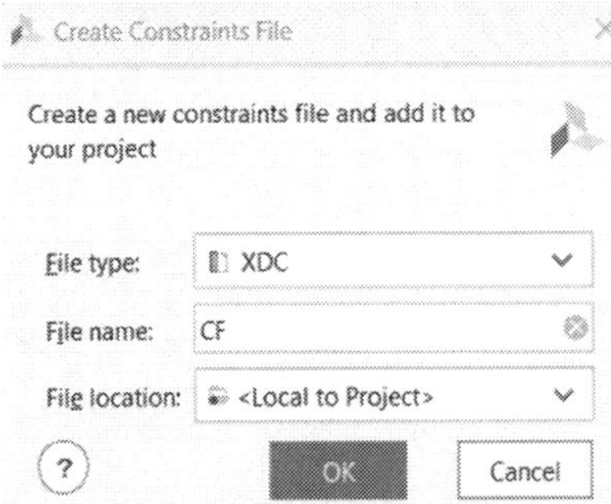

Figure 1.1.9 "Add Constraints File" screen

Once you have done this, the screen shown in Figure 1.1.8 should update to have contents in the box that previously said, "Use Add Files or Create File buttons below". Click "Next" once you see this happen.

You will then see the screen shown in Figure 1.1.10. This is an important step, since this is where we are telling the IDE what FPGA board we are using to program. If you get this step wrong, you won't be able to run any code, since Vivado is going to upload code to your board assuming your board was a different model. To get this step right, all you do is search "xc7a100tcsg324-1" in the search bar and click enter. Then underneath the search bar, under "Part", you should see the part, "xc7a100tcsg324-1", come up as shown in Figure 1.1.10. Double click this to proceed. You can also click it once and then click "Next" instead of double clicking it.

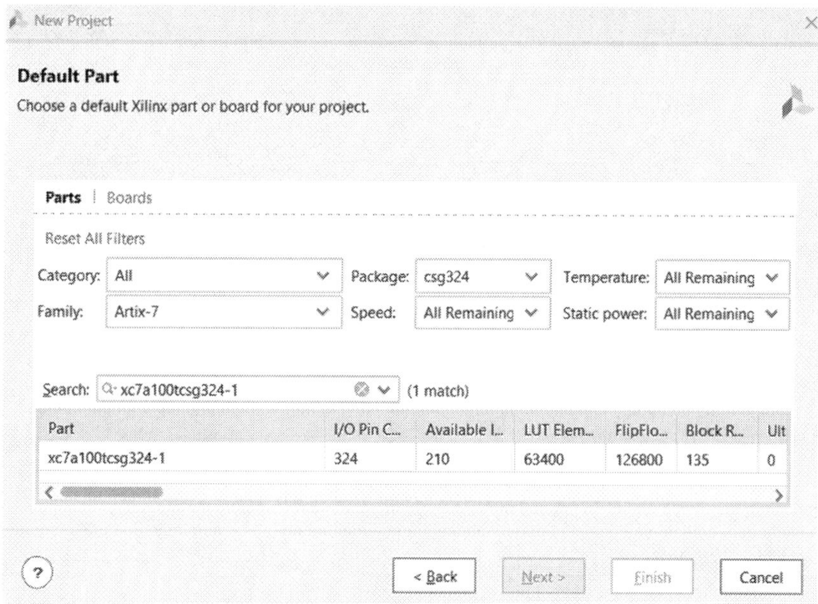

Figure 1.1.10 "Default Part" screen

Once you have done this, the screen 1.1.11 will come up. Click "Finish" to finish making the project. If more windows pop up, don't worry. Just click "Yes" or "OK" to them. When you are done, you should see your screen look like Figure 1.1.12.

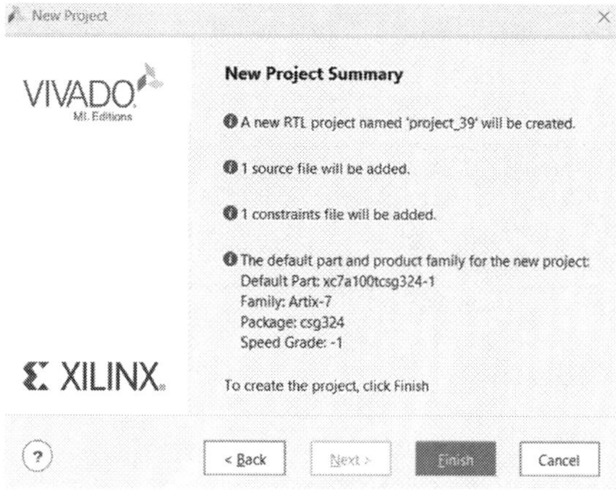

Figure 1.1.11 "New Project Summary" screen

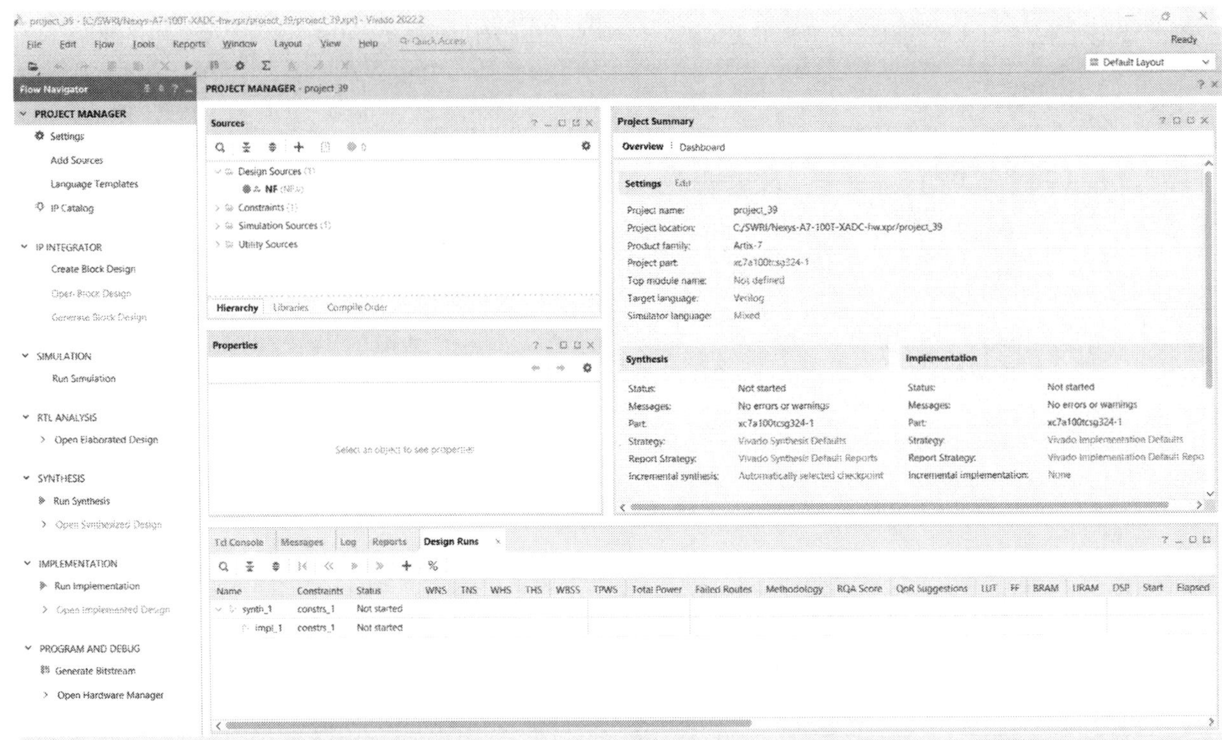

Figure 1.1.12 Verilog IDE ready for programming

1.2 Running a Project

Now that the project has been created, you are 50% done with getting credit for the first lab. All that remains now is to cut and paste the provided constraint file and provided source file into the IDE and upload the code to the board. So, to start off, under the "Sources" box, under "Design Sources", you will click the name of the file you created. The figure below shows the source file boxed with an arrow pointing to it. When you have located the source file, double click it. Note that it says "NF" because in the previous section, I named the source file "NF". If you named it something different, then that name will be present in the boxed region. Double click it regardless.

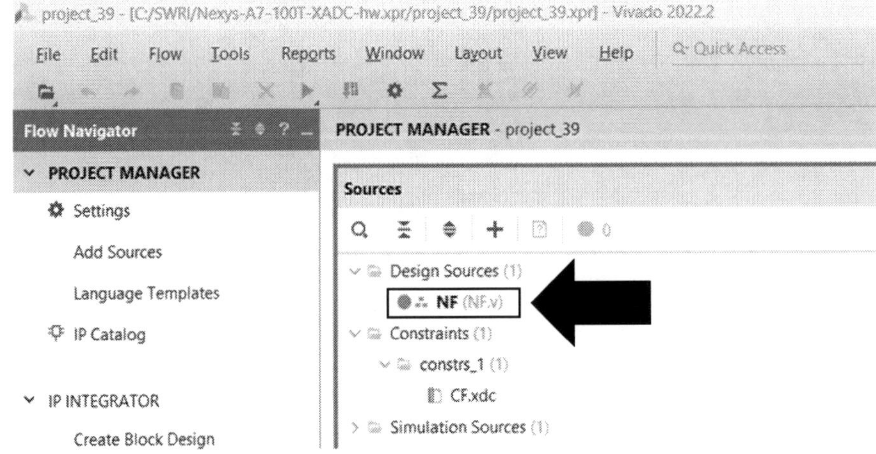

Figure 1.2.1 Source file location

After clicking the source file, your screen should look like Figure 1.2.2. In the right, there is now a space where you can write code in. For your convenience, a thick box has been inserted to surround the region you need to cut and paste the code into. Click into this region and copy and paste the provided source code. The source code is provided below. If you don't want to manually type it, scan the QR code to access the file.

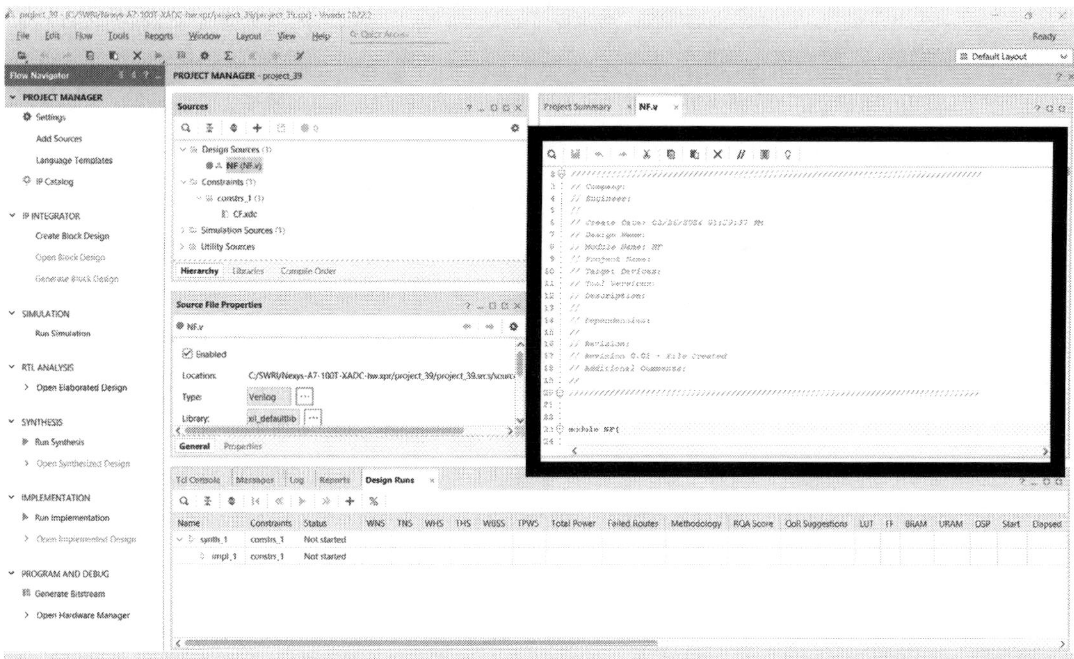

Figure 1.2.2 Source file programming location surrounded by box

Lab 1 Source Code

```
module mux2to1 (sel, I0, I1, out);
        input I0, I1, sel;
        output out;

        not(W0, sel);
        and(W1, I0, W0);
        and(W2, I1, sel);
        or(out, W1, W2);
endmodule
```

Now that you have cut and pasted the source file code into the IDE, we must do the same thing for the constraint file. To access the constraint file you created in section 1.1 of this chapter, you will need to navigate to the following area shown in Figure 1.2.3. double click on the boxed icon. Note that it says "CF.xdc" because I named my constraint file CF. If you named it something different then it won't say "CF" at the front. Double click it regardless. You will need to click on the symbol that is to the left of each folder to expand them if you don't already see the xdc file.

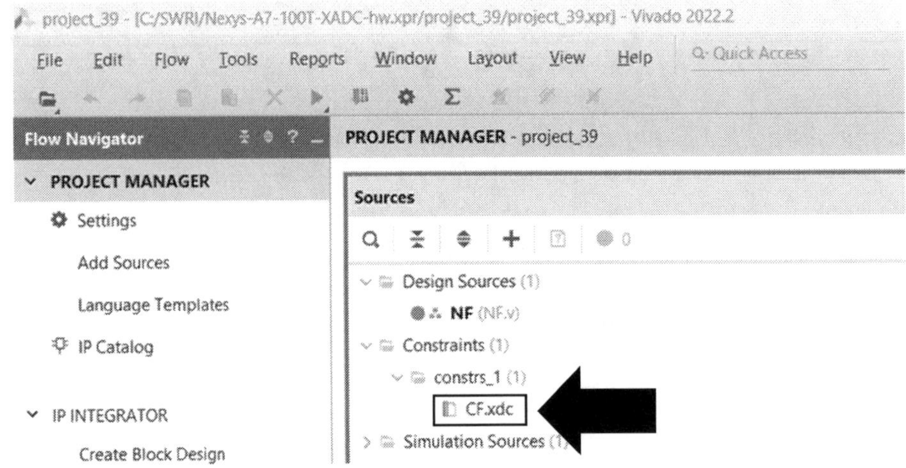

Figure 1.2.3 Constraint file location

After clicking the constraint file, your screen should look like Figure 1.2.4. In the right, there is now a space where you can write code in. For your convenience, Figure 1.2.4 has a thick box surrounding the region where you need to cut and paste the code into. Click into this region and copy and paste the provided constraint code. The provided constraint code is provided on the next page. If you don't want to manually type it, scan the following QR code to access the file.

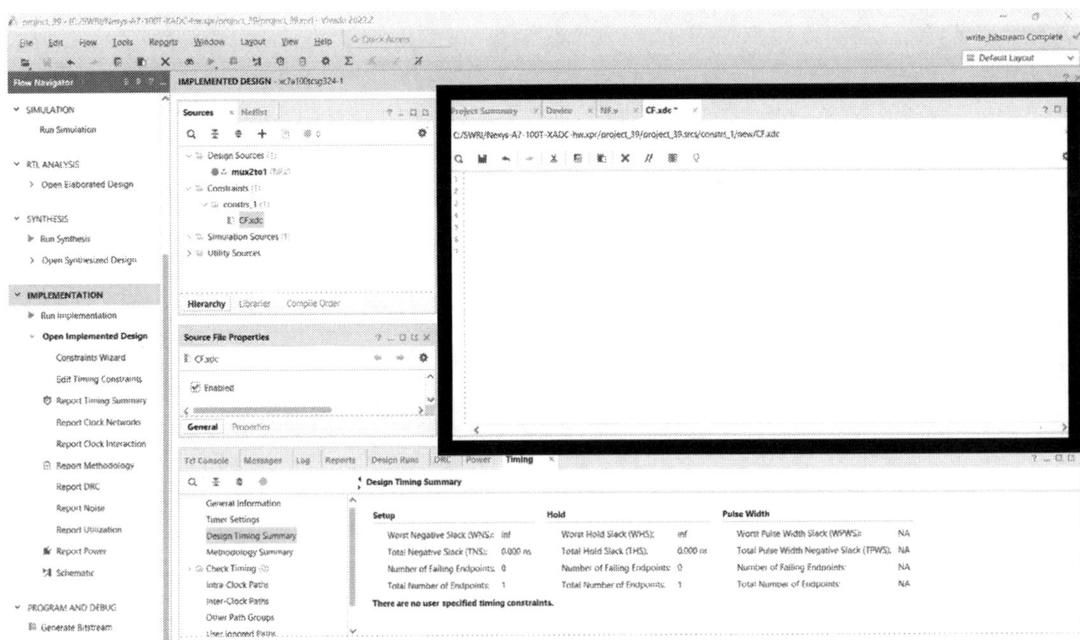

Figure 1.2.4 Constraint file programming location surrounded by box

Lab 1 Constraint Code

```
##Switches

set_property -dict { PACKAGE_PIN J15   IOSTANDARD LVCMOS33 } [get_ports { I0 }];
#IO_L24N_T3_RS0_15 Sch=sw[0]

set_property -dict { PACKAGE_PIN L16   IOSTANDARD LVCMOS33 } [get_ports { I1 }];
#IO_L3N_T0_DQS_EMCCLK_14 Sch=sw[1]

set_property -dict { PACKAGE_PIN M13   IOSTANDARD LVCMOS33 } [get_ports { sel }];
#IO_L6N_T0_D08_VREF_14 Sch=sw[2]

## LEDs

set_property -dict { PACKAGE_PIN H17   IOSTANDARD LVCMOS33 } [get_ports { out }];
#IO_L18P_T2_A24_15 Sch=led[0]
```

Now that both the source and constraint files have been finished, it is time to upload the project to your board. It is extremely simple to do this. Just navigate to the box labeled "Flow Navigator", scroll down, and click "Generate Bitstream". After doing this, if it asks you to save, then click "Save". Click "Yes" to whatever other windows pop up too. The figure below shows the flow manager in a box in case you have a hard time identifying it. An arrow is pointing to the "Generate Bitstream" icon you will need to click on. Remember if you don't see it in the flow navigator, you will need to use the bar to scroll down.

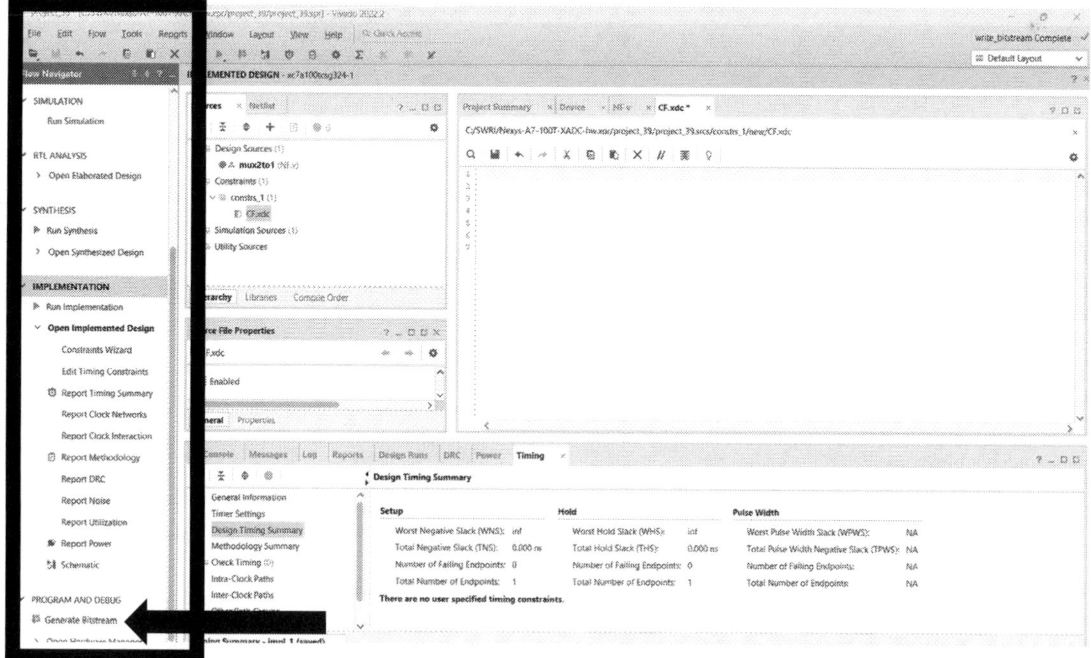

Figure 1.2.5 "Flow Navigator" and "Generate Bitstream" location

Once you have finished this, your computer will begin to create the bitstream. The bitstream is the information that will be uploaded into your FPGA enabling it to physically build the circuit described in the source code. You will need to wait for around 5 minutes before the bitstream is done generating. Yes, that's right, 1-5 minutes. In Micro 1, it was instant, but due to the FPGA being much more complex, it takes longer. When the bitstream generation is complete, a window will pop up. Just click "OK" or close it. Next, navigate to the hardware manager, open target, and click auto connect. Figure 1.2.6 shows where you need to go. Make sure your board is plugged in and the power switch is on. The power switch is located near the plug connecting to your computer.

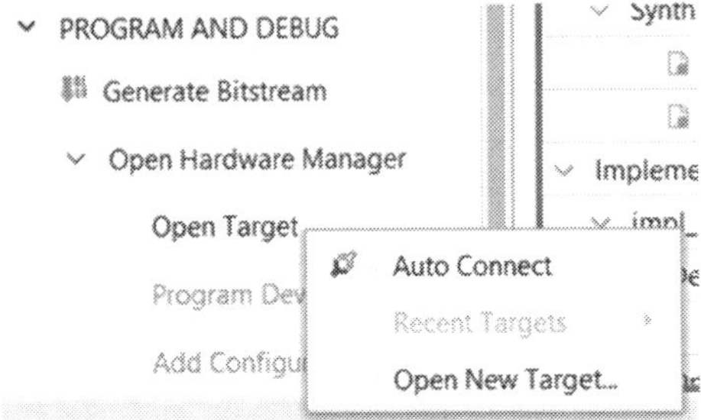

Figure 1.2.6 "Auto Connect" location

Next, once you have done this, you should see "Program device" appear in the top left of the hardware manager box. Click on "Program device". To help you locate where to click, there is an arrow pointing to it in Figure 1.2.7.

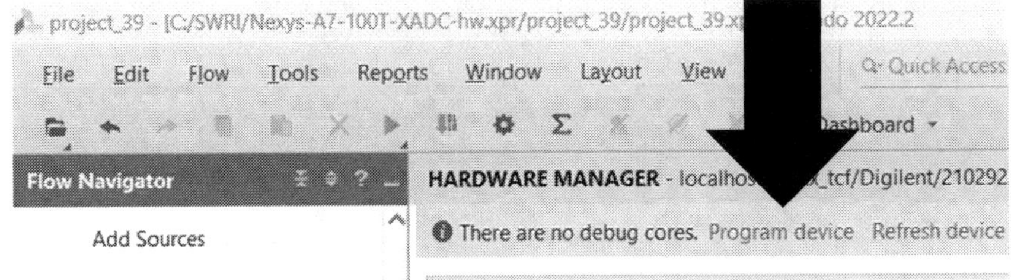

Figure 1.2.7 "Program device" location

Once you have clicked "Program device", you should see the window in Figure 1.2.8 pop up. Click program and you should be done with the Lab!

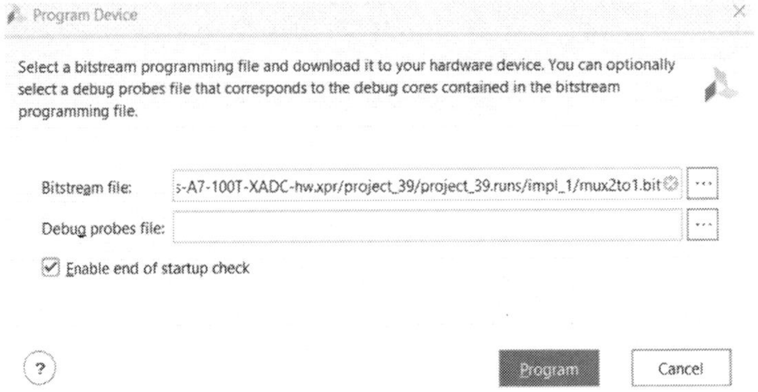

Figure 1.2.8 "Program device" location

1.3 Code Explained

In this Lab, so far you have essentially cut and pasted code into the IDE and uploaded it into the board without much explanation as to how that code was derived or even what it does. The main purpose of lab 1 was to get you acquainted with the process of creating a project and uploading it into your board after having finished the constraint and source file. Now in the real world, you are never just given the constraint and source file, so now it's time to explain the given source and constraint file, so you can go on to write the next one yourself.

Every source file has one purpose, which is to provide a description of the physical circuit to be built on the FPGA. The source file you were given was code describing a 2:1 multiplexer. The source file describes a 2:1 multiplexer by laying out a gate level design using what are called primitives in Verilog. Primitives are the pre-defined building blocks defined by Verilog. Primitives model logical gates. This is because gates, as you learned in the logic design section, are the building blocks of all digital systems. A primitive in Verilog will be named with the logical gate name followed by parenthesis and some variables as parameters. For primitives modeling gates, the very first parameter is always the output of the primitive. The parameters that follow are always inputs. The example below shows an "and" gate primitive being defined while showing the equivalent circuit.

and(Z,A,B) A B Z

Figure 1.3.1 2-input "and" primitive

From the figure, it is apparent that the first parameter is the output of the gate and the two that follow are the inputs. If we wanted to have a 3-input gate, we would simply define it as shown below.

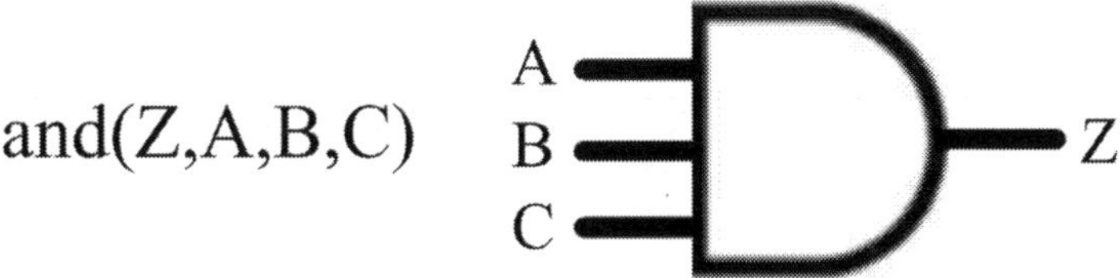

Figure 1.3.2 3-input "and" primitive

Now that you understand how a primitive works, let's revisit the source code that was given. Below shows the code again for your reference. From the source code, you can clearly see that on lines 5-8, primitives were defined. Try to imagine what piece of hardware corresponds to each primitive. After doing that, you can see the solution in the next figure.

Lab 1 Source Code

```
1 module mux2tol (sel, I0, I1, out);
2       input I0, I1, sel;
3       output out;
4
5       not(W0, sel);
6       and(W1, I0, W0);
7       and(W2, I1, sel);
8       or(out, W1, W2);
9 endmodule
```

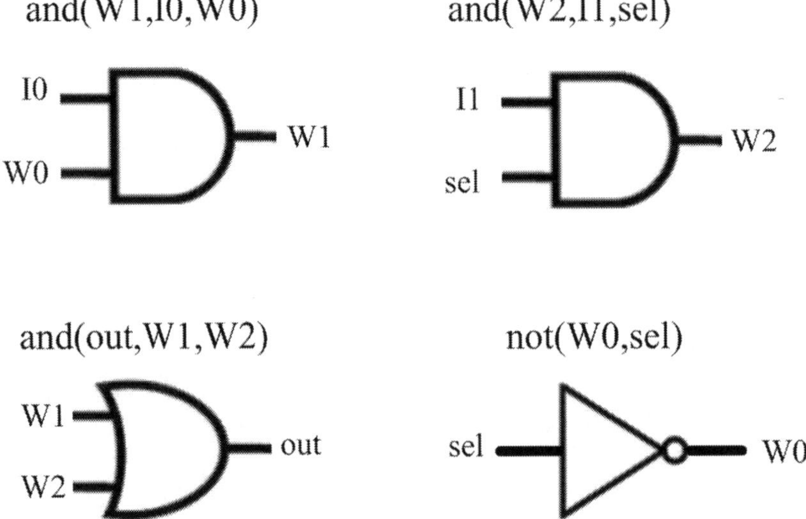

Figure 1.3.3 primitives from source code

Now for the "not" primitive, there will always only be two parameters since there are no such things as multiple input inverters. All the others followed the convention from Figure 1.3.1. If you refer to section 2.1 of the combinational logic review half of the book, we used logic design to build a 2:1 multiplexer from scratch using conventional circuit design techniques. At the end of section 2.1, we eventually derived a physical schematic of the 2:1 multiplexer. This schematic will be shown again labeled for your convenience. Notice how each wire gets assigned a name. The wires directly connected to the inputs and outputs are named the same as the input or output. The wires that are not directly connected to an input or output are given a different name. In this case, they are named "W0", "W1", and "W2". These three wires are called internal wires since they are internal to the design. Notice how every single gate shown is identical to the ones from Figure 1.3.3. They are all shown assembled together here. The compiler for Verilog knows how to assemble each primitive defined in lines 5-8 to generate the structure shown in Figure 1.3.4. If you are having trouble visualizing how a bunch of primitives combine, start by individually making each one, then connecting the wires that are the same together, then arrange the entire thing to be neater.

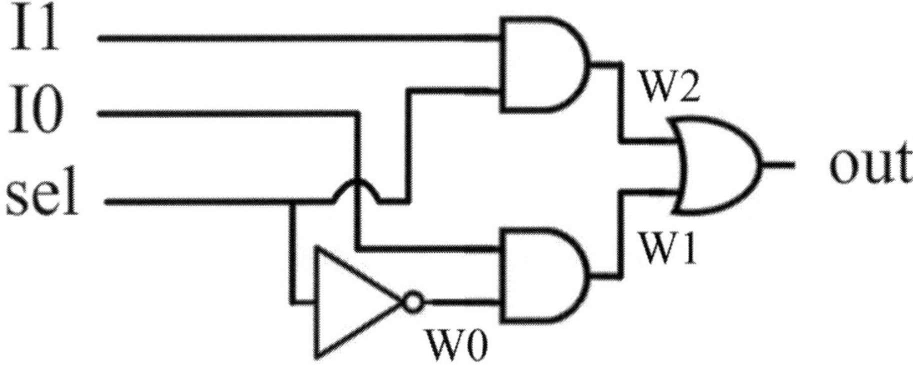

Figure 1.3.4 primitives from source code assembled

Now that you understand how lines 5-8 work in the source code, it is time to discuss lines 1,2,3 and 10. Line 1 defines the module and the inputs and outputs. Line 10 marks the end of the module A module declaration will always have the following structure.

```
module   Name(A,B,C...);
...
endmodule
```

Figure 1.3.5 module declaration

A module is used to create a physical piece of hardware. In our source code, we made one module to make the 2:1 multiplexer. Each time you create a module declaration, you will include the keyword "module" as shown in Figure 1.3.5. The list of variables in the parenthesis is called the sensitivity list, where A, B, and C represent general inputs and outputs. You will always list your inputs and outputs in the sensitivity list. In our source code, we had three inputs, "sel", "I1", and "I0". The only output was "out". Each of these were included in the sensitivity list. The module name will always be declared between the keyword "module" and between the sensitivity list. For our source code, the module name was "mux2to1". For each module declaration, there will need to be an "endmodule" to mark the end of the module. Line 10 of the source code achieves this effect. Each time you make a module declaration, the next step is to simple state directly which contents in the sensitivity list are outputs and which ones are inputs. Lines 2 and 3 of the source code achieve this effect. So, there you have it! The entirety of the source code has been discussed and explained. Now it is time to do the same thing for the constraint file that was given.

Every constraint file has one purpose, which is to physically map the inputs and outputs described in the source file to physical parts on the board. In the constraint file you were given, I0 was mapped to switch 0 on the board, I1 was mapped to switch 1 on the board, and I2 was mapped to switch 2 on the board. The output "out" was mapped to led 0 on the board. The Figure below shows the location of these parts on the board. Note that "SW" is the abbreviation for Switch. If you flip the three switches and observe the labeled LED in Figure 1.3.6, you will see that it behaves exactly like a 2:1 multiplexer. The select line is "SW 2", input 1 is "SW 1", input 0 is "SW 0", and the output of the mux is "led 0". Had the constraint file of been different, then the inputs and output could have been mapped differently.

Figure 1.3.6 Parts on board

Now you might be wondering how the constraint file was used to assign switches 0-2 as inputs and the rightmost led, led 0, as the output. Well, the constraint file is extremely simple compared to the source file. In the constraint file, a comment starts with a "#" symbol. The comments in the constraint file specify which component is being represented by what line. For example, the comment on line 4 says that line 3 corresponds to "sw[0]" or switch 0 in other words. For each line corresponding to a physical part on the board, you will insert the name of the assigned input or output in the "get_ports{}" field. For example, since we wanted to assign "I0" to switch 0, we wrote "I0" in the "get_ports{}" field of line 3. The same was done for the remaining inputs and outputs. Again, for example, line 14 maps the output we declared in the source file, "out", to "led 0" on board. We know that line 14 does this, since line 15 says in the comments that it does.

Lab 1 Constraint Code

```
1   ##Switches
2
3   set_property -dict { PACKAGE_PIN J15   IOSTANDARD LVCMOS33 } [get_ports { I0 }];
4   #IO_L24N_T3_RS0_15 Sch=sw[0]
5
6   set_property -dict { PACKAGE_PIN L16   IOSTANDARD LVCMOS33 } [get_ports { I1 }];
7   #IO_L3N_T0_DQS_EMCCLK_14 Sch=sw[1]
8
9   set_property -dict { PACKAGE_PIN M13   IOSTANDARD LVCMOS33 } [get_ports { sel }];
10  #IO_L6N_T0_D08_VREF_14 Sch=sw[2]
11
12  ## LEDs
13
14  set_property -dict { PACKAGE_PIN H17   IOSTANDARD LVCMOS33 } [get_ports { out }];
15  #IO_L18P_T2_A24_15 Sch=led[0]
```

The following figure will completely summarize the process done by the constraint file for lab 1. In the left is the constraint file code. As you can clearly see, each line is responsible for assigning an input or output to the physical location specified in the comments. For example, the first line has I0 in the "get_ports{}" field and the comment for that line says "sw[0]". This results in switch 0 being assigned to I0 as shown on the right. The same process was done for the remaining inputs and outputs.

Figure 1.3.7 Constraint file assigning inputs and outputs to the physical parts on the board

Now you might be wondering where we would be able to get lines corresponding to other switches or LEDs. What line would we use if we wanted to map "out" to led 10 instead of led 0? Well, the answer is that there is a general constraint file that is specific to the board we are using, and that general file has all possible lines already written. You just identify from the comments where the desired lines are and then fill out the "get_ports{}" field with your values. Since only four combined inputs and outputs were present, only four lines from the general constraint file were used. The rest were deleted as they were not needed. **If you want to see the full constraint file, scan the following QR code. You should always use this file as a template when making a new constraint file.**

1.4 Test Bench Creation

Before moving on, it is important to mention how to add a test bench file into the project. To do this, click the add Sources button as shown in Figure 1.4.1.

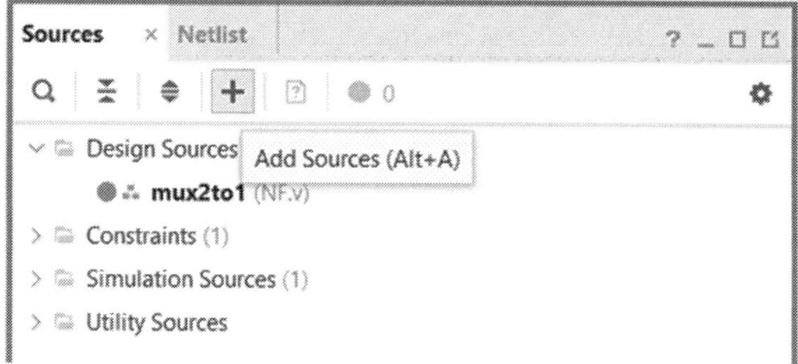

Figure 1.4.1 Add sources button location

After clicking the add Sources button, a window will appear asking you which option to select. Pick the option "Add or create simulation sources" and then click "Next". After doing that, you should see the window in Figure 1.4.2 appear on your screen. Then click "Create file".

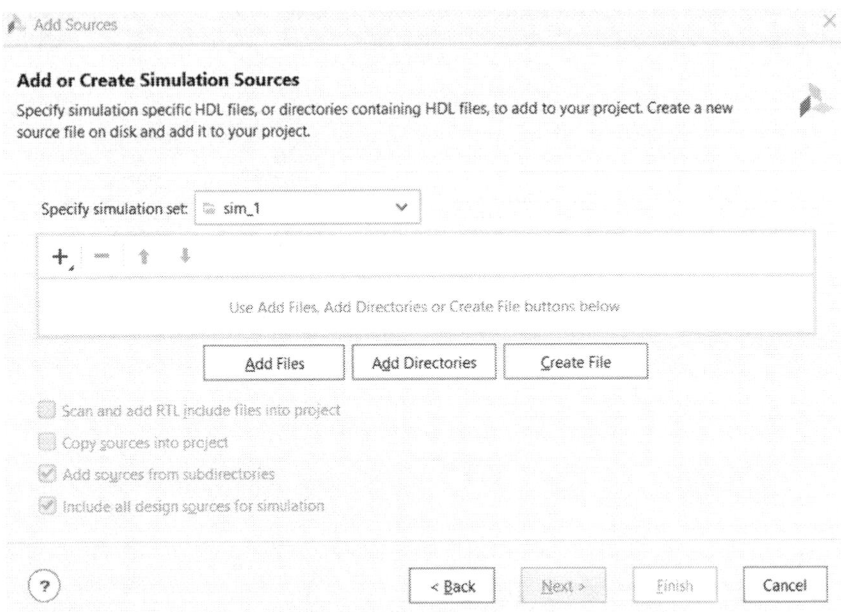

Figure 1.4.2 "Add or Create Simulation Sources" window

Once you have clicked "Created File", the window in Figure 1.4.3 should appear. Enter the File name you want your test bench to have. I typically name it "TB", since this file will be used to write the test bench. After naming it, click "OK".

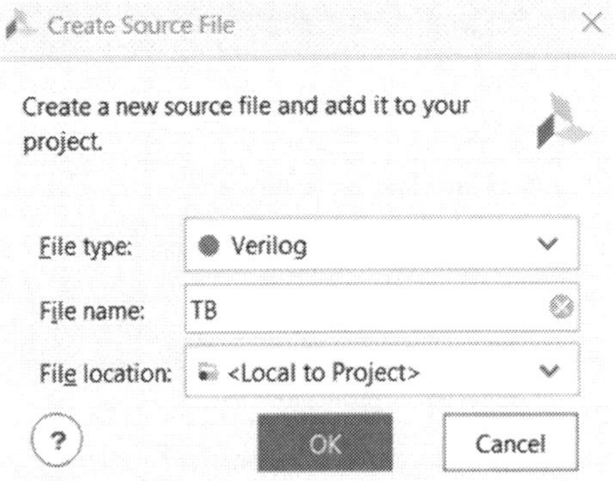

Figure 1.4.3 "Create Source File" window

Once you have clicked "OK" the window in Figure 1.4.3 should disappear and you will click "Finish" in the window from Figure 1.4.2. Click "OK" and "Yes" to whatever additional windows pop up. Once you have done this, to access the simulation file, navigate to the following region in Figure 1.4.4 and double click the test bench file. In Figure 1.4.4, the test bench file is named "TB" and is boxed with an arrow pointing to it. If you named it something else, then click that name when you see it.

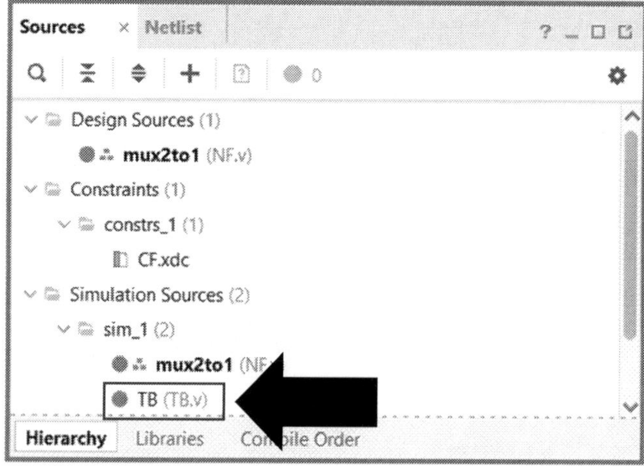

Figure 1.4.4 Test Bench location

Once you have clicked the test bench file, it should open to the right and your screen should look like Figure 1.4.5. You can begin to insert your test bench code in the boxed region in Figure 1.4.5. Do not worry about writing a test bench for now. That will be covered later. This section is just meant to get you acquainted with how to make the file for it. Detailed programming lessons on how to program both source files and test bench files will follow this lab.

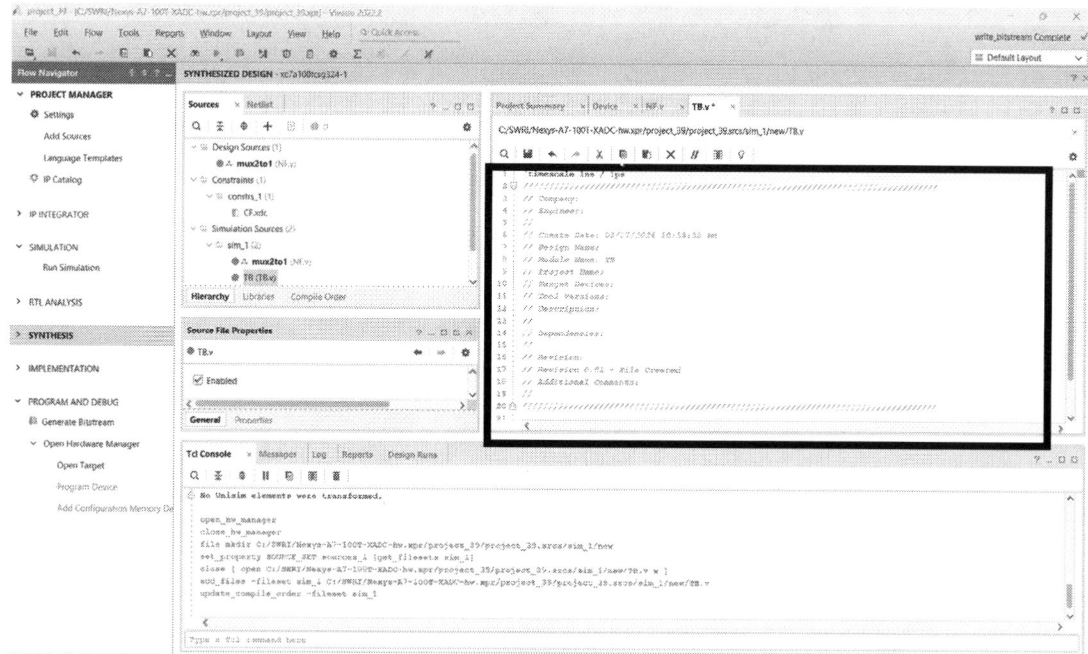

Figure 1.4.5 Test bench file ready for programming

1.5 Gate level Verilog schematic

Another extremely important tool to discuss is the RTL analysis tool in the flow navigator. The RTL analysis tool allows you to physically see the gate level schematic generated by your source file. This will be extremely useful for debugging your code, since if your code generates the wrong circuit, you will know. To access this schematic, go to the flow navigator, and under RTL analysis, click "Open Elaborated Design". If it asks you to save, click "Save". Say "OK" and "Yes" any other windows that pop up. Figure 1.5.1 shows where to click.

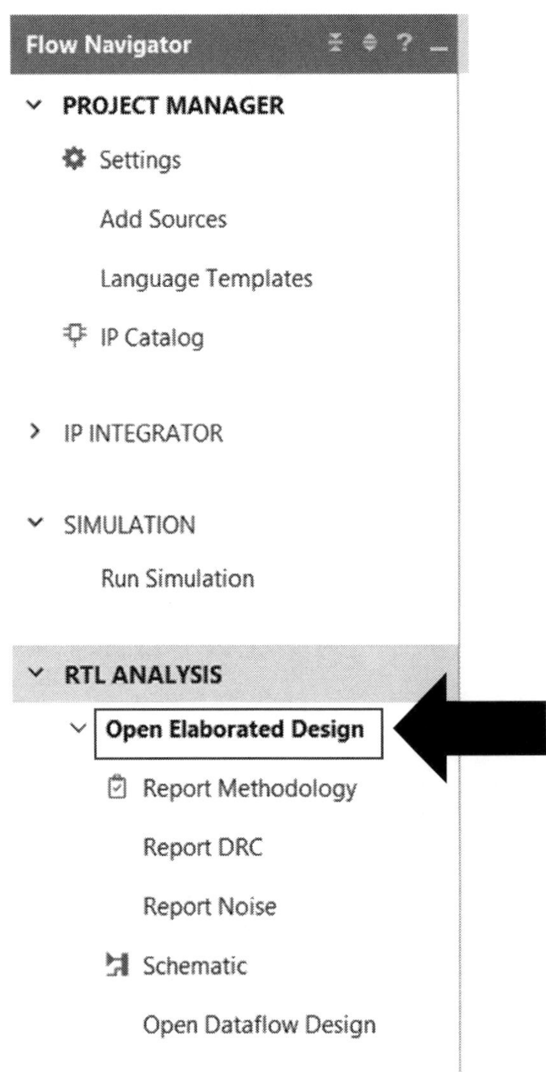

Figure 1.5.1 Elaborated design location

After opening the elaborated design for the source code provided, you should see the following schematic shown in Figure 1.5.2.

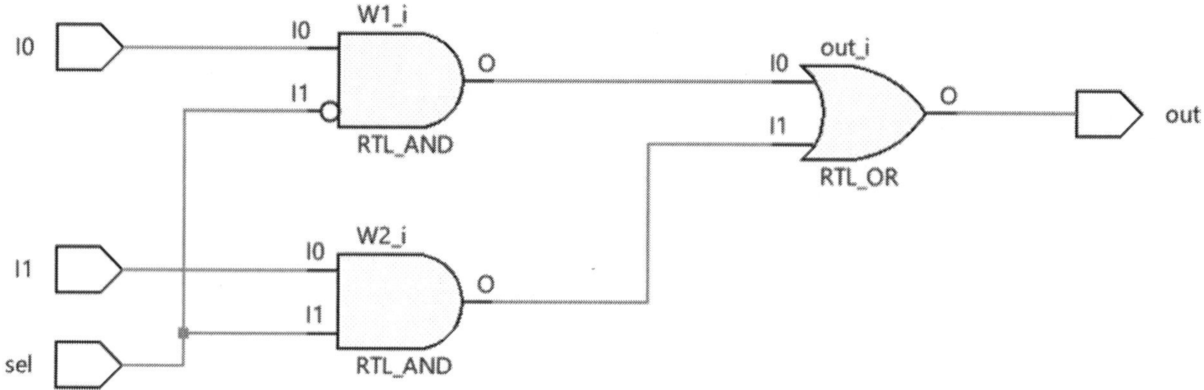

Figure 1.5.2 Lab 1 elaborated design

1.6 One Important Tip

The final and last tip before concluding lab 1 is how to make the source window appear again if you accidentally closed it. I remember when I first started programming in Verilog, Whenever I accidently would close my source files, I would have to close vivado and re-open the project to get it to come back. I easily wasted a few hours of my life for nothing because of that. Fortunately, because you have this book, you get to just have the answer instantly. To open the source file box again, navigate to the region shown in Figure 1.6.1 and click "Reset Layout".

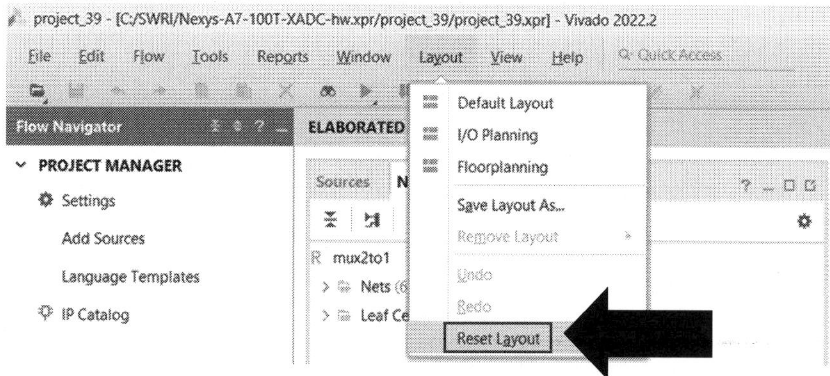

Figure 1.6.1 Reset layout location

If you are in the hardware or any other manager and want to reset, then you will need to exit before resetting the layout. Figure 1.6.2 shows where to click in this situation.

Figure 1.6.2 Exit hardware manager location

Lesson 1 – Introduction to Combinational Design in Verilog

In lab 1 you learned how to create a source file and got a crash course on how primitives work, but there are many other ways to build a circuit than with primitives. In general, there are two kinds of approaches when designing in Verilog. There are structural approaches and behavioral approaches. Structural approaches are when the designer comes up with the gate level schematic first and then manually converts their design into Verilog code. The source code from lab 1 was derived using a structural approach since the gate level design was developed by hand in section 2.2 of the logic design half of the book. Then after it was derived by hand, primitives were used to manually convert the gate level schematic into lines of Verilog code. Behavioral approaches are much more powerful than structural approaches, since with a behavioral approach, we can simply describe the overall behavior we want the circuit to have, and the IDE will construct the gate level schematic for us. This can save a HUGE amount of time, since we will no longer need to design the entire thing ourselves. In this lesson, you will be taught how to make a Verilog module to build combinational circuits using both structural and behavioral methods.

L1.1 Declaring a Verilog Module

In Verilog, the way we make individual circuits is with modules. We must first know the inputs and outputs of our circuit, then after that, we can declare a module to start designing it. The following figure shows how a module can generally be structured.

```
1    module Name (A, B,C);
2          input A, B;
3          output C;
...
...        // Insert design here
...
10   endmodule
```

Figure L1.1.1 Module declaration format

In the figure, the keyword "module" is always present in the declaration in line 1. The list of parameters in the parenthesis is called the sensitivity list. The sensitivity list is where you include the inputs and outputs. "A", "B", and "C" represent general inputs and outputs in the sensitivity list. The name of the module, represented by "Name", is always placed between the "module" keyword and the sensitivity list. In every module, the inputs and outputs must be directly stated. Lines 2 and 3 represent how this would happen should "A" and "B" of been assigned as inputs and "C" as an output. Then at the end of each module, there must be an "endmodule" line, as done in line 10. Note that the double slash, "//", is how comments are made in Verilog source files. There are other ways to declare a module but in truth, if you master the convention in Figure L1.1.1, then you can define any module, regardless of the complexity. For this reason, no other variations will be discussed. The following examples show how to declare a module.

Example 1

Declare a Verilog module that has "IN0", "X", and "Y" as inputs with "T" and "QR" as outputs. Name the module "Circuit3".

```
module Circuit3 (IN0, X, Y, T, QR);
    input IN0, X, Y;
    output T, QR;

    // Insert design here

endmodule
```

Example 2

Declare a Verilog module that has "IN0", "IN1", and "IN3" as inputs with "OUT1" and "OUT0" as outputs. Name the module "Circuit0".

```
module Circuit0 (IN0, IN1, IN2, OUT0, OUT1);
    input IN0, IN1, IN2;
    output OUT0, OUT1;

    // Insert design here

endmodule
```

L1.2 Primitives

If you read section 1.3 of lab 1, then you already have a great jump start on how built-in primitives work, but if you didn't, that's ok. This lesson will explain the basics a second time. Built-in primitives are great for structural design since they allow designers to work at the gate level. Since built-in primitives are structural in nature, we usually won't use them except for rare instances where we want to specify the exact gate level layout of our design. There are two kinds of primitives, user defined and built in. Built in primitives are ones that are built into Verilog. You will know when a primitive is built-in due to it having a keyword that is purple when declared in Vivado. Verilog has a built-in primitive for each logic gate. The structure of a basic built-in primitive is shown in Figure L1.2.1.

```
name(Output,Input0,Input1, ...)
```

Figure L1.2.1 Primitive declaration format

From the figure, the "name" represents where the primitive name would be placed. The name of the primitive is always written in lowercase and will always be the name of its corresponding logic gate. For example, the name of the built-in primitive for the xor gate is simply "xor". From the figure, the parentheses contain the parameters of the built-in primitive. The first parameter is always the output, which is why the first parameter is labeled "Output". The remaining parameters are always inputs, which is why they are labeled as "Input1" and "Input2". The "..." is included since any number of inputs could be specified. The examples below show how logic gates can be represented using primitives.

Example 1

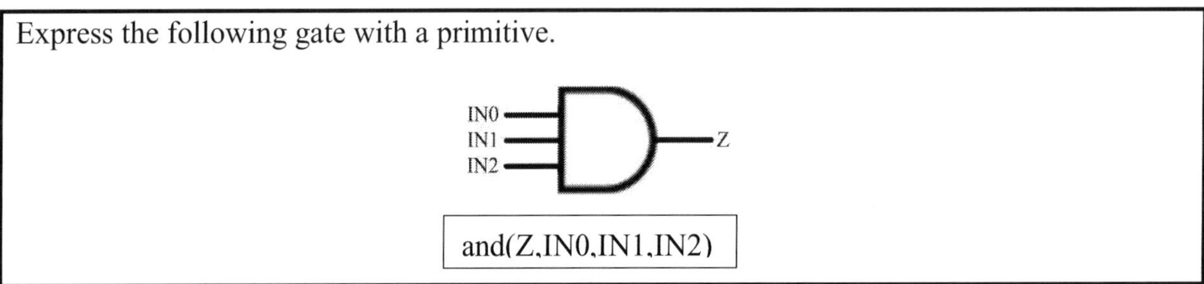

Example 2

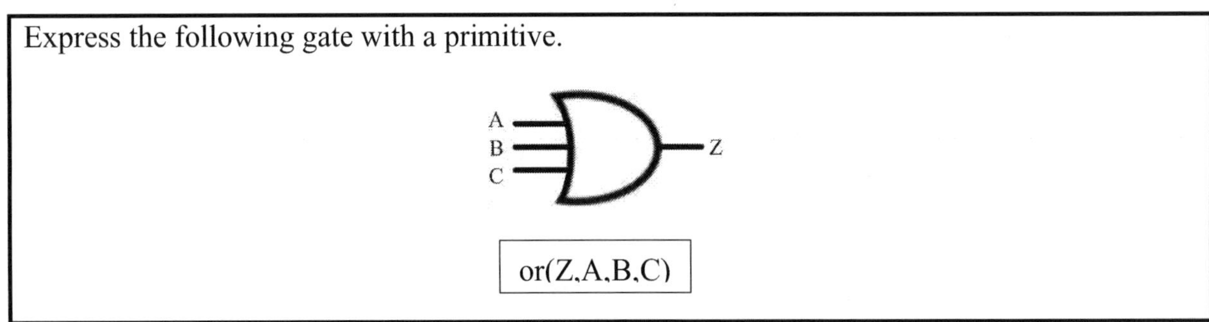

Example 3

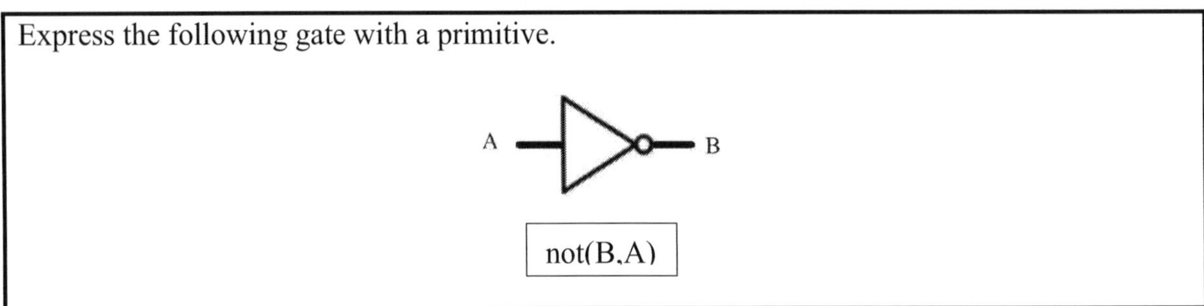

Primitives can also be assembled to form a larger combinational circuit. The example that follows demonstrates this.

Example 4

Write Verilog module named Circuit0 to build the following circuit using built-in primitives.

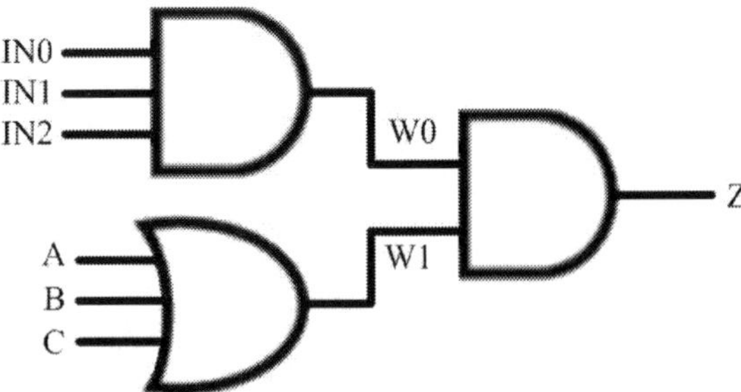

The first step is to define a module. From the provided circuit, the inputs are IN0, IN1, IN2, A, B, and C. There is one output Z. The module can be declared as shown below.

```
module Circuit0 (IN0, IN1, IN2, A, B, C, Z);
      input IN0, IN1, IN2, A, B, C,;
      output Z;


endmodule
```

The next step is to declare a primitive for each logic gate. The declaration for each is shown below.

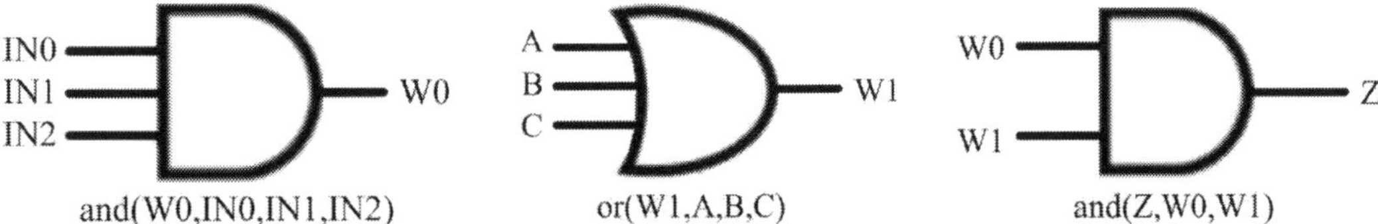

Lastly, to implement the circuit, we insert each primitive in the module. Nothing more needs to be done since the IDE will know how to generate the correct circuit using the three primitives.

```
module Circuit0 (IN0, IN1, IN2, A, B, C, Z);
      input IN0, IN1, IN2, A, B, C,;
      output Z;

      and(W0,IN0,IN1,IN2);
      or(W1,A,B,C);
      and(Z,W0,W1);

endmodule
```

The next kind of primitive to discuss are user defined primitives, or UPDs. A UDP is a primitive that is modeled in a table describing the combinational behavior. Then, once it is defined, it can be used just like a built-in primitive. A UDP can be made for any combinational piece of hardware that can be modeled in a table.

A UDP for a 2:1 mux is shown below. Lines 1-3 set up the module by defining the inputs and outputs. Then in lines 5-16, we make a table for the mux. For UDPs, the input columns of the table will always be assumed by the IDE to be in the same order as the sensitivity list. Since the inputs were ordered as "sel,A,B", the columns in the truth table were made in this order. We know that the output must be "Y", since every UDP can only have one output, which is always the first parameter in the sensitivity list. Verilog will know to create a 2:1 Multiplexer by directly implementing the truth table in lines 5-16. Since the UDP will directly implement the truth table, it is a behavioral method since it allowed us to bypass the creating and solving of K-Maps, saving presumably, 30 minutes of time.

UDP for a 2:MUX

```
1  primitive mux(Y,sel,A,B);
2     input sel, A, B;
3     output Y;
4
5     // Truth table for the 2-to-1 multiplexer
6     table
7        //  sel  A B : Y
8            0    0 0 : 0;  // When sel is 0, output Y is connected to input A
9            0    0 1 : 0;  // When sel is 0, output Y is connected to input A
10           0    1 0 : 1;  // When sel is 0, output Y is connected to input A
11           0    1 1 : 1;  // When sel is 0, output Y is connected to input A
12           1    0 0 : 0;  // When sel is 1, output Y is connected to input B
13           1    0 1 : 1;  // When sel is 1, output Y is connected to input B
14           1    1 0 : 0;  // When sel is 1, output Y is connected to input B
15           1    1 1 : 1;  // When sel is 1, output Y is connected to input B
16    endtable
17
18 endprimitive
```

This UDP can then be instantiated and used by a module as if it were built in. When a primitive is instantiated, it is like when a function is called in C++. The example below shows how you could use the UDP in a top-level module. More about instantiation will be covered later.

Example 5

Write Verilog module named Circuit0 to build the following circuit using primitives.

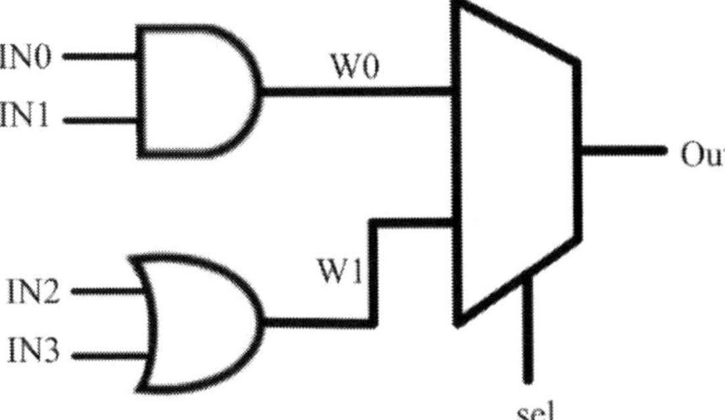

The first step is to define a module. From the provided circuit, the inputs are IN0, IN1, IN2, IN3 and sel. There is one output, "Out". The module can be declared as shown below.

```
module Circuit0 (IN0, IN1, IN2, IN3,sel, Out);
      input IN0, IN1, IN2, IN3, sel;
      output Out;

endmodule
```

The next step is to create a primitive for each component. A primitive declaration will be made for the two gates as shown below.

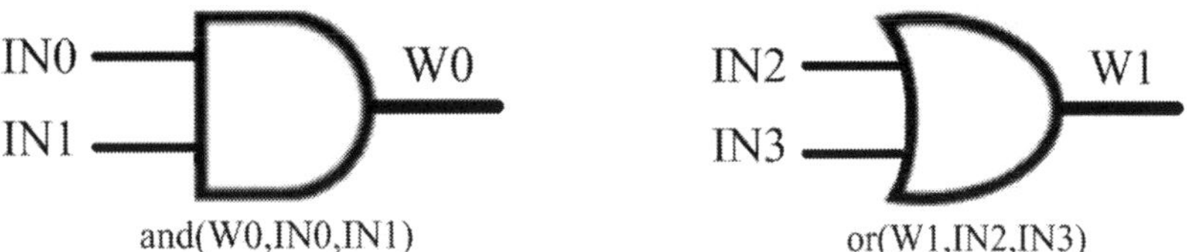

Now we add the two primitive decorations into the module in lines 5 and 6. Then we cut and paste the 2:1 mux UPD after the module. Next, we can write a declaration in line 7 calling (instantiating) the UPD into the module. Below shows the final code.

```
1   module Circuit0 (IN0, IN1, IN2, IN3,sel, Out);
2         input IN0, IN1, IN2, IN3,sel;
3         output Out;
4
5         and(W0,IN0,IN1);
6         or(W1,IN2,IN3);
7         mux(Out,sel,W0,W1);
8
9   endmodule
10
11  primitive mux(Y,sel,A,B);
...       // lines 12- 26
27  endprimitive
```

Since the first parameter of the module defined in line 11 is the output, the first parameter in line 7 will be "Out", since that is the output signal according to the schematic. Similarly, because the second parameter of the module defined in line 11 was the select line, we know to put "sel" as the second parameter in line 7. The same rationale was done for the remaining parameters.

L1.3 Assign Statements

Now that you have reviewed what primitives are, it is time to review the next fundamental concept, which is how to use assign statements. An assign statement is used to directly implement a Boolean equation. Assign statements are always used for combinational logic. They are also structural, since to implement a piece of hardware via an assign statement, we need to of already obtained the Boolean equation for it, meaning we have already solved the K-Maps to obtain the gate level description. The table below shows the logical operations and the equivalent Verilog operator. Examples of how a combinational network can be made using assign statements is shown below.

Logic Gate	Symbol	Boolean	Verilog Operator
AND	A, B	$X = A \cdot B$	$X = A \,\&\, B$
OR	A, B	$X = A + B$	$X = A \mid B$
NAND	A, B	$X = \overline{A \cdot B}$	$X = A \sim\!\& B$
NOR	A, B	$X = \overline{A + B}$	$X = A \sim\!\mid B$
XOR	A, B	$X = A \oplus B$	$X = A \,\hat{}\, B$
XNOR	A, B	$X = \overline{A \oplus B}$	$X = A \sim\hat{}\, B$
NOT	A	$X = \bar{A}$	$X = \sim A$

Figure L1.3.1 Table of logical gates and Verilog operators

Example 1

For the following truth table, make a Verilog module implementing the combinational circuit using assign statements.

Index	A	B	C	D	Z
0	0	0	0	0	1
1	0	0	0	1	0
2	0	0	1	0	1
3	0	0	1	1	0
4	0	1	0	0	0
5	0	1	0	1	0
6	0	1	1	0	1
7	0	1	1	1	X
8	1	0	0	0	X
9	1	0	0	1	0
10	1	0	1	0	0
11	1	0	1	1	X
12	1	1	0	0	1
13	1	1	0	1	X
14	1	1	1	0	1
15	1	1	1	1	1

The first step is to map the 1's and X's from the truth table into the K-Map. Since this is a 4-variable K-Map, we will map it into the template for the 4-Variable K-Map as discussed in the logic design section. Using the indices, we know which boxes in the K-Map should receive the 1's and X's. Refer to the logic design section if you need a refresher on this.

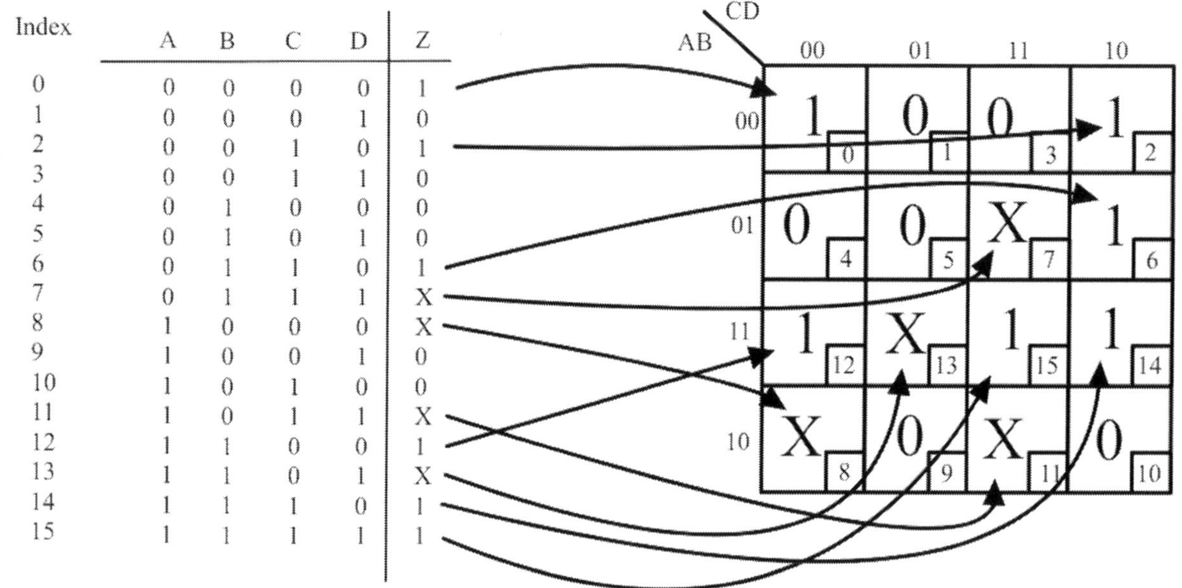

Once the values have been mapped from the truth table to the K-Map, we circle the terms to completely encompass the 1's as shown next. The don't care boxes with X's are circled only if them being circled allows for a large group of 1's. The more 1's included in a circle; the more terms reduced. The fewer large circles the better too.

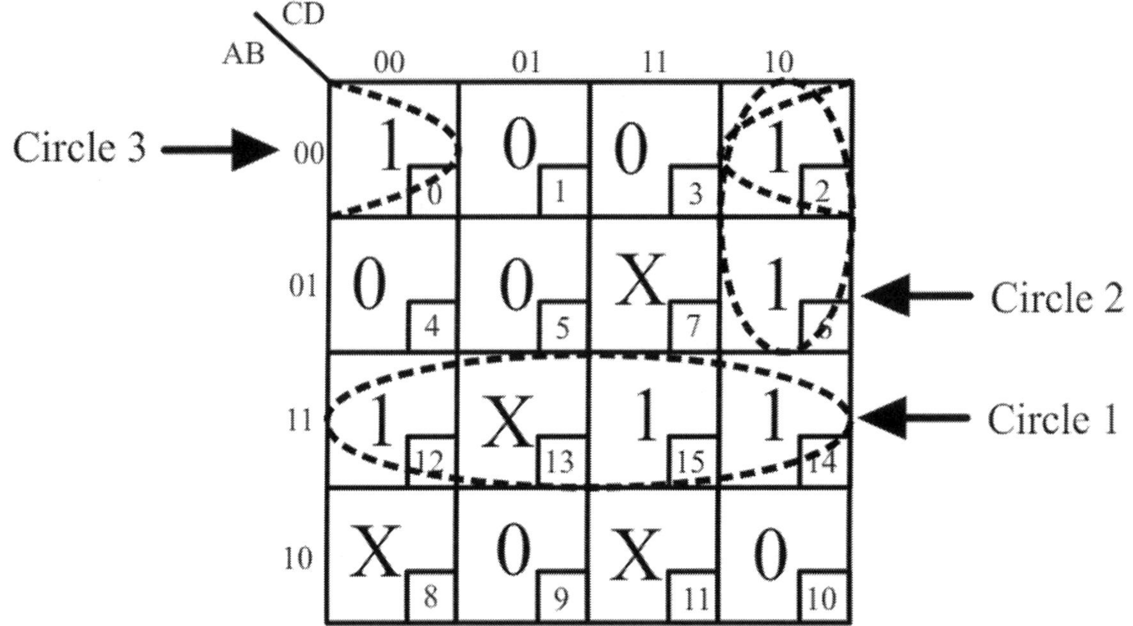

From the K-Map, we can obtain the following equations for each circle. Then after logically OR-ing them together, we can obtain the following equation for Z. If you are unsure how this was done from looking at the circled K-Maps, refer to section 2.1 of the logic design half. Hopefully, you can already obtain the equations for each circle in your head, but if not, you can use the tabular algorithm from section 2.1 to brute force your way to the answer any day of the week.

Circle 1: AB   Circle 2: A′CD′   Circle 3: A′B′D′

$$Z = AB + A'CD' + A'B'D'$$

Now that we have found the Boolean expression for Z, we can begin to create the Verilog module for it. From the equation, it is evident that the inputs are A,B,C, and D. It is evident that the only output is Z. Using this we can create the following module definition.

```
module Circuit0 (A, B, C, D, Z);
    input A, B, C, D;
    output Z;



endmodule
```

Now that the module definition has been made, all that remains is to insert an assignment statement for Z. This is done using the "assign" keyword and by using the Verilog operators. The final code is below.

```
module Circuit0 (A, B, C, D, Z);
    input A, B, C, D;
    output Z;

    assign Z = (A & B) | (A & ~C & ~D) | (~A & ~B & ~D);

endmodule
```

From example 1, it should be obvious now why using a structural approach is extremely inefficient. A UDP could of easily of been made to bypass the creation and solving of the K-Map. The example that follows will not emphasize this point, as the equations will be given to put more emphasis on the conversion of an equation to Verilog.

Example 2

For the following equations, make a Verilog module to implement them.

$$\text{Out0} = (ABC + BD) \mid (B')$$

$$\text{Out1} = (A'C \oplus D) \mid (B')$$

After defining a module and inserting two assignment expressions, the following will be obtained.

```
module Circuit0 (A, B, C, D, Out1,Out0);
    input A, B, C, D;
    output Out1, Out0;

    assign Out0 = (A&B&C | B&D) | ( ~B );
    assign Out1 = (~A&C ^ D) | ( ~B );

endmodule
```

From both examples 1 and 2, it should be evident that once the Boolean equation is obtained, the conversion to Verilog code is very simple. After obtaining the equations, all we do is replace the Boolean operators to show the Verilog equivalent. This is why the Boolean operator "+" is replaced with the Verilog operator "|". The terms that are implied to be AND-ed together in the equation receive the Verilog operator "&", since there is no implied AND-ing in Verilog syntax.

L1.4 "?" Operator

There is one last operator you need to be introduced to for now. This operator is the "?" operator. The "?" operator has only one purpose, which is to create multiplexers efficiently in a single statement. The "?" operator is considered a behavioral tool since it allows you to implement a multiplexer without solving any K-Maps or doing any circuit design. It is not as powerful as other behavioral methods, though it is still preferred by some people. The structure of the "?" operator is as follows.

$$\text{Out} = \text{condition} \ ? \ \text{V1} : \text{V0}$$

Figure 1.4.1 Assign statement with "?" operator

If the condition is equal to one, then "Out" will be assigned the value of V1. If the condition is equal to zero, then "Out" will be assigned the value of V0. If we use the "?" operator, we can write the following code to quickly implement a 2:1 multiplexer. Note how the condition statement, we use a double equal sign, "==". For every conditional statement in Verilog, a double equal sign must be used. So remember that to assign a variable a value, you use a single equal sign and to test an expression, you use a double equal sign.

2:1 Mux Using "?" Operator

```
module mux2to1 (sel, I0, I1, out);
      input I0, I1, sel;
      output reg out;

      assign out = (sel == 1) ? I1 : I0;

endmodule
```

The "?" operator can also be used to implement a 4:1 or 8:1 mux without much trouble too. This would be done by inserting two new expressions using the "?" operator in place of "V1" and V2".

L1.5 Lesson 1 Problems

It is highly recommended to attempt all these problems, since they are foundational and will prepare you well for the following lab chapters. The solutions will also be provided at the end.

L.1.1 Problems

Problem 1) Declare a Verilog module to represent the following block diagram. The inputs are going in through the left and the outputs are going out the right.

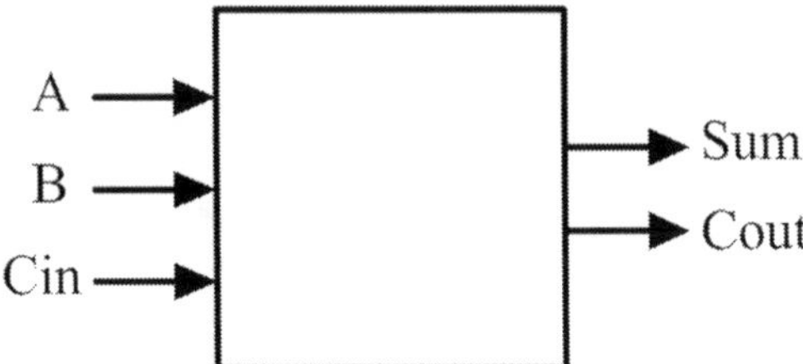

Problem 2) Declare a Verilog module to represent the following block diagram. The inputs are going in through the left and the outputs are going out the right.

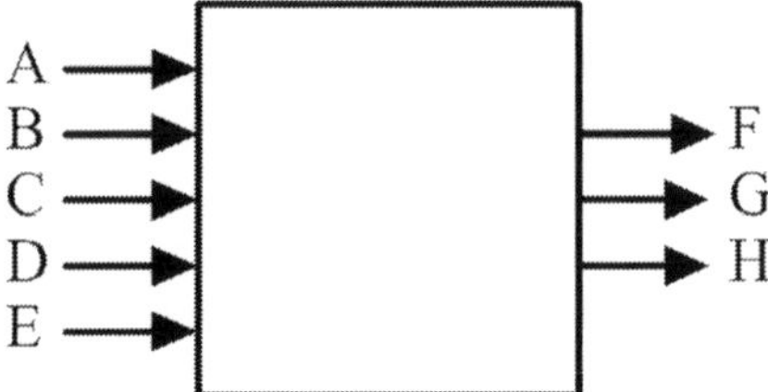

L.1.2 Problems

Problem 1) Use primitives to express each of the following gates.

Problem 2) For the following truth table, derive the gate-level schematic and then use built in primitives to implement it in a Verilog module.

A	B	Cin	Sum	Cout
0	0	0	0	0
0	0	1	0	1
0	1	0	0	1
0	1	1	1	0
1	0	0	0	1
1	0	1	1	0
1	1	0	1	0
1	1	1	1	1

Problem 3) Repeat problem 2 but use a UDP instead.

Problem 4) What kind of a design approach was used in problems 2 and 3 respectively? Which one was faster and easier?

L.1.3 Problems

Problem 1) For the Boolean expressions obtained in problem 2 of section L1.2, create a Verilog module implementing it with assign statements.

Problem 2) What kind of design approach was used when implementing the Boolean expressions with an assign statement? Structural or behavioral? Explain why.

L.1.4 Problems

Problem 1) Write an assign statement for a 4:1 multiplexer through use of the "?" operator.

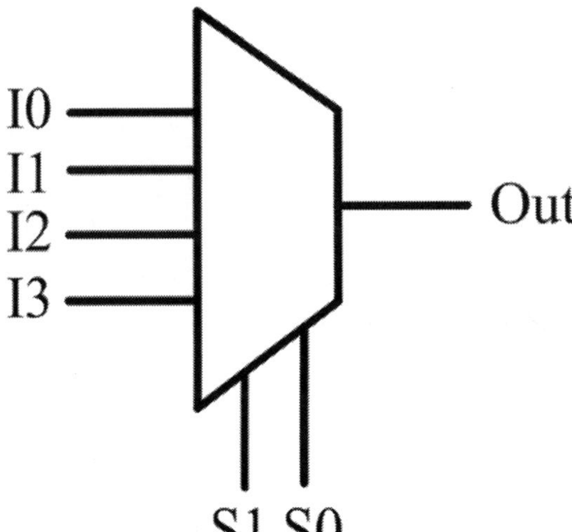

Solutions

Section L1.1 Problem 1

```
module Circuit0 (A, B, Cin, Sum, Cout);
      input A, B, Cin;
      output Sum, Cout;

endmodule
```

Section L1.1 Problem 2

```
module Circuit0 (A, B, C, D, E, F, G , H);
      input A, B, C, D, E;
      output F, G , H;

endmodule
```

Section L1.2 Problem 1

```
nand(Out0,IN0,IN1)
```

```
xnor(F,A,B,C)
```

```
nor(F,A,In,X)
```

Section L1.2 Problem 2

From the truth table, the following K-Maps and equations are obtained.

A	B	Cin	Cout	Sum
0	0	0	0	0
0	0	1	0	1
0	1	0	0	1
0	1	1	1	0
1	0	0	0	1
1	0	1	1	0
1	1	0	1	0
1	1	1	1	1

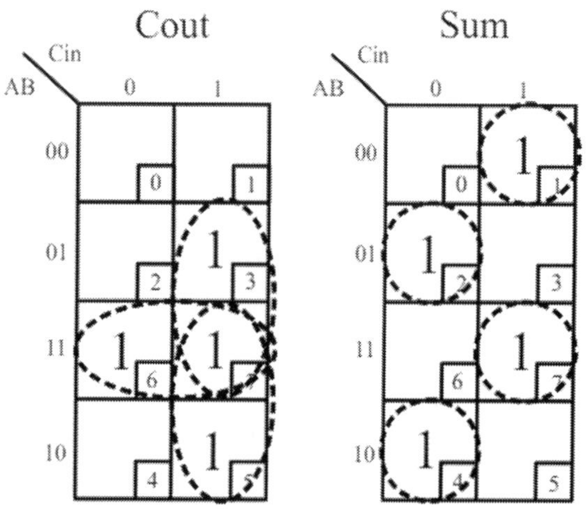

Cout

AB \ Cin	0	1
00	0	1
01	2	1 3
11	1 6	1 7
10	4	1 5

Sum

AB \ Cin	0	1
00	0	1 1
01	1 2	3
11	6	1 7
10	1 4	5

$$\text{Cout} = AB + AC_{in} + BC_{in}$$

$$\text{Sum} = A'B'C_{in} + A'BC'_{in} + ABC_{in} + AB'C'_{in}$$

Converting each equation into hardware yields the following.

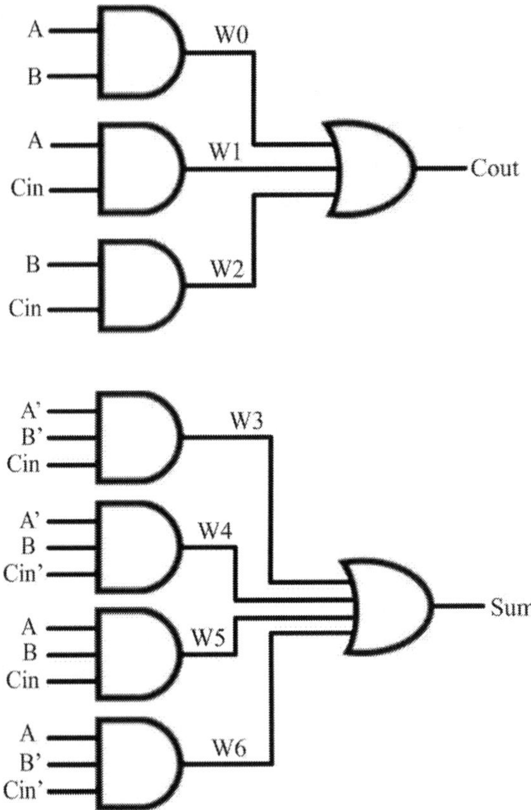

The following code can be made after converting the schematic into Verilog using built-in primitives.

```
module Full_Adder (A, B, Cin, Sum, Cout);
    input A, B, Cin;
    output Sum, Cout;

    // Cout Hardware
    and(W0,A,B);
    and(W1,A,Cin);
    and(W2,B,Cin);
    or(Cout,W0,W1,W2);

    // Sum Hardware
    and(W3,~A,~B,Cin);
    and(W4,~A,B,~Cin);
    and(W5,A,B,Cin);
    and(W6,A,~B,~Cin);
    or(Sum,W3,W4,W5,W6);

endmodule
```

Section L1.2 Problem 3

Since a UDP can only have one output, two UDPs were defined. One for the "Sum" output and one for the "Cout" output. The final code is below.

```
module Full_Adder (A, B, Cin, Sum, Cout);
      input A, B, Cin;
      output Sum, Cout;

      Sum(Sum,A,B,Cin);
      Cout (Cout,A,B,Cin);
endmodule

primitive Sum (Sum, A, B, Cin);
   input A, B, Cin;
   output Sum;

   table // Truth table
     //  A  B  Cin  Sum
         0  0  0  :  0;
         0  0  1  :  1;
         0  1  0  :  1;
         0  1  1  :  0;
         1  0  0  :  1;
         1  0  1  :  0;
         1  1  0  :  0;
         1  1  1  :  1;
   endtable
endprimitive

primitive Cout (Cout, A, B, Cin);
   input A, B, Cin;
   output Cout;

   table // Truth table
     //  A  B  Cin  Cout
         0  0  0  :  0;
         0  0  1  :  0;
         0  1  0  :  0;
         0  1  1  :  1;
         1  0  0  :  0;
         1  0  1  :  1;
         1  1  0  :  1;
         1  1  1  :  1;
   endtable
endprimitive
```

Section L1.2 Problem 4

A structural approach was taken in problem 2 and a behavioral approach was taken in problem 3. Implementing the circuit using the UDP in problem 3 was easier, since no K-Maps or circuit design was performed.

Section L1.3 Problem 1

The implementation of the Boolean equations as shown below yielded the following code.

$$\mathrm{Cout} = \mathrm{AB} + \mathrm{AC_{in}} + \mathrm{BC_{in}}$$

$$\mathrm{Sum} = \mathrm{A'B'C_{in}} + \mathrm{A'BC'_{in}} + \mathrm{ABC_{in}} + \mathrm{AB'C'_{in}}$$

```
module Full_Adder (A, B, Cin, Sum, Cout);
    input A, B, Cin;
    output Sum, Cout;

    assign Sum = (~A ^ ~B ^ Cin) | (~A ^ B ^ ~Cin) | (A & B & Cin) | (A & ~B & ~Cin);
    assign Cout = (A & B) | (A & Cin) | (B & Cin);

endmodule
```

Section L1.3 Problem 2

A structural approach was used, since to obtain the Boolean equations, manual circuit design with K-Maps needed to be performed.

Section L1.4 Problem 1

We start by making a statement for when S1 is equal to 1 as shown below.

$$\mathrm{Out} = (\mathrm{S1} == 1)\ ?\ (\mathrm{Expression\ 1}) : (\mathrm{Expression\ 2})$$

When "S1" is 1, then "Out" will be assigned the value in "Expression 1". If "S1" is 1, then "Out" can only be assigned to "I2" or "I3" depending on the value of "S0". This means we need to make "Expression 1" have a final value of "I2" when "S0" is 0 and "I3" when "S0" is 1. Inserting the following for "Expression 1" achieves this effect.

$$\mathrm{Out} = (\mathrm{S1} == 1)\ ?\ \big((\mathrm{S0} == 1) ?\ \mathrm{I3} : \mathrm{I2}\big) : (\mathrm{Expression\ 2})$$

Using similar logic for when "S1" is 0 leads to "Expression 2" being replaced in a similar manner. The final assignment statement is below.

$$\boxed{\mathrm{Out} = (\mathrm{S1} == 1)\ ?\ \big((\mathrm{S0} == 1) ?\ \mathrm{I3} : \mathrm{I2}\big) : \big((\mathrm{S0} == 1) ?\ \mathrm{I1} : \mathrm{I0}\big)}$$

Lab 2 – Instantiation and Modularization

In this chapter, you will be tasked with completing the second lab. First, the problem you are expected to solve in the lab will be explained, then for the remainder of the chapter, a similar problem will be solved from start to finish. Once you understand how the similar problem was solved, you must go back and attempt the initial problem yourself.

2.1 Lab 2 Description

For your second assignment, you will be tasked with making a 4:1 multiplexer using instantiation. In the logic design portion of the book, a 2:1 multiplexer was designed from scratch by making a truth table and solving the equations manually. If we were to try to make a 4:1 multiplexer using these same traditional methods discussed in the logic design half of the book, we would find that it is nearly impossible due to the K-Maps being too large to solve. Since a 4:1 multiplexer or larger cannot be efficiently made using truth tables, then how are they made? Well, the answer is through modularization. Modularization is the key to making complex digital designs possible, since it allows us to combine multiple easily constructed smaller units to form a sophisticated component that would otherwise be challenging to build. For example, in a 4:1 mux, these "smaller units" would be 2:1 multiplexers. The way a group of 2:1 multiplexers would be combined to form a 4:1 multiplexer is shown below.

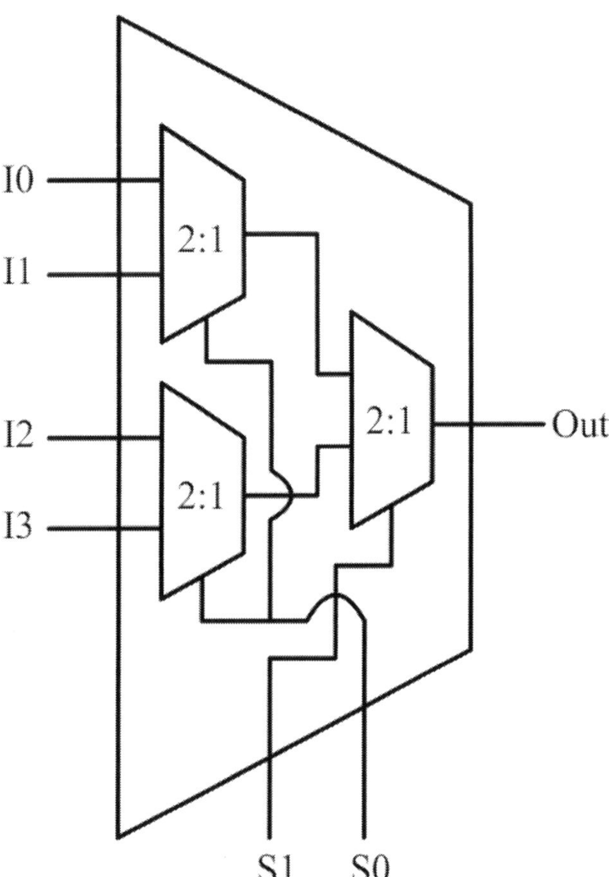

Figure 2.1.1 4:1 multiplexer made using 2:1 multiplexers

Now your task in this lab is to use Verilog to combine these 2:1 multiplexers together to form a 4:1 multiplexer. The code for the 2:1 multiplexer has already been provided, so your only task is to use Verilog to assemble multiple of them together in the configuration shown in Figure 2.1.1. Now unlike lab 1, where the solution was provided for you to just cut and paste, you will be required to write the source and constraint file yourself. To give you sufficient preparation, an extremely similar problem will be solved and explained completely. Once you have understood how the provided example was solved, going back, and making a 4:1 multiplexer using instantiation should be very straight forward.

2.2 Modular Adder Via Instantiation

So, the problem that will be demonstrated is how to build a simple 4-bit adder through modularization. To begin, an adder is a combinational piece of hardware that takes in two binary numbers and then instantly reflects the sum at the output. For a 4-bit adder, the block diagram would be the following.

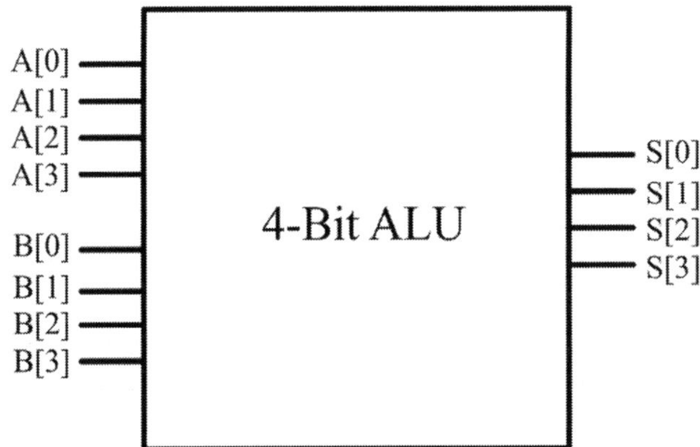

Figure 2.2.1 4-bit adder block diagram

The first binary number will be received through A[3]-A[0] and the second binary number will be received through B[3]-B[0]. The sum of the two binary numbers will be sent out through S[3]-S[0]. A much more compact way of representing the block diagram is through using vector notation. For example, A[3], A[2], A[1], and A[0] could be expressed with A[3:0] instead. The block diagram below shows how this would look when done for all the inputs and outputs.

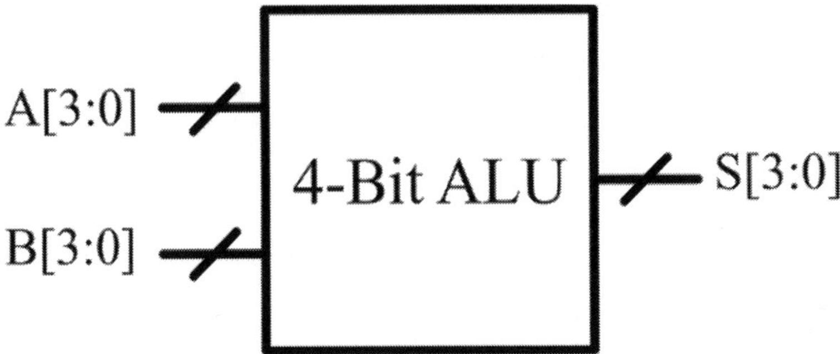

Figure 2.2.2 Better 4-bit adder block diagram

In case you are still not aware of how the 4-bit ALU should work, the following discussion should make it clear. Supposed we wanted to use our 4-bit adder to add together 5 and 3. The result should be 8, correct? To do this, we would need to use inputs A[3]-A[0] to send in a binary equivalent for 5 and we would need to use inputs B[3]-B[0] to send in a binary equivalent for 3. Then once this has been done, the output pins, S[3]-S[0] should reflect the binary equivalent of 8. The figure below shows what each block diagram would look like when modelling this situation.

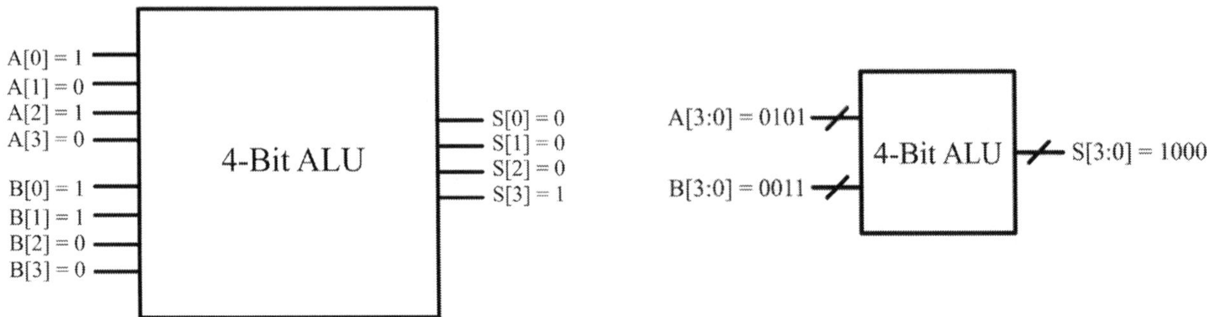

Figure 2.2.3 5 and 3 being added to produce 8

In the figure, in both representations, the binary equivalent of 5, 0101, was input through the input bus for number A and the binary equivalent of 3, 0011, was input though the input bus for number B. The sum was 1000, which is the binary expression for 8. If you do not understand how to express decimal numbers in their binary equivalent, then refer to section 2.9 of the logic design half of the book. In section 2.9, the algorithm for converting decimal numbers like 52 or 5 into binary representations is discussed.

Now that the behavior of the combination adder has been described, it is time to think about how to design circuitry for it. Suppose we were to naively assume that because this is a combinational device, we could make a truth table, solve equations and be done. Any combinational piece of hardware can be expressed through a truth table, right? The figure below shows what kind of truth table someone would make if they tried to do this.

A[3]	A[2]	A[1]	A[0]	B[3]	B[2]	B[1]	B[0]	S[3]	S[2]	S[1]	S[0]
0	0	0	0	0	0	0	0	0	0	0	0
0	0	0	0	0	0	0	1	0	0	0	1
0	0	0	0	0	0	1	0	0	0	1	0
0	0	0	0	0	0	1	1	0	0	1	1
…	…	…	…	…	…	…	…	…	…	…	…
1	1	1	1	1	1	1	1	X	X	X	X

Figure 2.2.4 Truth table for 4-bit adder

A person trying to write out every possible row would eventually realize that since there are 8 inputs, there would be 2^8 or 256 rows that they would need to fill out and realize it's not possible. Suppose one stubborn fool stayed there for 6 hours straight filling out the entire table. At the end of those 6 hours, they would say to themselves "Ha! The table is finally done! But now how do I make a K-Map to solve the 8-variable table?". The truth is that 8-variable K-Maps are never taught in university due to them being too complex. In some universities a 5 variable K-map might occasionally be discussed but never will anything more be discussed due to it being impossible to solve without a supercomputer. Suppose the same fool researched how to solve an 8-variable K-Map and actually attempted it. They could easily spend years of their life filling out the K-Maps. It is for this reason that complex combinational devices are never made using truth tables. Instead, they are made though modular designs that combine groups of simpler combinational devices. These simpler devices are small enough to be modelled using a truth table that is solvable by hand.

From section 2.1 of this chapter, you learned that a 2:1 mux could be used in a modular design to implement a 4:1 mux. So, what kind of smaller device can be used to make a 4-bit adder in a modular design? Well, the device that is used is called a full adder. A full adder is a simple combinational piece of hardware that when combined can implement a 4-bit adder. The truth table of the full adder is shown below. The derivation of the full adder truth table based on the rules of binary addition will not be discussed due to being a quite lengthy discussion and not the central focus of this lab.

A	B	Cin	Cout	Sum
0	0	0	0	0
0	0	1	0	1
0	1	0	0	1
0	1	1	1	0
1	0	0	0	1
1	0	1	1	0
1	1	0	1	0
1	1	1	1	1

Figure 2.2.5 Truth table for Full Adder

If you did your due diligence and attempted the problems in lesson 1, you made a module for a full adder using three different methods. You used two structural approaches, one way making it using built-in primitives and another way making it with assign statements. You also used one behavioral approach using a user defined primitive. Each of these methods works equally well, however the time it took to create all three is different. Instead of re-using one of these three methods, a different and even better behavioral method will be introduced. This method is to create a module specifically for the Half adder by using a combinational always block to directly implement the truth table. This method will be even faster than a UDP, since although we can do this for a UDP, a UDP is limited to one output, meaning that for truth tables with multiple outputs, multiple UDPs must be defined for each output. This can lead to unnecessarily long code, which is why this new behavioral approach will be shown. The code implementing the truth table from Figure 2.2.5 using a combinational always block is shown on the next page.

Full Adder Via Combinational Always Block

```
1  module FullAdder(A,B,Cin,Sum,Cout);
2  input A,B,Cin;
3  output reg Sum,Cout;
4  
5  // Combinational logic to implement Full Adder truth table
6  always @(*) begin
7     if({A,B,Cin} == 3’b000) {Cout, Sum} = 2’b00;
8     if({A,B,Cin} == 3’b001) {Cout, Sum} = 2’b01;
9     if({A,B,Cin} == 3’b010) {Cout, Sum} = 2’b01;
10    if({A,B,Cin} == 3’b011) {Cout, Sum} = 2’b10;
11    if({A,B,Cin} == 3’b100) {Cout, Sum} = 2’b01;
12    if({A,B,Cin} == 3’b101) {Cout, Sum} = 2’b10;
13    if({A,B,Cin} == 3’b110) {Cout, Sum} = 2’b10;
14    if({A,B,Cin} == 3’b111) {Cout, Sum} = 2’b11;
15 end
16 
17 endmodule
```

From the code, it should be obvious enough how the truth table from Figure 2.2.5 was implemented but if it’s not obvious, the following discussion should offer some clarity. To start off, the module was defined using the methodology discussed in lesson 1, however there is one difference, which is that the outputs have been defined as registers on line 3 through the use of "reg". The reason why this was done is because the values in the always block that are assigned values must be registers. From the code, it is evident that only "Cout" and "Sum" are being assigned values, which is why they must be defined as registers.

There are 8 if-statements in lines 7-14 that implement each of the 8 rows in the truth table. For example, to implement the first row of the truth table, the first statement in line 7 checks to see if the values of A, B, and Cin are 0, 0, and 0 respectively. If this is true, then Cout and Sum will be assigned a value of 0 and 0 respectively. Again, in case it’s not clear, to implement the sixth row of the truth table, the statement in line 12 checks to see if the values of A, B, and Cin are 1, 0, and 1 respectively. If this is true, then Cout and Sum will be assigned a value of 1 and 0 respectively.

If you are unsure as to where the "3’bxxx" and "2’bxx" terms came from, just memorize that this is the syntax used to represent a binary number. The number before the tick represents the number of bits to be included and the letter "b" lets Verilog know that this is a binary number. For example, say for hypothetical outputs X1, X2, X3, X4, X5, we wanted to assign 1 to "X1", 0 to "X2", 1 to "X3", 1 to "X4", and 0 to "X5". We would write "{X1,X2,X3,X4,X5} = 5’b10110". If we wanted to perform this when hypothetical inputs I0 and I1 were 1 and 0 respectively, we would use the following line: "if({I0,I1} == 2’b10) {X1,X2,X3,X4,X5} = 5’b10110;". Armed with this information about how a combinational always block works, you should feel empowered enough to implement any truth table by simply modifying the always block shown for the full adder.

Now that the module for the full adder has been completely discussed, the next question is how to combine multiple of these modules together to form a 4-bit adder. The way a group of full adders would be combined to form a 4-bit adder is shown below. To simulate the exact circuit shown, scan the QR code.

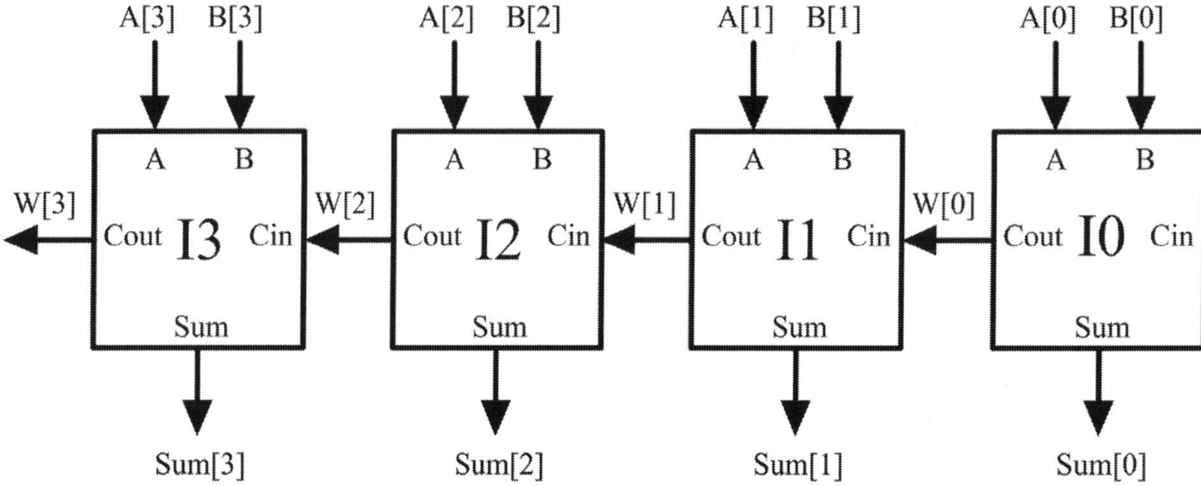

Figure 2.2.6 4-bit adder made from full adders

Now that it is known how to combine multiple full adders together to create a 4-bit adder, the question that remains is how to do it in Verilog? Well fortunately it is a very straightforward process. All it involves is creating a top-level module for the 4-bit adder, pasting the module we made for the full adder underneath, and then instantiating four instances of the full adder module into the top-level module. The step-by-step process will be shown from start to finish.

So, to create a module for the 4-bit adder, we need to remember that there are 8 total inputs and four total outputs. Fortunately, Verilog allows for arrays to be made, so rather than having eight inputs A0, A1, A2, A3, B0, B1, B2, B3 with four outputs S0, S1, S2, S3, we can simply make arrays. The code below shows how we can define a module for a 4-bit adder using arrays for the inputs and outputs.

4-Bit Adder Top Level Module

```
module FourBitAdder(A,B,Sum);
input [3:0] A,B;
output [3:0] Sum;



endmodule
```

The next step is to simply cut and paste the module we made for the full adder into the source file. The code on the following page shows this.

4-Bit Adder Continued

```
module FourBitAdder(A,B,Sum);
input [3:0] A,B;
output [3:0] Sum;
// This line will be filled later

// First Instantiation
// Second Instantiation
// Third Instantiation
// Fourth Instantiation

endmodule

module FullAdder(A,B,Cin,Sum,Cout);
input A,B,Cin;
output reg Sum,Cout;

// Combinational logic to implement Full Adder truth table
always @(*) begin
   if({A,B,Cin} == 3'b000) {Cout, Sum} = 2'b00;
   if({A,B,Cin} == 3'b001) {Cout, Sum} = 2'b01;
   if({A,B,Cin} == 3'b010) {Cout, Sum} = 2'b01;
   if({A,B,Cin} == 3'b011) {Cout, Sum} = 2'b10;
   if({A,B,Cin} == 3'b100) {Cout, Sum} = 2'b01;
   if({A,B,Cin} == 3'b101) {Cout, Sum} = 2'b10;
   if({A,B,Cin} == 3'b110) {Cout, Sum} = 2'b10;
   if({A,B,Cin} == 3'b111) {Cout, Sum} = 2'b11;
end

endmodule
```

The next step is to declare the instantiations of the full adder. The general format of module instantiation is below.

Name of Module Being Instantiated	Instance Name	(Parameters)

Figure 2.2.7 Module instantiation format

The name of the module being instantiated always starts the line. Then we must include the instance name followed by the list of parameters. When we instantiated user defined primitives in lesson 1, we could get away with not having an instance name, however Verilog syntax requires an instance name when instantiating modules.

I will demonstrate the rationale of how the instantiation is done for each full adder in the schematic. Figure 2.2.8 shows it being done for the first full adder. Since we are instantiating the full adder module, we write start the instantiation line with "FullAdder". We give it an instance name of "I0" since that is the name it received in the schematic. Then for the first parameter, we know that it must be the input going into port A of the full adder, since that's what the first parameter was in line 13 where the FullAdder module was defined. Line 13 is included with an arrow pointing down to make it easier to see what parameter corresponds to what. Looking at the schematic, we clearly see that "A[0]" is what is going into the A port, so we write A[0] as the first parameter. For the remaining parameters, the same rationale is used. For the third parameter, since it corresponds to the Cin port and no input is connected in the schematic, we simply put "0" for it. The process being repeated for the remaining full adder instantiations is also shown next.

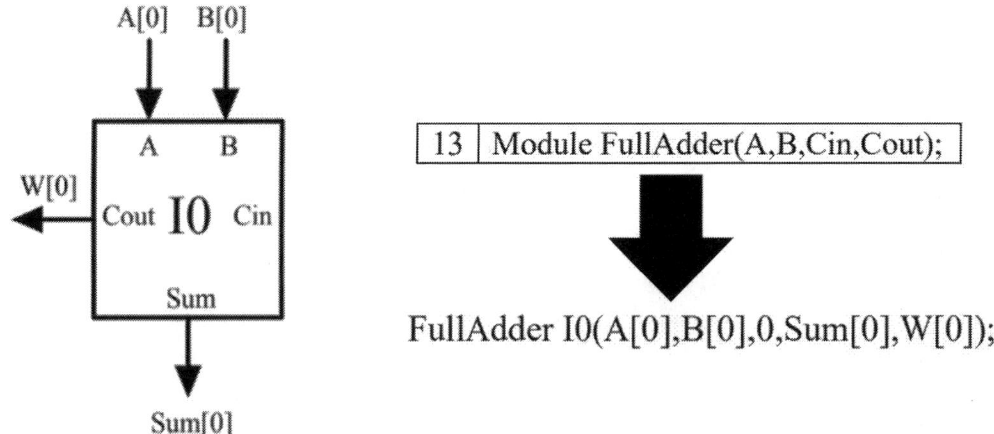

Figure 2.2.8 I0 instantiation

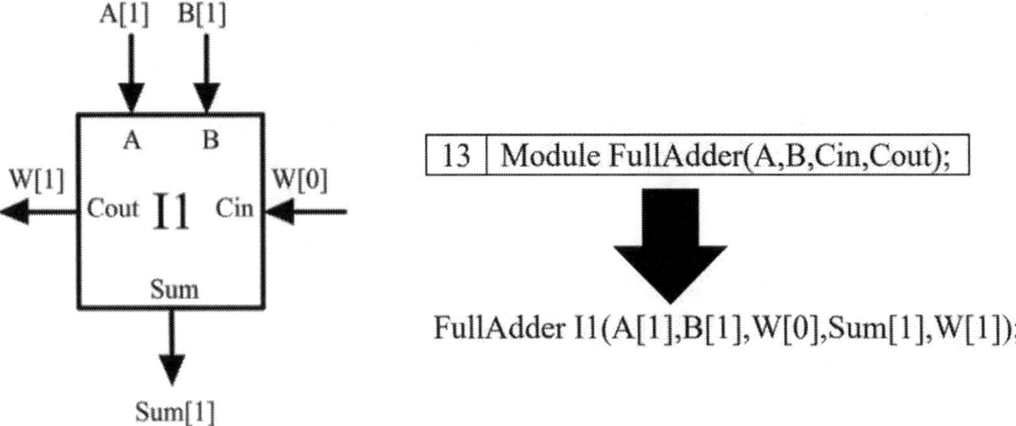

Figure 2.2.9 I1 instantiation

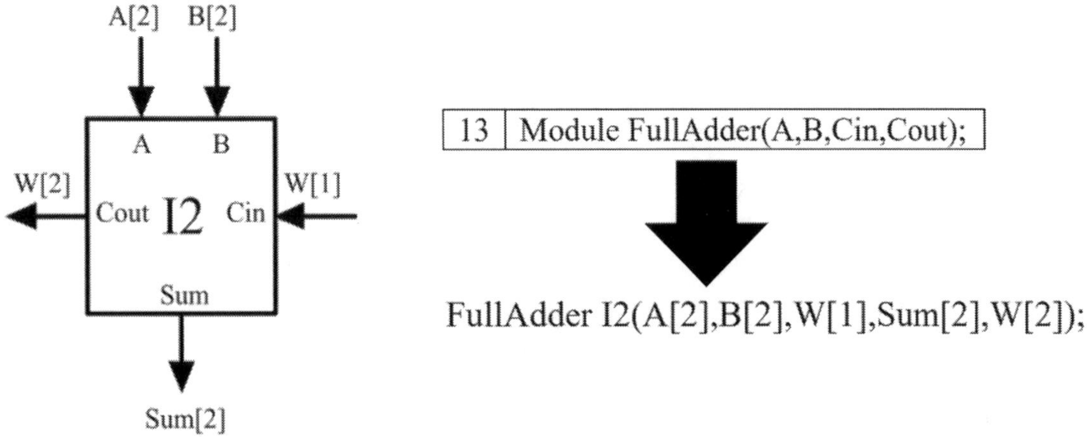

Figure 2.2.10 I2 instantiation

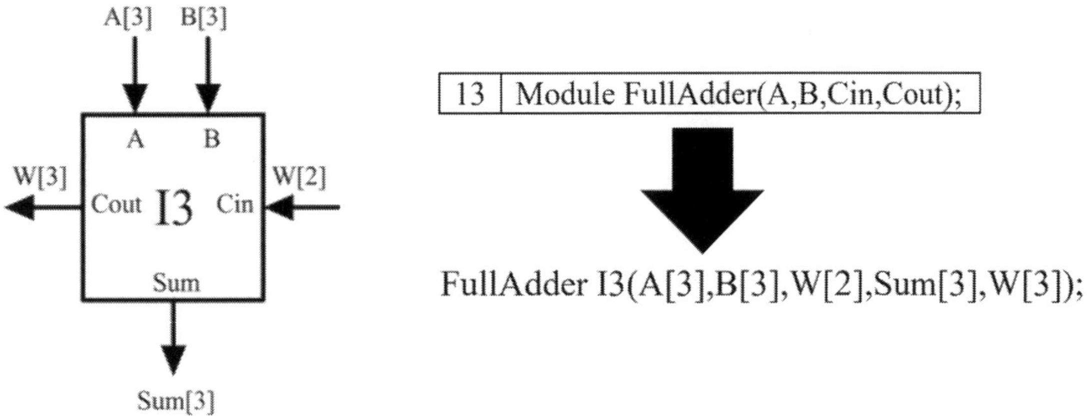

Figure 2.2.11 I3 instantiation

Now that we have all four instantiations completed, we must copy and paste them into the code and declare an array for wires W[0], W[1], W[2], and W[3]. This array must be declared because Verilog syntax mandates defining each internal signal used when instating modules. The final code after implementing these steps is shown on the following page.

Final Source File for 4-bit Adder

```
module FourBitAdder(A,B,Sum);
input [3:0] A,B;
output [3:0] Sum;
wire [3:0] W; // This line defines the internal signals

FullAdder I0(A[0],B[0],0,Sum[0],W[0]);       // First Instantiation
FullAdder I1(A[1],B[1],W[0],Sum[1],W[1]); // Second Instantiation
FullAdder I2(A[2],B[2],W[1],Sum[2],W[2]); // Third Instantiation
FullAdder I4(A[3],B[3],W[2],Sum[3],W[3]); // Fourth Instantiation

endmodule

module FullAdder(A,B,Cin,Sum,Cout);
input A,B,Cin;
output reg Sum,Cout;

// Combinational logic to implement Full Adder truth table
always @(*) begin
   if({A,B,Cin} == 3'b000) {Cout, Sum} = 2'b00;
   if({A,B,Cin} == 3'b001) {Cout, Sum} = 2'b01;
   if({A,B,Cin} == 3'b010) {Cout, Sum} = 2'b01;
   if({A,B,Cin} == 3'b011) {Cout, Sum} = 2'b10;
   if({A,B,Cin} == 3'b100) {Cout, Sum} = 2'b01;
   if({A,B,Cin} == 3'b101) {Cout, Sum} = 2'b10;
   if({A,B,Cin} == 3'b110) {Cout, Sum} = 2'b10;
   if({A,B,Cin} == 3'b111) {Cout, Sum} = 2'b11;
end

endmodule
```

So, there you have it! This code can now be ready cut and pasted into the IDE and used as a source file. All that needs to be done now before uploading to the board is to create a constraint file.

2.3 Making a Constraint File

Now that the source file for the 4-bit adder is complete, the only remaining step now is to make a constraint file that maps the inputs and outputs to the board. There are only three steps for this. The first step is to decide where to map each input and output too, the second step is to copy the lines that are needed from the constraint file, then the last step is to insert the name of each input into the "getports" portion of each line after uncommenting the line. Suppose we want to map the inputs as shown in the figure below.

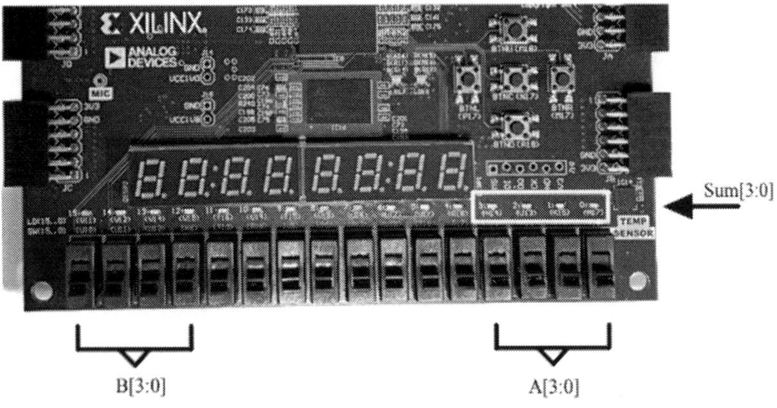

Figure 2.3.1 Input Assignment

Since we want to assign inputs B[3:0] to Switches 15-12, A[3:0] to Switches 3-0, and Sum[3:0] to LEDs 3-0, we would need to copy the respective lines from the general file and uncomment them. Below shows which lines from the general file would need to be copied. We know which lines are needed based on the comments to the right. The desired lines are boxed.

```
##Switches

#set_property -dict { PACKAGE_PIN J15   IOSTANDARD LVCMOS33 } [get_ports { SW[0] }]; #IO_L24N_T3_RS0_15 Sch=sw[0]
#set_property -dict { PACKAGE_PIN L16   IOSTANDARD LVCMOS33 } [get_ports { SW[1] }]; #IO_L3N_T0_DQS_EMCCLK_14 Sch=sw[1]
#set_property -dict { PACKAGE_PIN M13   IOSTANDARD LVCMOS33 } [get_ports { SW[2] }]; #IO_L6N_T0_D08_VREF_14 Sch=sw[2]
#set_property -dict { PACKAGE_PIN R15   IOSTANDARD LVCMOS33 } [get_ports { SW[3] }]; #IO_L13N_T2_MRCC_14 Sch=sw[3]
#set_property -dict { PACKAGE_PIN R17   IOSTANDARD LVCMOS33 } [get_ports { SW[4] }]; #IO_L12N_T1_MRCC_14 Sch=sw[4]
#set_property -dict { PACKAGE_PIN T18   IOSTANDARD LVCMOS33 } [get_ports { SW[5] }]; #IO_L7N_T1_D10_14 Sch=sw[5]
#set_property -dict { PACKAGE_PIN U18   IOSTANDARD LVCMOS33 } [get_ports { SW[6] }]; #IO_L17N_T2_A13_D29_14 Sch=sw[6]
#set_property -dict { PACKAGE_PIN R13   IOSTANDARD LVCMOS33 } [get_ports { SW[7] }]; #IO_L5N_T0_D07_14 Sch=sw[7]
#set_property -dict { PACKAGE_PIN T8    IOSTANDARD LVCMOS18 } [get_ports { SW[8] }]; #IO_L24N_T3_34 Sch=sw[8]
#set_property -dict { PACKAGE_PIN U8    IOSTANDARD LVCMOS18 } [get_ports { SW[9] }]; #IO_25_34 Sch=sw[9]
#set_property -dict { PACKAGE_PIN R16   IOSTANDARD LVCMOS33 } [get_ports { SW[10] }]; #IO_L15P_T2_DQS_RDWR_B_14 Sch=sw[10]
#set_property -dict { PACKAGE_PIN T13   IOSTANDARD LVCMOS33 } [get_ports { SW[11] }]; #IO_L23P_T3_A03_D19_14 Sch=sw[11]
#set_property -dict { PACKAGE_PIN H6    IOSTANDARD LVCMOS33 } [get_ports { SW[12] }]; #IO_L24P_T3_35 Sch=sw[12]
#set_property -dict { PACKAGE_PIN U12   IOSTANDARD LVCMOS33 } [get_ports { SW[13] }]; #IO_L20P_T3_A08_D24_14 Sch=sw[13]
#set_property -dict { PACKAGE_PIN U11   IOSTANDARD LVCMOS33 } [get_ports { SW[14] }]; #IO_L19N_T3_A09_D25_VREF_14 Sch=sw[14]
#set_property -dict { PACKAGE_PIN V10   IOSTANDARD LVCMOS33 } [get_ports { SW[15] }]; #IO_L21P_T3_DQS_14 Sch=sw[15]


## LEDs

#set_property -dict { PACKAGE_PIN H17   IOSTANDARD LVCMOS33 } [get_ports { LED[0] }]; #IO_L18P_T2_A24_15 Sch=led[0]
#set_property -dict { PACKAGE_PIN K15   IOSTANDARD LVCMOS33 } [get_ports { LED[1] }]; #IO_L24P_T3_RS1_15 Sch=led[1]
#set_property -dict { PACKAGE_PIN J13   IOSTANDARD LVCMOS33 } [get_ports { LED[2] }]; #IO_L17N_T2_A25_15 Sch=led[2]
#set_property -dict { PACKAGE_PIN N14   IOSTANDARD LVCMOS33 } [get_ports { LED[3] }]; #IO_L8P_T1_D11_14 Sch=led[3]
#set_property -dict { PACKAGE_PIN R18   IOSTANDARD LVCMOS33 } [get_ports { LED[4] }]; #IO_L7P_T1_D09_14 Sch=led[4]
#set_property -dict { PACKAGE_PIN V17   IOSTANDARD LVCMOS33 } [get_ports { LED[5] }]; #IO_L18N_T2_A11_D27_14 Sch=led[5]
```

Figure 2.3.2 Identifying lines to use

Now after copying these lines into our constraint file, the only remaining step is to assign all eight inputs and all four outputs to their respective lines by filling in the "getports" field. The following figure shows this process completed below.

```
##Switches

set_property -dict { PACKAGE_PIN J15   IOSTANDARD LVCMOS33 } [get_ports { A[0] }]; #IO_L24N_T3_RS0_15 Sch=sw[0]
set_property -dict { PACKAGE_PIN L16   IOSTANDARD LVCMOS33 } [get_ports { A[1] }]; #IO_L3N_T0_DQS_EMCCLK_14 Sch=sw[1]
set_property -dict { PACKAGE_PIN M13   IOSTANDARD LVCMOS33 } [get_ports { A[2] }]; #IO_L6N_T0_D08_VREF_14 Sch=sw[2]
set_property -dict { PACKAGE_PIN R15   IOSTANDARD LVCMOS33 } [get_ports { A[3] }]; #IO_L13N_T2_MRCC_14 Sch=sw[3]

set_property -dict { PACKAGE_PIN H6    IOSTANDARD LVCMOS33 } [get_ports { B[0] }]; #IO_L24P_T3_35 Sch=sw[12]
set_property -dict { PACKAGE_PIN U12   IOSTANDARD LVCMOS33 } [get_ports { B[1] }]; #IO_L20P_T3_A08_D24_14 Sch=sw[13]
set_property -dict { PACKAGE_PIN U11   IOSTANDARD LVCMOS33 } [get_ports { B[2] }]; #IO_L19N_T3_A09_D25_VREF_14 Sch=sw[14]
set_property -dict { PACKAGE_PIN V10   IOSTANDARD LVCMOS33 } [get_ports { B[3] }]; #IO_L21P_T3_DQS_14 Sch=sw[15]


## LEDs

set_property -dict { PACKAGE_PIN H17   IOSTANDARD LVCMOS33 } [get_ports { Sum[0] }]; #IO_L18P_T2_A24_15 Sch=led[0]
set_property -dict { PACKAGE_PIN K15   IOSTANDARD LVCMOS33 } [get_ports { Sum[1] }]; #IO_L24P_T3_RS1_15 Sch=led[1]
set_property -dict { PACKAGE_PIN J13   IOSTANDARD LVCMOS33 } [get_ports { Sum[2] }]; #IO_L17N_T2_A25_15 Sch=led[2]
set_property -dict { PACKAGE_PIN N14   IOSTANDARD LVCMOS33 } [get_ports { Sum[3] }]; #IO_L8P_T1_D11_14 Sch=led[3]
```

Figure 2.3.3 4-bit adder constraint file

So, there you have it! This constraint file can then be cut and pasted into the IDE and a project can uploaded to the board while using the previous source file.

Now that you have reviewed the entire process for instantiating four full adders to create a 4-bit adder, your job is to use what you have learned in this chapter instantiate three 2:1 multiplexers to create a 4:1 multiplexer. The code for the 2:1 multiplexer is shown again for your reference. Remember, you must create a top-level module for the 4:1 multiplexer, then copy the code for the 2:1 multiplexer below it, define the internal wires, then create three lines instantiating the 2:1 multiplexer module in the top-level module. That is all you need to do to complete lab 2. If you have trouble in any of these steps, refer to the portion of this chapter where the exact same thing was done for the example problem.

2:1 Multiplexer Code

```
module mux2to1 (sel, I0, I1, out);
    input I0, I1, sel;
    output out;

    not(W0, sel);
    and(W1, I0, W0);
    and(W2, I1, sel);
    or(out, W1, W2);
endmodule
```

Lesson 2 – Introduction to Sequential Design in Verilog

In this lesson, you will learn about the basics of sequential circuit design in Verilog. In lesson 1, you learned how to implement the methods discussed in the combinational review from the logic design half of the book. In this lesson, you will learn how to do the same for sequential circuits. This chapter will discuss how to implement a state machine given a state table or diagram. Next the importance of clocking will be covered. After that, some strategies on how to avoid doing all the work yourself by using behavioral methods will be discussed. There will also be problems with solutions at the end.

L2.1 Sequential Always-Block

Before demonstrating how to implement a state machine from a state diagram using Vivado, some foundational topics must be discussed. The very first topic that needs to be covered is the sequential always-block. A sequential always-block is a lot like the combinational always block discussed in Lab 2, however it is used for sequential circuits rather than combinational. The basic structure of an always-block is below.

```

always @(xxxedge A) begin
// Instructions
end

```

Figure L2.1.1 always-block structure

In Figure L2.1.1, "xxxedge" can be either "posedge" or "negedge". "A" represents the input signal that is in the sensitivity list. The block is always used to execute instructions after an edge change is detected. If the always block had "posedge A" in the sensitivity list, then on the rising edge of the clock signal A, the instructions written in the block will execute. If the always-block had "negedge A" in the sensitivity list, then on the falling edge of the clock signal A, the instructions written in the block will execute. In the following figure, the arrows show where the instructions would be executed should the always block be a negative edge or positive edge one.

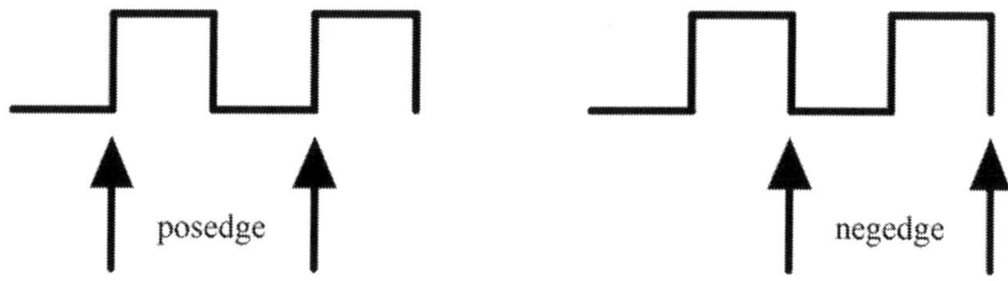

Figure L2.1.2 posedge vs negedge

Now that you know the basic structure of an always-block, it is time to discuss the kind of instructions that can be executed in always blocks. To start off, assignment statements will be covered. In an always block, there are two assignment operators. There is the "=" operator and there is the "<=" operator. The "=" sign is used in blocking assignments. Assignments using this operator will be executed before the remaining assignments. The example below demonstrates this.

Example 1

Draw the timing diagram for the following always block. Assume both registers have an initial value of zero.

```
always @(posedge Clock) begin
 reg0 = 1’b1;
 reg1 = 1’b1;
end
```

Knowing that on the positive edge, reg0 changes to 1 and that immediately after, reg1 will change to 1, we can draw the following diagram.

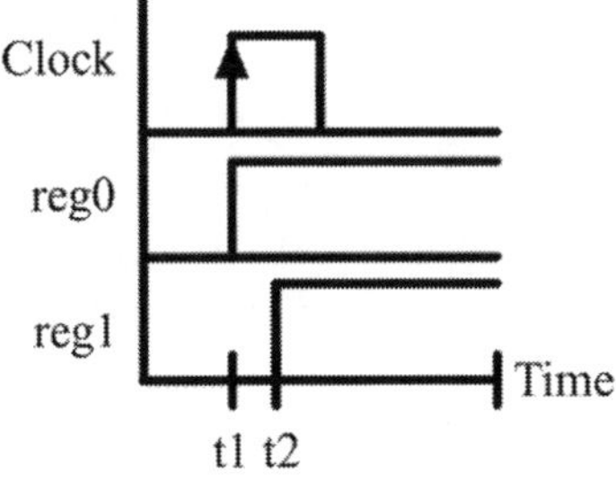

The "<=" sign is used in non-blocking assignments. Assignments using this operator will be executed in parallel with other statements using this operator. The example below demonstrates this.

Example 2

Draw the timing diagram for the following always block. Assume both registers have an initial value of zero.

```
always @(posedge Clock) begin
 reg0 <= 1’b1;
 reg1 <= 1’b1;
end
```

Knowing that on the positive edge, reg0 and reg2 change to 1 in parallel, we can draw the following diagram.

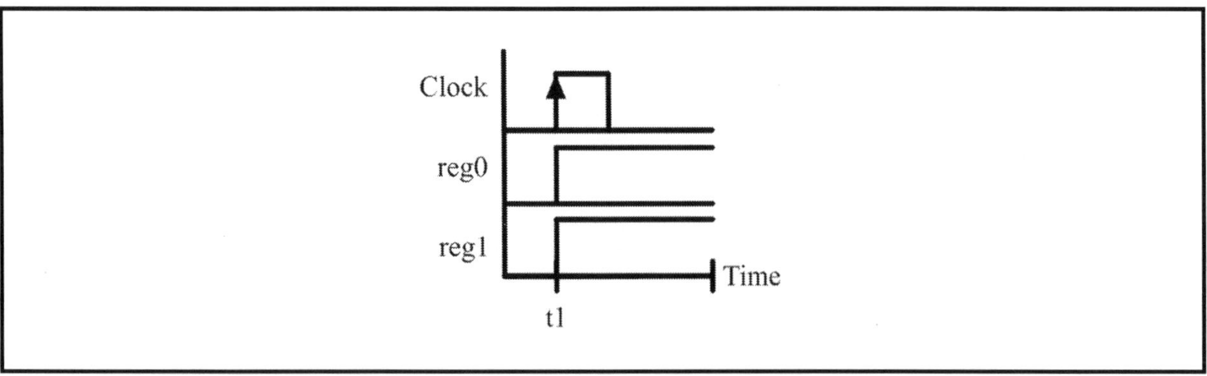

Though typically considered poor practice, non-blocking and blocking statements can also be placed in the same always block. The example below shows how this could look like.

Example 3

Draw the timing diagram for the following always block. Assume all registers have an initial value of zero.

```
always @(posedge Clock) begin
 reg0 = 1'b1;
 reg1 <= 1'b1;
 reg2 <= 1'b1;
end
```

Since we know that reg0 will change first, and then some very short delay later, reg1 and reg2 will change in parallel, we can draw the following.

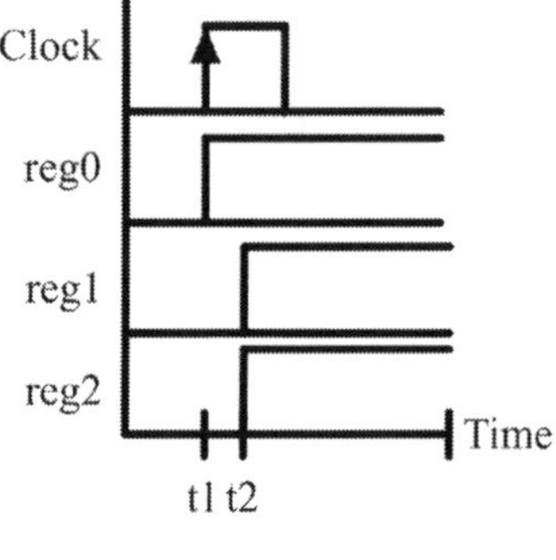

In general, it is best practice to use all blocking statements in always-blocks intended for combinational logic and to use all non-blocking statements in always-blocks intended for sequential logic. Seldom is it a good idea to mix blocking and non-blocking statements together.

The next important topic to discuss is the use of multiple blocks. In general, it is best to have a single always-block that uses non-blocking assignments. Introducing multiple always-blocks or using blocking assignments can create errors or undesired behavior. The example that follows will illustrate this.

Example 4

Suppose reg0 and reg1 are initialized to 1 and 0 respectively. Out of the two programs, which would be ideal for creating a program that causes reg0 and reg1 to swap values with each clock edge.

```
1  always @(posedge Clock) begin
2      reg0 <= reg1;
3      reg1 <= reg0;
4  end
5
```

```
1  always @(posedge Clock) begin
2      reg0 = reg1;
3  end
4
5  always @(posedge Clock) begin
6      reg1 = reg0;
7  end
```

The program on the left would simultaneously change the contents of each register creating the desired behavior. The program on the right would choose to evaluate one always block first due to the instructions being blocking. Assuming the block from lines 1-3 executes first, since reg1 is initially 0, reg0 will be assigned 0 in the instruction on line 3. Then an instant later, the instruction in line 6 will execute and reg 1 will be assigned the value of reg0, which was 0. The result of the right program would be both registers having a value of 0. Had the other always block of executed first, then the result would have been both registers having a value of 1.

Lastly, before moving on, there are two practices that need to be stated when using always blocks. The first is that the variable on the left side of an always block assignment must be declared as a register. If it is not declared as anything or declared as a wire, you will receive an error. The second rule to follow is to never use two blocks to change the contents of the same register. Doing this will result in a multiple driver error. Example 5 shows a program with these two errors and the program after having these errors fixed.

Example 5

The program on the left has two errors. The program on the right shows the corrected code.

```
module Ciruit0(A,B,C,Clock);
   input Clock;
   output A; // error
   output B;
   output C;

   always @(posedge Clock) begin
      A <= B;
   end

   always @(posedge Clock) begin
      A <= C; // error
   end
endmodule
```

```
module Ciruit0(A,B,C,Clock);
   input Clock;
   output reg A; // fixed
   output B;
   output C;

   always @(posedge Clock) begin
      A <= B;
   end

   // removal of block fixed multi-driver error

endmodule
```

In the example, since variable A is on the lefthand side of each assignment in the always block, it must be declared as a register. Since A has two always-blocks assigning a value to it, one must be removed to remedy the multi diver error.

L2.2 Case Statement

The next important topic to introduce is the syntax and function of case statements. Case statements are the same as if-statements, however they are often more desirable due to their compact nature. The general structure of a case statement is shown below.

```

always @(posedge clock) begin
   case(State)
   0  : begin
      // Instructions to be executed when State == 0
   end

   1  : begin
      // Instructions to be executed when State == 1
   end

   // More Cases
   endcase
end
```

Figure L2.2.1 case statement structure

In Figure L2.2.1, the line "case(State)" marks the beginning of the case statement structure. The end of the case statement is marked by "endcase". The "x : begin" lines where "x" is a number, mark the beginning of the code that should execute when the variable "State" is equal to "x". Each "x : begin" statement has a corresponding "end" line to mark the end to the code to be executed. In case it is still not clear, the following example should clarify how to use a case statement and its similarities to an if statement.

Example 1

Use a case statement to make a module such that whenever State is 0, Reg1 will be assigned a value of 3 on the next clock edge. Make it when State is 1, Reg1 will be assigned a value of 4 on the next clock edge. Repeat the same thing with if statements instead. Assume Reg1 is a 6-bit output and that the only input is the clock.

```
module Circuit0 (reg1, Clock);
  output reg [5:0] reg1;
  input Clock;

  reg [5:0] State = 0;

  always @(posedge Clock) begin
    case(State)
      0: begin
        reg1 <= 6'd3;
      end
      1: begin
        reg1 <= 6'd4;
      end
    endcase
  end

endmodule
```

```
module Circuit0 (reg1, Clock);
  output reg [5:0] reg1;
  input Clock;

  reg [5:0] State = 0;

  always @(posedge Clock) begin
    if (State == 0) begin
      reg1 <= 6'd3;
    end

    if (State == 1) begin
      reg1 <= 6'd4;
    end

  end

endmodule
```

From example 1, it is apparent that there essentially is no functional difference between a case statement and an if statement. This means that in theory, you could just use one 100% of the time and be perfectly fine having never learned the other. This however is strongly discouraged since sometimes using case statements will result in code that is easier to understand and vice versa.

L2.3 State Machine Done Via Always Block & Case Statements

Now that the syntax rules of an always block and case statement have been laid out, it is time to discuss the procedure of implementing a state machine using Verilog. In the sequential review of the logic design half of the book, state machines were implemented through making a state diagram, converting the diagram into a table, making K-Maps for the state table, and then finally obtaining the equations. In the old days, this tedious process always had to be performed to implement a state machine. Now however, using Verilog, we can build any state machine without having to perform any circuit design at all! Now don't get too carried away, since although Verilog can automate the tedious process of making the state table, K-Maps, and extracting equations, you still must come up with the original state diagram yourself. Every other stage in the design process is still bypassed completely.

Figure L2.3.1 shows a Mealy state diagram for a sequence detector where the output Z turns to 1 when two ones are received in a row through the input. Overlapping targets are allowed. The deprivation of this exact same state diagram was discussed in section 3.5 of the logic design half of the book. To efficiently communicate the process of how to convert the state diagram into Verilog code, the steps will be listed and then the final code will be shown and discussed in detail.

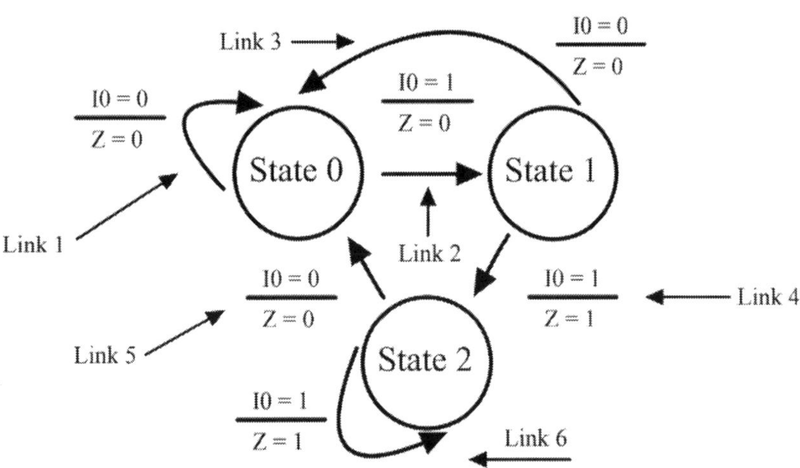

Figure L2.3.1 Pure Mealy Diagram

Pure Mealy Machine to Verilog Code Steps
1) Declare a module for the state machine based on inputs and outputs. Make a register to hold the state and always have an input for the clock.
2) Make a sequential always block to calculate the state transitions as a function of current inputs.
3) Make a combinational always block to calculate the outputs as a function of both the current state and current inputs.

Final Code for Figure L2.3.1 Mealy Diagram

```
1  module Circuit0 (I0,Z,Clock);
2     input wire I0, Clock;
3     output reg Z;
4  
5     reg [1:0] State;
6  
7     always @(*) begin
8        if(State == 0 && I0 == 0) Z = 0;   // Link 1
9        if(State == 0 && I0 == 1) Z = 0;   // Link 2
10 
11       if(State == 1 && I0 == 0) Z = 0;   // Link 3
12       if(State == 1 && I0 == 1) Z = 1;   // Link 4
13 
14       if(State == 2 && I0 == 0) Z = 0;   // Link 5
15       if(State == 2 && I0 == 1) Z = 1;   // Link 6
16    end
17 
18    always @(posedge Clock) begin
19       case(State)
20       0  :  begin
21          if(I0 == 0) State <= 0;   // Link 1
22          if(I0 == 1) State <= 1;   // Link 2
23       end
24       1  :  begin
25          if(I0 == 0) State <= 0;   // Link 3
26          if(I0 == 1) State <= 2;   // Link 4
27       end
28       2  :  begin
29          if(I0 == 0) State <= 0;   // Link 5
30          if(I0 == 1) State <= 2;   // Link 6
31       end
32       endcase
33    end
34 
35 endmodule
```

Lines 1-5 complete the first step. Line 1 list in the sensitivity list all the inputs and outputs. Lines 2-3 specify which parameters in the sensitivity list are inputs and outputs. Since output Z is to be used in the lefthand side of an always block, it is declared as a register type. Line 5 creates a register to store the state. Since there are three states, we declare the state register to be two bits long on line 5. Lines 18-33 complete the second step. For example, for state 4 of the diagram, when the input I0 is 1, the arrow points to state 2. Thinking about this in terms of case and if statements will result in the following: "In the case where state is 1, if I0 is 1, then the next state is 2." From this description, we can write line 26 in the case where state equals 1. The same logic was used for the remaining 5 if statements. Lines 7-16 complete the final step, since they effectively make the output Z a function of both the current state and input. For example, looking at the diagram, if the state is 2 and the input is 1, then the link has the output Z as 1. From this observation, we can write line 15 to complete the output transition for link 6. The same methodology was applied for the remaining 5 output transitions.

It is important to note that since this is a mealy machine, the inputs can instantly change the outputs regardless of the clock. The state still must receive a clock pulse to update. The block diagram for a pure Mealy machine is shown below in Figure L2.3.2.

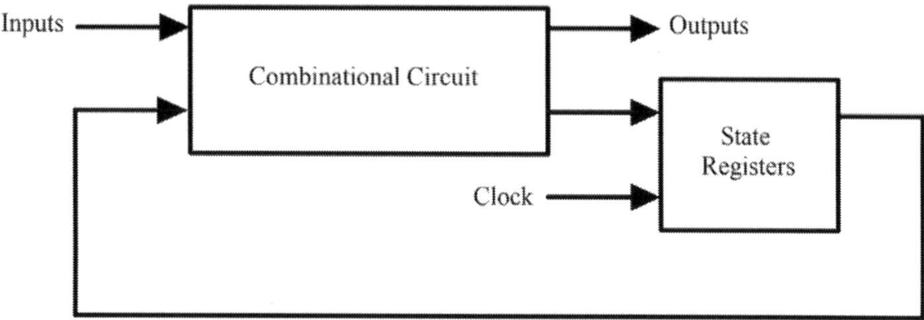

Figure L2.3.2 Pure Mealy Block Diagram.

Now that the process has been shown completely for a Mealy Machine, it is time to explain how it would be different for the Moore machine shown in Figure L2.3.3. The Moore diagram shown is a sequence detector where the output Z turns to 1 when the third 1 is received through the input. The deprivation of this exact state diagram was discussed in section 3.5 of the logic design half of the book. The steps are listed, and the final code follows with a detailed description.

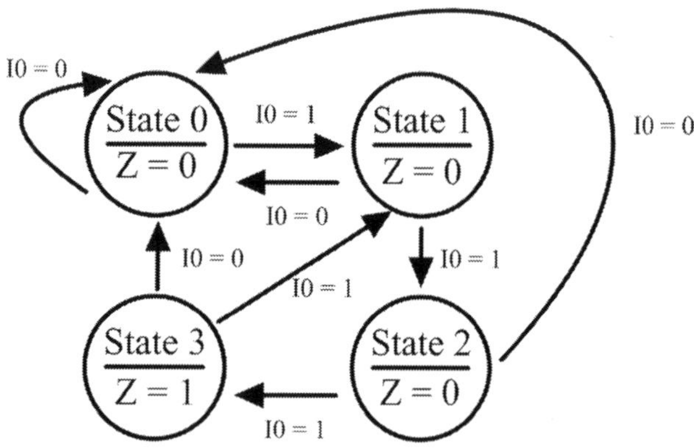

Figure L2.3.3 Pure Moore Diagram

Pure Moore Machine to Verilog Code Steps
1) Declare a module for the state machine based on inputs and outputs. Make a register to hold the state and always have an input for the clock. 2) Make a sequential always block to calculate the state transitions as a function of the current inputs.

3) Make a combinational always block to calculate the outputs as a function of both the current state.

Final Code for Figure L2.3.3 Moore Diagram

```
1  module Circuit0 (I0,Z,Clock);
2     input wire I0, Clock;
3     output reg Z;
4  
5     reg [1:0] State;
6  
7     always@(*) begin
8        if(State == 0) Z = 0;
9        if(State == 1) Z = 0;
10       if(State == 2) Z = 0;
11       if(State == 3) Z = 1;
12    end
13 
14    always @(posedge Clock) begin
15       case(State)
16       0  :  begin
17          if(I0 == 0) State <= 0;
18          if(I0 == 1) State <= 1;
19       end
20       1  :  begin
21          if(I0 == 0) State <= 0;
22          if(I0 == 1) State <= 2;
23       end
24       2  :  begin
25          if(I0 == 0) State <= 0;
26          if(I0 == 1) State <= 3;
27       end
28       3  :  begin
29          if(I0 == 0) State <= 0;
30          if(I0 == 1) State <= 1;
31       end
32      endcase
33    end
34 
35 endmodule
```

So, the only difference between the process for this Moore machine and the previous Mealy machine is that for the third step, we create a combinational always block that is a function of only the current state. Lines 7-12 achieve this effect. Lines 1-5 completed step 1 and line 14-33 completed step 2 for the Moore diagram in the above code. Both steps 1 and two were identical to the mealy machine, so no further explanation is needed.

It is important to note that since this is a Moore machine, the outputs cannot instantly change. The outputs are calculated by the state and even if the inputs change, no change will be reflected in the circuit without a change in the state. The inputs only indirectly affect the outputs by affecting what the next state will be. The block diagram of a Moore machine is shown below in Figure L2.3.4.

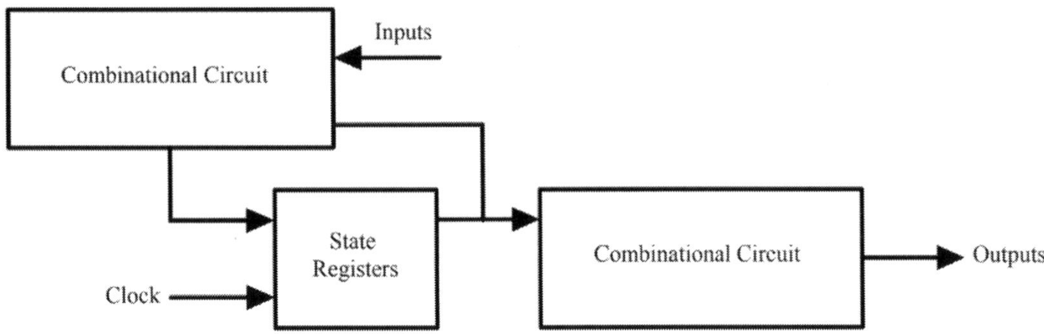

Figure L2.3.4 Pure Moore Block Diagram.

The final situation to discuss is the situation of how to build a hybrid state diagram in Verilog. A hybrid state diagram is one that has both Mealy and Moore components. Fortunately, the process is almost the same as for the previous examples. In fact, steps 1 and 2 are identical to the previous two examples. The steps are summarized below. Figure L2.3.5 shows the hybrid state diagram that will be used for the discussion. The final code and explanation will be shown next.

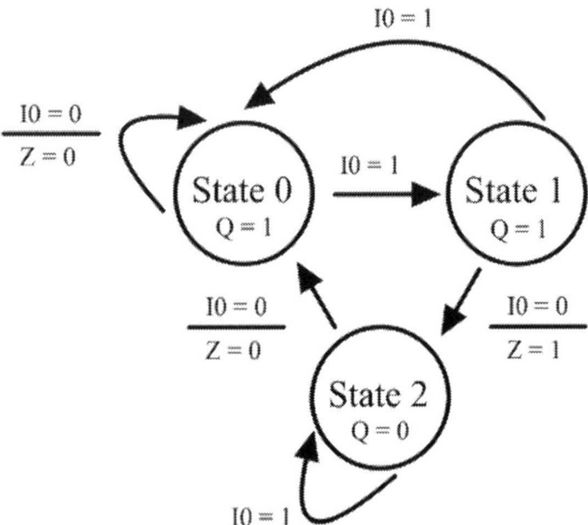

Figure L2.3.5 Hybrid State Diagram

Hybrid Machine to Verilog Code Steps
1) Declare a module for the state machine based on inputs and outputs. Make a register to hold the state and always have an input for the clock. 2) Make a sequential always block to calculate the state transitions as a function of current inputs.

3) Make a combinational always block to calculate the Mealy outputs as a function of both the current state and current inputs.

4) Make a combinational always block to calculate the Moore outputs as a function of only the current state.

Final Code for Figure L2.3.5 Hybrid Diagram

```
module Circuit0 (I0,Z,Q,Clock);
   input wire I0, Clock;
   output reg Z,Q;

   reg [1:0] State;

   always@(*) begin
        if(State == 0) Q = 1;
        if(State == 1) Q = 1;
        if(State == 2) Q = 0;
   end

   always@(*) begin
        if(State == 0 && I0 == 0) Z = 0;
        if(State == 0 && I0 == 1) ; // not specified in diagram
        if(State == 1 && I0 == 0) Z = 1;
        if(State == 1 && I0 == 1) ; // not specified in diagram
        if(State == 2 && I0 == 0) Z = 0;
        if(State == 2 && I0 == 1) ; // not specified in diagram
   end

   always @(posedge Clock) begin
      case(State)
      0  :  begin
         if(I0 == 0) State <= 0;
         if(I0 == 1) State <= 1;
      end
      1  :  begin
         if(I0 == 0) State <= 2;
         if(I0 == 1) State <= 0;
      end
      2  :  begin
         if(I0 == 0) State <= 0;
         if(I0 == 1) State <= 2;
      end
      endcase
   end

endmodule
```

Lines 1-5 complete step 1 and lines 22-27 complete step 2. Since both steps were identical to the previous examples, no elaboration is needed. Step 3 is completed through lines 13-20. In the diagram, no output was specified for the links where the input was 1, so those lines are left blank. The remaining lines were done using the methodology discussed in the example for the pure Mealy machine. For example, in the state diagram, when the state is 1 and the link contains I0 = 0, then the output Z was 1. Using this observation, we can write line 16 as shown in the final code. The statements for the two remaining Mealy outputs were done using the same rationale in lines 14 and 18. Step 4 is completed through lines 7-11. The line of reasoning for each if statement was very simple. From the diagram, states 0 and 1 had Q = 1 and only state 2 had Q = 0. From this observation, lines 8-10 were written.

Now that you have seen how to make a source file for three examples, you can make a constraint file for each example and upload a project for any one of them to an FPGA. Now if you were to do this, you will find that the state machines won't behave as expected. This is simply because if you were to map the "Clock" input directly to the 100MHz clock in the constraint file, the state machine will move to new states too fast for you to see or understand what's happening. The solution to this problem involves making custom slower clocks, which will be discussed in the next section.

L2.4 Custom Clock

From L2.3, it was shown how to make a source file implementing a state diagram. Now if you were to make a constraint file and upload a project to an FPGA for any of the three source files made in L2.3, you will run into problems. The reason is because by default, the hardware synthesized will run on a 100Mhz clock, which is way too fast to see what's going on. The solution to this problem is to create either a slower clock through a clock divider or a clock that is based on an incoming input signal. Both methods work just fine and will be discussed.

To start off, I will discuss how to make a clock that is based on an incoming signal. Say for example that we wanted to press a button on the FPGA board and each time we pressed that button, the state machine would update. To think about how this would be accomplished, let's consider if we want it to trigger on the falling edge or rising edge? Well, to make it update the instant the button is released, it would need to trigger on the falling edge. From the timing diagram, we can see that the falling edge of the button occurs when the button changes from 1 to 0, between t1 and t2. Using this piece of information, we can continuously sample the two most recent inputs of the button and store them in a register, "Reg0". We know that if Reg0 is equal to 10, then a falling edge has occurred and all the code that must execute on the falling edge of the button should occur in the if statement checking the value of Reg0. The code that follows shows how to implement this.

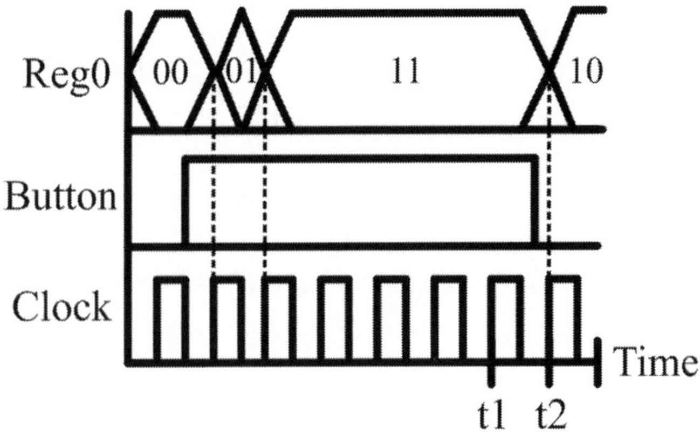

Figure L2.4.1 Timing diagram

Button Falling Edge Code

```
reg [1:0] Reg0;

always @(posedge Clock) begin
      Reg0[0] <= Button;
      Reg0[1] <= Reg0[0];

      if (Reg0 == 2'b10) begin
      // Code that executes on the falling edge of the button
      end
end
```

Now suppose we wanted to include this method to finalize the source file for the pure Moore machine in section L2.3. We would simply use the following code shown below. As you can see the only modification was the addition of a button input and the implementation of the falling edge code using the register "Reg0". This source file is ready to have a constraint file made for it and uploaded to the board now.

Final Moore Sequence Detector with Button Clock

```
module Circuit0 (I0,Z,Clock,Button);
   input wire I0, Clock, Button;
   output reg Z;

   reg [1:0] State;
   reg [1:0] Reg0;

   always@(*) begin
      if(State == 0) Z = 0;
      if(State == 1) Z = 0;
      if(State == 2) Z = 0;
      if(State == 3) Z = 1;
   end
```

```

    always @(posedge Clock) begin
        Reg0[0] <= Button;
        Reg0[1] <= Reg0[0];
        if( Reg0 == 2'b10) begin
            case(State)
            0  :  begin
                if(I0 == 0) State <= 0;
                if(I0 == 1) State <= 1;
            end
            1  :  begin
                if(I0 == 0) State <= 0;
                if(I0 == 1) State <= 2;
            end
            2  :  begin
                if(I0 == 0) State <= 0;
                if(I0 == 1) State <= 3;
            end
            3  :  begin
                if(I0 == 0) State <= 0;
                if(I0 == 1) State <= 1;
            end
            endcase
        end
    end
endmodule
```

The next step is to discuss how to create a custom clock that is a specific frequency. To do this, we will need to divide the 100MHz clock using counters. Suppose we want to divide the 100MHz clock by 10 to create a 10 MHz clock. To do this, we would need to make a counter that increments on each rising clock edge of the 100MHz clock. On the rising edge of the 100MHz clock where the counter finally reaches 4, the counter is set to zero and the new divided clock toggles. The figure below illustrates how this would work.

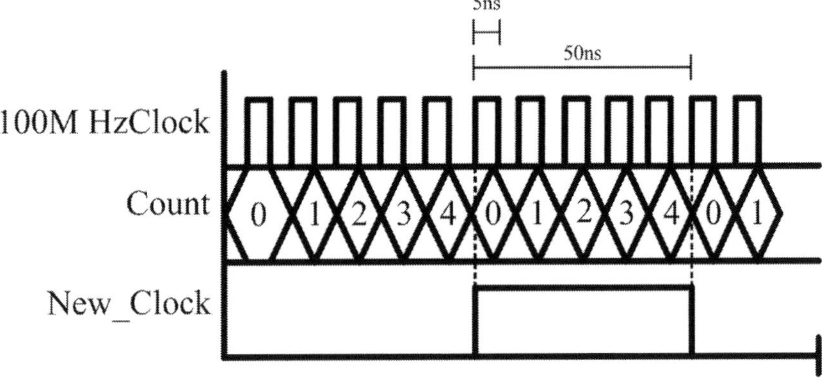

Figure L2.4.2 Timing Diagram

From the timing diagram, it should be apparent that the formula for the frequency of the new clock is $\frac{100M}{(count+1)*2}$. Since a maximum count of 4 was used, the frequency of the new clock was 10M Hz. The code to implement this exact clock divider is shown below.

Custom 10M HZ clock divider

```
1  module CLK100MHZ_divider(CLK100MHZ, New_Clock);
2     input wire CLK100MHZ;      // Input clock signal
3     output reg New_Clock;        // Divided clock output
4  
5     reg [31:0] count = 0; // [31:0] is large enough to hold any value
6  
7     always @(posedge CLK100MHZ) begin
8        count <= count + 1;  // Increment count
9        if (count == 31'd4) begin
10          New_Clock <= ~New_Clock; // Toggle New Clock
11          count <= 31'b0;       // Reset count
12       end
13    end
14 endmodule
```

Using this clock divider, you can change the condition in line 13 to be any integer value, meaning that you can generate a clock of any frequency of your choosing. The remaining lines can remain completely unaltered. This clock divider module is something that is going to be re-used repeatedly through the course, so knowing how to make a clock with it is important. Fortunately, it is easy to use due to only line 13 needing to be altered.

L2.5 Lesson 2 Problems

The problems and solutions for the topics in the lesson are presented in this section. There are a lot of problems with making circuitry to implement state diagrams and the reason is because it is extremely important. The entire end goal of logic design was to learn how to do this one thing using traditional methods. In just this one lesson, you learned how to use Verilog to implement any state machine in under 10 minutes, something that would have previously taken hours using the methods discussed in logic design. When attempting the L2.3 and L2.4 problems, the power of the FPGA should be made evident due to the extremely fast implementation and physical construction of the state machines. Even if at first it takes a long time to implement a given state diagram using Verilog, with experience it will easily be doable in under 10 minutes, even for large state machines with 20 plus states.

L.2.1-2.2 Problems

Problem 1) Make a module that uses a sequential always block and case statement to increment cases with each falling clock edge (cases go from 0,1,2,3,4). In cases 0, 2, and 3, an output Z equals 2. In case 4, a 3-bit register named count is incremented by 2. Assume that when case 4 is reached, the next case is 0. Nothing happens in the other cases.

Problem 2) Make a module that uses a sequential always block and case statement to go from cases 0,1,2 and 3. When case 3 is reached. If an input "Y" is 0, then the next case is 0. When case 3 is reached and the input "Y" is 1, go to case 3. When in state 4, do nothing.

L.2.3 Problems

Problem 1) For the following Moore diagram, make a source file.

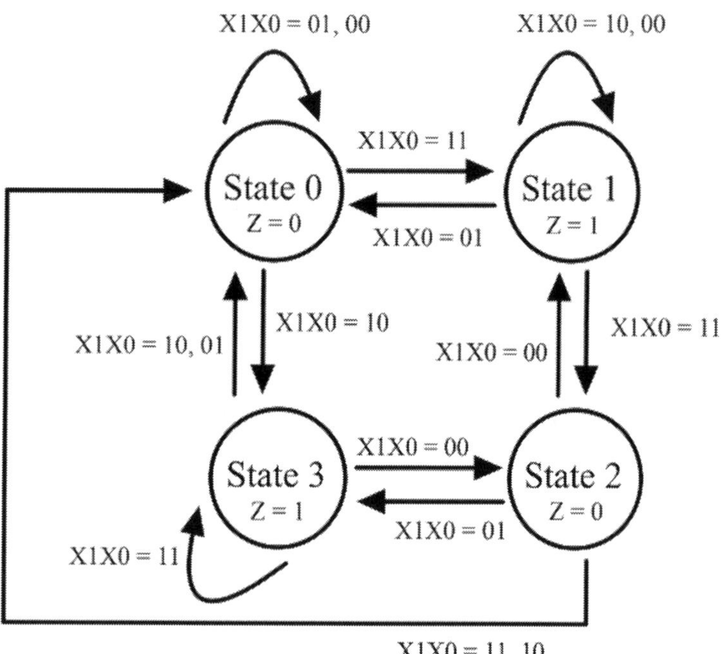

Problem 2) For the following Moore diagram, make a source file.

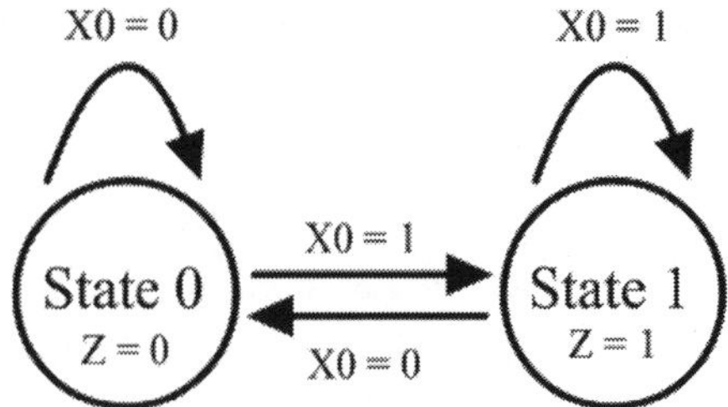

Problem 3) For the following Mealy diagram, make a source file.

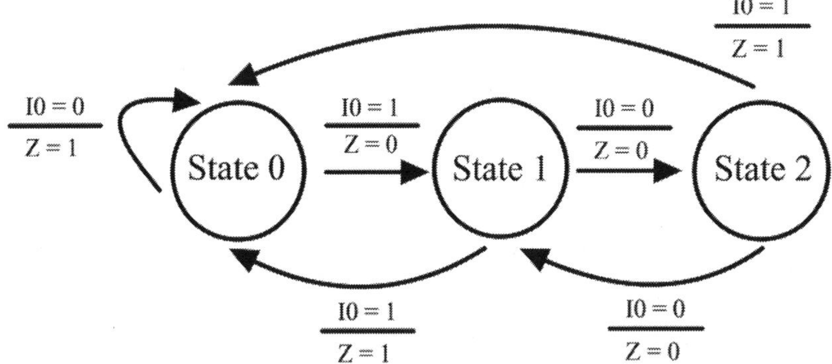

Problem 4) For the following hybrid diagram, make a source file.

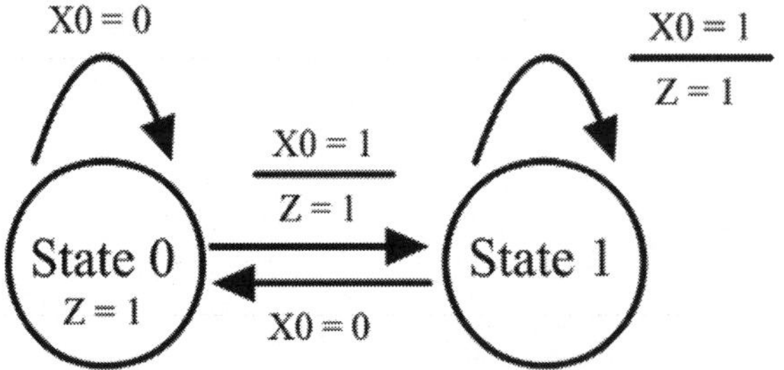

Problem 5) For the following hybrid diagram, make a source file.

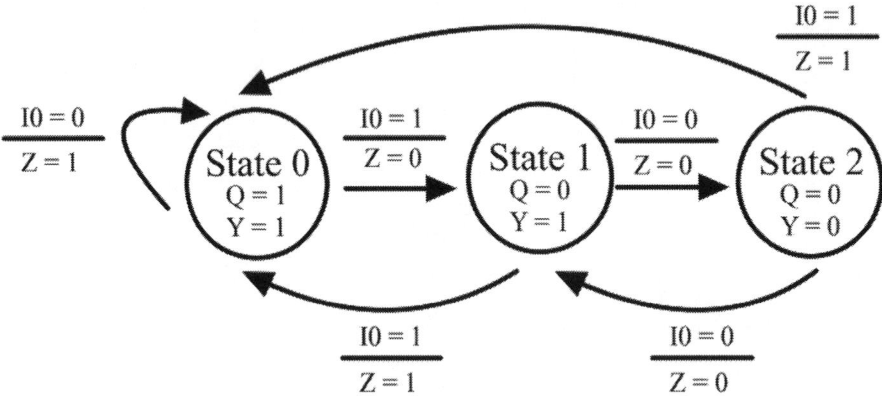

L.2.4 Problems

Problem 1) For the source file made in problem 1 of the L.2.3 problem set, have the state machine be clocked by a button or switch. Ideally make a constraint file and upload it to your FPGA to verify functionality before viewing the solution.

Problem 2) For the source file made in problem 5 of the L.2.3 problem set, have the state machine be clocked using a 1HZ clock. Ideally make a constraint file and upload it to your FPGA to verify functionality before viewing the solution.

Solutions

L2.1 - 2.2 Problems

Problem 1)

```
module Circuit0 (Z, Clock);
   input wire Clock;
   output reg [1:0] Z;

   reg [2:0] CASE;
   reg [2:0] Count;

   always @(negedge Clock) begin
      case(CASE)
      0  :  begin
         Z <= 2;
         CASE <= 1;
      end
      1  :  begin
         Z <= 2;
         CASE <= 2;
      end
      2  :  begin
         Z <= 2;
         CASE <= 3;
      end
      3  :  begin
         Z <= 2;
         CASE <= 4;
      end
      4  :  begin
         Count <= Count + 2;
         CASE <= 0;
      end
      endcase
   end
endmodule
```

Problem 2)

```
module Circuit0 (Y, Clock);
   input wire Clock,Y;

   reg [2:0] CASE;

```

```
    always @(posedge Clock) begin
      case(CASE)
      0  :  begin
         CASE <= 1;
      end
      1  :  begin
         CASE <= 2;
      end
      2  :  begin
         CASE <= 3;
      end
      3  :  begin
         if(Y == 0) CASE <= 0;
         if(Y == 1) CASE <= 4;
      end
      4  :  begin
      end
      endcase
   end
endmodule
```

L2.4 Problems

Problem 1) Given in L2.5 problem 1 solution.

Problem 2)

```
module Circuit0 (I0,Z,Clock);
   input wire I0,Clock;
   output reg Z;

   reg State;

   always @(*) begin
      if(State == 0) Z <= 0;
      if(State == 1) Z <= 1;
   end

   always @(posedge Clock) begin
      case(State)
      0  :  begin
         if(I0 == 0) State <= 0;
         if(I0 == 1) State <= 1;
         end
      1  :  begin
         if(I0 == 0) State <= 0;
         if(I0 == 1) State <= 1;
```

```
    end
    endcase
    end
endmodule
```

Problem 3)

```
module Circuit0 (I0,Z,Clock);
   input wire I0,Clock;
   output reg Z;

   reg [1:0] State;

   always @(posedge Clock) begin
         case(State)
         0  :  begin
            if(I0 == 0) begin
               State <= 0;
               Z <= 1;
            end
            if(I0 == 1) begin
               State <= 1;
               Z <= 0;
            end
         end
         1  :  begin
            if(I0 == 0) begin
               State <= 2;
               Z <= 0;
            end
            if(I0 == 1) begin
               State <= 0;
               Z <= 1;
            end
         end
         2  :  begin
            if(I0 == 0) begin
               State <= 1;
               Z <= 0;
            end
            if(I0 == 1) begin
               State <= 0;
               Z <= 1;
            end
         end
         endcase
    end
```

```
endmodule

```

Problem 4)

```
module Circuit0 (I0,Z,Clock);
   input wire I0,Clock;
   output reg Z;

   reg State;

   always @(*) begin
      if(State == 0) Z <= 1;
   end

   always @(posedge Clock) begin
      case(State)
      0  :  begin
         if(I0 == 0) State <= 0;
         if(I0 == 1) begin
            State <= 1;
            Z <= 1;
         end
         end
      1  :  begin
         if(I0 == 0) State <= 0;
         if(I0 == 1) begin
            State <= 1;
            Z <= 1;
         end
         end
         endcase
     end
endmodule
```

Problem 5) Given in L2.5 problem 2 solution.

L2.5 Problems

Problem 1)

```
module Circuit0 (X0,X1,Z,Clock,Button);
   input wire X0, X1, Clock, Button;
   output reg Z;

   reg [1:0] State;
   reg [1:0] Reg0;
```

```

    always@(*) begin
      if(State == 0) Z = 0;
      if(State == 1) Z = 1;
      if(State == 2) Z = 0;
      if(State == 3) Z = 1;
    end

    always @(posedge Clock) begin
      Reg0[0] <= Button;
      Reg0[1] <= Reg0[0];
      if( Reg0 == 2'b10) begin
        case(State)
        0  :  begin
          if(X1 == 0 && X0 == 0) State <= 0;
          if(X1 == 0 && X0 == 1) State <= 0;
          if(X1 == 1 && X0 == 0) State <= 3;
          if(X1 == 1 && X0 == 1) State <= 1;
        end
        1  :  begin
          if(X1 == 0 && X0 == 0) State <= 1;
          if(X1 == 0 && X0 == 1) State <= 0;
          if(X1 == 1 && X0 == 0) State <= 1;
          if(X1 == 1 && X0 == 1) State <= 2;
        end
        2  :  begin
          if(X1 == 0 && X0 == 0) State <= 1;
          if(X1 == 0 && X0 == 1) State <= 3;
          if(X1 == 1 && X0 == 0) State <= 0;
          if(X1 == 1 && X0 == 1) State <= 0;
        end
        3  :  begin
          if(X1 == 0 && X0 == 0) State <= 2;
          if(X1 == 0 && X0 == 1) State <= 0;
          if(X1 == 1 && X0 == 0) State <= 0;
          if(X1 == 1 && X0 == 1) State <= 3;
        end
        endcase
     end
    end
endmodule
```

Problem 2)

```
module Circuit0 (I0,Z,Y,Q,Clock,Button);
    input wire I0,Clock,Button;
```

```
    output reg Z,Y,Q;

    reg [1:0] State;
    reg [1:0] Reg0;

    always@(*) begin
        if(State == 0) begin
            Y <= 1;
            Q <= 1;
        end
        if(State == 1) begin
            Y <= 1;
            Q <= 0;
        end
        if(State == 2) begin
            Y <= 0;
            Q <= 0;
        end
    end

    always @(posedge Clock) begin
        Reg0[0] <= Button;
        Reg0[1] <= Reg0[0];
        if( Reg0 == 2'b10) begin
            case(State)
            0  :  begin
                if(I0 == 0) begin
                    State <= 0;
                    Z <= 1;
                end
                if(I0 == 1) begin
                    State <= 1;
                    Z <= 0;
                end
            end
            1  :  begin
                if(I0 == 0) begin
                    State <= 2;
                    Z <= 0;
                end
                if(I0 == 1) begin
                    State <= 0;
                    Z <= 1;
                end
            end
            2  :  begin
```

```
                if(I0 == 0) begin
                    State <= 1;
                    Z <= 0;
                end
                if(I0 == 1) begin
                    State <= 0;
                    Z <= 1;
                end
            end
            endcase
        end
    end
endmodule
```

Lab 3 – Counters

In this third lab, you will be expected to create a an 8-bit up down counter that has a clear and load feature. To give you a complete understanding of how to make a counter, this chapter will discuss how a similar 3-bit counter can be made down to the gate level. Once the gate level design for the 3-bit counter has been completely discussed, a behavioral approach will be discussed.

3.1 Lab 3 Description

In this third lab, you will be expected to create a an 8-bit up down counter that has a clear and load feature. As a refresher, a counter is a chain of registers whose stored binary value increments by one on each rising clock edge. For example, in a 3-bit counter, the output would change from 000, 001, 010, 011, 100, 101, 110, 111. The binary numbers increment starting from 0 and increment by 1 with each clock cycle. If you do not know how to represent a number in binary, revisit the section on unsigned binary, so you can understand why "000, 001, 010, 011, 100, 101, 110, 111" is the same as "0,1,2,3,4,5,6,7". There will be 5 inputs to your counter, one 8-bit input to load in a value, and four button inputs to change the state of the counter. There will be one output, which is an 8-bit value that is to be displayed on the LEDs of your board. The block diagram of the counter is below and a table explaining each signal is provided.

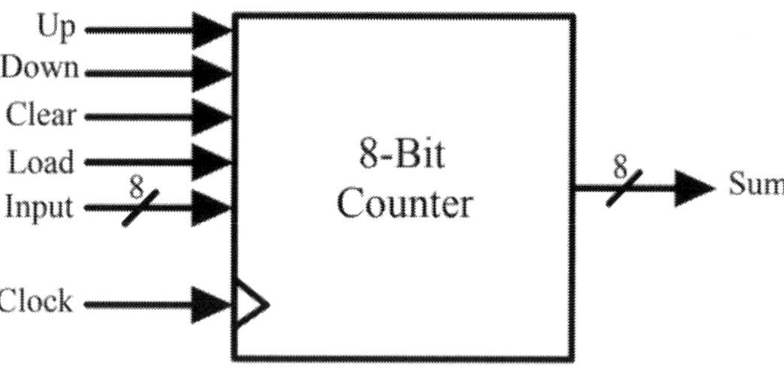

Figure 3.1.1 8-Bit Counter

Table of Signals

Signal Name	Input/Output Mapping	Behavior
UP	Input: A switch on the board	When this switch is active, the 8 LEDs should increase the binary value by one with each clock cycle. EX: 00000000 00000001,00000010, 00000011, … 11111111.
Down	Input: A switch on the board	When this switch is active, the 8 LEDs should decrease the binary value by one with each clock cycle. EX: 11111111,11111110,11111101,11111100, … 00000000.
Load	Input: A switch on the board	When this switch is active, the 8 LEDs should change to reflect the binary value input through the 8 switches. EX: Input is 11001100, then on the next clock cycle the LEDs will become 11001100.
Input	Input: 8 switches on the board	This is what is used to manually change the LED's. whenever the Load switch is active, the LEDs change to whatever value is present at this 8-bit input.

clock	Input: The internal 100MHZ clock	The clock oscillates at a 100M Hz square wave within the board.
Sum	Output: 8 LEDs on the board	The 8 LEDs light up to show the value of the sum output.

3.2 Gate Level 3-Bit Counter

So, to prepare you for making your own 8-bit counter, the circuitry for a 3-bit one will be discussed in detail. The schematic below shows the gate level hardware needed to create a 3-bit up/down counter with a load and clear option. Since we want to store a 3-bit value, 3 registers are used. Since we want to be able to count up, count down, clear, and load in a value, we will need an array for each situation and consequently must have a 4:1 mux for each register. To satisfy the array loaded when a Clear is performed, a 0 is present at the first input of each mux. The Load [2:0] Array is directly coming in from input switches. The Up[2:0] array is always one greater than the Sum[2:0] output. The Down[2:0] array is always one less than the Sum[2:0] output. For example, if we want to increase the output, we set the select line to steer in the Up[2:0] array. Then on each clock edge, Sum[2:0] will be updated with Up[2:0] and the combinational circuitry will change the Up[2:0] array to be one greater. On the next clock edge, the process continues, resulting in the output, the Sum[2:0] array continuously being incremented by one. To simulate this exact circuit, scan the QR code. A computer will allow for a full screen view, so consider sending the QR code link to your computer. Note that in the simulation, an enable signal was added for control.

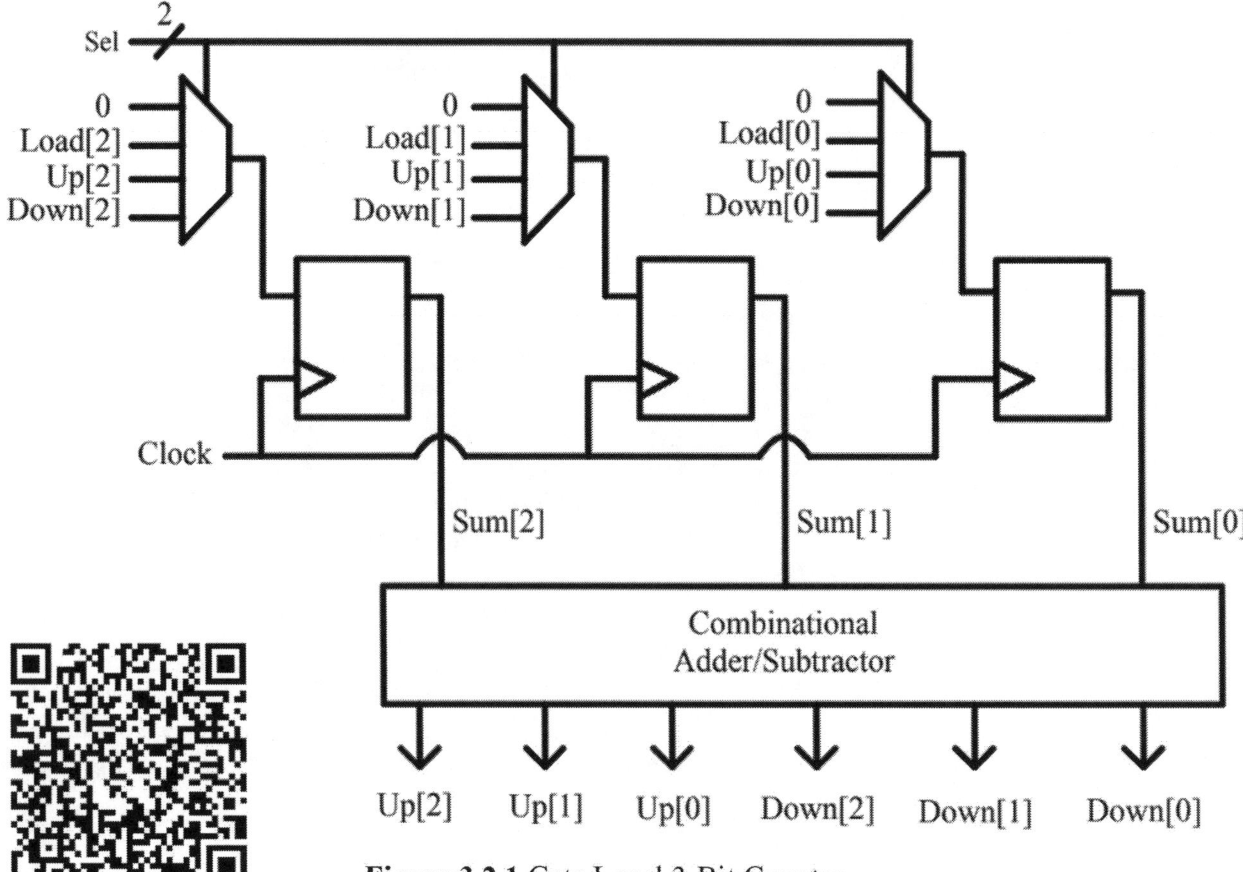

Figure 3.2.1 Gate Level 3-Bit Counter

So, now that the schematic for the circuit has been discussed, it is time to go thought the process of making a source file for it. To begin directly converting the schematic given in Figure 3.2.1 into code, we will simply make a module for each block, and then make one top level module instantiating everything. A module will need to be made for a 4:1 mux, for a D flip-flop, and for a combinational adder/subtractor. The most challenging of these three by far is the combinational adder/subtractor, so that will be covered first.

If you recall in lab 2, you learned how to build a 4-bit adder by instantiating multiple copies of the half adder circuit. The 4-bit adder would then perform binary addition by instantly adding two input arrays, A and B. That same code from lab 2 can easily be modified to make the 3-bit adder module shown below. If you do not understand how this code was derived, revisit lab 2 where it is explained completely.

Final Source File for 3-bit Adder

```
module ThreeBitAdder(A,B,Sum);
input [2:0] A,B;
output [2:0] Sum;
wire [2:0] W; // This line defines the internal signals

FullAdder I0(A[0],B[0],0,Sum[0],W[0]);       // First Instantiation
FullAdder I1(A[1],B[1],W[0],Sum[1],W[1]); // Second Instantiation
FullAdder I2(A[2],B[2],W[1],Sum[2],W[2]); // Third Instantiation

endmodule

module FullAdder(A,B,Cin,Sum,Cout);
input A,B,Cin;
output reg Sum,Cout;

// Combinational logic to implement Full Adder truth table
always @(*) begin
   if({A,B,Cin} == 3'b000) {Cout, Sum} = 2'b00;
   if({A,B,Cin} == 3'b001) {Cout, Sum} = 2'b01;
   if({A,B,Cin} == 3'b010) {Cout, Sum} = 2'b01;
   if({A,B,Cin} == 3'b011) {Cout, Sum} = 2'b10;
   if({A,B,Cin} == 3'b100) {Cout, Sum} = 2'b01;
   if({A,B,Cin} == 3'b101) {Cout, Sum} = 2'b10;
   if({A,B,Cin} == 3'b110) {Cout, Sum} = 2'b10;
   if({A,B,Cin} == 3'b111) {Cout, Sum} = 2'b11;
end

endmodule
```

So now that we have the 3-bit adder, you may be thinking: "Well what about the 3-bit subtractor?". Well as it turns out, we don't need to make any new hardware and the reason why is because rather than making a brand-new piece of circuitry to subtract, we can re-use the 3-bit adder to subtract by adding a negative number to a positive number. To subtract the sum by 1, we just add -1 to it. In signed binary, -1 is represented by 111, so to subtract the sum by 1, we would add 111 to it using the three-bit adder. Armed with this information, we can write a top-level module for the combinational adder/subtractor to be the following. If you are unsure why -1 in decimal equals 111 in signed binary, refer to the signed binary section of the logic design review.

Top Level Module For Combinational Adder/Subtractor

```
module Adder_AND_Subtractor(Sum,Up,Down);
   input [2:0] Sum;
   output [2:0] Up,Down;

   ThreeBitAdder IN0 (Sum,3'b001,Up);      // Add 1 to Sum[2:0]
   ThreeBitAdder IN1 (Sum,3'b111,Down);  // Add -1 to Sum[2:0]
endmodule

// Insert 3-bit adder and full adder modules
```

This top-level module takes in a 3-bit input, labeled Sum, and outputs one 3-bit value that is one greater than the input and one 3-bit value that is one less than the input. These outputs are named Up and Down respectively.

Now that the module for the adder/subtractor has been made. All that remains is to create a module for the multiplexer and D flip-flop. Neither of these things are new material, so the code for each will be shown without elaboration for their derivation.

Module for 4:1 Mux

```
module MUX4TO1(I0, I1, I2, I3, Sel, Out);
   input I0, I1, I2, I3;
   input [1:0] Sel;
   output reg Out;

   always @(*) begin
      if(Sel == 2'b00) Out = I0;
      if(Sel == 2'b01) Out = I1;
      if(Sel == 2'b10) Out = I2;
      if(Sel == 2'b11) Out = I3;
   end
endmodule
```

Module for D flip-fop

```
module DFF(D,Q,Clock);
   input wire D, Clock;
   output reg Q;

   always @(posedge Clock) begin
      Q <= D;
   end
endmodule
```

The final step is to create a source file that has a top-level Counter module instantiating the other modules together, uses a custom clock, and has the desired inputs and outputs. Since instantiation has already been covered, no super in depth explanation using diagrams or anything like that will be here. Only a general description of the source code will be provided. If you are unsure how the top-level Counter module instantiates the other modules and want to know how instantiation works, refer to lab 2. In the meantime, the final source file for the 3-bit counter is below. The clock divider module was included too.

Final 3-bit Counter Code

```
`timescale 1ns / 1ps

module Counter(Sel,Sel_Val,Load,Clock,New_Clock,Sum);
   input Clock;
   input [1:0] Sel;
   input [2:0] Load;
   output [2:0] Sum;

   output wire [1:0] Sel_Val;
   output wire New_Clock;

   assign Sel_Val = Sel;

   wire [2:0] Load,Up,Down,W;

   DFF IN0(W[0],Sum[0],New_Clock);
   DFF IN1(W[1],Sum[1],New_Clock);
   DFF IN2(W[2],Sum[2],New_Clock);

   MUX4TO1 IN00(1'b0,Load[0],Up[0],Down[0],Sel,W[0]);
   MUX4TO1 IN01(1'b0,Load[1],Up[1],Down[1],Sel,W[1]);
   MUX4TO1 IN02(1'b0,Load[2],Up[2],Down[2],Sel,W[2]);

   Adder_AND_Subtractor IN000(Sum,Up,Down);

```

```
   CLK100MHZ_divider(Clock,New_Clock);
endmodule

module MUX4TO1(I0,I1,I2,I3,Sel,Out);
   input I0,I1,I2,I3;
   input [1:0] Sel;
   output reg Out;

   always @(*) begin
      if(Sel == 2'b00) Out = I0;
      if(Sel == 2'b01) Out = I1;
      if(Sel == 2'b10) Out = I2;
      if(Sel == 2'b11) Out = I3;
   end
endmodule

module DFF(D,Q,Clock);
   input wire D, Clock;
   output reg Q;

   always @(posedge Clock) begin
      Q <= D;
   end
endmodule

module Adder_AND_Subtractor(Sum,Up,Down);
   input [2:0] Sum;
   output [2:0] Up,Down;

   ThreeBitAdder IN0 (Sum,3'b001,Up);      // Add 1 to Sum[2:0]
   ThreeBitAdder IN1 (Sum,3'b111,Down);  // Add -1 to Sum[2:0]
endmodule

module ThreeBitAdder(A,B,Sum);
   input [2:0] A,B;
   output [2:0] Sum;
   wire [2:0] W; // This line defines the internal signals

   FullAdder I0(A[0],B[0],0,Sum[0],W[0]);       // First Instantiation
   FullAdder I1(A[1],B[1],W[0],Sum[1],W[1]); // Second Instantiation
   FullAdder I2(A[2],B[2],W[1],Sum[2],W[2]); // Third Instantiation
endmodule

module FullAdder(A,B,Cin,Sum,Cout);
   input A,B,Cin;
   output reg Sum,Cout;
```

```
72
73     // Combinational logic to implement Full Adder truth table
74     always @(*) begin
75        if({A,B,Cin} == 3'b000) {Cout, Sum} = 2'b00;
76        if({A,B,Cin} == 3'b001) {Cout, Sum} = 2'b01;
77        if({A,B,Cin} == 3'b010) {Cout, Sum} = 2'b01;
78        if({A,B,Cin} == 3'b011) {Cout, Sum} = 2'b10;
79        if({A,B,Cin} == 3'b100) {Cout, Sum} = 2'b01;
80        if({A,B,Cin} == 3'b101) {Cout, Sum} = 2'b10;
81        if({A,B,Cin} == 3'b110) {Cout, Sum} = 2'b10;
82        if({A,B,Cin} == 3'b111) {Cout, Sum} = 2'b11;
83     end
84  endmodule
85
86  module CLK100MHZ_divider(CLK100MHZ, New_Clock);
87     input wire CLK100MHZ;      // Input clock signal
88     output reg New_Clock;      // Divided clock output
89
90     reg [31:0] count = 0; // large enough register to hold 49999999
91
92     always @(posedge CLK100MHZ) begin
93        count <= count + 1;  // Increment count
94        if (count == 31'd49999999) begin
95           New_Clock <= ~New_Clock; // Toggle New Clock
96           count <= 31'b0;      // Reset count
97        end
98     end
99  endmodule
```

In lines 3-12 of the code, the inputs and outputs are defined. The outputs defined on lines 9-10 are only present to further show what is going on. On line 94, the value 49999999 was used to generate a 1 Hz clock using the methods dissed in lesson 2. On line 10, we can declare the custom clock we made as an output that will be mapped to an LED. Doing this will allow us to see the 1 HZ clock on an LED. Lines 9 and 12 allow us to make an output to keep track of the select line which too can be mapped to the LEDs. Line 14 declares the internal wires needed for instantiation. Lines 16-27 are where the instantiations are done, marking the end of the top-level module of the counter. I would recommend looking at Figure 3.2.1 to see how the instantiation relates to the schematic. The remaining lines are the previous modules all copied and pasted in. If you want to understand how each of these modules work, then refer to the pervious labs and lessons where they were derived or where similar variations were derived. The QR code will allow you to download the source and constraint code so you can upload it to your board.

3.3 Alternate Behavioral Method

Although the methodology discussed in section 3.2 can very well be applied to implement an 8-bit version of the counter, doing so would be very time consuming, since it is a structural approach after all. If you wish to design the schematic for an 8-bit counter yourself and manually convert the design into Verilog code as done in section 3.2, you may, however this approach could easily take over an hour. If you do choose that route, you will need to modify the 3-bit counter by adding 5 more registers, 5 more multiplexers, and make the combinational adder circuitry compatible for 8 bits instead of just three. You may want to use the website circuit verse to simulate your structural design before converting it into Verilog code. Section 3.2 was intended to give you a great foundational understanding of how a counter behaves. Using the knowledge gained from section 3.2, implementing a behavioral version should not be hard.

A great behavioral approach is to create a design using a sequential always-block. This always-block would only need to include four conditional if-statements. There would be one statement to handle counting up, another for counting down, a third for when the clear switch is activated, and a final one for when the switch to load an 8-bit input is active. It's important to note that the clock used in this always block should be a custom clock that is slow enough to see changes. The entire code for such an approach, including the provided custom clock module, should require less than 35 lines. This means that you only need to write around 15 lines of code to finish the source file using this approach. Remember to use the non-blocking operator, "<=", in the sequential always block.

Lab 4 – Memory Circuits

Knowing how to make a memory chip is extremely important in Verilog. In many projects where a signal is sampled thousands of times per second and a huge number of mathematical calculations are performed, memory will be needed to store each sample and the calculation result. A Fourier transform is a perfect example of such an instance where a memory module would be needed. In this fourth lab, you will be expected to create a memory chip that has 32 locations and can store an 8-bit value in each location. Like the previous labs, to give you preparation, a similar problem to this lab will be discussed fully, all the way to the gate level. Then multiple behavioral approaches will be discussed.

4.1 Lab 4 Description

In this lab, you will create a memory chip that has 32 locations and can store an 8-bit value in each location. You will need to have a five-bit address line ($2^5 = 32$) to choose which of the 32 locations to read or write from. You will need to have an 8-bit input to write data in the memory chip. You will also need to have a load input to control when the value at the 8-bit input is written into the selected address. You will also need to have a separate input that clears the value in the selected address. The outputs will be the current address and the current 8-bit value. The block diagram of the circuit is below.

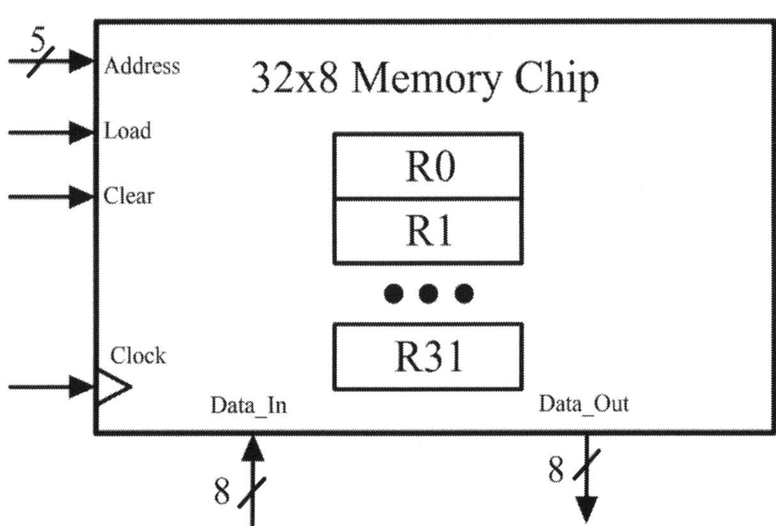

Figure 4.1.1 32x8 Memory Chip

Table of Signals

Signal Name	Input/Output Mapping	Behavior
Address	Input: 5 switches on the board Output: 5 LEDs on the board	These 5 switches control the address that is selected. They will be mapped to LEDs too, so the current address can be visually seen.
Load	Input: A switch or button on the board	When this signal is high, on the next clock edge, the value present at the Data_In input is loaded (stored) into the memory location selected by the Address input.

Clear	Input: A switch or button on the board	When this signal is high, on the next clock edge, the memory location selected by the Address input has its contents reset to zero.
Data_In	Input: 8 switches on the board	These switches are used to send data in. For example, if we want to load in 00001111, then we have the top four switches open (Zero) and the bottom four closed (one).
clock	Input: The internal 100MHZ clock	The clock oscillates at a 100M Hz square wave within the board.
Data_Out	Output: 8 LEDs on the board	The current value stored in the selected memory location is shown using these 8 LEDs. For example, if 10001100 is stored in location 15 and the address line is set to 15, then the LEDs will be 10001100.

4.2 Memory Chip Structural Vs Behavioral Approach

So, to prepare you for making a 32x8 Memory Chip, the circuitry for a 4x4 Memory Chip will be shown. The schematic below shows the gate level hardware needed to make a 4x4 Memory Chip. Each row stores a 4-bit value. A demultiplexer is used to enable the row selected by the address using the Clear and Load input. When Clear is 0 and Load is 1, Data_In is steered to the input of all the rows and the Address input only allows the selected row to be updated. When Clear is 1 and load is 0, the multiplexer at the top steers zero into all rows, and the row selected by the address will have its contents updated to 0.

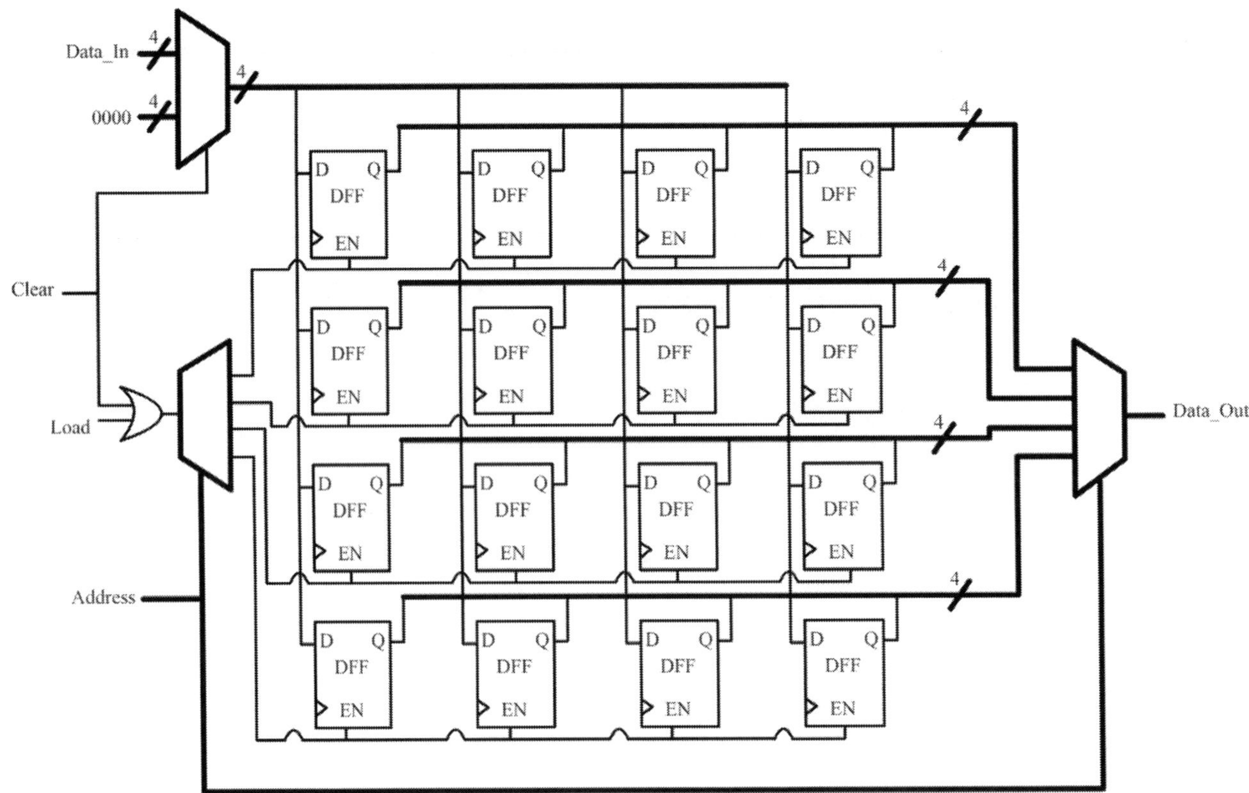

Figure 4.1.2 4x4 Memory Chip

To simulate the exact 4x4 memory circuit in Figure 4.1.2, scan the following QR code. You may want to access the link using a computer to use the full screen.

The schematic in Figure 4.1.2 can easily be implemented using a structural approach. There would need to be an instantiation for each multiplexer, for the decoder, the logical OR gate, and 16 instantiations for each flip-flop. Now although it is feasible to implement a 4x4 memory chip using a structural approach, what about for chips that are large enough to have practical use? For example, what about a 1024x16 chip? Well in such a chip, there would be well over 16,000 flip-flops, so a structural design would be well over 16,000 lines long! Clearly this is not at all practical, so how are memory circuits made in Verilog? Well, the answer is through using multidimensional arrays in a behavioral implementation. The format of a multidimensional array is shown below.

Multidimensional Array Declaration Format
reg [X:0] name [Y:0];   // (Y+1) total (X+1)-bit values

In the format, X+1 determines the length of each binary value to be stored. Y+1 determines how many total values we would want to store. For example, if we wanted to have 256 total 16-bit values, we would set Y to 255 and X to 15. Using an always block in conjunction with multidimensional arrays can easily implement a memory chip. The code below shows how a 256x16 chip can be implemented.

256x16 Memory Chip

```
module memory_chip(Clock, Address, Load, Clear, Data_in, Data_out);
   input wire Clock, Load, Clear;
   input wire [7:0] Address;
   input wire [15:0] Data_in;
   output wire [15:0] Data_out;

   reg [15:0] memory [255:0];        // 256 total 16-bit values

   always @(posedge Clock) begin
      if (Load) memory[Address] <= Data_in;
      if (Clear) memory[Address] <= 16'h0000;
   end

   assign Data_out = memory[Address];

endmodule
```

The code shown for the 256x16 memory chip can easily be modified to implement any size chip. Exploiting this fact and using the code as a template for your lab and other projects requiring storage would be a great approach.

In lines 10 and 11, all 16 bits of an address are assigned a value. Now suppose, we wanted to specifically assign a value to only bits 7:0? Well, the way this can be solved is through the following assignment format.

Multidimensional Array Assignment Format

```
memory[Address][X:0] <= Value;  // assigns Value to bits X:0 of the Address
```

What if we wanted to assign specific bits to a value? For example, what if we wanted to assign value1 to bits [15:12], value2 to bits [11:7], and the remaining bits to value3? Well, this could easily be achieved through using the concatenation notation as shown below. Value1 would be in the left, value2 would be next, and value3 would be last. In practice there can be any number of values concatenated together, so there could easily be more values, implied by the "..." symbol.

Assignment using Concatenation

```
memory[Address] <= {Value1,Value2, Value3...};  // assigns all values concatenated
```

Now what if we wanted to assign a value to the most significant bits and value to the least significant while keeping the remaining bits unchanged? The example that follows demonstrates how such a rare instance could be delt with.

Example 1

Assign 4'hA to the most significant bits of memory, 4'h9 to the least significant bits while keeping the rest unchanged. Assume the memory has 16-bit values stored at each address.

```
memory [Address] <= {4'hA, memory [Address][11:4], 4'h9};
```

In place of Value2 were bits 11:4 of the selected address. Bits 11:4 were calculated knowing that bits 15:12 and 3:0 were taken by 4'hA and 4'h9.

4.3 Memory Chip Via Modularization

Now although using a multidimensional array is a great way to make a memory chip fast, this isn't always how dedicated memory chips are made. In the real world, large memory chips are typically made through modularization. This section will explain in detail how this occurs. If you are enrolled in a computer organization and architecture course, then this section will be very useful.

The figure below shows how an 8x8 memory chip can be made using multiple 4x4 chips. The most significant bits of the Data_In input go to the chips on the left and the least significant ones to the right. The most significant bits of the address always go into a decoder to select which row to enable. Since there are only two rows, only a 1-bit decoder is used. Had there been 4 rows to create a 16x8 chip, then a 2-bit decoder would be needed. Had here of been 8 rows to create a 32x8 chip, then a 3-bit decoder would be needed. An 8-bit multiplexer is used to select the output. The select line of the mux is the same input going into the decoder. The QR code below will allow you to simulate the exact circuit. Using a computer is best if you want a full screen view.

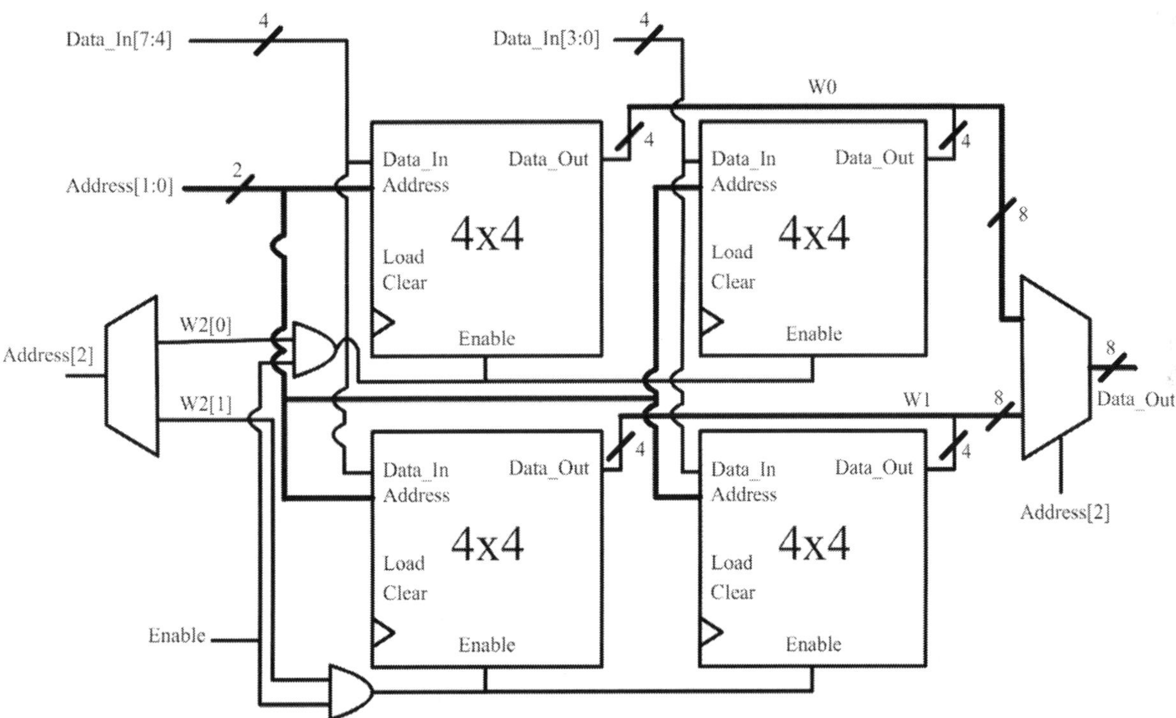

Figure 4.3.1 8x8 Memory Chip

It is important to note that any size chip can be made by combining smaller chips together. The number of smaller chips needed to make a larger chip will always be equal to $\frac{\text{R1}}{\text{R2}} * \frac{\text{C1}}{\text{C2}}$, where R1 is the address size of the larger chip, R2 is the address size of the smaller chip, C1 is the bit length of the larger chip, and C2 is the bit length of the smaller chip. For example, if we want to make a 512x32 chip from 16x16 bit chips. We would know that the number of 16x16 bit chips required would be $\frac{512}{16} * \frac{32}{16} = 64$. The notation of a memory chip is always written as (Rows) X (Columns) and the decoder size will always be equal to $\log_2(\text{Rows})$ for a chip that is not made from other chips. For example, a 512x32 chip that is not made from other chips would have a decoder size that is $\log_2(512) = 9$. For chips made from smaller chips, the size of an additional decoder is always equal to $\log_2\left(\frac{\text{R1}}{\text{R2}}\right)$. The example below should offer more clarity of how these rules can be applied.

Example 2

a) Determine the decoder size needed for a 16x4 memory chip.

$$\text{Decoder Size} = \log_2(\text{Rows}) = \log_2(16) = \text{4-bit decoder}$$

b) How many 16x4 chips can be used to make a 1024x32 chip?

$$\text{Total chips} = \frac{\text{R1}}{\text{R2}} * \frac{\text{C1}}{\text{C2}} = \frac{1024}{16} * \frac{32}{4} = 512 \text{ chips}$$

d) In making a 1024x32 chip from 16x4 chips, what size decoder is needed to select among the rows of 16x4 chips?

$$\text{Decoder Size} = \log_2\left(\frac{\text{R1}}{\text{R2}}\right) = \log_2\left(\frac{1024}{16}\right) = \text{6-bit decoder}$$

The Verilog code for the circuit in Figure 4.3.1 is provided below. If you wish, you may modify it to implement a 32x8 memory unit for your lab. This method will give you great knowledge of how to modularize memory chips, however it is still much slower than the behavioral method discussed in section 4.2.

8x8 Chip From 4x4 Chips

```
`timescale 1ns / 1ps

module memory8x8(Clock, Address, Load, Clear, Data_in, Data_out, Enable);
   input wire Clock, Load, Clear, Enable;
   input wire [2:0] Address;
   input wire [7:0] Data_in;
   output wire [7:0] Data_out;
```

```
    wire [7:0] W0,W1;
    wire [1:0] W2;

memory4x4 IN0(Clock,Address[1:0],Load,Clear,Data_in[7:4],W0[7:4],W2[0]&&Enable);
memory4x4 IN1(Clock,Address[1:0],Load,Clear,Data_in[3:0],W0[3:0],W2[0]&&Enable);
memory4x4 IN2(Clock,Address[1:0],Load,Clear,Data_in[7:4],W1[7:4],W2[1]&&Enable);
memory4x4 IN3(Clock,Address[1:0],Load,Clear,Data_in[3:0],W1[3:0],W2[1]&&Enable);
MUX2TO1_8BIT IN4(W0,W1,Address[2],Data_out);
DECODER2TO1 IN5(Address[2],W2[0],W2[1]);
endmodule

module memory4x4(Clock, Address, Load, Clear, Data_in, Data_out, Enable);
    input wire Clock, Load, Clear, Enable;
    input wire [1:0] Address;
    input wire [3:0] Data_in;
    output wire [3:0] Data_out;

    reg [3:0] memory [3:0];      // 4 total 4-bit values
    integer i = 0;

    initial begin
        for(i = 0; i < 4; i = i+1) begin
            memory[i] <= 4'h0;
        end
    end

    always @(posedge Clock) begin
        if (Enable == 1) begin
            if (Load) memory[Address] <= Data_in;
            if (Clear) memory[Address] <= 4'h0;
        end
    end

    assign Data_out = memory[Address];

endmodule

module MUX2TO1_8BIT(I0,I1,Sel,Out);
    input wire [7:0] I0,I1;
    input wire Sel;
    output wire [7:0] Out;

    assign Out = Sel ? I1 : I0;
endmodule
```

```
module DECODER2TO1(In,Out0,Out1);
   input wire In;
   output wire Out0, Out1;

   assign Out0 = ~In;
   assign Out1 = In;
endmodule
```

4.4 Memory Chip Vs ROM

The final topic to discuss is the difference between a ROM and a memory chip. A ROM stands for "Read Only Memory". A ROM, like its name implies, has memory that can be accessed, but not written into. This is because a ROM is a huge combinational circuit that can be modeled by a truth table. Since a ROM is combinational, any memory chip containing a clock or register, by definition, cannot be a ROM. ROMs have many applications in digital circuits where speed is needed. For example, a cosine function could be implemented in a huge ROM rather than being calculated on the fly. This is extremely useful, since it is often much faster to have the answer for each possible case pre-solved, than to perform signed floating-point arithmetic on the fly. The example below shows how a small ROM can be implemented.

Example 3

```
module ROM (address,data);
   input wire [2:0] address,   // 3 bits for addressing 8 locations
   output reg [7:0] data       // 8-bit data from each location

   // Define the ROM content
   always @(address) begin
      case (address)
         3'b000: data = 8'b00000001;
         3'b001: data = 8'b00000010;
         3'b010: data = 8'b00000100;
         3'b011: data = 8'b00001000;
         3'b100: data = 8'b00010000;
         3'b101: data = 8'b00100000;
         3'b110: data = 8'b01000000;
         3'b111: data = 8'b10000000;
         default: data = 8'b00000000; // Default case
      endcase
   end

endmodule
```

Now you may be wondering how a practical ROM could be made? For a well-executed cosine function to be implemented using a ROM, we would need thousands of thousands of rows to cover as many inputs as possible. In practical applications, we would not write all these lines ourselves as done in example 3, since that would waste weeks of time. In practice, a computer program such as MAT-Lab or C is used to generate a text file having done this for you. This text file can then be used in a Verilog module. The code below shows how this can be done for the previous example.

Example 4

```
1  module ROM (Address,Data);
2     input wire [2:0] Address;    // 3 bits for addressing 8 locations
3     output reg [7:0] Data;       // 8-bit data from each location
4
5     // Declare the ROM memory array
6     reg [7:0] memory[0:7];
7
8     // Initialize memory from a file at compile-time
9     initial begin
10       $readmemb("memory_contents.mem", memory);
11    end
12
13    // Output the data corresponding to the input address
14    always @(Address) begin
15       Data = memory[Address];
16    end
17
18 endmodule
```

To create a mem file in Verilog, you simply create a new source file but change the file type as shown below. Once created, click on the memory file under the design sources and paste in the text file contents. Note that in line 10 of example 4, the first parameter of the read function, "$readmemb", is the name of the memory file.

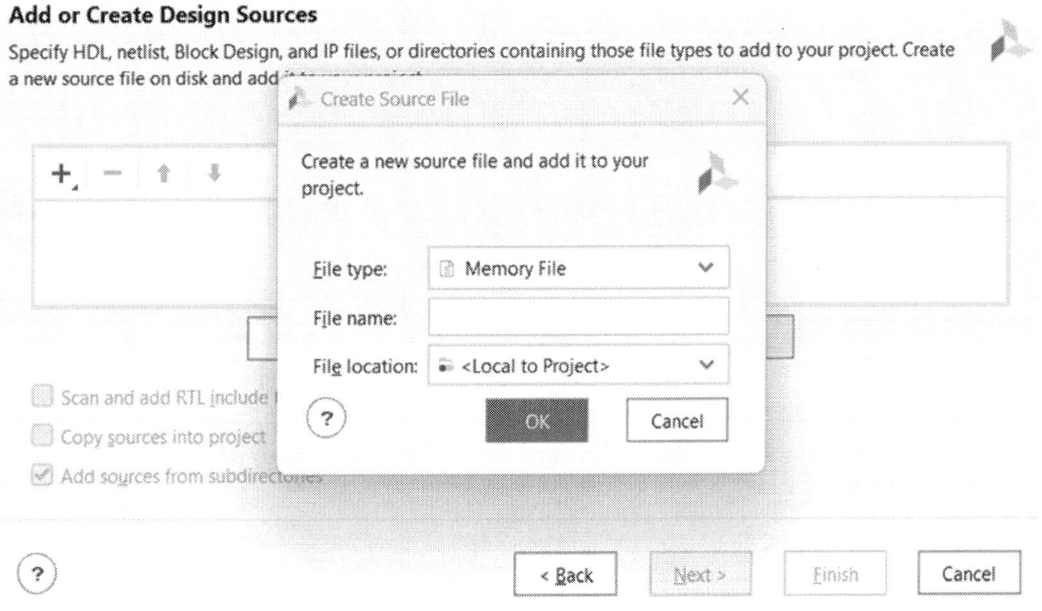

Figure 4.4.1 Memory File Creation

The text below shows the contents of what a memory file could look like. The text file only needs to have the ROM contents, since Verilog knows how to interpret the file based on the order of the contents. For example, if the text file below were used in example 4, the program will know to assign 00000001 to the very first location of the ROM, 00000010 to the second location of the ROM, and so on.

Memory File Contents

```
00000001
00000010
00000100
00001000
00010000
00100000
01000000
10000000
```

Practical Lesson 1 – Button Debouncing

In the problems for section L2.4 of lesson 2, you were asked to implement a state machine with a button input as a clock. If you did your due diligence and uploaded the solution to your board, then you likely noticed that sometimes when the button was pressed, it would not register correctly. Now you may have been tempted to say that the board was just broken but this isn't the case. When the button is pressed or released, the momentum sometimes causes it to bounce back up or down a few micrometers, temporarily changing the state of the signal. This phenomenon is called button bouncing. This unstable signal will cause the circuit to behave as if you pressed the button multiple times, which is not good. The timing diagram below shows the signal the FPGA will receive whenever you press a button.

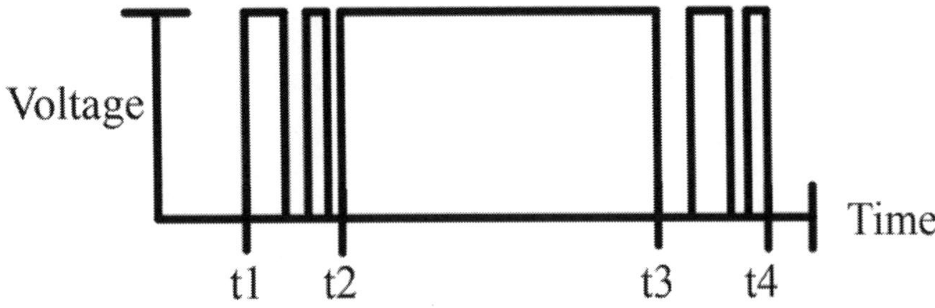

Figure PL1.1 Button Press Timming Diagram

At time t1 is when the button is pressed and at time t2 is when the button is stabilized. Then sometime later at t3, the button is released and stabilizes at time t4. The time to stabilize is very small and is usually within the order of microseconds. Now how might we prevent the unstable signal from reaching the FPGA? Well, the answer is to temporarily stop reading after the first rising or falling edge has been detected. Then after enough time has elapsed such that the signal is stabilized, we can start reading again. By using a counter, we can set a flag to control when we begin reading. The figure below shows what the timing diagram would look like with flags included to prevent the reading after each edge has been detected.

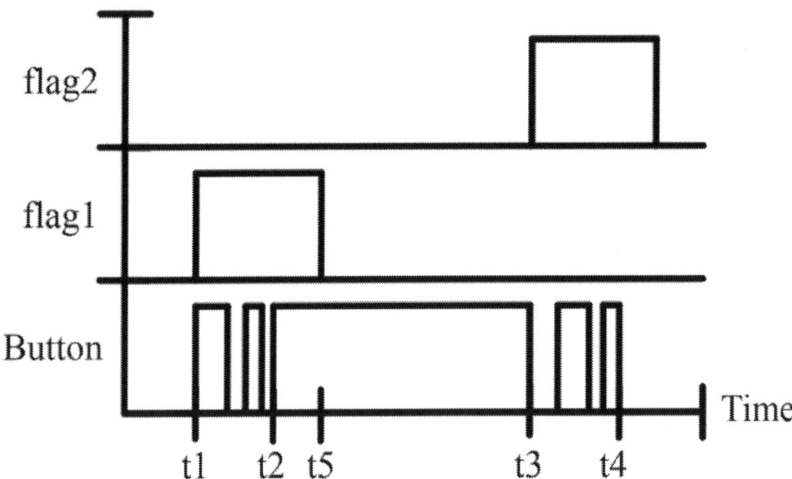

Figure PL1.2 Button Press Timming Diagram with Flags

At time t1, the button is pressed, and the first one is detected, causing flag1 to turn on. During the time that flag1 is on, the circuit stops reading for a fixed time until the signal stabilizes. Once the waiting time has elapsed, flag1 turns off and the circuit resumes reading at time t5. At time t3, when the button is released, the first zero is detected, causing flag2 to turn on. During the time flag2 is on, the circuit stops reading for a fixed time until the signal stabilizes. The sometime after t4, flag2 is disabled and the circuit begins waiting for a new button press. The code that was supposed to execute on the press of the button would typically execute at time t3 or after t4 when flag2 is set to zero again.

The code below shows how the state machine from lesson 2 could use a button for a clock that is debounced. Lines 24-40 were added to debounce the button. Lines 24-29 make it such that during the time a flag is on is on, a counter will count to a fixed number before setting the flags and count to zero. Line 31 sets flag1 to turn on at the first rising edge of the button. Line 32 set flag2 to one on the first falling edge. Lines 34-37 read the current state of the button when both flags are off. Reg0 technically did not need to be two bits but was done so anyway to allow for the two most recent inputs to be seen. This made it easier to identify a falling or rising edge in simulation, since 01 is a rising edge and 10 is a falling edge. Again, having Reg0 record the most current two values instead of the most current value was a subjective choice. Line 40 causes the state machine to update on the instance flag2 is set to one. The remaining lines were identical to the code discussed in lesson 2. Refer to lesson 2 if you wish for an explanation of the remaining lines.

Final Moore Sequence Detector with Debounced Button Clock

```
1   module Circuit0 (I0,Z,Clock,Button,State,Reg0);
2      input wire I0, Clock, Button;
3      output reg Z;
4      output reg [1:0] State;
5      output reg [1:0] Reg0;
6
7      reg flag1 = 0;
8      reg flag2 = 0;
9      reg [31:0] Count = 0;
10
11     initial begin
12        Reg0 = 0;
13        State = 0;
14     end
15
16     always@(*) begin
17        if(State == 0) Z = 0;
18        if(State == 1) Z = 0;
19        if(State == 2) Z = 0;
20        if(State == 3) Z = 1;
21     end
22
```

```
  always @(posedge Clock) begin
    if(flag1 || flag2) Count <= Count + 1;
    if(Count == 31'd5000000) begin // Delay for 20th of a second
      flag1 <= 0;
      flag2 <= 0;
      Count <= 0;
    end

    if(Reg0[0] == 0 && Button == 1 && flag2 == 0) flag1 <= 1;
    if(Reg0[0] == 1 && Button == 0 && flag1 == 0) flag2 <= 1;

    if(flag1 == 0 && flag2 == 0) begin // Read when flags are zero
      Reg0[0] <= Button;
      Reg0[1] <= Reg0[0];
    end

    // Execute code when flag2 turns to 1
    if(Reg0[0] == 1 && Button == 0 && flag1 == 0) begin
      case(State)
      0  :  begin
        if(I0 == 0) State <= 0;
        if(I0 == 1) State <= 1;
      end
      1  :  begin
        if(I0 == 0) State <= 0;
        if(I0 == 1) State <= 2;
      end
      2  :  begin
        if(I0 == 0) State <= 0;
        if(I0 == 1) State <= 3;
      end
      3  :  begin
        if(I0 == 0) State <= 0;
        if(I0 == 1) State <= 1;
      end
      endcase
    end
  end

endmodule
```

To further demonstrate the functionality of this code, some waveforms from a test bench will be shown in the following figure. In a future lesson, you will be taught how to write a test bench, but for now just focus on interpreting the results on this one. The test shows the behavior of the circuit when two button presses off different lengths are applied. One is long enough that the button is still held down after the first flag was set to zero. The other is short enough that the button already ended before flag2 could even turn on. The test waveform clearly shows a fully functional circuit, since with each button press, the state updates according to the input I0. If you recall, the circuit was a sequence detector.

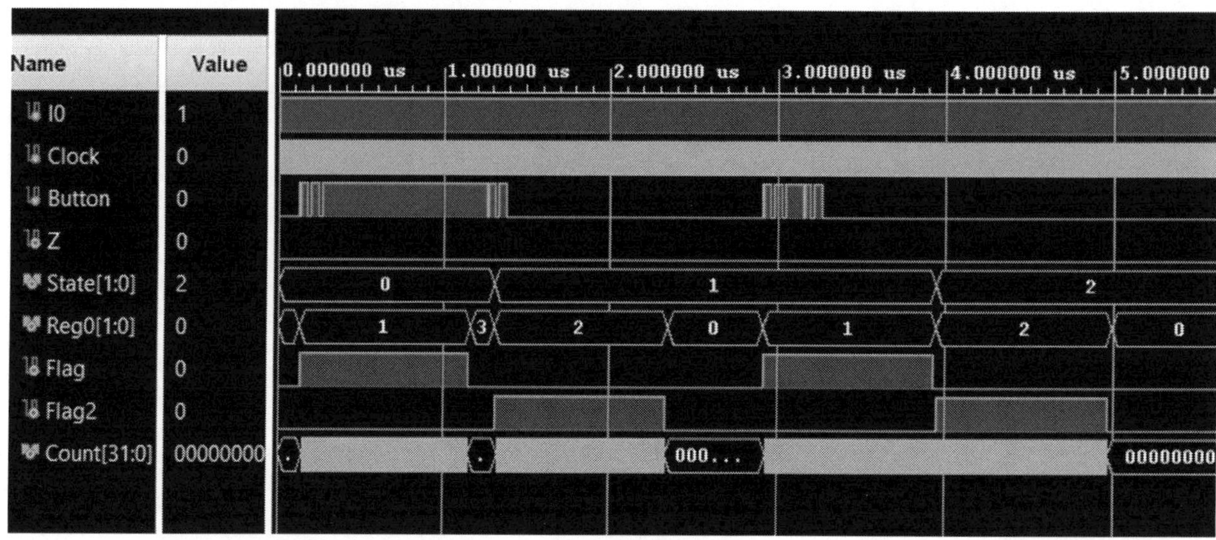

Figure PL1.3 Test Bench Waveforms of Debounced Button Code

Now this circuit clearly is working very well but what could possibly make it go wrong? Well, there is only really one way for the debounced button to give an incorrect result. This is when is button is pressed two times fast enough such that the second button press occurred during the time that reading was disabled. On line 25, the count was set to 5000000 to give a wait time for a 20th of a second. This means that the time for flag1 and flag 2 combined is a 10th of a second. This means that if a button is pressed less than a 10th of a second after a previous press, it will likely not be detected. The solution to this is by changing the maximum count. If we changed the count to 500000, then it is fine to press the button 100th of a second after a previous press. Now with this solution, why not have the count be as low as possible? Well, the reason is because although a lower count allows for more inputs to be accurately read in quick succession, the less time that is spent waiting for the button to stabilize. At the end of the day, it is a compromise between accurate readings and the quickness of readings. If you want to read inputs in quick succession and aren't as concerned about button debouncing, set the count low. If you want more accurate readings and are fine receiving inputs at a slower rate, set the count high.

Lab 5 – Intro to Seven-Segment Display

Seven-segment displays are an important tool in digital design since they are used to display numerical outputs to the user. In this Lab, you will be expected to display a hex number using the seven-segment display and control which of the eight displays shows it. To give you preparation, a very similar example will be shown and discussed.

5.1 Lab description

In this Lab, you will display a number using the seven-segment displays. The number displayed will come from four input switches. For example, if the four input switches have a value of 0011, then the number 3 should appear on the seven-segment display. If the switches have a value of 1111, then the hex number F should appear on the seven-segment display. On the rising edge of a slow clock, the number will vanish from the current display and appear on the display to the left. This will make the number move left with each clock edge. The number will start at the rightmost seven-segment and slowly move to the leftmost one. To begin, the structure of the seven-segment display needs to be discussed. The block diagram of the circuit for an individual seven segment display is shown below.

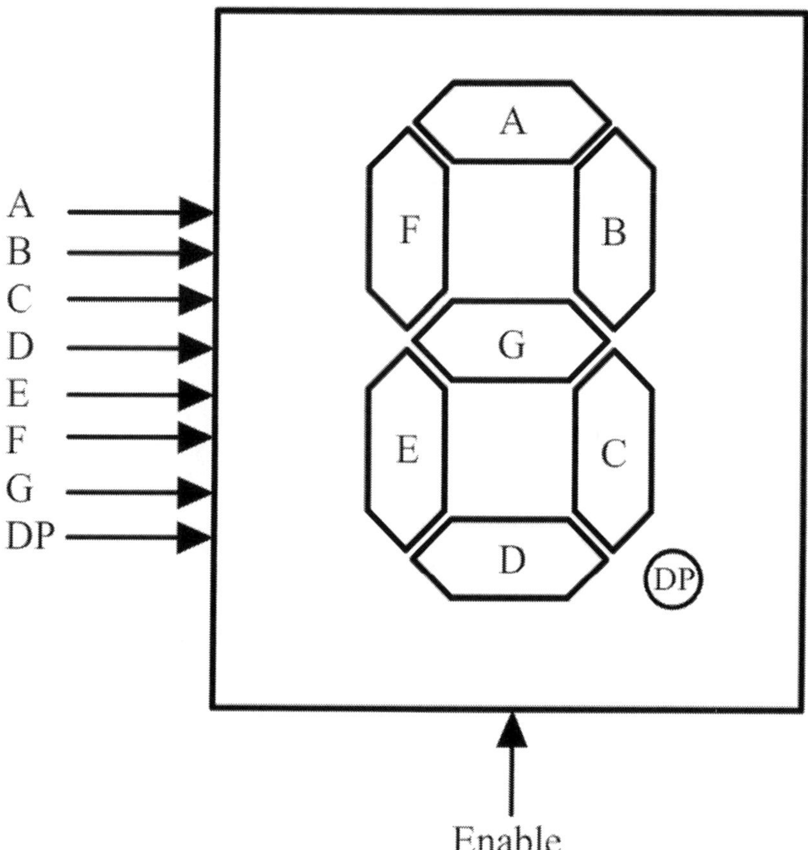

Figure 5.1.1 Seven-segment display block diagram

For each LED, there is an active-low input wire to control if it is on or off. There is also an active-low enable signal to control if the seven-segment display will show anything.

The figure below shows how to create the number two with a seven-segment display. In the figure, {DP, G, F, E, D, C, B, A} = {1, 0, 1, 0, 0, 1, 0, 0} and Enable = 0. Since only C, F, and DP are 1, only the LEDs corresponding to those inputs are turned off. The enable signal is obviously 0 to ensure the switch is lit up due to it being active low. If the enable signal was 1, then none of the LEDs would be on, regardless of the inputs.

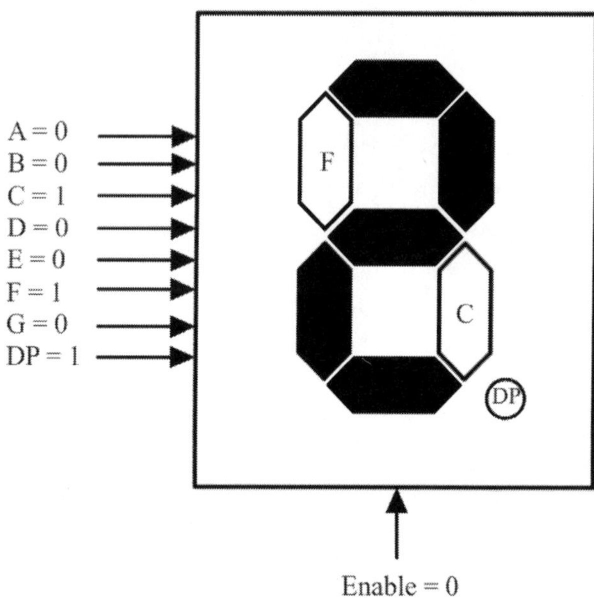

Figure 5.1.2 Making 2 on Seven-segment display

Now that you understand how a single seven-segment display works, it is time to discuss the inconvenient way the seven segments are connected. The figure below shows how all eight seven-segment displays are connected. Now since there are eight different seven segments, there are eight different enable signals for each. Now you might logically think that there would be eight different input arrays {DP, G, F, E, D, C, B, A} for each seven-segment but this unfortunately is not how the board was designed. All eight share the same input array.

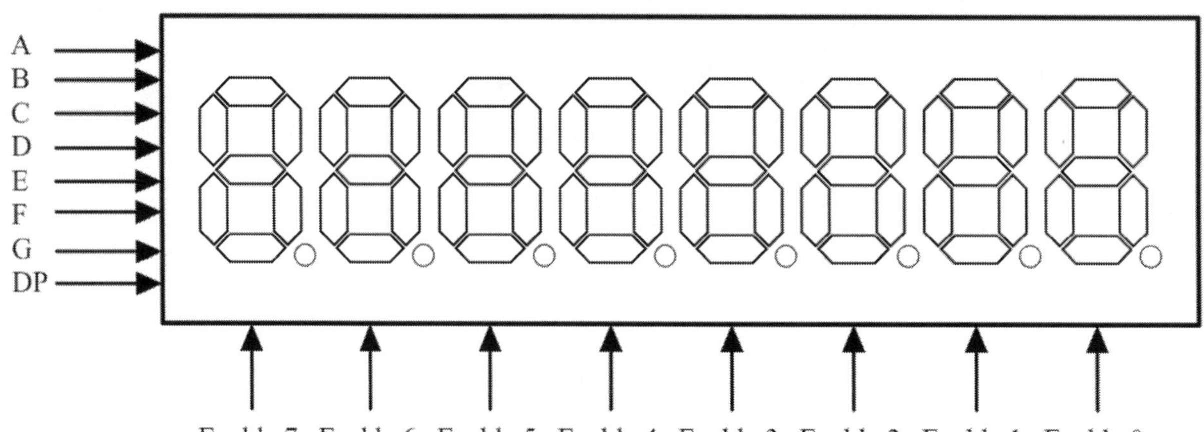

Figure 5.1.3 Complete seven-segment display block diagram

Since all eight seven-segment displays share the same thing inputs, this means that if we make a 2 by setting {DP, G, F, E, D, C, B, A} = {1, 0, 1, 0, 0, 1, 0, 0} and Enable = 0 for all enable signals, all eight displays will show a 2. The figure below shows this.

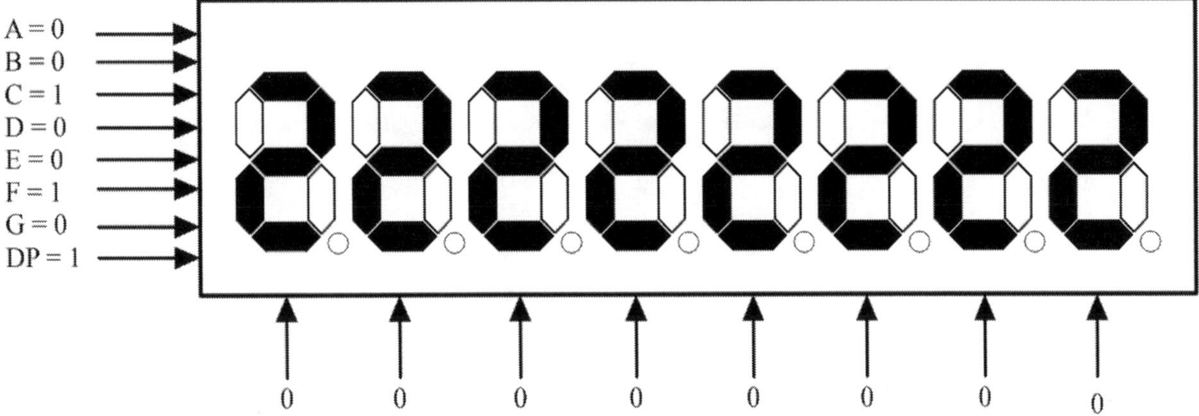

Figure 5.1.4 Complete seven-segment display block diagram

The reason why this is extremely inconvenient is because although displaying a single number is very straightforward, displaying a number like 5472 takes a more complicated approach. The next lab will teach you how to display numbers like 5472 but in the meantime, try thinking about what could be done to display 5472. For this lab, you don't need to worry about this, since only a single number will be displayed at a time.

5.2 Displaying & Moving Input Number Using 3 Seven-Segments

To give you preparation for your lab, an example will be shown how to display numbers 0-3 on the segment displays. The numbers will come from a 2-bit input switch. Only one number will be shown at a time and on each edge of a slow clock, the position will move back and forth between the first and fifth seven-segment display. To start, the very first step is to declare a module with all the inputs and outputs as shown in the code below.

Module Declaration

```
module Circuit0 (DP,G,F,E,D,C,B,A,Enable,Clock,SW);
   input wire Clock;
   input wire [1:0] SW;
   output reg DP,G,F,E,D,C,B,A;
   output reg [7:0] Enable;

   // Contents

endmodule
```

The outputs were declared as registers since they will be assigned values in always-blocks. The inputs were all declared as wires since they will not be assigned a value in an always block.

Now that the module has been declared with the necessary inputs and outputs, the next step is to create a combinational circuit that takes in the switches as an input and then generates the desired output for the {DP, G, F, E, D, C, B, A} array. The figure below shows the truth table completed for this step.

SW[1]	SW[0]	DP	G	F	E	D	C	B	A
0	0	1	1	0	0	0	0	0	0
0	1	1	1	0	0	1	1	1	1
1	0	1	0	1	0	0	1	0	0
1	1	1	0	1	1	0	0	0	0

Figure 5.2.1 Decoder for Circuit

In the truth table, the values for the {DP, G, F, E, D, C, B, A} array are set according to each input. For example, when the switches are 00, the {DP, G, F, E, D, C, B, A} array is set such that the number 0 will show on the display. Again, when the switches are 01, the {DP, G, F, E, D, C, B, A} array is set such that the number 1 will show on the display. The same thing was done for when the switches are 10 and 11. The code below shows the truth table being implemented using a combinational always block.

Module with Combinational Circuit

```
module Circuit0 (DP,G,F,E,D,C,B,A,Enable,Clock,SW);
  input wire Clock;
  input wire [1:0] SW;
  output reg DP,G,F,E,D,C,B,A;
  output reg [7:0] Enable;

  always@(*) begin
    if(SW == 2'b00) {DP,G,F,E,D,C,B,A} = 8'b11000000; // Make 0 with LEDs
    if(SW == 2'b01) {DP,G,F,E,D,C,B,A} = 8'b11001111; // Make 1 with LEDs
    if(SW == 2'b10) {DP,G,F,E,D,C,B,A} = 8'b10100100; // Make 2 with LEDs
    if(SW == 2'b11) {DP,G,F,E,D,C,B,A} = 8'b10110000; // Make 3 with LEDs
  end

endmodule
```

The final step is to add code that causes the Enable [7:0] array to switch between the first and fifth seven-segment. The code and explanation are shown in the pages that follow.

Final Code

```
1  module Circuit0 (DP,G,F,E,D,C,B,A,Enable,Clock,SW);
2     input wire Clock;
3     input wire [1:0] SW;
4     output reg DP,G,F,E,D,C,B,A;
5     output reg [7:0] Enable;
6
7     wire Slow_Clock;
8     CLK100MHZ_divider(Clock, Slow_Clock);
9
10    initial begin
11       Enable = 8'b11111110;
12    end
13
14    always@(*) begin
15       if(SW == 2'b00) {DP,G,F,E,D,C,B,A} = 8'b11000000; // Make 0 with LEDs
16       if(SW == 2'b01) {DP,G,F,E,D,C,B,A} = 8'b11001111; // Make 1 with LEDs
17       if(SW == 2'b10) {DP,G,F,E,D,C,B,A} = 8'b10100100; // Make 2 with LEDs
18       if(SW == 2'b11) {DP,G,F,E,D,C,B,A} = 8'b10110000; // Make 3 with LEDs
19    end
20
21    always@(posedge Slow_Clock) begin
22       if(Enable == 8'b11111110) Enable <= 8'b11101111; // If seg1 is active, go to seg5
23       if(Enable == 8'b11101111) Enable <= 8'b11111110; // If seg5 is active, go to seg1
24    end
25 endmodule
26
27 module CLK100MHZ_divider(CLK100MHZ, New_Clock);
28    input wire CLK100MHZ;     // Input clock signal
29    output reg New_Clock;      // Divided clock output
30
31    reg [31:0] count = 0; // [31:0] is large enough to hold any value
32
33    always @(posedge CLK100MHZ) begin
34       count <= count + 1;  // Increment count
35       if (count == 31'd49999999) begin
36          New_Clock <= ~New_Clock; // Toggle New Clock
37          count <= 31'b0;      // Reset count
38       end
39    end
40 endmodule
```

When we want only the first seven-segment to be on, we use 11111110 for the Enable array. When we want only the fifth segment to be on, we use 11101111 for the Enable array. Using this information, we can create an always block that causes the enable array to switch between these two values, as done on lines 21-24. Lines 10-12 set to Enable array to initially start at 11111110.

This is important, since if you do not initialize it, it will start at a value that is not covered by an if statement. Lines 7-8 create a slow clock by using the clock divider module in lines 27-40.

5.3 Final Remarks & Tips

Now that you have seen how to write code to display numbers 0-3 on the seven-segment display while moving the location of the number between the fifth and first position, you should be ready to make your own code for the lab. Remember that the goal of the lab is to display numbers 0-F on the seven-segment display while moving the location of the number from left to right. The number will start at the rightmost seven-segment and gradually move left until it reaches the leftmost one. When it reaches the leftmost one, on the next slow clock edge, it starts over again at the far right.

If you wish, you may re-use the code from the example as a template for your lab. You will need to change the switch input to a four-bit value instead of a two-bit value. Then you will need to modify the always block in lines 14-19 of the final example code to cover all 16 possibilities. Also note that now the if statements will need to have 4'b in front of the binary number in the conditional expression. Once this has been done, you will need to then modify the always block in lines 21-24 to cover all eight possibilities. For example, in the first case where the enable array is 11111110, the array should change to 11111101. In summary, you can complete the lab by writing 25 lines of code. Sixteen of these lines will be in the combinational always block, eight will be in the sequential always block, and one will be written modifying the switch input. For the sixteen lines in the combinational always block, consider making a truth table by hand as done in the example.

The source and constraint file for the example can be accessed by scanning the QR code below. It is highly recommended to copy and paste the code into your IDE and then upload it onto your board so you can see the example explained to you in action.

Lab 6 – Multiplexing with Seven-Segment Display

This lab will be like the previous lab since you will still use the seven-segment displays. In the last lab, you learned how to display a single number. In this lab, you will learn how to display multiple numbers. To give you preparation, a very similar example will be shown and discussed.

6.1 Lab Description

For your lab, you will use eight switches to provide an 8-bit value as an input. The FPGA will then display the hex equivalent of this 8-bit value using the first and second seven-segment displays. The FPGA will also display the bitwise inversion of the input using the fifth and sixth displays. The block diagram below shows an example of what you should see when the switches feed in the value 10101111.

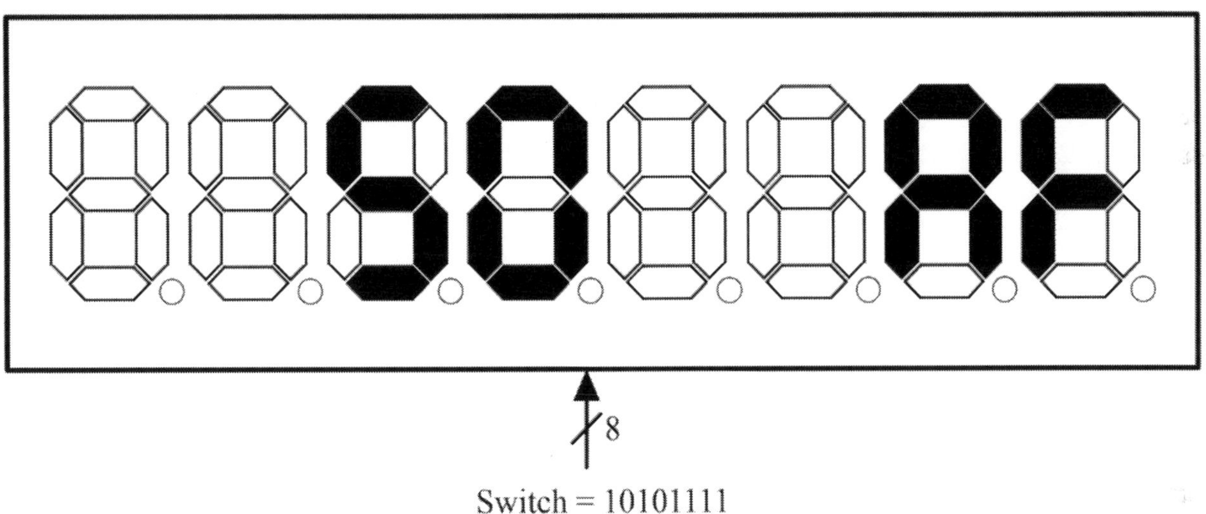

Figure 6.1.1 Seven segment with switch = 10101111

We know that the hexadecimal equivalent of 10101111 is AF, so AF is displayed in the two rightmost displays. The bitwise inversion of 10101111 is 01010000 and the hexadecimal equivalent of 01010000 is 50, so 50 is displayed in the sixth and fifth displays. If you do not understand how to convert a binary number into hexadecimal. Refer to the unsigned binary chapter in the logic design half of the book.

6.2 Multiplexing Using Sequential Always Block

If you don't already know how to display multiple digits as shown in Figure 6.1.1, take a break for a few minutes and think about how it could be done. Hopefully you managed to figure it out but in case you didn't, don't worry. It's actually a very simple solution. The way it is done is through a method called multiplexing. Multiplexing is when you have the input array send in one number and the enable array only allows for the number to be shown on one display. Then, very quickly, both the input and enable array simultaneously to change to display a different number in a different segment. If you have a fast enough clock to display different numbers in different locations, it will appear as if multiple digits are being displayed at once. In case it is not clear, the example that follows will show how a number like 792 could be displayed.

Interval 0

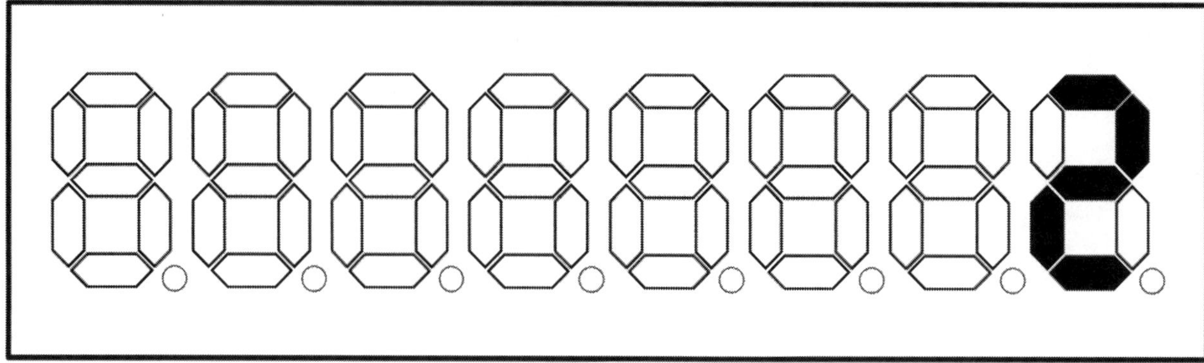

Interval 1

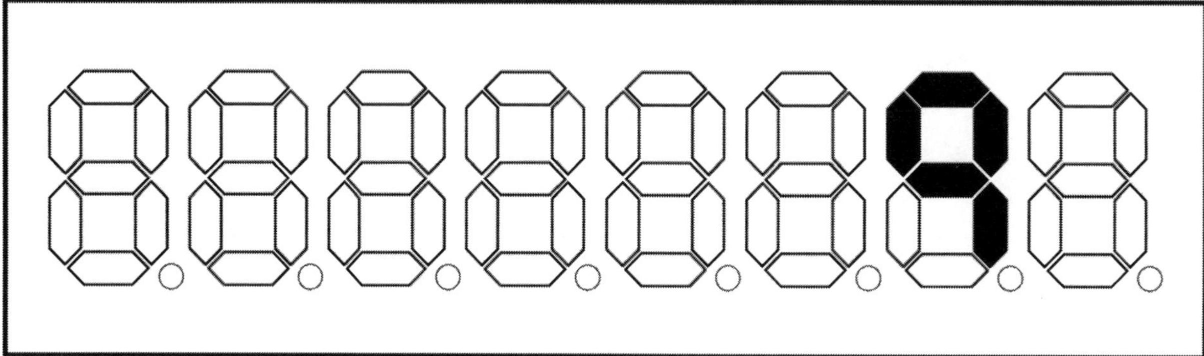

Interval 2

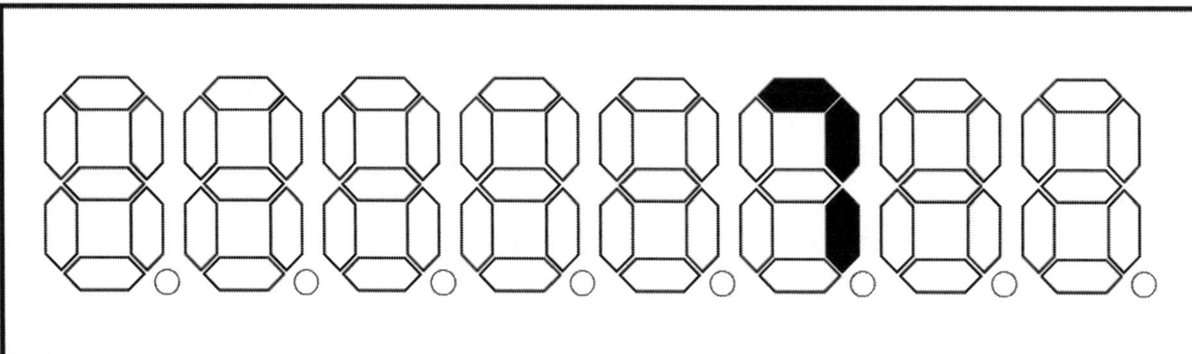

Figure 6.2.1 Multiplexing displays to make 792

In the example shown in Figure 6.2.1, there are three intervals that repeat. During interval 0, the enable array is set to 11111110 and the input array {DP, G, F, E, D, C, B, A} is set to make a 2 on the LEDs. Then immediately after interval 0 ends, interval 1 begins. During interval 1, the enable array is set to 11111101 and the input array {DP, G, F, E, D, C, B, A} is set to make a 9 on the LEDs. Then immediately after interval 1 ends, interval 2 begins. During interval 2, the enable array is set to 11111011 and the input array {DP, G, F, E, D, C, B, A} is set to make a 7 on the LEDs. Then immediately after interval 2 ends, interval 0 begins and the cycle repeats. The time spent in each interval is extremely small because the display needs to be changing fast enough to create the illusion that all three digits are on at once, even though, only a single digit is ever on at any given time. The process of rapidly changing the values of the input and enable array is called multiplexing.

So, what kind of code could be used to achieve this effect? If your bold, try thinking about it yourself before viewing the example. If not that's ok. Well in truth, there are many ways to multiplex the seven segment displays, but one of the simplest ways is to use a sequential always block with eight case statements. The code below shows an example program for how this could be done.

Multiplexing Code

```
module Circuit0 (DP,G,F,E,D,C,B,A,Enable,Clock,SW);
   input wire Clock;
   input wire [3:0] SW;
   output reg DP,G,F,E,D,C,B,A;
   output reg [7:0] Enable;

   reg [3:0] Location = 0;
   reg [3:0] Digit;

   wire Clk_Multi;
   CLK100MHZ_divider(Clock, Clk_Multi);

   always@(*) begin
      if(Digit == 4'b0000) {DP,G,F,E,D,C,B,A} = 8'b11000000; // Make 0 with LEDs
      if(Digit == 4'b0001) {DP,G,F,E,D,C,B,A} = 8'b11001111; // Make 1 with LEDs
      if(Digit == 4'b0010) {DP,G,F,E,D,C,B,A} = 8'b10100100; // Make 2 with LEDs
      if(Digit == 4'b0011) {DP,G,F,E,D,C,B,A} = 8'b10110000; // Make 3 with LEDs
      if(Digit == 4'b0100) {DP,G,F,E,D,C,B,A} = 8'b10011001; // Make 4 with LEDs
      if(Digit == 4'b0101) {DP,G,F,E,D,C,B,A} = 8'b10010010; // Make 5 with LEDs
      if(Digit == 4'b0110) {DP,G,F,E,D,C,B,A} = 8'b10000010; // Make 6 with LEDs
      if(Digit == 4'b0111) {DP,G,F,E,D,C,B,A} = 8'b11111000; // Make 7 with LEDs
      if(Digit == 4'b1000) {DP,G,F,E,D,C,B,A} = 8'b10000000; // Make 8 with LEDs
      if(Digit == 4'b1001) {DP,G,F,E,D,C,B,A} = 8'b10011000; // Make 9 with LEDs
      if(Digit == 4'b1010) {DP,G,F,E,D,C,B,A} = 8'b10001000; // Make A with LEDs
      if(Digit == 4'b1011) {DP,G,F,E,D,C,B,A} = 8'b10000011; // Make b with LEDs
      if(Digit == 4'b1100) {DP,G,F,E,D,C,B,A} = 8'b11000110; // Make C with LEDs
```

```
        if(Digit == 4'b1101) {DP,G,F,E,D,C,B,A} = 8'b10100001; // Make d with LEDs
        if(Digit == 4'b1110) {DP,G,F,E,D,C,B,A} = 8'b10000110; // Make E with LEDs
        if(Digit == 4'b1111) {DP,G,F,E,D,C,B,A} = 8'b10001110; // Make F with LEDs
    end

always@(posedge Clk_Multi) begin
    Location <= Location + 1;
    case(Location)
        0:  begin
                Enable <= 8'b11111110;
                Digit <= 5;
            end
        1:  begin
                Enable <= 8'b11111101;
                Digit <= SW + 1;
            end
        2:  begin
                Enable <= 8'b11111011;
                Digit <= 7;
            end
        3:  begin
                Enable <= 8'b11110111;
                Digit <= SW;
            end
        4:  begin
                Enable <= 8'b11101111;
                Digit <= 15;
            end
        5:  begin
                Enable <= 8'b11011111;
                Digit <= 5;
            end
        6:  begin
                Enable <= 8'b10111111;
                Digit <= 7;
            end
        7:  begin
                Enable <= 8'b01111111;
                Digit <= 2;
                Location <= 0;
            end
    endcase
end
endmodule

module CLK100MHZ_divider(CLK100MHZ, New_Clock);
```

```
73      input wire CLK100MHZ;       // Input clock signal
74      output reg New_Clock;       // Divided clock output
75
76      reg [31:0] count = 0; // [31:0] is large enough to hold any value
77
78      always @(posedge CLK100MHZ) begin
79         count <= count + 1;   // Increment count
80         if (count == 31'd10000) begin
81            New_Clock <= ~New_Clock; // Toggle New Clock
82            count <= 31'b0;       // Reset count
83         end
84      end
85   endmodule
```

In the code, lines 1-8 declare the module and registers. Lines 10-11 create a multiplexer clock by instantiating the clock divider module on lines 72-85. It's important to note that on line 80, the count was set to 10,000 to create a clock of a specific frequency. If the frequency is too slow, we would visibly see only one seven-segment at a time. If the frequency is too fast, then the seven-segment would not even have time to turn on, resulting in nothing showing in the display. By setting the count to 10000, we obtain a frequency that is fast enough to trick our eyes into seeing multiple digits at once but also slow enough to give the LEDs time to turn on. Lines 13-30 create the combinational circuit to convert a 4-bit input into an appropriate {DP,G,F,E,D,C,B,A} array. You should already understand how lines 13-30 work since you were instructed to create these 16 lines yourself in the previous lab.

The sequential block that does the multiplexing is on lines 32-69. In this always block, there are 8 cases for each display. In each case, only one display is enabled at a time. For example, in case 0, when location is 0, only the rightmost display is enabled. Again, in case 1, when location is 1, only the second rightmost display is enabled. In each case the desired digit to be shown is also present. For example, in case 0, the digit 5 will be shown in the enabled display. In case 1, the digit coming in from the switch + 1 will be shown in the enabled display. Line 33 always causes the block to increment each case with each clock edge. In the final case, the location register is set to 0, thereby returning to case 0 to resume the process.

6.3 Final Remarks & Tips

It is important to know that although the multiplexing code shown had specific values for the digit and enable array, both values can be modified to accommodate almost any program requiring a value to be displayed using the seven-segments. Form example, suppose we want to have the leftmost seven-segment off. We would simply manipulate line 64 to have the enable array to be 11111111 instead of 01111111. Again, for example, if we wanted to display the number 7 in the rightmost display instead of 5, we would change line 37 accordingly. Due to the general flexibility of this code, you may want to use it as a template for your sixth lab. Remember that in the lab description, only certain segments were supposed to be enabled. You will need to have some cases assign 11111111 to the enable array to achieve this effect. For the digits, you will need to assign the switch input to the digit in the correct cases. Remember that in your lab, you will have an 8-bit switch array. To display the 8-bit hex number, you will need to have one case that handles the lower 4 bits and another to handle the upper 4 bits. Another extremely important tip is to use the bitwise inversion operator "~". Using this operator will allow you to easily assign the inversion of a 4-bit switch input to the digit register.

In summary, if you choose to use the example code as a template, you will need to modify 4 lines to assign 11111111 to the enable array in cases where the displays should be off. There will be 2 lines modified to assign the 8-bit hex value to two seven segments. There will be two lines modified to assign the inverted 8-bit hex value to two seven segments. Lastly, the line declaring the switch as an input will need to be modified to accommodate an 8-bit input rather than a 4-bit input. In total, you can complete the lab by modifying just 9 lines! Not even making a single new line. This code is so flexible and general that even the previous lab could easily be done using this template too. To implement the previous lab using the multiplexing code, a slower clock would be used in the sequential always block, in each case, the digits would all be assigned to the switch, and the enable array would be unchanged in all cases. The QR code below contains the source and constraint file for the example code. It is highly recommended that you upload it to your board to see the discussed code in action. Once you have done that, then you can begin modifying it to achieve the desired behavior mentioned in the lab description.

Practical Lesson 2 – Test Bench

In this lesson, you will learn how to simulate code using a test bench. Simulation is extremely important since you can verify code instantly without uploading anything to your board. This means that when testing code, you no longer must wait a for the bitstream to generate each time you want to verify functionality. For large programs where the bitstream generation might take 30 minutes or longer, simulation is extremely important. Simulation can also help you visualize what is happening at a level that would not have been possible otherwise. It is also important to note that although simulation is a great tool, there are times where simulation will not accurately predict code functionality. In other words, simulation may tell you that your code works, but when you upload it to your board, you find that it doesn't work. From my experience, there is only around a 5% chance of this happening, but it is still an important fact to know. This chapter will go through the process of writing a test bench for two programs from past sections.

PL2.1 General Steps

Before we begin, it is important to highlight all the steps involved in making a test bench. The steps will be the same for every source file, no matter what the source file is for.

Testbench Creation Steps
1) Make sure that all registers are initialized in the module to be simulated.
2) Declare a register for each input and a wire for each output of the original module. Make sure to use the same name as the original module.
3) Instantiate the module using the dot notation. If you did step 1 correctly, then all you need to do is copy the name of each input or output twice in each line of the instantiation sensitivity list. One time outside the parenesis, to the right of the dot, and once in the parenthesis.
4) Make an initial begin block setting all inputs to zero. If there are any clocks, then make an always statement.
5) Make an initial begin statement modifying the inputs to test the module.

PL2.2 State Machine Simulation

The first program that will be simulated is a state machine from lesson 2. It is important to note that the procedure for making a test bench is identical for all source files regardless of the source file functionality. This means that making a test bench for a source file in this section will have an identical procedure for any other source file. In other words, pay attention here because if you understand how to make a test bench for this program, you can do it for any other program too. The source file that follows is what we will simulate. The source file is for a state machine that detects a sequence and has an output of z = 1 with every third 1 received through the input.

State Machine

```
1   module Circuit0 (I0,Z,Clock);
2      input wire I0, Clock;
3      output reg Z;
4
5      reg [1:0] State;
6
7      ////// Step 1 initialize all the registers //////
8      initial begin
9         Z = 0;
10        State = 0;
11     end
12     ////////////////////////////////////////////////////////////
13
14     always@(*) begin
15        if(State == 0) Z = 0;
16        if(State == 1) Z = 0;
17        if(State == 2) Z = 0;
18        if(State == 3) Z = 1;
19     end
20
21     always @(posedge Clock) begin
22        case(State)
23        0  :  begin
24           if(I0 == 0) State <= 0;
25           if(I0 == 1) State <= 1;
26        end
27        1  :  begin
28           if(I0 == 0) State <= 0;
29           if(I0 == 1) State <= 2;
30        end
31        2  :  begin
32           if(I0 == 0) State <= 0;
33           if(I0 == 1) State <= 3;
34        end
35        3  :  begin
36           if(I0 == 0) State <= 0;
37           if(I0 == 1) State <= 1;
38        end
39       endcase
40     end
41  endmodule
```

The first step has already been done in lines 8-11 of the source file. If the source file doesn't have all its register contents initialized, then the simulation will fail.

The second step is to look at the inputs and outputs of the module to be simulated and declare a register for each input and a wire for each output. It is important to use the same names as the original module. In our source file, lines 2-3 show the inputs and outputs. Starting test bench by making registers and wires based off the inputs and outputs of lines 2-3 yields the code below.

Testbench Step 2

```
`timescale 1ns / 1ps

module TestBench;
// Inputs
   reg I0;
   reg Clock;

// Outputs
   wire Z;

endmodule
```

Now that this has been done, the next step is to instantiate the module to be simulated. When instantiation was done in the past, the order of the inputs and outputs in the instantiation sensitivity list mattered. This past method will still work; however, a better way is through using the dot notation. The dot notation makes the order irrelevant. The code below shows the instantiation being done through the dot notation.

Testbench Step 3

```
1  `timescale 1ns / 1ps
2  
3  module TestBench;
4     // Inputs
5     reg I0;
6     reg Clock;
7  
8     // Outputs
9     wire Z;
10 
11    Circuit0 IN0(
12    .I0(I0),
13    .Z(Z),
14    .Clock(Clock)
15    );
16 
17 endmodule
```

For each line in the instantiation sensitivity list, lines 12-14, know that the name outside of the parenthesis is the name of the actual variable in the sensitivity list of the original module. The name inside the parenthesis is the name of the wire or register the testbench is using to monitor that variable. Although the name inside the parenthesis technically could be anything, it is best to make it the same as the name in the original module, as done in the code above. If you do step 1 right, then you won't ever need to worry about that, since the name of both will be the same for each line, as done in the code shown for step 3.

The next step is to set all inputs to zero and generate a clock with an always statement. The code below shows this being done in lines 17-22. In line 22, the #5 indicates that every 5 ns the clock will toggle. This is a great delay time, since it will simulate a clock that is identical to the 100M Hz clock.

Testbench Step 4

```
1  `timescale 1ns / 1ps
2
3  module TestBench;
4     // Inputs
5     reg I0;
6     reg Clock;
7
8     // Outputs
9     wire Z;
10
11    Circuit0 IN0(
12    .I0(I0),
13    .Z(Z),
14    .Clock(Clock)
15    );
16
17    initial begin
18       I0 = 0;
19       Clock = 0;
20    end
21
22    always #5 Clock = !Clock;
23
24 endmodule
```

The final step is to create an initial begin statement that manually sets the value of the input to values that we want. The code that follows is final and shows this step completed in lines 25-34. It is important to note that a delay of 10ns was chosen so that each bit of input data occupies one clock period, leading to a stable read on the rising edge. Choosing a smaller delay, such as a 5ns delay would occasionally result in the input, I0, changing during the rising edge of the clock, which is not ideal.

Testbench Step 5

```
`timescale 1ns / 1ps

module TestBench;
   // Inputs
   reg I0;
   reg Clock;

   // Outputs
   wire Z;

   Circuit0 IN0(
   .I0(I0),
   .Z(Z),
   .Clock(Clock)
   );

   // Clock generation
   initial begin
      I0 = 0;
      Clock = 0;
   end

   always #5 Clock = !Clock;

   initial begin
      #10 I0 = 0;
      #10 I0 = 1;
      #10 I0 = 0;
      #10 I0 = 1;
      #10 I0 = 1;
      #10 I0 = 1;
      #10 I0 = 0;
      #10 I0 = 1;
   end
endmodule
```

Running the simulation using the testbench step 5 code will yield the following waveform. If you are unsure how to run a testbench once you have written the file for it, refer to Lab 1.

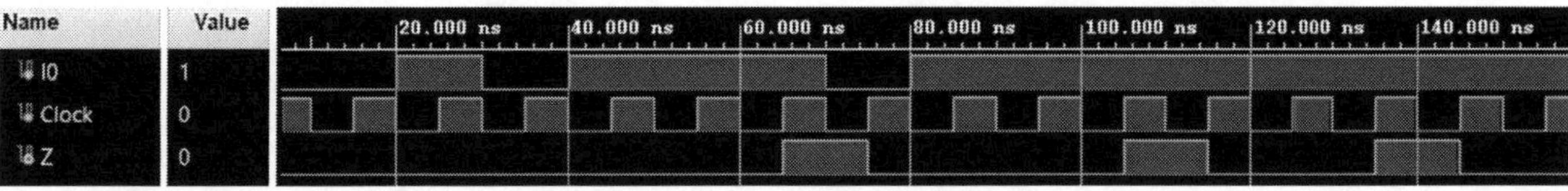

Figure PL2.2.1 Testbench Waveform

PL2.3 Internal Signals

Now although the waveform in the previous figure does a great job showing the behavior of the inputs and outputs, it doesn't show the internal register that holds the state. Fortunately, internal signals can be easily monitored through declaring a wire of the following format.

Internal Signal Monitoring

```
wire [bit-length] (Name) = (Module Name).(Internal Register Name)

or

wire [bit-length] (Name) = (Module Name).(Instantiation Name).(Internal Register Name)
```

Using the top format, we can add the following line in our step 5 testbench code. As shown below in line 10. We use the top format since we are not viewing an internal signal that was from an instantiated submodule. More on this will be discussed later.

```
1   `timescale 1ns / 1ps
2
3   module TestBench;
4      // Inputs
5      reg I0;
6      reg Clock;
7
8      // Outputs
9      wire Z;
10     wire [1:0] State = Circuit0.State;
11
...    ...
```

Running the simulation with this line added will result in the following waveform. From the waveform in Figure PL2.3.1, it is apparent that the state machine is fully functional, since each time a one or zero is received, it goes to the correct state. The state diagram will be provided again in Figure PL2.3.2 for your convenience. Make sure to look at the state diagram and waveform to see for yourself that the simulation is indeed correctly showing the behavior of the state machine.

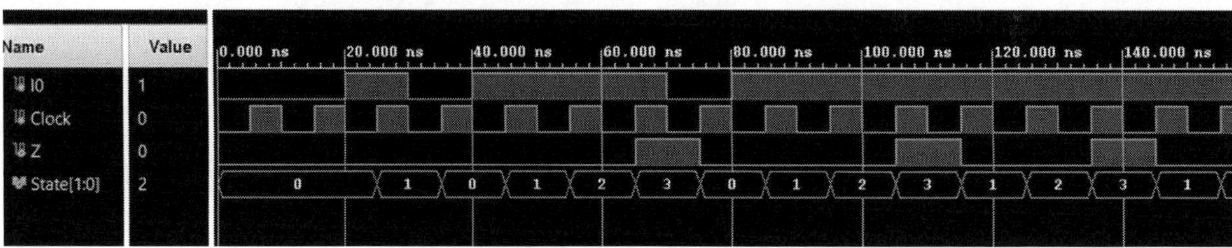

Figure PL2.3.1 Testbench Waveform

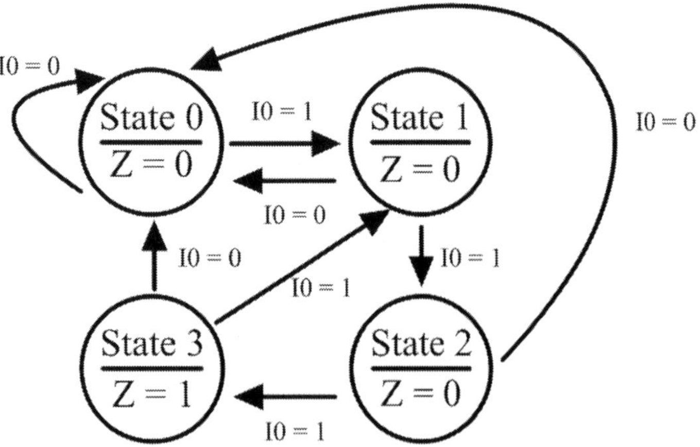

Figure PL2.3.2 State Machine Diagram

PL2.4 Counter Simulation

The second example that will be discussed is the simulation of the counter made in section 3.2 of Lab 3. The source file is provided again here for your convenience. Note that the source file here has been modified to have an initial-begin block in each module that has registers. Also, in line 111, the clock divider module has been modified to have a count of 5 instead of 49999999. For the program to generate correctly, 49999999 should be used, but to make simulation more convenient, we changed it to 5. The reason why it's more convenient to have the clock divided less during simulation is because then we get to see the result faster. If we divided it with 49999999, then we would need to simulate enough time to cover 49999999 clock edges before seeing a change. Although the simulation is fast, that will take a few minutes, which is why changing it to 5 is better.

3-bit Counter Code

```
1   `timescale 1ns / 1ps
2
3   module Counter(Sel,Sel_Val,Load,Clock,New_Clock,Sum);
4      input Clock;
5      input [1:0] Sel;
6      input [2:0] Load;
7      output [2:0] Sum;
8
9      output wire [1:0] Sel_Val;
10     output wire New_Clock;
11
12     assign Sel_Val = Sel;
13
14     wire [2:0] Load,Up,Down,W;
15
16     DFF IN0(W[0],Sum[0],New_Clock);
17     DFF IN1(W[1],Sum[1],New_Clock);
18     DFF IN2(W[2],Sum[2],New_Clock);
```

```

    MUX4TO1 IN00(1'b0,Load[0],Up[0],Down[0],Sel,W[0]);
    MUX4TO1 IN01(1'b0,Load[1],Up[1],Down[1],Sel,W[1]);
    MUX4TO1 IN02(1'b0,Load[2],Up[2],Down[2],Sel,W[2]);

    Adder_AND_Subtractor IN000(Sum,Up,Down);

    CLK100MHZ_divider IN001(Clock,New_Clock);
endmodule

module MUX4TO1(I0,I1,I2,I3,Sel,Out);
   input I0,I1,I2,I3;
   input [1:0] Sel;
   output reg Out;

   initial begin
      Out = 0;
   end

   always @(*) begin
      if(Sel == 2'b00) Out = I0;
      if(Sel == 2'b01) Out = I1;
      if(Sel == 2'b10) Out = I2;
      if(Sel == 2'b11) Out = I3;
   end
endmodule

module DFF(D,Q,Clock);
    input wire D, Clock;
    output reg Q;

    initial begin
      Q = 0;
    end

    always @(posedge Clock) begin
       Q <= D;
    end
endmodule

module Adder_AND_Subtractor(Sum,Up,Down);
    input [2:0] Sum;
    output wire [2:0] Up,Down;

    ThreeBitAdder IN0 (Sum,3'b001,Up);       // Add 1 to Sum[2:0]
    ThreeBitAdder IN1 (Sum,3'b111,Down);  // Add -1 to Sum[2:0]
```

```
endmodule

module ThreeBitAdder(A,B,Sum);
  input [2:0] A,B;
  output wire [2:0] Sum;
  wire [2:0] W; // This line defines the internal signals

  FullAdder I0(A[0],B[0],0,Sum[0],W[0]);       // First Instantiation
  FullAdder I1(A[1],B[1],W[0],Sum[1],W[1]); // Second Instantiation
  FullAdder I2(A[2],B[2],W[1],Sum[2],W[2]); // Third Instantiation
endmodule

module FullAdder(A,B,Cin,Sum,Cout);
  input A,B,Cin;
  output reg Sum,Cout;

  initial begin
    Sum = 0;
    Cout = 0;
  end

  // Combinational logic to implement Full Adder truth table
  always @(*) begin
    if({A,B,Cin} == 3'b000) {Cout, Sum} = 2'b00;
    if({A,B,Cin} == 3'b001) {Cout, Sum} = 2'b01;
    if({A,B,Cin} == 3'b010) {Cout, Sum} = 2'b01;
    if({A,B,Cin} == 3'b011) {Cout, Sum} = 2'b10;
    if({A,B,Cin} == 3'b100) {Cout, Sum} = 2'b01;
    if({A,B,Cin} == 3'b101) {Cout, Sum} = 2'b10;
    if({A,B,Cin} == 3'b110) {Cout, Sum} = 2'b10;
    if({A,B,Cin} == 3'b111) {Cout, Sum} = 2'b11;
  end
endmodule

module CLK100MHZ_divider(CLK100MHZ, New_Clock);
  input wire CLK100MHZ;     // Input clock signal
  output reg New_Clock;     // Divided clock output

  initial begin
    New_Clock = 0;
  end

  reg [31:0] count = 0; // large enough register to hold 49999999

  always @(posedge CLK100MHZ) begin
    count <= count + 1;  // Increment count
```

```
        if (count == 31'd5) begin // Should be 49999999
          New_Clock <= ~New_Clock; // Toggle New Clock
          count <= 31'b0;       // Reset count
        end
      end
endmodule
```

The test bench below shows steps 2-5 completed for the counter source file. Step 2 is completed with lines 1-11. Step 3 is completed though lines 14-19. Notice how in step 3, the names of the inputs and outputs made in step 2 are mentioned twice. One time outside the parenthesis and one time inside the parenthesis for each input or output name. Lines 21-28 complete step 4 by initializing the inputs to zero and making a clock using an always statement. Lastly, lines 31-42 set the values of the input to test the behavior of the circuit.

3-bit Counter Test Bench

```
1   `timescale 1ns / 1ps
2
3   module Counter_tb;
4
5     // Inputs
6     reg Clock;
7     reg [1:0] Sel;
8     reg [2:0] Load;
9
10    // Outputs
11    wire [2:0] Sum;
12
13    // Instantiate the Unit Under Test (UUT)
14    Counter uut (
15      .Sel(Sel),
16      .Load(Load),
17      .Clock(Clock),
18      .Sum(Sum)
19    );
20
21    initial begin
22      Clock = 0;
23      Sel = 0;
24      Load  = 0;
25    end
26
27    // Clock generation
28    always #10 Clock = ~Clock; // Toggle clock every 10ns
29
30    // Initial setup and input stimulus
```

```
    initial begin
        #1000;
        Sel = 2'b10; // Count up at t = 1000ns
        #1000;
        Load = 3'b111;
        Sel = 2'b01; // Load in 7 to sum
        #1000;
        Sel = 2'b11; // Count down at t = 2000ns
        #1000;
        Sel = 2'b00; // Clear to sum to 0
        $finish;
    end

endmodule
```

When the simulation is done using the testbench file, the waveform below is generated. From the simulation, it is apparent that the module is completely functional since, it counts up, then loads in a value, then counts down, and then finally sets the output to zero, just as it was supposed to.

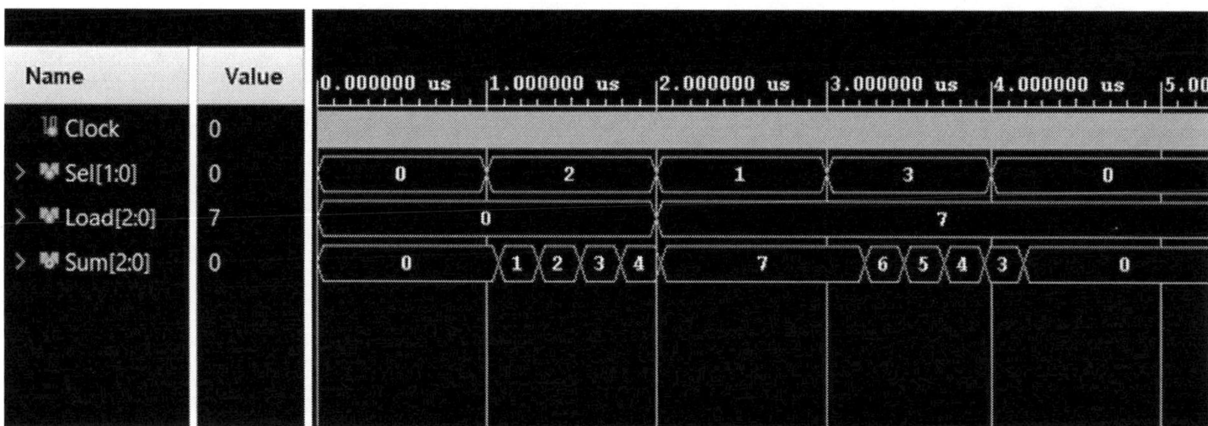

Figure PL2.4.1 Testbench Waveform

The QR code below will take you to a folder where you can access both the source file and test bench file. If you wish, you may copy it into your IDE to see it in action.

Lab 7 – State Machine from Equations Vs ROM

In this lab, you will learn how to build a state machine by extracting equations from an SM chart. In addition to this, you will also do it using a ROM. To give you sufficient preparation, a complete example of each will be discussed.

7.1 Lab Description

For your lab, you will need to write a Verilog module to implement the state machine below. First, you will need to obtain the equations from the chart directly, instantiate two flip-flops, one for Q0, one for Q1, and make a module based on the equations. After you have gotten the program working with equations, you will need to redo it again with a ROM. To implement the state machine with a ROM, you will need to use its state transition table, which is provided in Figure 7.1.2 of the next page.

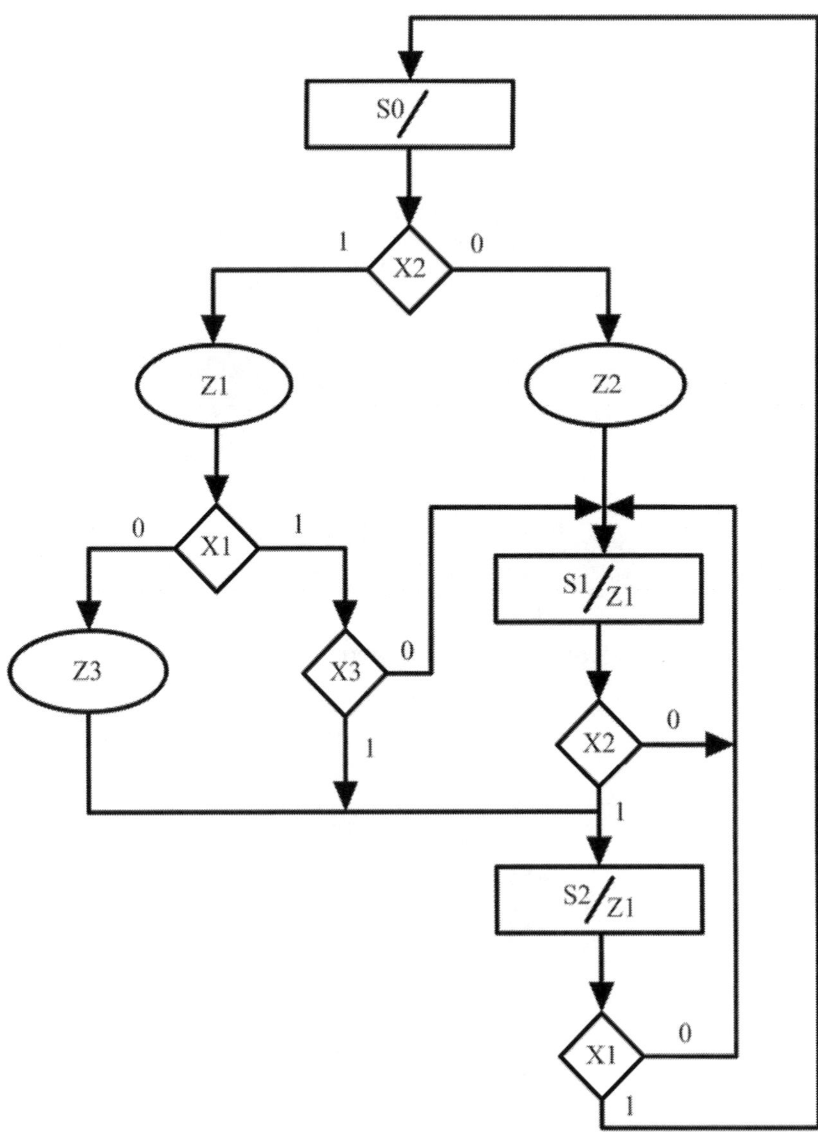

Figure 7.1.1 State Chart

Normally, the state table would be in one piece, however, to make it fit on the page it was broken up into two pieces. The half on the top handles the first four possible input cases and the bottom half handles the last four possible input cases. Although not required, I would recommend comparing the state chart from Figure 7.1.1 with the state table from Figure 7.1.2 to understand how they correlate.

Present State	Next State & Output			
	X3X2X1 = 000	X3X2X1 = 001	X3X2X1 = 010	X3X2X1 = 011
S0 = 00	**Box 0** S1 = 01 Z3Z2Z1 = 010	**Box 1** S1 = 01 Z3Z2Z1 = 010	**Box 2** S2 = 10 Z3Z2Z1 = 101	**Box 3** S1 = 01 Z3Z2Z1 = 001
S1 = 01	**Box 8** S1 = 01 Z3Z2Z1 = 001	**Box 9** S1 = 01 Z3Z2Z1 = 001	**Box 10** S2 = 10 Z3Z2Z1 = 001	**Box 11** S2 = 10 Z3Z2Z1 = 001
S2 = 10	**Box 16** S1 = 01 Z3Z2Z1 = 001	**Box 17** S0 = 00 Z3Z2Z1 = 001	**Box 18** S1 = 00 Z3Z2Z1 = 001	**Box 19** S0 = 00 Z3Z2Z1 = 001
S3 = 11	**Box 24** X	**Box 25** X	**Box 26** X	**Box 27** X

Present State	Next State & Output			
	X3X2X1 = 100	X3X2X1 = 101	X3X2X1 = 110	X3X2X1 = 111
S0 = 00	**Box 4** S1 = 01 Z3Z2Z1 = 010	**Box 5** S1 = 01 Z3Z2Z1 = 010	**Box 6** S2 = 10 Z3Z2Z1 = 101	**Box 7** S2 = 10 Z3Z2Z1 = 001
S1 = 01	**Box 12** S1 = 01 Z3Z2Z1 = 001	**Box 13** S1 = 01 Z3Z2Z1 = 001	**Box 14** S2 = 10 Z3Z2Z1 = 001	**Box 15** S2 = 10 Z3Z2Z1 = 001
S2 = 10	**Box 20** S1 = 01 Z3Z2Z1 = 001	**Box 21** S0 = 00 Z3Z2Z1 = 001	**Box 22** S1 = 01 Z3Z2Z1 = 001	**Box 23** S0 = 00 Z3Z2Z1 = 001
S3 = 11	**Box 28** X	**Box 29** X	**Box 30** X	**Box 31** X

Figure 7.1.2 State Table

7.2 Example of Equation Implementation

This section will demonstrate how to implement the state chart below with equations. It is important to pay attention since if you fully understand this section, then you should have no problem replicating the process for the one in the lab description. In section 3.8 of the logic design section, you learned how to convert an SM chart into equations and in section L1.3 of the digital design section, you learned how to make a Verilog module from equations. This section will make use of the lessons from both of those past sections, so if you want a refresher on all the steps that will follow, refer to those sections.

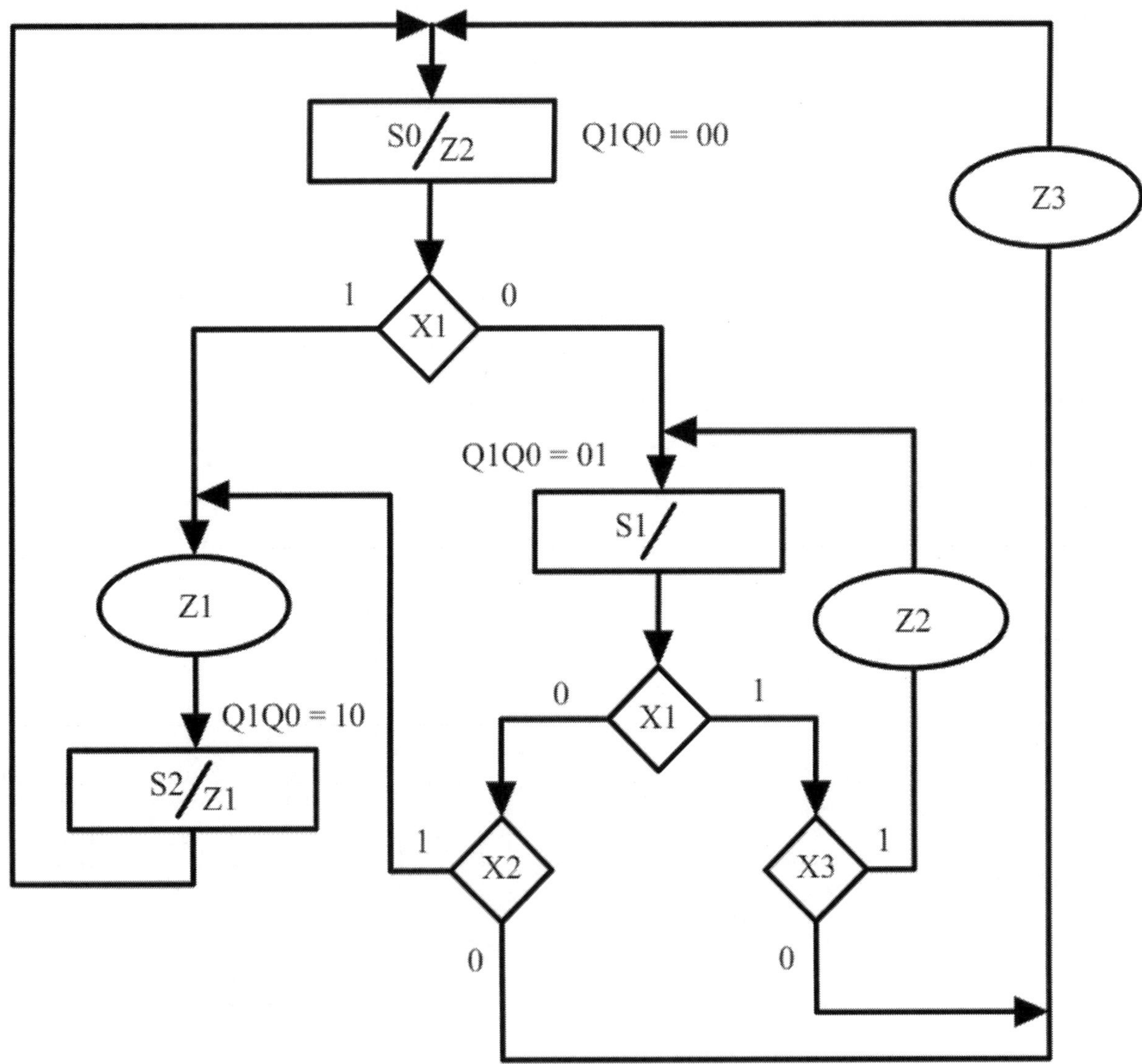

Figure 7.2.1 State Chart

In Figure 7.2.1, near each state box is the value of each state written in terms of Q1 and Q0. Remember that Q1 holds bit 1 and Q0 holds bit 0. For example, in state 0, Q1Q0 = 00. In state 1, Q1Q0 = 01. In state 2, Q1Q0 = 10. Writing each state in terms of Qn is always the first step. The second step is to identify all the relevant paths as shown in the figure below.

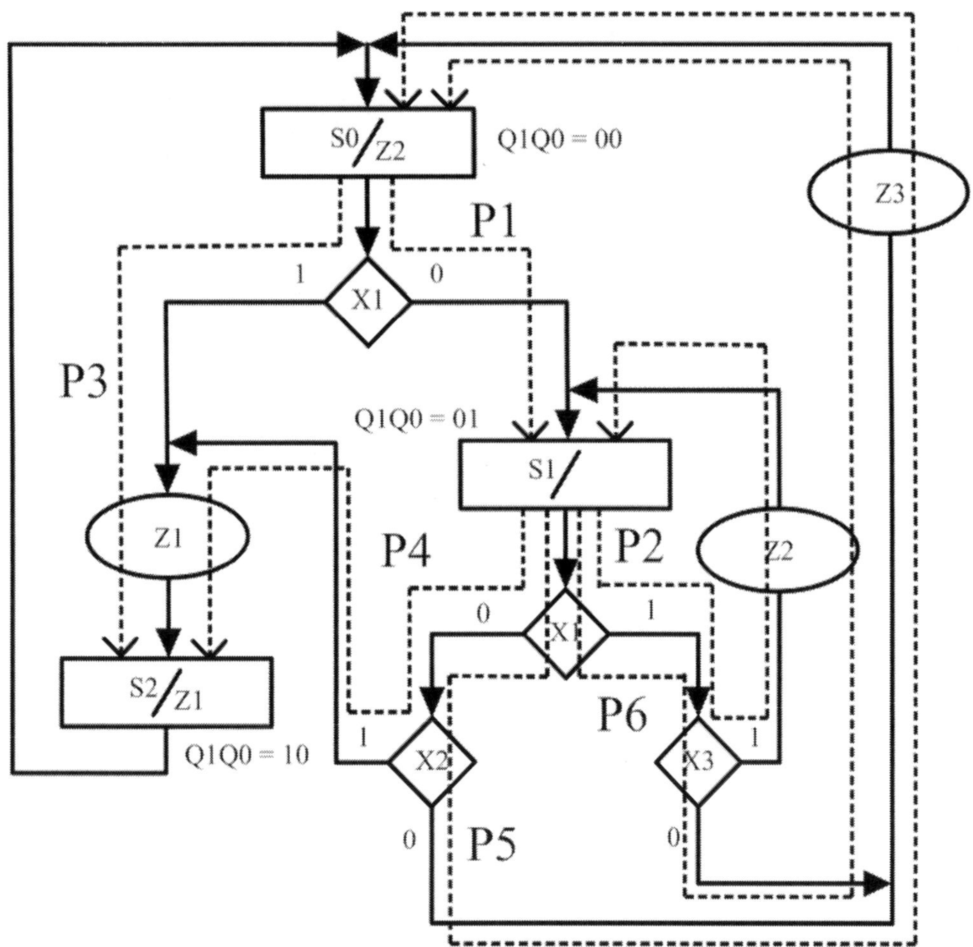

Figure 7.2.2 State Chart with Paths Identified

Since all the paths have been identified, all that remains is to generate the terms for each path and then generate the equations using the terms.

Finding the term for P1

Since P1 starts at state 0 where Q1Q0 = 00 and goes through X1 = 0, the terms concatenated have a binary value of Q1Q0X1 = 000. Copying the final term based of the binary value results in the final term for P1 being Q1'Q0'X1'.

Finding the term for P2

Since P2 starts at state 1 where Q1Q0 = 01 and goes through X1X3 = 11, the terms concatenated have a binary value of Q1Q0X1X3 = 0111. Copying the final term based of the binary value results in the final term for P2 being Q1'Q0X1X3.

Finding the term for P3

Since P3 starts at state 0 where Q1Q0 = 00 and goes through X1 = 1, the terms concatenated have a binary value of Q1Q0X1 = 001. Copying the final term based of the binary value results in the final term for P3 being Q1'Q0'X1.

Finding the term for P4

Since P4 starts at state 1 where Q1Q0 = 01 and goes through X1X2 = 01, the terms concatenated have a binary value of Q1Q0X1X2 = 0101. Copying the final term based of the binary value results in the final term for P2 being Q1'Q0X1'X2.

Finding the term for P5

Since P5 starts at state 1 where Q1Q0 = 01 and goes through X1X2 = 00, the terms concatenated have a binary value of Q1Q0X1X2 = 0100. Copying the final term based of the binary value results in the final term for P2 being Q1'Q0X1'X2'.

Finding the term for P6

Since P6 starts at state 1 where Q1Q0 = 01 and goes through X1X3 = 10, the terms concatenated have a binary value of Q1Q0X1X3 = 0110. Copying the final term based of the binary value results in the final term for P6 being Q1'Q0X1X3'.

Summary of P1-P6 terms

P1 = Q1'Q0'X1'

P2 = Q1'Q0X1X3

P3 = Q1'Q0'X1

P4 = Q1'Q0X1'X2

P5 = Q1'Q0X1'X2'

P6 = Q1'Q0X1X3'

Finding Q1+ and Q0+ Equations

To find the expression for Q0+, we need to first identify which states have Q0 = 1. Only state 1 has Q0 = 1, so only the terms for paths going into state 1 will be included, i.e. for P1 and P2. Logically OR-ing these terms together yields the following expression for Q0+.

Q0+ = Q1'Q0'X1' + Q1'Q0X1X3

To find the expression for Q1+, we need to first identify which states have Q1 = 1. Only state 2 has Q1 = 1, so only the terms for paths going into state 2 will be included, i.e. for P3 and P4. Logically OR-ing these terms together yields the following expression for Q1+.

Q1+ = Q1'Q0'X1 + Q1'Q0X1'X2

Finding Z1, Z2 and Z3 Equations

Looking at state 2, the Moore term for Z1 is Q1Q0'. The Mealy output for Z1 occurs during paths P3 and P4. Logically OR-ing together the terms for these paths with the Moore term yields the following expression for Z1.

$$Z1 = Q1'Q0'X1 + Q1'Q0X1'X2 + Q1Q0'$$

Looking at state 0, the Moore term for Z2 is Q1'Q0'. The Mealy output for Z2 occurs during path P2. Logically OR-ing together the term for P2 with the Moore term yields the following expression for Z2.

$$Z2 = Q1'Q0X1X3 + Q1'Q0'$$

For Z3, there are no Moore outputs. The Mealy outputs occur during paths P5 and P6. Logically OR-ing together the term for these paths yields the following expression for Z3.

$$Z3 = Q1'Q0X1'X2' + Q1'Q0X1X3'$$

Now that all the equations have been generated, the next step is to write a module in Verilog to implement the state machine. Since there are two bits used to hold the state, a D flip-flop will need to be made for Q1 and for Q0. Then a combinational network will be made to implement all the equations we came up with. The block diagram below shows it all.

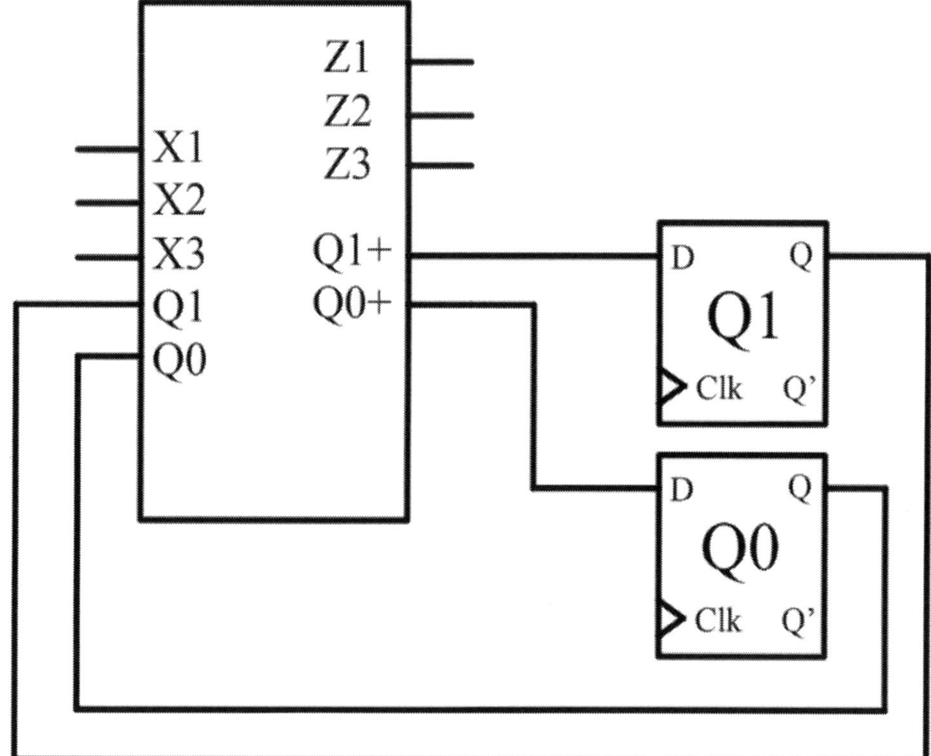

Figure 7.2.3 State Machine Block Diagram

Fortunately, the procedure to implement the state machine as shown in Figure 7.2.3 is extremely simple after having already obtained the equations. The code below shows the Verilog implementation of the SM chart from Figure 7.2.1. To begin, there are four modules used to implement the state machine. There is a module for the combinational network on lines 16-26. There is a module for a D flip-flop on lines 28-34. There is also a module used to create a button clock on lines 36-66. Lastly, there is a top-level module instantiating the supporting modules during lines 3-14. Every one of these modules was made using methodology from previous chapters. The top-level module was created using the methods covered in Lab 2. The combinational network module was created using the methods discussed in Lesson 1. The D flip-flop was made using an always block, so Lesson 2 can explain how that works. Lastly, the button clock module was made using methodology discussed in Lesson 2 and Practical Lesson 1. Refer to any of these chapters for additional clarity. The source and constraint files can be downloaded from the link embedded in the QR code that follows.

Final State Machine Code with Equations

```
1   `timescale 1ns / 1ps
2
3   module Top(X1,X2,X3,Z1,Z2,Z3,Clock,Button,Button_Clock,Q1,Q0);
4      input X1,X2,X3,Clock,Button;
5      output wire Z1,Z2,Z3,Button_Clock,Q1,Q0;
6
7      wire Q1P,Q0P;
8
9      Combinational_Network IN0(X1,X2,X3,Q1,Q0,Z1,Z2,Z3,Q1P,Q0P);
10     DFF IN1(Q1P,Q1,Button_Clock);
11     DFF IN2(Q0P,Q0,Button_Clock);
12
13     Button_Clock IN3(Clock,Button,Button_Clock);
14  endmodule
15
16  module Combinational_Network(X1,X2,X3,Q1,Q0,Z1,Z2,Z3,Q1P,Q0P);
17     input X1,X2,X3,Q1,Q0;
18     output Z1,Z2,Z3,Q1P,Q0P;
19
20     assign Z1 = ~Q1&~Q0&X1 | ~Q1&Q0&~X1&X2 | Q1&~Q0;
21     assign Z2 = ~Q1&Q0&X1&X3 | ~Q1&~Q0;
22     assign Z3 = ~Q1&Q0&~X1&~X2 | ~Q1&Q0&X1&~X3;
23
24     assign Q1P = ~Q1&~Q0&X1 | ~Q1&Q0&~X1&X2;
25     assign Q0P = ~Q1&~Q0&~X1 | ~Q1&Q0&X1&X3;
26  endmodule
27
28  module DFF(D,Q,Clock);
29      input wire D, Clock;
30      output reg Q;
```

```

    always @(posedge Clock) begin
        Q <= D;
    end
endmodule

module Button_Clock(Clock,Button,Button_Clock);
   input Clock,Button;
   output reg Button_Clock;

   reg flag1 = 0;
   reg flag2 = 0;
   reg [31:0] Count = 0;
   reg [1:0] Reg0 = 0;

   always @(posedge Clock) begin
      if(flag1 || flag2) Count <= Count + 1;
      if(Count == 31'd5000000) begin // Delay for 20th of a second
         flag1 <= 0;
         flag2 <= 0;
         Count <= 0;
      end

      if(Reg0[0] == 0 && Button == 1 && flag2 == 0) flag1 <= 1;
      if(Reg0[0] == 1 && Button == 0 && flag1 == 0) flag2 <= 1;

      if(flag1 == 0 && flag2 == 0) begin // Read when flags are zero
         Reg0[0] <= Button;
         Reg0[1] <= Reg0[0];
      end

      // Execute code when flag2 turns to 1
      if(Reg0[0] == 1 && Button == 0 && flag1 == 0) begin
         Button_Clock <= !Button_Clock;
     end
   end
endmodule
```

7.3 Example of ROM Implementation

The second part of your lab was to implement the state table from the lab description with a ROM. To give you preparation, this section will implement the state table below with a ROM. Note that the state table below corresponds to the same state machine expressed by the state chart from Figure 7.2.1. Note that each box has been labeled in bold.

Present State	Next State & Output			
	X3X2X1 = 000	X3X2X1 = 001	X3X2X1 = 010	X3X2X1 = 011
S0 = 00	**Box 0** S1 = 01 Z3Z2Z1 = 010	**Box 1** S2 = 10 Z3Z2Z1 = 011	**Box 2** S1 = 01 Z3Z2Z1 = 010	**Box 3** S2 = 10 Z3Z2Z1 = 011
S1 = 01	**Box 8** S0 = 00 Z3Z2Z1 = 100	**Box 9** S0 = 00 Z3Z2Z1 = 100	**Box 10** S2 = 10 Z3Z2Z1 = 001	**Box 11** S0 = 00 Z3Z2Z1 = 100
S2 = 10	**Box 16** S0 = 00 Z3Z2Z1 = 001	**Box 17** S0 = 00 Z3Z2Z1 = 001	**Box 18** S0 = 00 Z3Z2Z1 = 001	**Box 19** S0 = 00 Z3Z2Z1 = 001
S3 = 11	**Box 24** X	**Box 25** X	**Box 26** X	**Box 27** X

Present State	Next State & Output			
	X3X2X1 = 100	X3X2X1 = 101	X3X2X1 = 110	X3X2X1 = 111
S0 = 00	**Box 4** S1 = 01 Z3Z2Z1 = 010	**Box 5** S2 = 10 Z3Z2Z1 = 011	**Box 6** S1 = 01 Z3Z2Z1 = 010	**Box 7** S2 = 10 Z3Z2Z1 = 011
S1 = 01	**Box 12** S0 = 00 Z3Z2Z1 = 100	**Box 13** S1 = 01 Z3Z2Z1 = 010	**Box 14** S2 = 10 Z3Z2Z1 = 001	**Box 15** S1 = 01 Z3Z2Z1 = 010
S2 = 10	**Box 20** S0 = 00 Z3Z2Z1 = 001	**Box 21** S0 = 00 Z3Z2Z1 = 001	**Box 22** S0 = 00 Z3Z2Z1 = 001	**Box 23** S0 = 00 Z3Z2Z1 = 001
S3 = 11	**Box 28** X	**Box 29** X	**Box 30** X	**Box 31** X

Figure 7.3.1 State Table

Normally, the state table would be in one piece however to make it fit on the page, it was broken up into two pieces. The half on the top handles the first four possible input cases and the bottom half handles the last four possible input cases. I would recommend comparing the state chart from Figure 7.2.1 with the state table from Figure 7.3.1 to understand how they correlate.

Since we are going to make a state machine with a ROM, it is important to first start off by reviewing the physical structure of the circuit before writing any Verilog. The figure on the following page shows the physical structure of the circuit. From the figure, it should be apparent that the ROM is a combinational piece of hardware that has five inputs and five outputs. Three of the inputs to the ROM are the three inputs X1, X2, and X3. The other two inputs are the current state bits, Q0 and Q1. Three of the outputs are the outputs Z1, Z2, and Z3. The other two outputs are the next state bits, Q0+ and Q1+.

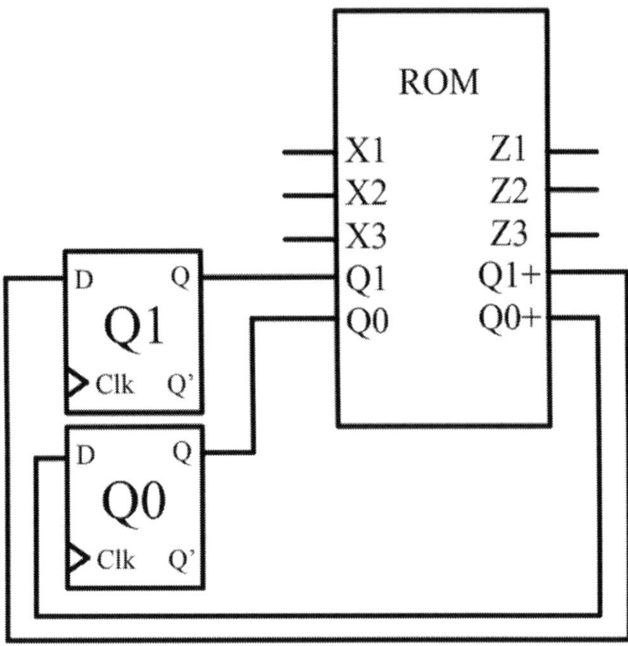

Figure 7.3.2 State Machine with ROM

Since the ROM is a combinational piece of hardware, it can be modeled with a truth table as shown below. The entire truth table was made by directly copying the values from the state table in Figure 7.3.1. For example, in the state table, when S0 = 00 and X3X2X1 = 000, the outputs are supposed to be S1 = 01 and Z3Z2Z1 = 010. From these outputs in box 0, we know to have {Q1+, Q0+, Z3, Z2, Z1} = {01010} in row 0 of the truth table as shown below. It's important to note that the row number corresponds to the box number. Look at the state table from Figure 7.3.1 and try to see how each situation was copied into the table below. It's important that you know how it was copied, since you will need to do it for your lab's state table.

Row	Q1	Q0	X3	X2	X1	Q1+	Q0+	Z3	Z2	Z1
0	0	0	0	0	0	0	1	0	1	0
1	0	0	0	0	1	1	0	0	1	1
2	0	0	0	1	0	0	1	0	1	0
3	0	0	0	1	1	1	0	0	1	1
4	0	0	1	0	0	0	1	0	1	0
5	0	0	1	0	1	1	0	0	1	1
6	0	0	1	1	0	0	1	0	1	0
7	0	0	1	1	1	1	0	0	1	1
8	0	1	0	0	0	0	0	1	0	0
9	0	1	0	0	1	0	0	1	0	0
10	0	1	0	1	0	1	0	0	0	1
11	0	1	0	1	1	0	0	1	0	0

12	0	1	1	0	0	0	0	1	0	0
13	0	1	1	0	1	0	1	0	1	0
14	0	1	1	1	0	1	0	0	0	1
15	0	1	1	1	1	0	1	0	1	0
16	1	0	0	0	0	0	0	0	0	1
17	1	0	0	0	1	0	0	0	0	1
18	1	0	0	1	0	0	0	0	0	1
19	1	0	0	1	1	0	0	0	0	1
20	1	0	1	0	0	0	0	0	0	1
21	1	0	1	0	1	0	0	0	0	1
22	1	0	1	1	0	0	0	0	0	1
23	1	0	1	1	1	0	0	0	0	1
24	1	1	0	0	0	X	X	X	X	X
25	1	1	0	0	1	X	X	X	X	X
26	1	1	0	1	0	X	X	X	X	X
27	1	1	0	1	1	X	X	X	X	X
28	1	1	1	0	0	X	X	X	X	X
29	1	1	1	0	1	X	X	X	X	X
30	1	1	1	1	0	X	X	X	X	X
31	1	1	1	1	1	X	X	X	X	X

Figure 7.3.3 ROM truth table

Using the ROM truth table, a source file can be written for it in Verilog. The code below shows the final implementation of the state machine using a ROM. It is important to note that the only difference from the previous solution with equations is that the combinational network module was replaced with a ROM module. There is absolutely no difference otherwise. This makes sense because a ROM technically is a combinational network after all.

The ROM module is very simple to understand. Lines 16-18 declare the module with the inputs and outputs. Line 20 creates a chain of 32 5-bit registers to store the ROM contents in. Lines 22-55 directly implement all 32 rows of the truth table. Note that the don't care rows were given a value of zero. It is recommended to look at the truth table and compare each row with each line of the initial begin block, so you can see how truly easy it was to implement the ROM from the truth table. And lastly, line 57 is used to assign an output to {Q1P, Q0P, Z3, Z2, Z1} based off the inputs {Q1, Q0, X3, X2, X1}.

Final State Machine Code with ROM

```
1  `timescale 1ns / 1ps
2  
3  module Top(X1,X2,X3,Z1,Z2,Z3,Clock,Button,Button_Clock,Q1,Q0);
4     input X1,X2,X3,Clock,Button;
5     output wire Z1,Z2,Z3,Button_Clock,Q1,Q0;
6  
7     wire Q1P,Q0P;
8  
```

```
    ROM IN0(X1,X2,X3,Q1,Q0,Z1,Z2,Z3,Q1P,Q0P);
    DFF IN1(Q1P,Q1,Button_Clock);
    DFF IN2(Q0P,Q0,Button_Clock);

    Button_Clock IN3(Clock,Button,Button_Clock);
endmodule

module ROM(X1,X2,X3,Q1,Q0,Z1,Z2,Z3,Q1P,Q0P);
    input X1,X2,X3,Q1,Q0;
    output Z1,Z2,Z3,Q1P,Q0P;

    reg [4:0] ROM [31:0]; // 32 5-bit values

    initial begin
        ROM[0] = 5'b01010;
        ROM[1] = 5'b10011;
        ROM[2] = 5'b01010;
        ROM[3] = 5'b10011;
        ROM[4] = 5'b01010;
        ROM[5] = 5'b10011;
        ROM[6] = 5'b01010;
        ROM[7] = 5'b10011;
        ROM[8] = 5'b00100;
        ROM[9] = 5'b00100;
        ROM[10] = 5'b10001;
        ROM[11] = 5'b00100;
        ROM[12] = 5'b00100;
        ROM[13] = 5'b01010;
        ROM[14] = 5'b10001;
        ROM[15] = 5'b01010;
        ROM[16] = 5'b00001;
        ROM[17] = 5'b00001;
        ROM[18] = 5'b00001;
        ROM[19] = 5'b00001;
        ROM[20] = 5'b00001;
        ROM[21] = 5'b00001;
        ROM[22] = 5'b00001;
        ROM[23] = 5'b00001;
        ROM[24] = 5'b00000;
        ROM[25] = 5'b00000;
        ROM[26] = 5'b00000;
        ROM[27] = 5'b00000;
        ROM[28] = 5'b00000;
        ROM[29] = 5'b00000;
        ROM[30] = 5'b00000;
        ROM[31] = 5'b00000;
```

```
    end

assign {Q1P,Q0P,Z3,Z2,Z1} = ROM [{Q1,Q0,X3,X2,X1}];

endmodule

module DFF(D,Q,Clock);
    input wire D, Clock;
    output reg Q;

    always @(posedge Clock) begin
        Q <= D;
    end
endmodule

module Button_Clock(Clock,Button,Button_Clock);
    input Clock,Button;
    output reg Button_Clock;

    reg flag1 = 0;
    reg flag2 = 0;
    reg [31:0] Count = 0;
    reg [1:0] Reg0 = 0;


    always @(posedge Clock) begin
        if(flag1 || flag2) Count <= Count + 1;
        if(Count == 31'd5000000) begin // Delay for 20th of a second
            flag1 <= 0;
            flag2 <= 0;
            Count <= 0;
        end

        if(Reg0[0] == 0 && Button == 1 && flag2 == 0) flag1 <= 1;
        if(Reg0[0] == 1 && Button == 0 && flag1 == 0) flag2 <= 1;

        if(flag1 == 0 && flag2 == 0) begin // Read when flags are zero
            Reg0[0] <= Button;
            Reg0[1] <= Reg0[0];
        end

        // Execute code when flag2 turns to 1
        if(Reg0[0] == 1 && Button == 0 && flag1 == 0) begin
            Button_Clock <= !Button_Clock;
        end
    end
```

```

endmodule
```

The source and constraint file for the solution with a ROM can be downloaded from the link embedded in the QR code below. It is recommended to upload the ROM solution onto your board after having done so with the equation solution, so you can see that both programs work the same. Doing this will solidify to yourself the fact that a state machine can be done either way.

7.4 Extra Help & Tips

To give you some extra help, some of the solutions were provided in your lab hanout in class. This section will go over the steps for those solutions to give you some additional help. The two previous sections should have been enough, but in case you still need more help, this section will offer more clarity.

To start off, in your lab, you need to use the given SM chart to generate equations for Q1+, Q0+, Z3, Z2, and Z1. The solutions for Q0+ and Z1 will be given to you and the steps will be shown below. To start, the figure below shows the given SM chart with some of the paths labeled.

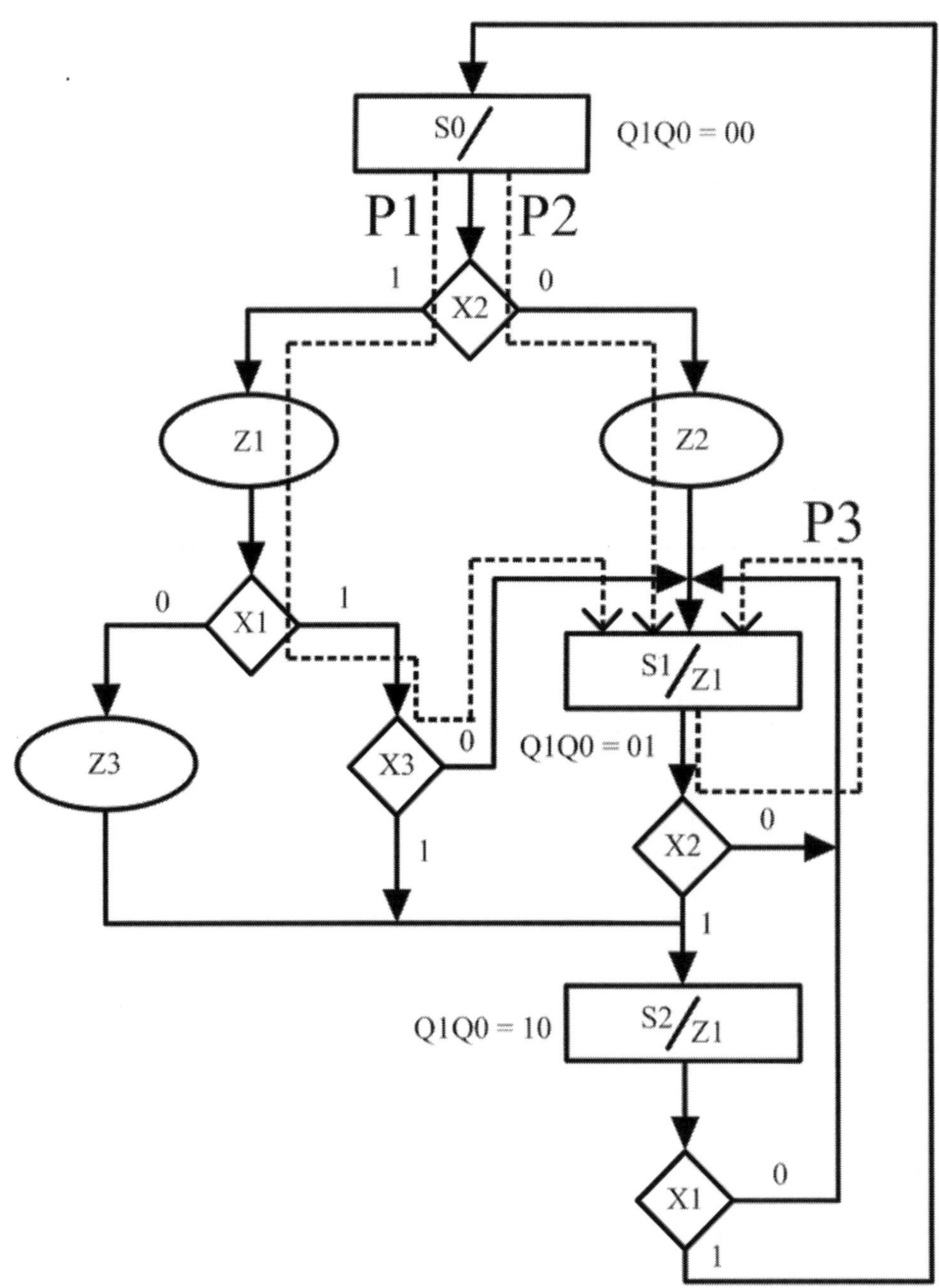

Figure 7.4.1 State Chart with Paths Identified

Finding the term for P1

Since P1 starts at state 0 where Q1Q0 = 00 and goes through X3X2X1 = 011, the terms concatenated have a binary value of Q1Q0X3X2X1 = 00011. Copying the final term based of the binary value results in the final term for P1 being Q1'Q0'X3'X2X1.

Finding the term for P2

Since P2 starts at state 0 where Q1Q0 = 00 and goes through X2 = 0, the terms concatenated have a binary value of Q1Q0X2 = 000. Copying the final term based of the binary value results in the final term for P2 being Q1'Q0'X2'.

Finding the term for P3

Since P3 starts at state 1 where Q1Q0 = 01 and goes through X2 = 0, the terms concatenated have a binary value of Q1Q0X2 = 010. Copying the final term based of the binary value results in the final term for P3 being Q1'Q0X2'.

Finding Q0+

To find the expression for Q0+, we need to first identify which states have Q0 = 1. Only state 1 has Q0 = 1, so only the terms for paths going into state 1 will be included, i.e. for P1, P2 and P3. Logically OR-ing these terms together yields the following expression for Q0+.

Q0+ = Q1'Q0'X3'X2X1 + Q1'Q0'X2' + Q1'Q0X2'

Finding Z1

For Z1, there are two Moore outputs. One in state 1 and one in state 2. The terms for these states are Q1'Q0 + Q1Q0' respectively. There is a Mealy output along both paths where the state is 0 and X2 = 1. The term for this is Q1'Q0'X2. Logically OR-ing the terms for each state and path together yields the following expression for Z1.

Z1 = Q1'Q0'X2 + Q1'Q0 + Q1Q0'

So, there you have it! You have been given for free two out of five equations. Once you obtain the equations for Q1+, Z2, and Z3, you can make the source file very easily and be done. It is recommended to use the code from the QR code link in section 7.2 as a template. Using that code as a template, you need to only modify 5 lines by replacing the equations from the combinational network module with the equations for your own problem. The constraint file does not need to be altered at all. So just come up with the equations, modify 5 lines and you're done! If you're fast, you could finish in under 10 minutes. Once you have finished, re-attempt the problem by making a source file that uses a ROM. This should not take too long to do either assuming you use the code from section 7.3 as a template and already have the ROM truth table extracted from the state table.

Practical Lesson 3 – Frequency Counter

In many applications in industry, determining the frequency of a signal is of high importance. For example, some motors may output a square wave whose frequency is in direct proportion to the speed of rotation, so to know the rotation speed, you must have a way of measuring the frequency. This chapter will demonstrate how to create a source file that can be used to calculate the frequency of an incoming square wave.

So, to start off, it is important to first discuss the procedure for calculating a square wave by hand. Before we can even think about writing any Verilog, we must first understand how to calculate the frequency by hand. The frequency of a square wave is equal to one divided by the period. Remember that the period is equal to the time it takes to complete a single cycle. The figure below shows this.

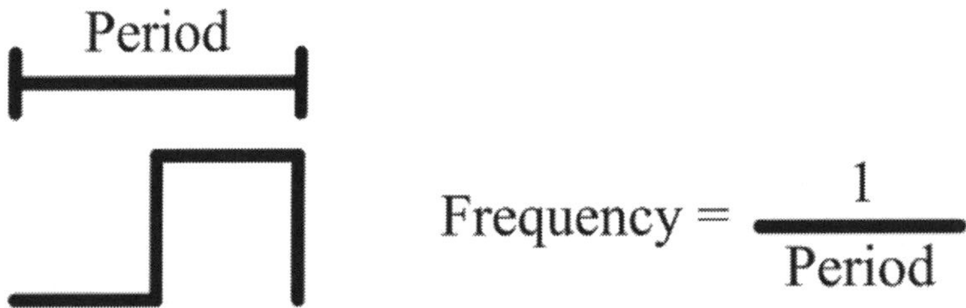

Figure L3.1.1 Frequency from Period

So, from Figure L3.1.1, it should be apparent that the frequency of a square wave can be easily calculated once the period has been recorded. Well as it turns out, recording the period is a lot more difficult than recording the time it takes to complete a half period. The figure below shows how the frequency can be calculated from the half period.

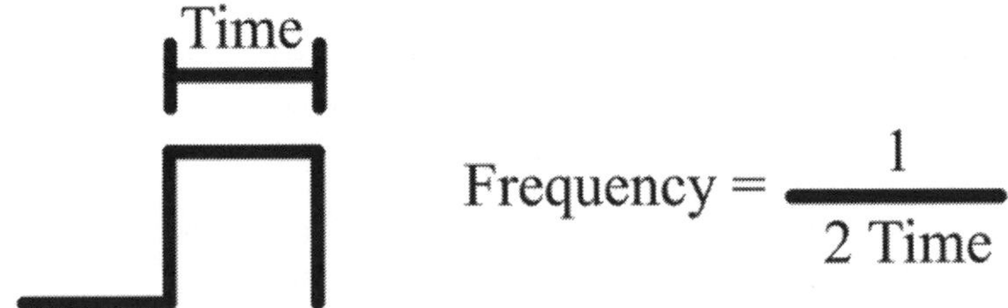

Figure L3.1.2 Frequency from Half Period

Now that you know how to calculate the frequency from the half period, it is time to discuss how to record the half period. Assuming we have an always block that executes on each rising clock edge of the 100MHz clock, we can use a counter to count up whenever the signal is one. Whenever the signal is zero, the count is zero. The figure that follows shows an example of this.

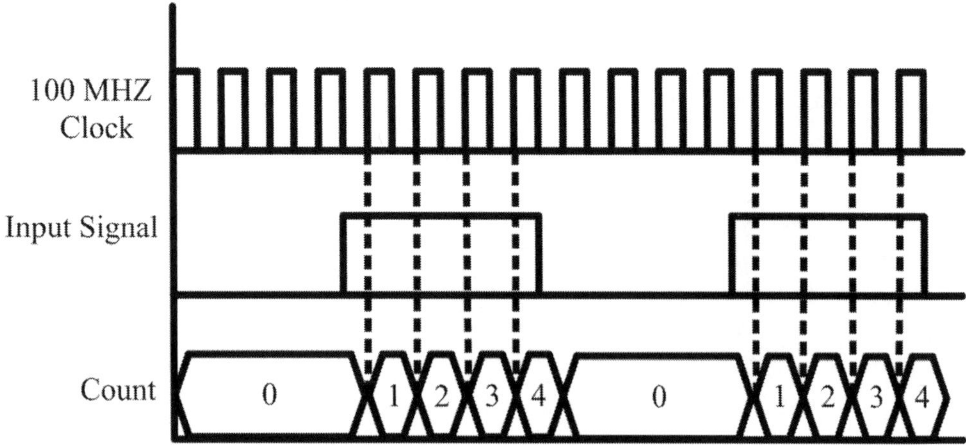

Figure L3.1.3 Count Register Updating

From Figure L3.1.3, it is apparent that the input signal has a half period that is equal to four periods of the 100MHZ clock. Since we know that the 100MHZ clock has a period of 10ns, then this means that the half period of the input signal is 40ns. From the formula in Figure L3.1.2, we can determine the frequency as shown in the equation below.

$$f = \frac{1}{2 * 40n} = 12{,}500{,}000 \text{ HZ}$$

Figure L3.1.4 Frequency Calculation

Now how can we replace the numbers in the frequency formula in Figure L3.1.2 with values that can calculate the frequency using the count register? Well since the count register shows the number of 100MHZ cycles that have occurred during the time it takes to complete a half period, and we know the time of each 100MHZ cycle is 10ns, we can use the following formula.

$$f = \frac{1}{2 * (\text{Count} * 10n)}$$

Figure L3.1.5 Frequency Formula Un-simplified

Simplifying the formula by substituting the nano prefix with 10^{-9} and evaluating the rest yields the following equation below.

$$f = \frac{50000000}{\text{Count}}$$

Figure L3.1.6 Frequency Formula Simplified

The final step is to write Verilog code to implement a counter that behaves in the manner shown in Figure L3.1.3 and to implement a division module that can perform unsigned binary division very quickly. The code below shows both these things being done.

Final Frequency Counter Code

```
module frequency(Signal,Clock,Frequency);
   input wire Signal,Clock;
   output wire [15:0] Frequency;

   wire [31:0] A,B,Value;
   reg [31:0] Count,CountR,CountOld = 0;
   reg OldSignal = 0;

   initial begin
      Count = 0; // must be initalized for simulation
      CountR = 0;
   end

   always @(posedge Clock) begin
      if(Signal == 1) Count <= Count + 1;
      if(Signal == 0) Count <= 0;
      OldSignal <= Signal;
      if(OldSignal == 1 && Signal == 0) CountR <= Count;
   end

   division IN0(32’d50050000,CountR,Frequency);
endmodule

module division(A,B,Res2);

   //the size of input and output ports of the division module is generic.
   parameter WIDTH = 32;
   //input and output ports.
   input wire [WIDTH-1:0] A;
   input wire [WIDTH-1:0] B;
   output wire [WIDTH-1:0] Res2;
   //internal variables
   reg [WIDTH-1:0] Res = 0;
   reg [WIDTH-1:0] a1,b1;
   reg [WIDTH:0] p1;
   integer i;

   always@ (A or B)
   begin
      //initialize the variables.
      a1 = A;
```

```
42       b1 = B;
43       p1= 0;
44       for(i=0;i < WIDTH;i=i+1)   begin //start the for loop
45          p1 = {p1[WIDTH-2:0],a1[WIDTH-1]};
46          a1[WIDTH-1:1] = a1[WIDTH-2:0];
47          p1 = p1-b1;
48          if(p1[WIDTH-1] == 1)   begin
49             a1[0] = 0;
50             p1 = p1 + b1;   end
51          else
52             a1[0] = 1;
53       end
54       Res = a1;
55    end
56
57    assign Res2 = Res;
58 endmodule
```

To replicate the behavior in Figure L3.1.3, line 15 increments the count whenever the signal is one and line 16 sets the count to 0 whenever the signal is 0. Lines 17 and 18 are only present to shift the value of the count register into the division module after the falling edge of the input signal. This is an essential step, since if you remember in Figure L3.1.3, only, 4, the value of the count register that was present during the falling edge of the input signal was used in the calculation.

Line 21 instantiates the division module. The number 50050000 was used instead of 50000000 since the clock on my board turned out to be slightly different than 100MHZ. Your clock is likely not exactly 100 MHz either, so you may need to change the number though trial and error. The division module is implemented in lines 24-58. Don't worry about understanding how the division module was formed. The main purpose of this chapter was to understand how to implement a frequency counter, not to design an ALU that can do division. The QR codes that follow give the Verilog files and show a video demonstration. If you upload the code to your board and test it with a function generator, make sure to use 3.3Vpp with a DC offset of 1.65V. Using a larger peak to peak voltage or DC offset may damage the FPGA and cause erroneous results.

Files

Video

Lab 8 – Non-Sequential Counter

In this Lab, you will build an arbitrary counter using a state machine. To give you preparation, an example will be solved using fundamental design methods. No examples containing behavioral methods will be shown, since doing so would make it way too easy. If you understand the fundamentals of what's going on, then you should be able to easily make a behavioral implementation and finish very quickly by yourself.

8.1 – Lab Description

For your lab, you will implement an arbitrary counter that counts from C A 4 5 7 3 F 6 9 and back to C. The state diagram is below for your reference. Your board will need to use a single seven segment display to show the state. You should also have the binary equivalent shown on LEDs. From the diagram, you should expect to see the seven-segment change from C, A, 4, 5, 7, 3, F, 6, 9, and back to C. You should expect the LEDs to change from 1100, 1010, 0100, 0101, 0111, 0011, 1111, 0110, 01001 and back to 1100.

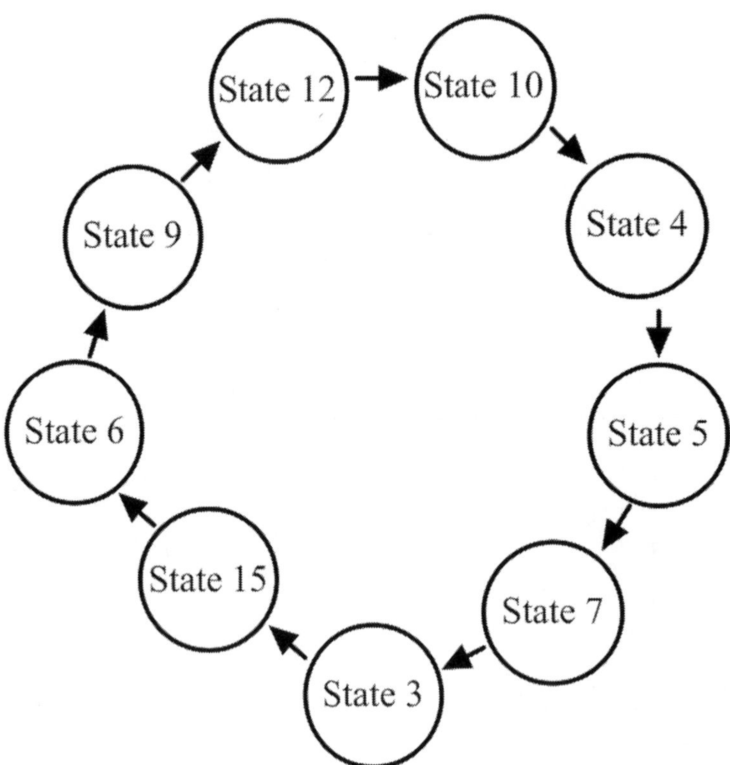

Figure 8.1.1 State Diagram for Arbitrary Counter

8.2 – Arbitrary Counter Example

The example that will be solved is how to make an arbitrary counter that counts in the following order: 0, 7, 4, 5, 2, 1. To begin, the state diagram is shown below in Figure 8.2.1. From the state diagram, it should be noted that there are no external inputs or outputs! That's right, none are needed since the three registers holding the current state will be tied to the output. We know that three registers are needed, since the largest state, 7, requires three bits to be represented in unsigned binary as 111.

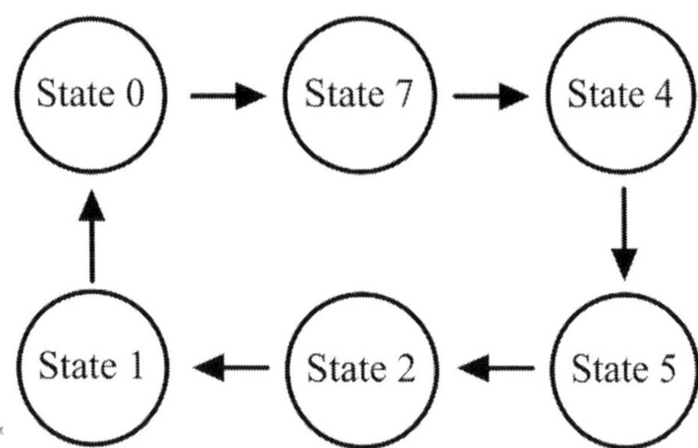

Figure 8.2.1 State Diagram for Arbitrary Counter

The state diagram is a good starting point when designing an arbitrary counter, but a state table is much more essential. The state table representing the state machine from Figure 8.2.1 is shown below in Figure 8.2.2.

Row	Q_2	Q_1	Q_0	$+Q_2$	$+Q_1$	$+Q_0$
0	0	0	0	1	1	1
1	0	0	1	0	0	0
2	0	1	0	0	0	1
3	0	1	1	X	X	X
4	1	0	0	1	0	1
5	1	0	1	0	1	0
6	1	1	0	X	X	X
7	1	1	1	1	0	0

Figure 8.2.2 State Diagram for Arbitrary Counter

Making the state table in Figure 8.2.2 using the state diagram in Figure 8.2.1 is something that you should have learned in the logic design portion of the book. If you don't know how it was done, the following text will clarify how it was done. To start, looking at the diagram in Figure 8.2.1, when the state is 0, then the next state is 7. Using this information, when the state is 0, i.e when $\{Q_2, Q_1, Q_0\} = 000$, we know that the next state is 7, i.e that $\{+Q_2, +Q_1, +Q_0\} = 111$, and can fill out row 0 in the table accordingly. Rows 3 and 6 had don't cares in the output since in the state diagram, states 3 and 6 were not present. The remaining rows were done using the same though process as row 0.

The next step is to solve the equations using K-Maps as shown below. The K-Maps were made by copying the output into the corresponding box. For example, the output of +Q2 was 1 when $\{Q_2, Q_1, Q_0\} = 000$ in row 0. For this reason, a 1 is placed in the top right box that corresponds to row 0. The little number in the corner of each box indicates the corresponding row. Also, note that the little number is the decimal equivalent of the value of $\{Q_2, Q_1, Q_0\}$. For all three K-Maps, boxes 3 and 6 have a don't care since rows 2 and 6 had don't cares in the table from Figure 8.2.2. If you don't understand how to map a truth table to a K-Map and extract the equations, refer to the logic design section where it was demonstrated many times.

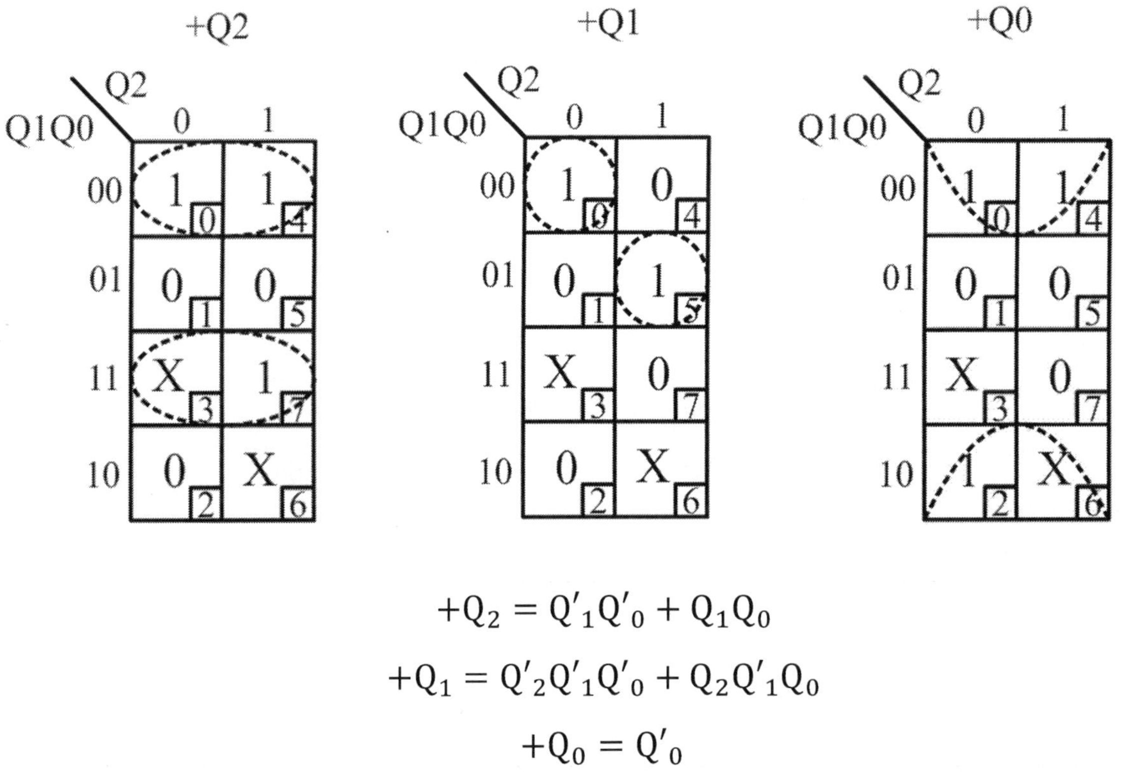

$$+Q_2 = Q'_1Q'_0 + Q_1Q_0$$

$$+Q_1 = Q'_2Q'_1Q'_0 + Q_2Q'_1Q_0$$

$$+Q_0 = Q'_0$$

Figure 8.2.3 K-Maps and Equations for Arbitrary Counter

Now that the equations have been generated, we are ready to construct a Verilog module based on them. The subsequent code illustrates how to accomplish this. The setup includes a total of five modules: a D flip-flop module is defined between lines 22-29; a combinational network module that implements the equations spans lines 31-38; a clock divider module designed to produce a slow clock covers lines 40-53; another combinational network module, which converts a binary number into an array suitable for a seven-segment display to show the corresponding number, occupies lines 55-69; and finally, a top-level module that integrates all components is outlined in lines 3-20.

Arbitrary Counter Code

```
`timescale 1ns / 1ps

module Top(Clock,Q2,Q1,Q0,DP,G,F,E,D,C,B,A,AN);
   input Clock;
   output Q2,Q1,Q0;
   output DP,G,F,E,D,C,B,A;
   output [7:0] AN;

   assign AN = ~8'h01;

   wire Q2P,Q1P,Q0P,New_Clock;

   DFF IN0(Q0P,Q0,New_Clock);
   DFF IN1(Q1P,Q1,New_Clock);
   DFF IN2(Q2P,Q2,New_Clock);

   Combinational_Network IN3(Q2,Q1,Q0,Q2P,Q1P,Q0P);
   CLK100MHZ_divider IN4(Clock, New_Clock);
   Seven_Seg IN5({Q2,Q1,Q0},DP,G,F,E,D,C,B,A);
endmodule

module DFF(D,Q,Clock);
    input D, Clock;
    output reg Q;

    always @(posedge Clock) begin
        Q <= D;
    end
endmodule

module Combinational_Network(Q2,Q1,Q0,Q2P,Q1P,Q0P);
   input Q2,Q1,Q0;
   output Q2P,Q1P,Q0P;

   assign Q2P = ~Q1&~Q0 | Q1&Q0;
   assign Q1P = ~Q2&~Q1&~Q0 | Q2&~Q1&Q0;
   assign Q0P = ~Q0;
endmodule

module CLK100MHZ_divider(CLK100MHZ, New_Clock);
   input wire CLK100MHZ;      // Input clock signal
   output reg New_Clock;       // Divided clock output

   reg [31:0] count = 0; // [31:0] is large enough to hold any value

```

```
   always @(posedge CLK100MHZ) begin
      count <= count + 1;  // Increment count
      if (count == 31'd49999999) begin
         New_Clock <= ~New_Clock; // Toggle New Clock
         count <= 31'b0;      // Reset count
      end
   end
endmodule

module Seven_Seg(Digit,DP,G,F,E,D,C,B,A);
   input [2:0] Digit;
   output reg DP,G,F,E,D,C,B,A;

   always@(*) begin
      if(Digit == 3'b000) {DP,G,F,E,D,C,B,A} = 8'b11000000; // Make 0 with LEDs
      if(Digit == 3'b001) {DP,G,F,E,D,C,B,A} = 8'b11001111; // Make 1 with LEDs
      if(Digit == 3'b010) {DP,G,F,E,D,C,B,A} = 8'b10100100; // Make 2 with LEDs
      if(Digit == 3'b011) {DP,G,F,E,D,C,B,A} = 8'b10110000; // Make 3 with LEDs
      if(Digit == 3'b100) {DP,G,F,E,D,C,B,A} = 8'b10011001; // Make 4 with LEDs
      if(Digit == 3'b101) {DP,G,F,E,D,C,B,A} = 8'b10010010; // Make 5 with LEDs
      if(Digit == 3'b110) {DP,G,F,E,D,C,B,A} = 8'b10000010; // Make 6 with LEDs
      if(Digit == 3'b111) {DP,G,F,E,D,C,B,A} = 8'b11111000; // Make 7 with LEDs
   end
endmodule
```

To give you a better understanding of the exact circuit the code above is meant to model, the schematic will be shown on the following page. The big box represents the top-level module so all the inputs and outputs from the top-level modules sensitivity list are present. For example, there is an input for the Clock and an output for Q2, Q1, Q0, DP, G, F, E, D, C, B, A, AN. Within the top-level module box, all the instantiations are shown. There are 3 D flip-flops that hold the state, the output of each flip-flop goes into the combinational network to calculate the new state, to the combinational network for the seven-segment display, and lastly, to the LEDs. There is also a clock divider that takes in the Clock input and creates a new clock to go into the 3 flip-flops. On the page after the schematic are two QR codes. One to simulate a version of the circuit shown in Figure 8.2.4 and one to obtain the source and constraint file for the Verilog implementation.

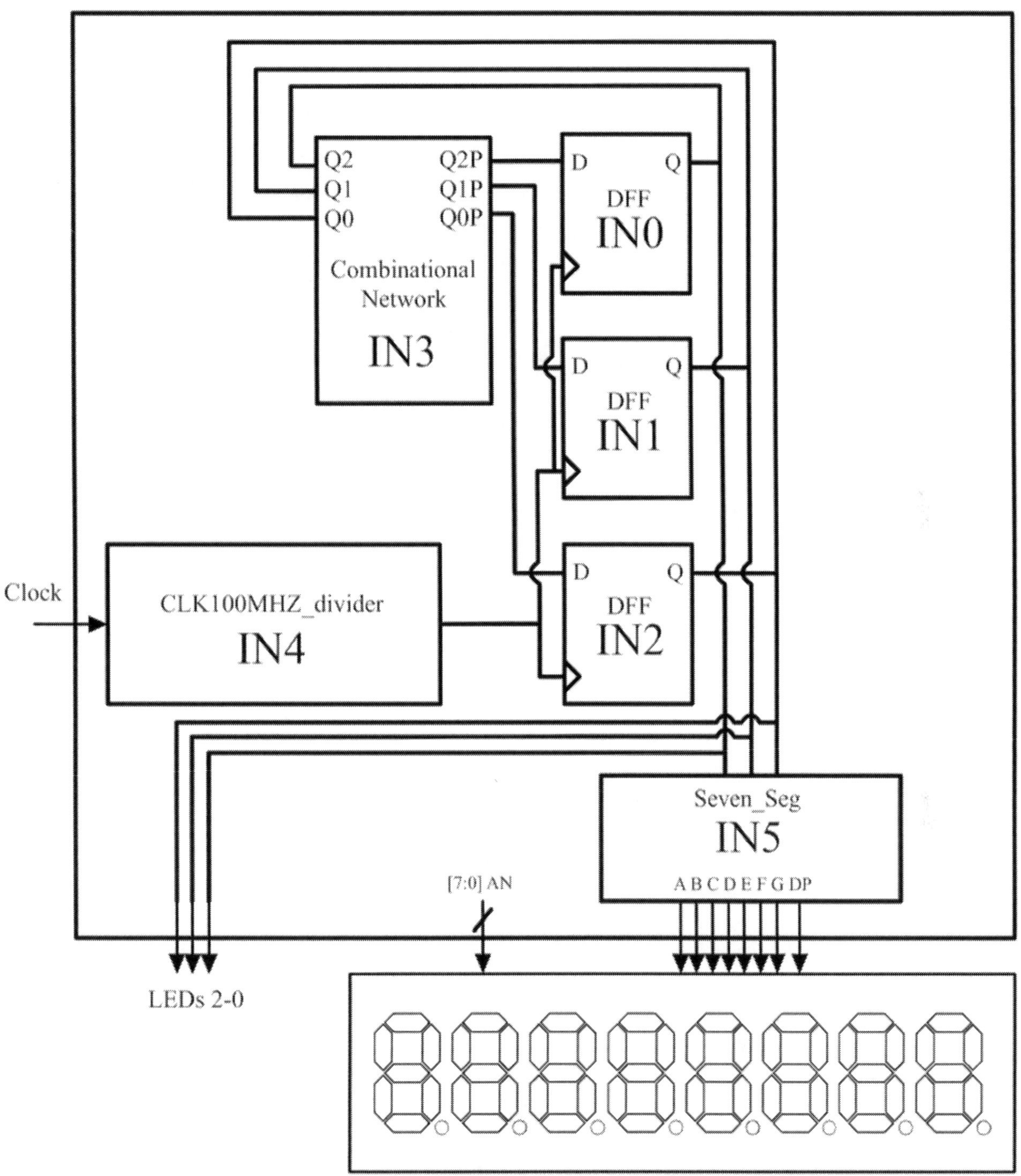

Figure 8.2.4 Arbitrary Counter Schematic

Verilog Files

Schematic Simulation

8.3 – Final Comments & Tips

So, for your lab, you essentially are making a different version of the circuit shown in the demonstration. If you choose to solve the lab with a structural approach, use the provided code as a template, modify the combinational network module that deals with the equations, and modify the combinational network that deals with the seven-segment display. Since your problem has F as the highest number, you must modify both modules to be compatible with four bits. In other words, make the combinational network that deals with the equations have an equation for $+Q_3, +Q_2, +Q_1,$ and $+ Q_0$. Also modify the seven-segment combinational network to be able to display letters A-F. If you choose to follow the structural approach as done in the demonstration, then the hardest part of this lab will be making the equations with K-Maps. Around 85% of your time will be spent making the state table, making K-Maps, and solving them.

Now of course, you don't have to use the structural methodology shown in the demonstration. You could very well do the entire thing behaviorally, which may be much faster. It is completely up to you. It isn't a bad idea to do it structurally though, since if you are successful, it means you have a complete understanding of what's going on.

Lab 9 – Comparator

In this lab, you will make a Verilog source file that will compare two 4-bit binary values, value 1 and value 2. You will need to use the seven-segment display to show the numbers being compared and the result. To give you some preparation, a gate level design for a comparator will be discussed.

9.1 – Lab Description

For your assignment, you will use 4 switches to enter in value V1 and another 4 switches to enter in value V2. V1 will be displayed in the rightmost seven segment display and V2 will be displayed in the display immediately to the left of V1. On the leftmost display, the result of the comparison will be displayed. The following figures show some example inputs and the expected behavior. When V1 = V2, the result is always "E", when V1 < V2, the result is always "L", and when V1 > V2, the result is always "G".

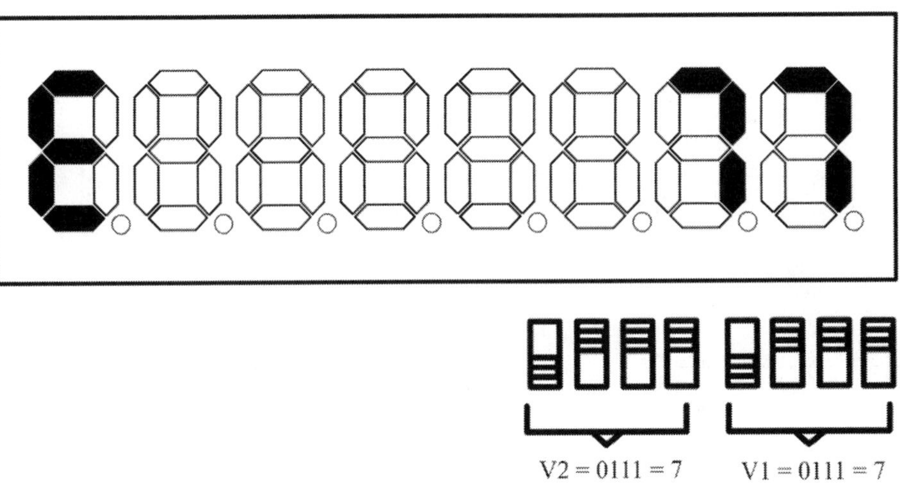

Figure 9.1.1 V1 = V2

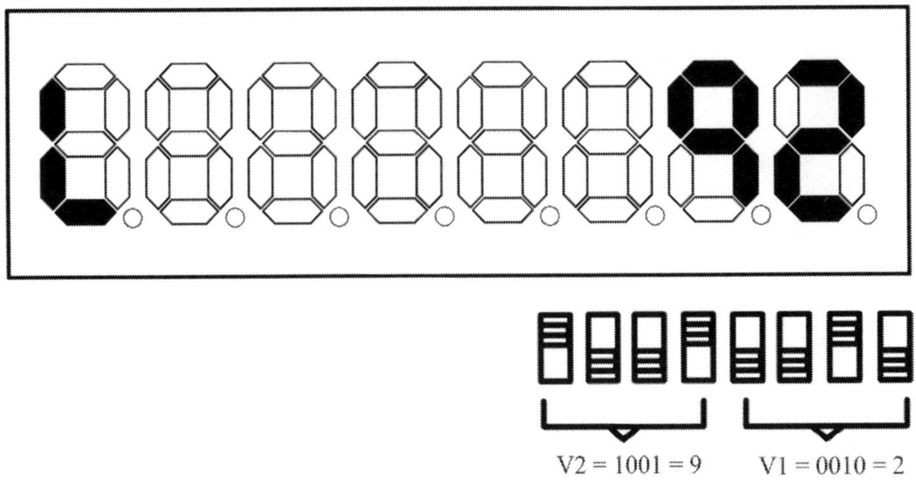

Figure 9.1.2 V1 < V2

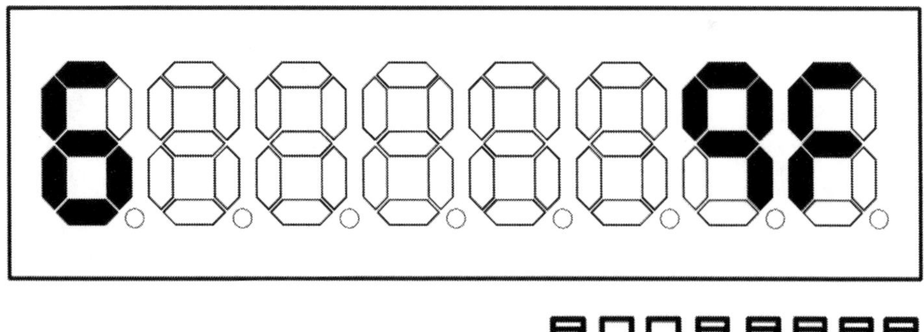

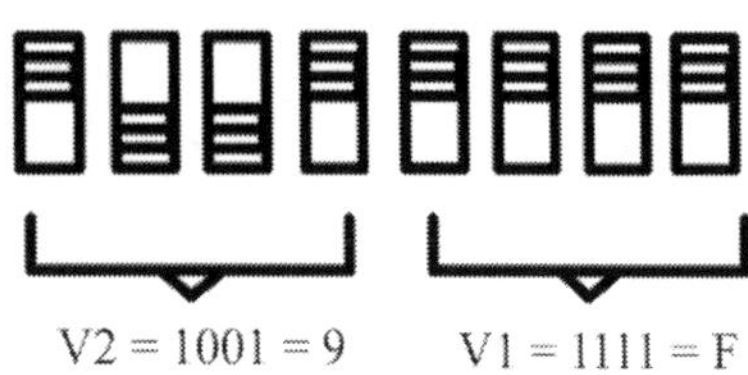

Figure 9.1.3 V1 > V2

9.2 – Comparator Fundamentals

For preparation, the fundamentals of how a comparator works will be reviewed. To start off, a traditional comparator is a combinational piece of hardware that takes in two inputs, A and B, and has three outputs. One output E indicates A = B, another output L indicates A < B, and the last output G indicates A > B. The truth table for a simple 1-bit comparator is below. At no time will more than one output be active, since only one situation is possible at a time.

A	B	E (A=B)	L (A<B)	G (A>B)
0	0	1	0	0
0	1	0	0	1
1	0	0	1	0
1	1	1	0	0

Figure 9.2.1 1-bit Comparator truth table

Now using K-Maps to obtain the expression for the three puts, we obtain the following equations for a 1-bit comparator.

One bit comparator equations

$$E = A'B' + AB$$

$$L = A'B$$

$$G = AB'$$

The approach for a 1-bit comparator was simple enough, so how would it be done for a 2-bit comparator? Well, you would just make a truth table for it as shown below and find the equations.

A1	A0	B1	B0	E (A=B)	L (A<B)	G (A>B)
0	0	0	0	1	0	0
0	0	0	1	0	1	0
0	0	1	0	0	1	0
0	0	1	1	0	1	0
0	1	0	0	0	0	1
0	1	0	1	1	0	0
0	1	1	0	0	1	0
0	1	1	1	0	1	0
1	0	0	0	0	0	1
1	0	0	1	0	0	1
1	0	1	0	1	0	0
1	0	1	1	0	1	0
1	1	0	0	0	0	1
1	1	0	1	0	0	1
1	1	1	0	0	0	1
1	1	1	1	1	0	0

Figure 9.2.2 2-bit Comparator truth table

Now what about for a 3-bit or 4-bit comparator? Could a truth table be made for those? Well not really since the truth tables get exponentially bigger. The 1-bit comparator table had 4 rows. The 2-bit already has 16 rows. If we tried making a table for a 3-bit comparator, we would need $2^{2(3)} =$ 64 rows! For a 4-bit comparator, we would need $2^{2(4)} = 256$ rows! A table with 256 rows is impossible to solve without a supercomputer, so it is not feasible to use this approach for applications of any value. So how is it done? Well, the answer is through modifying the 1-bit comparator and through modularization.

To think about how the 1-bit comparator can be modified to be modularized, we need to think about how numbers are compared in our heads. Typically, when we see something like 547 and 782, we start by looking at the most significant numbers and if one is greater than the other, we already know the answer. In the case of 547 and 782, we would compare 5 and 7 and already know which is greater without having to compare anything else. This same principle can be applied to the 1-bit adder by adding inputs PG and PL to indicate if the solution is known.

So how could we get the hardware for the modified 1-bit comparator? Well, the truth table that follows models the behavior. Rows 0-1 describe what should happen when the result isn't already known, i.e. when PG and PL are 0. In these rows, the output is determined by comparing A and B. Rows 4-7 describe what should happen when the result has already been determined that A is greater than B, i.e. when PG is 1. In these rows, G is always the only output. Rows 8-11 describe what should happen when the result has already been determined that A is less than B, i.e. when PL is 1. In these rows, L is always the only output. Rows 12-15 do not matter since at no time will PG and PL be 1 at the same time. This makes sense because A cannot be both greater than and less than B at the same time.

Row	PL	PG	A	B	E	L	G
0	0	0	0	0	1	0	0
1	0	0	0	1	0	1	0
2	0	0	1	0	0	0	1
3	0	0	1	1	1	0	0
4	0	1	0	0	0	0	1
5	0	1	0	1	0	0	1
6	0	1	1	0	0	0	1
7	0	1	1	1	0	0	1
8	1	0	0	0	0	1	0
9	1	0	0	1	0	1	0
10	1	0	1	0	0	1	0
11	1	0	1	1	0	1	0
12	1	1	0	0	X	X	X
13	1	1	0	1	X	X	X
14	1	1	1	0	X	X	X
15	1	1	1	1	X	X	X

Figure 9.2.3 Modified 1-bit Comparator

Figure 9.2.4 shows a 2-bit comparator using the modified 1-bit comparator described by the table in Figure 9.2.3. For example, in Figure 9.2.4, if A1 was 1 and B1 was 0, the first comparator would output $\{E, L, G\} = 001$ resulting in the second comparator receiving PG = 1. Since PG = 1, the second comparator would automatically output $\{E, L, G\} = 001$, regardless of A0 and B0, to correctly indicate that A was greater than B. Again, for example, if A1 was 0 and B1 was 1, the first comparator would output $\{E, L, G\} = 010$ resulting in the second comparator receiving PL = 1. Since PL = 1, the second comparator would automatically output $\{E, L, G\} = 010$, regardless of A0 and B0, to correctly indicate that A was less than B. Again, for example, if A1 and B1 were both 0 then the first comparator would output $\{E, L, G\} = 100$ and since the second comparator would receive 0 for both PL and PG, it would calculate the final answer based on A0 and B0.

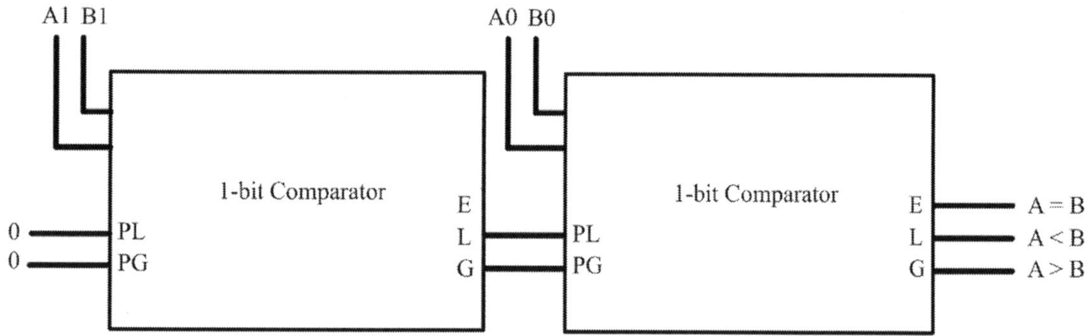

Figure 9.2.4 2-bit Comparator Using Modified 1-bit Comparator

Using the QR code below, you can simulate a 4-bit comparator using the modified 1-bit comparator from Figure 9.2.3 and Figure 9.2.4. If you didn’t understand the modified 1-bit comparator, then you may want to use the QR code to simulate it individually. If you understand that the end goal was to add gates to propagate the answer recorded by PG and PL while having the answer, originally be determined by A and B when PG and PL are 0, you should be able to understand.

9.3 – Behavioral approach

I understand that the structural approach in section 9.2 is not the most appealing, since although it is a simple procedure to implement, it takes time. For example, to make a module for the modified comparator, you would need to solve the K-Maps and make a Verilog module for it. Then to implement a 4-bit comparator, you would need to instantiate four copies of the modified comparator modules. Although this is very simple to do, this takes time. For this reason, you will be given an example of how a behavioral approach can quickly implement the comparator described by Figure 9.2.3.

If you remember from the truth table in Figure 9.2.3, there were only three cases that mattered. The first was what to do if PG and PL were both 0. The next was what to do if PG and PL were 0 and 1. The next was what to do if PG and PL were 1 and 0. The simple module below quickly implements the modified 1-bit comparator.

Modular 1-bit comparator

```
module One_Bit_Comparator(A,B,PG,PL,L,G,E);
  input A,B,PG,PL;
  output reg L,G,E;

  always@(*) begin
    if({PG,PL} == 2’b00) begin
      if(A > B) {L,G,E} = 3’b010;
      if(A == B) {L,G,E} = 3’b001;
      if(A < B) {L,G,E} = 3’b100;
    end
    if({PG,PL} == 2’b01) {L,G,E} = 3’b100;
    if({PG,PL} == 2’b10) {L,G,E} = 3’b010;
  end
endmodule
```

9.4 – Final Tips

So, for your lab, you will need to write a module for a four-bit comparator but ironically, the most challenging part doesn't even have anything to do with this. The hardest part is to use the seven-segment to display the results. To give you a good starting point, you may use the code provided below as a template. To start, you will need to make a module for a 4-bit comparator. The module will take in Number1 and Number2 and output L1, G1, and E1. You may choose to make the 4-bit comparator through a structural approach or through a behavioral approach. If you choose a structural approach, refer to Figure 9.2.4 and the QR code that shows a 4-bit comparator completely built. If you choose a behavioral approach, refer to section 9.3 as an example. Note that if you use a behavioral approach to implement the 4-bit comparator directly, you can completely avoid making a module for the modularized 1-bit comparator. If you do it correctly, it will take no more than 10 lines! Once you have finished the comparator, you will need to instantiate it on line 17. Once that is completed, study the rest of the top-level module and finish lines 38, 50, 55, and 56. The QR code containing the source file and constraint file is below.

Comparator Template

```
1  `timescale 1ns / 1ps
2
3  module Top(DP,G,F,E,D,C,B,A,Enable,Clock,Number1,Number2,L1,G1,E1);
4    input wire Clock;
5    input wire [3:0] Number1,Number2;
6    output reg DP,G,F,E,D,C,B,A;
7    output reg [7:0] Enable;
8    output wire L1,G1,E1;
9
10   reg [3:0] Location = 0;
11   reg [3:0] Digit;
12   reg [1:0] X;
13   reg Disp_R;
14
15   wire Clk_Multi;
16   CLK100MHZ_divider(Clock, Clk_Multi);
17   // Instantiate Four_Bit_Comparator Module
18
19   always@(*) begin
20     if(Digit == 4'b0000 & Disp_R == 1'b0) {DP,G,F,E,D,C,B,A} = 8'b11000000; // Make 0 with LEDs
21     if(Digit == 4'b0001 & Disp_R == 1'b0) {DP,G,F,E,D,C,B,A} = 8'b11001111; // Make 1 with LEDs
22     if(Digit == 4'b0010 & Disp_R == 1'b0) {DP,G,F,E,D,C,B,A} = 8'b10100100; // Make 2 with LEDs
23     if(Digit == 4'b0011 & Disp_R == 1'b0) {DP,G,F,E,D,C,B,A} = 8'b10110000; // Make 3 with LEDs
24     if(Digit == 4'b0100 & Disp_R == 1'b0) {DP,G,F,E,D,C,B,A} = 8'b10011001; // Make 4 with LEDs
25     if(Digit == 4'b0101 & Disp_R == 1'b0) {DP,G,F,E,D,C,B,A} = 8'b10010010; // Make 5 with LEDs
26     if(Digit == 4'b0110 & Disp_R == 1'b0) {DP,G,F,E,D,C,B,A} = 8'b10000010; // Make 6 with LEDs
27     if(Digit == 4'b0111 & Disp_R == 1'b0) {DP,G,F,E,D,C,B,A} = 8'b11111000; // Make 7 with LEDs
28     if(Digit == 4'b1000 & Disp_R == 1'b0) {DP,G,F,E,D,C,B,A} = 8'b10000000; // Make 8 with LEDs
29     if(Digit == 4'b1001 & Disp_R == 1'b0) {DP,G,F,E,D,C,B,A} = 8'b10011000; // Make 9 with LEDs
30     if(Digit == 4'b1010 & Disp_R == 1'b0) {DP,G,F,E,D,C,B,A} = 8'b10001000; // Make A with LEDs
31     if(Digit == 4'b1011 & Disp_R == 1'b0) {DP,G,F,E,D,C,B,A} = 8'b10000011; // Make b with LEDs
32     if(Digit == 4'b1100 & Disp_R == 1'b0) {DP,G,F,E,D,C,B,A} = 8'b11000110; // Make C with LEDs
33     if(Digit == 4'b1101 & Disp_R == 1'b0) {DP,G,F,E,D,C,B,A} = 8'b10100001; // Make d with LEDs
34     if(Digit == 4'b1110 & Disp_R == 1'b0) {DP,G,F,E,D,C,B,A} = 8'b10000110; // Make E with LEDs
```

```
        if(Digit == 4’b1111 & Disp_R == 1’b0) {DP,G,F,E,D,C,B,A} = 8’b10001110; // Make F with LEDs
        if(X == 2’b00 & Disp_R == 1’b1) {DP,G,F,E,D,C,B,A} <= 8’b10000110; // E
        if(X == 2’b01 & Disp_R == 1’b1) {DP,G,F,E,D,C,B,A} <= 8’b10000010; // G
        if(/* Fill In */) {DP,G,F,E,D,C,B,A} <= 8’b11000111; // L
    end

always@(posedge Clk_Multi) begin
    Location <= Location + 1;
    case(Location)
        0:  begin
                Enable <= 8’b11111110;
                {Digit,Disp_R} <= {Number1,1’b0};
            end
        1:  begin
                Enable <= 8’b11111101;
                // Assign value to display Number2
            end
        3:  begin
                Enable <= 8’b01111111;
                if({L1,G1,E1} == 3’b001) {X,Disp_R} <= {2’b00,1’b1};
                // Assign value for when G1 = 1;
                // Assign value for when L1 = 1;
                Location <= 0;
            end
    endcase
end
endmodule

module CLK100MHZ_divider(CLK100MHZ, New_Clock);
    input wire CLK100MHZ;      // Input clock signal
    output reg New_Clock;      // Divided clock output

    reg [31:0] count = 0; // [31:0] is large enough to hold any value

    always @(posedge CLK100MHZ) begin
        count <= count + 1;  // Increment count
        if (count == 31’d10000) begin
            New_Clock <= ~New_Clock; // Toggle New Clock
            count <= 31’b0;        // Reset count
        end
    end
endmodule

// Make Four_Bit_Comparator Module – Behavioral approach recommended
```

Lab 10 – VGA

Having the ability to process images with FPGAs is a highly valuable skill, given the diverse and complex display methods available. On the simpler end, a monitor might use VGA or HDMI to transmit pixel information directly. Conversely, more complex systems, like a portable camera, may transmit pixel information over an Ethernet cable using MIPI encoding. This introduction to video processing will focus on the simplest method: transmitting raw RGB values to a VGA display without any encoding. In advanced systems, images are compressed using sophisticated encoding schemes to save space and enable faster transmission. This section will describe the lab assignment and, for preparation, demonstrate how to manually display an image pixel by pixel.

10.1 - Lab Description

For this assignment, you will be tasked with displaying solid green on a VGA monitor. Then a few seconds later, the color should change to blue. Again a few seconds later, the color should change to red. Then a few seconds later, the color should change back to green and repeat. The entire goal is to have the screen alternate between those colors indefinitely.

10.2 – Manual Image with VGA

To start, a VGA display can be treated as a black box with five inputs and a single output. Each of those five inputs will come from the FPGA and the output is the image generated on the screen. The block diagram for a VGA monitor receiving it's signals from an FPGA is shown below.

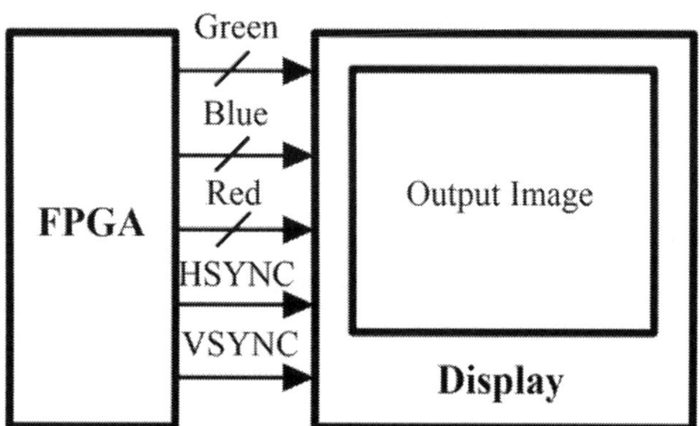

Figure 10.2.1 VGA Display Block Diagram

From Figure 10.2.1, three multiple bit signals are used to represent the red, green, and blue intensity for each pixel. For the FPGA used by this book, these signals are 4 bits wide, however in some other devices, it may be a different length. The higher the binary value of these color signals, the brighter the color. The other two signals, VSYNC and HSYNC, are synchronization signals used to specify which pixel to update using the current red, green, and blue values. Note that HSYNC stands for horizontal synchronization and VSYNC stands for vertical synchronization.

Before discussing these synchronization signals, it is important to go over how the VGA display generates an image. A standard VGA display has a 640x480 pixel resolution, for a total of

307,200 pixels. Each pixel is updated starting from the top left corner, moving to the right. Once the end of a line is reached, the process moves to the beginning of the next line below, updating pixels from left to right again. This sequence continues until all the pixels on the entire screen are updated. The image below shows how this is done.

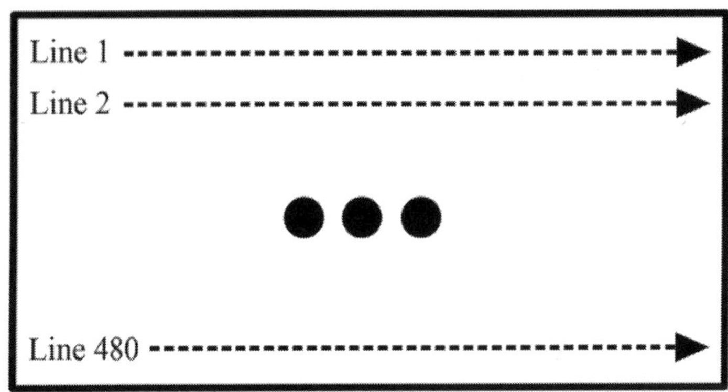

Figure 10.2.2 VGA Display Being Updated

Now let's look at the horizontal synchronization signal first. The diagram below shows the waveform required to generate a single horizontal line of pixels. The critical thing is the timing, which according to VGA standard, intervals A, B, C, and D should 16, 96, 48, and 640 periods of a 25.175MHZ clock respectively. The reason why is not something that needs to be understood. Just know that the physicist who designed VGA made it such that all displays must receive the signal shown in Figure 10.2.3. Our job as engineers is to replicate the HSYNC signal shown in Figure 10.2.3 and feed it into the VGA display as shown in Figure 10.2.1.

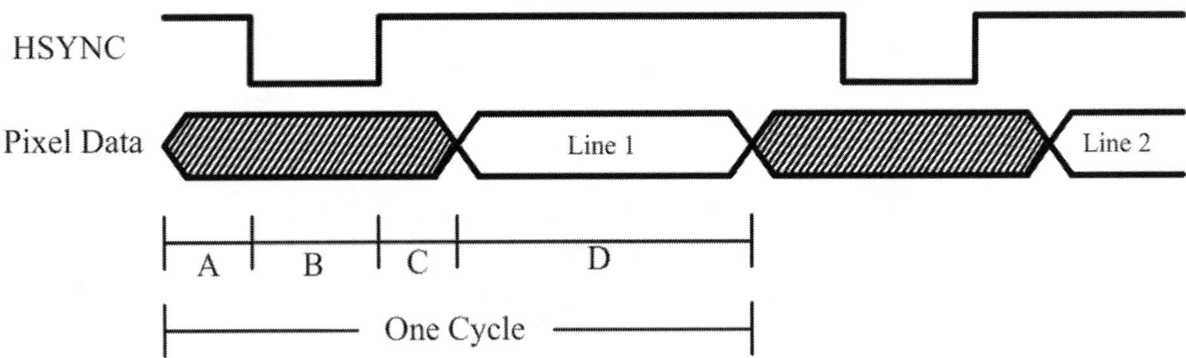

Figure 10.2.3 VGA Display Horizontal Synchronization Timming

The VSYNC does the same thing, except that the timing is done in terms of HSYNC cycles. Figure 10.2.4 shows the VSYNC waveform required to generate a single frame. For Figure 10.2.4, know that intervals A, B, C, and D, are 10, 2, 33, and 480 HSYNC cycles worth of time respectively. In other words, there are 525 cycles of HSYNC for each cycle of VSYNC. Again, the reason for these intervals is not something that is to be understood, just accepted as VGA protocol. Our job is to replicate the VSYNC signal and connect our FPGA as shown in figure 10.2.1.

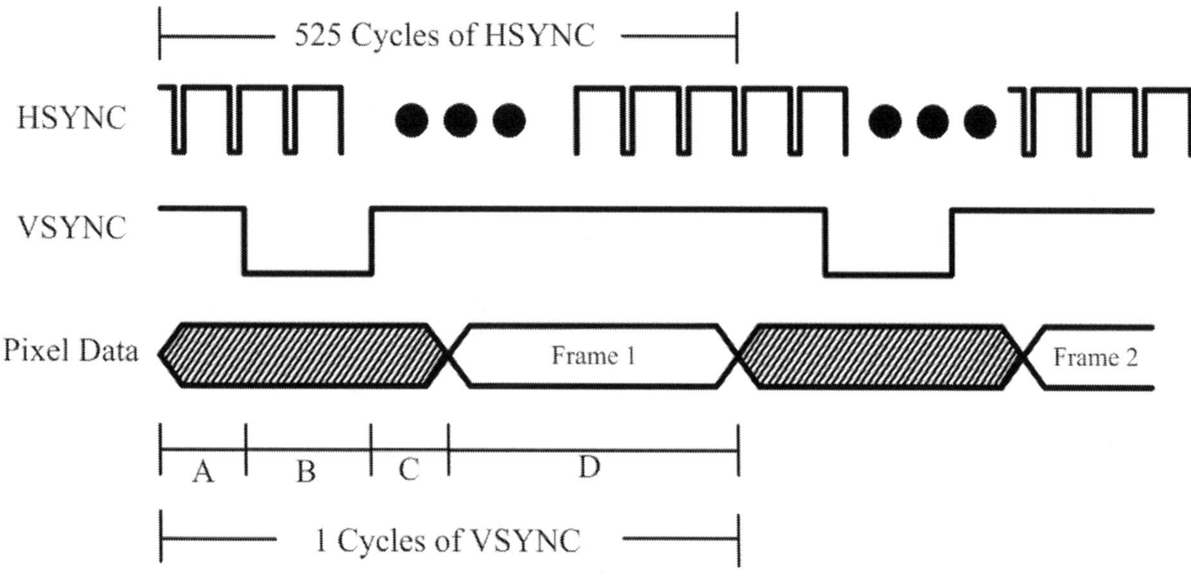

Figure 10.2.4 VGA Display Vertical Synchronization Timming

Now that you know the exact timing that both VSYNC and HSYNC use, it is time to summarize how the entire process works. In Figure 10.2.5, it should be apparent that the time it takes to complete a single cycle of the HSYNC signal is equal to the time it takes to complete a single line, which is 800 clock cycles. It should also be apparent that the time it takes to complete a single cycle of VSYNC is equal to the time it takes to complete a single frame, which is the same as 525 cycles of HSYNC. Both HSYNC and VSYNC are periodic signals that repeat indefinitely during a video. In other words, the first frame is generated by the first cycle of VSYNC, the second frame is generated by the second cycle of VSYNC, and so on.

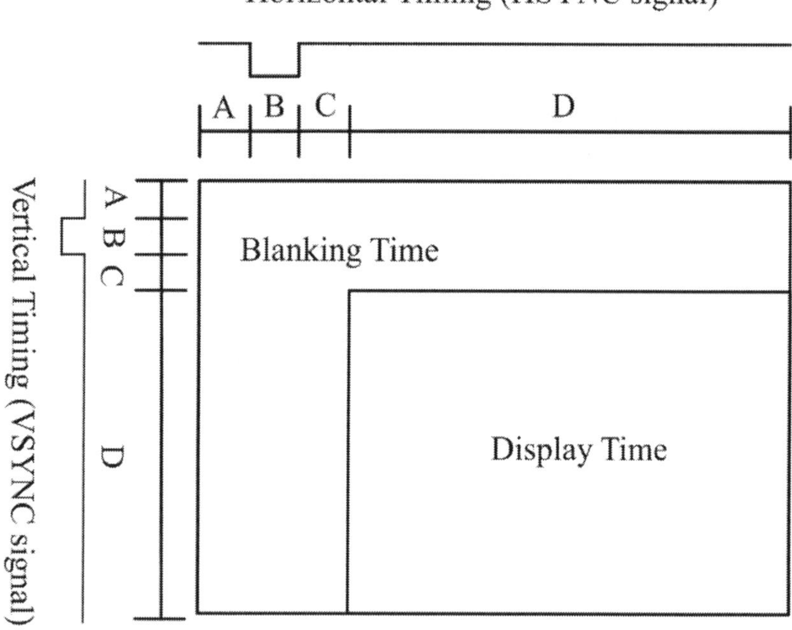

Figure 10.2.5 VGA Timming

Now that it has been covered what synchronization signals need to be injected into the VGA display, we can now write a module to replicate them. To begin, the code below shows how to replicate the waveform for the horizontal sync shown in Figure 10.2.3.

HSYNC Generation

```
`timescale 1ns / 1ps

module VGA(Clock,HSYNC);
   input Clock;
   output reg HSYNC;

   wire Pixel_Clock;
   reg [9:0] hs = 0;
   reg [3:0] hs_Interval = 0;

   CLK100MHZ_divider IN0(Clock, Pixel_Clock);

   always @(posedge Pixel_Clock) begin
      if(hs < 799) hs <= hs + 1; // incriment horizontal count
      if(hs == 799) hs <= 0; // end of the line and reset the horizontal count
   end

   // This sets HSYNC low during hs_Interval = B, and high every other time
   always @(*) begin
      if(hs_Interval == 4'hB) HSYNC = 0;
      else HSYNC = 1;
   end

   // This combinational always block updates hs_Interval for simulation purposes
   always @(*) begin
      if(hs < 16) hs_Interval <= 4'hA; // 16 clock cycles long
      if(hs > 15 && hs < 112) hs_Interval <= 4'hB; // 96 clock cycles long
      if(hs > 111 && hs < 160) hs_Interval <= 4'hC; // 48 clock cycles long
      if(hs > 159 && hs < 800) hs_Interval <= 4'hD; // 640 clock cycles long
   end

endmodule

module CLK100MHZ_divider(CLK100MHZ, New_Clock);
   input wire CLK100MHZ;      // Input clock signal
   output reg New_Clock;

   // Initialize Clock to 0 for simulation purposes
   initial begin
      New_Clock = 1'b0;
   end
```

```
42
43    // Divided clock output
44    reg [31:0] count = 0; // [31:0] is large enough to hold any value
45    always @(posedge CLK100MHZ) begin
46       count <= count + 1;  // Increment count
47       if (count == 32'd1) begin
48          New_Clock <= ~New_Clock; // Toggle New Clock
49          count <= 32'b0;          // Reset count
50       end
51    end
52 endmodule
```

Lines 34-52 create a 25 MHz clock using the clock divider module, and line 11 instantiates it into the top-level module. It is fine to use a 25MHZ clock instead of a 25.175MHZ clock. Lines 13-16 make a register named "hs" periodically cycle from 0 to 799. The time intervals from Figure 10.2.3 are shown again for your convenience using the inequality below. Using the inequality below, lines 25-30 keep track of the interval with the register "hs_Interval". Lines 19-22 make it so that HSYNC is zero only during interval B and one everywhere else, implementing the HSYNC waveform specified in Figure 10.2.3.

$$\text{Interval} = \begin{cases} A, & hs < 16 \\ B, & 15 < hs < 112 \\ C, & 111 < hs < 160 \\ D, & 159 < hs < 800 \end{cases}$$

Figure 10.2.6 Interval as a function of register "hs"

To simulate the code above to see for yourself that we have indeed flawlessly replicated the waveform from Figure 10.2.3, use the following QR code. When you launch the simulation, change the radix of the hs signal to be in unsigned decimal. You will see that each region lasts for the exact amount of clock cycles specified by the inequality above.

The next step is to replicate the VSYNC waveform described by Figure 10.2.4. If you're highly ambitious, you may want to attempt this part yourself. Regardless, the code that follows generates the vertical sync waveform and the explanation is provided.

HSYNC & VSYNC Generation

```
`timescale 1ns / 1ps

module VGA(Clock,HSYNC,VSYNC);
   input Clock;
   output reg HSYNC,VSYNC;

   wire Pixel_Clock;
   reg [9:0] hs = 0;
```

```
    reg [9:0] vs = 0;
    reg [3:0] hs_Interval = 0; // register for simulation purposes
    reg [3:0] vs_Interval = 0; // register for simulation purposes

    CLK100MHZ_divider IN0(Clock, Pixel_Clock);

    always @(posedge Pixel_Clock) begin
        if(hs < 799) hs <= hs + 1; // incriment horizontal count
        if(hs == 799) begin // the end of a line
            if(vs < 524) vs <= vs + 1; // incriment vertical count
            if(vs == 524) vs <= 0; // reset vertical count
            hs <= 0; // reset horizontal count
        end
    end

    // This sets HSYNC low during hs_Interval = B, and high every other time
    always @(*) begin
        if(hs_Interval == 4'hB) HSYNC = 0;
        else HSYNC = 1;
    end

    // This sets VSYNC low during vs_Interval = B, and high every other time
    always @(*) begin
        if(hs_Interval == 4'hB) VSYNC = 0;
        else VSYNC = 1;
    end

    // This combinational always block updates hs_Interval for simulation purposes
    always @(*) begin
        if(hs < 16) hs_Interval <= 4'hA; // 16 clock cycles long
        if(hs > 15 && hs < 112) hs_Interval <= 4'hB; // 96 clock cycles long
        if(hs > 111 && hs < 160) hs_Interval <= 4'hC; // 48 clock cycles long
        if(hs > 159 && hs < 800) hs_Interval <= 4'hD; // 640 clock cycles long
    end

    // This combinational always block updates vs_Interval for simulation purposes
    always @(*) begin
        if(vs < 10) vs_Interval <= 4'hA; // 10 line cycles long
        if(vs > 9 && vs < 12) vs_Interval <= 4'hB; // 2 line cycles long
        if(vs > 11 && vs < 45) vs_Interval <= 4'hC; // 33 line cycles long
        if(vs > 44 && vs < 525) vs_Interval <= 4'hD; // 480 line cycles long
    end

endmodule

module CLK100MHZ_divider(CLK100MHZ, New_Clock);
```

```
55     input wire CLK100MHZ;      // Input clock signal
56     output reg New_Clock;
57
58     // Initialize Clock to 0 for simulation purposes
59     initial begin
60        New_Clock = 1'b0;
61     end
62
63     // Divided clock output
64     reg [31:0] count = 0; // [31:0] is large enough to hold any value
65     always @(posedge CLK100MHZ) begin
66        count <= count + 1;  // Increment count
67        if (count == 32'd1) begin
68           New_Clock <= ~New_Clock; // Toggle New Clock
69           count <= 32'b0;          // Reset count
70        end
71     end
72  endmodule
```

To replicate the VSYNC waveform, the previous code was modified by adding lines 9, 11, 18, 19, 31-34, and 45-50. Line 9 defines register "vs" and line 11 defines register "vs_Interval". Lines 18 and 19 are part of the if statement that determines when the current line ends, allowing the "vs" register to increment each time a line ends and to reset after detecting 525 lines. Lines 31-34 make it so that VSYNC is zero only during interval B and one everywhere else, implementing the VSYNC waveform specified in Figure 10.2.4. Using the inequality below, lines 45-50 keep track of the interval with the register "vs_Interval".

$$\text{Interval} = \begin{cases} A, & vs < 10 \\ B, & 9 < vs < 12 \\ C, & 11 < vs < 45 \\ D, & 44 < vs < 525 \end{cases}$$

Figure 10.2.7 Interval as a function of register "vs"

To simulate the code above to see for yourself that we have indeed flawlessly replicated the waveforms from Figure 10.2.4, use the following QR code. When you launch the simulation, change the radix of the hs and vs signals to be in unsigned decimal. You will see that each region lasts for the exact number of clock cycles specified

Now that HSYNC and VSYNC have been replicated, the hardest part is complete. The next step is to input the appropriate pixel values during the display time. To illustrate the end goal clearly, I'll show what the final waveform should look like when zoomed into the portion where the display period is just starting. This waveform is shown in Figure 10.2.8.

The display time occurs when both HSYNC and VSYNC are in interval D. On the waveform, this means when "hs_Interval" and "vs_Interval" are both equal to D. Conversely, the blanking time is anytime "hs_Interval" or "vs_Interval" is not equal to D. According to the VGA standard, as specified in Figures 10.2.3 and 10.2.4, the pixel data is active only during the display time and zero during the blanking time. During the display time, each tick of the pixel clock shifts a new set of RGB values into the VGA display, which can be seen in the waveform below.

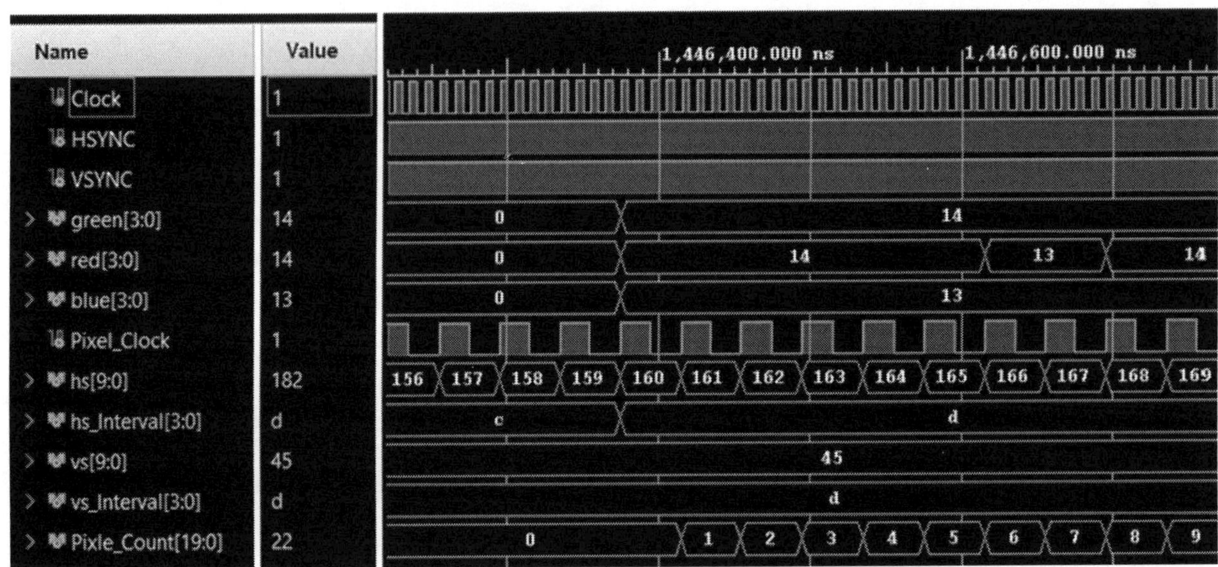

Figure 10.2.8 Waveform showing the start of display region

For example, looking at the waveform in Figure 10.2.8, when the display interval begins at hs = 160, the first set of RGB information is updated and sent to the VGA display. The display assigns the leftmost pixel in line 1 an RGB value of {Green, Red, Blue} = {14, 14, 13}. According to the waveform, the first six pixels of line 1 will have this RGB value. However, when the 7th pixel is displayed at Pixel_Count = 6, it will have an RGB value of {Green, Red, Blue} = {14, 13, 13}. This RGB updating process continues for the first line until the 640th pixel is reached at Pixel_Count = 639. Then, it resets and continues the process for line 2, from Pixel_Count = 640 to Pixel_Count = 1279. This cycle continues indefinitely until the first frame is finished at Pixel_Count = 307,199. Remember that there are 307,200 pixels per frame, and since Pixel_Count is indexed starting at 0, its final value should be 307,199, not 307,200.

Now that we understand how to inject signals into the VGA display through the color channels to manually create an image, the question now is what circuitry should be made? Well, the answer is to create three clocked ROMS to store 307,200 values for each color. Then by having the "Pixel_Count" and "Pixel_Clock" tied to the address and clock of each ROM, the correct RGB values will be shifted out during the display time with each tick of the pixel clock. The schematic that follows shows the structural design that needs to be made. Note that in addition to the ROMs, there are multiplexers to reset all color channels to zero when a reset signal is high. This will be important for setting the colors to zero during the blanking period. This is extremely important, since not doing that will result in a corrupt image.

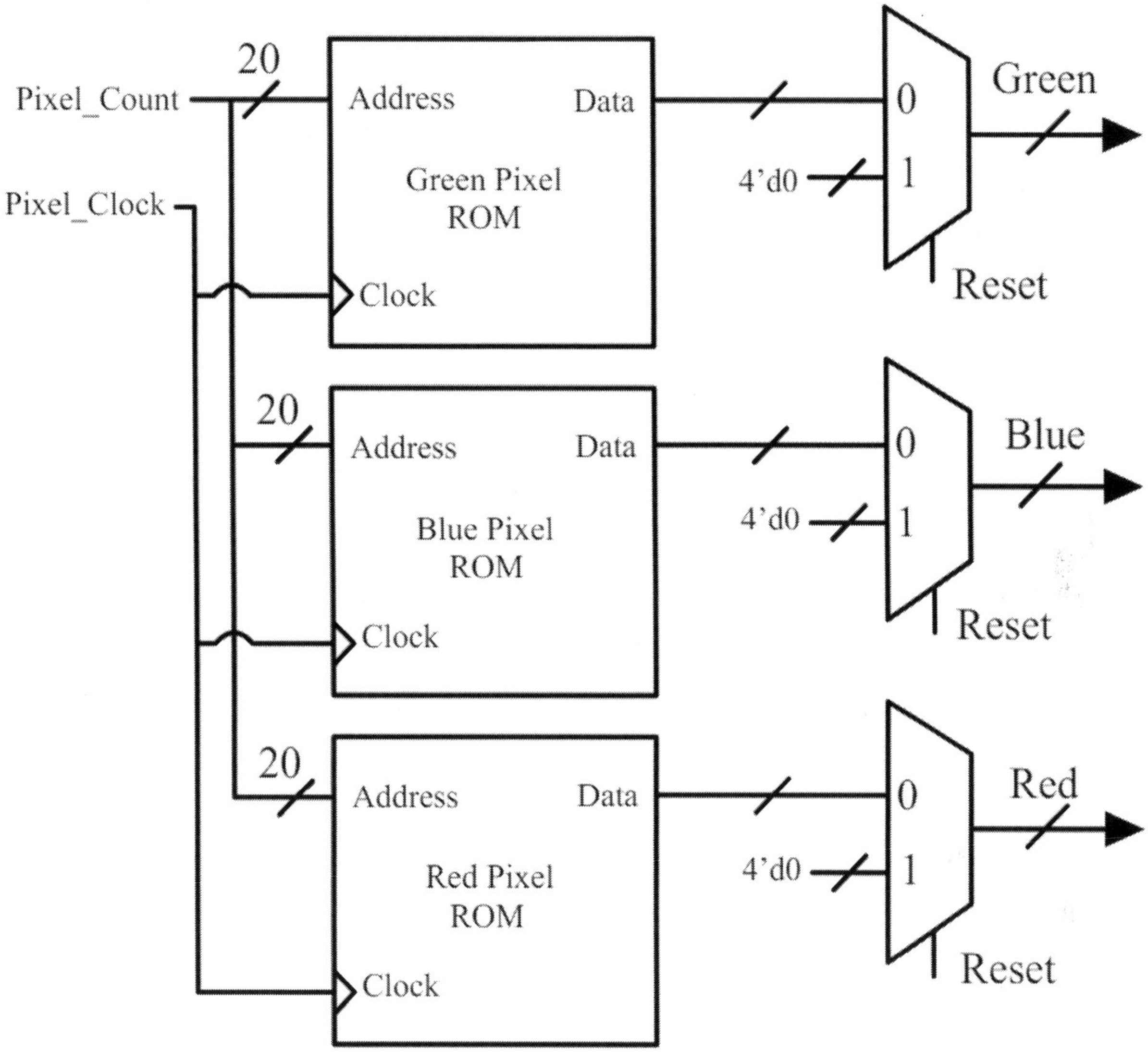

Pixel_Count
Pixel_Clock
20
Address
Data
Green Pixel
ROM
Clock
4'd0
0
1
Green
Reset
20
Address
Data
Blue Pixel
ROM
Clock
4'd0
0
1
Blue
Reset
20
Address
Data
Red Pixel
ROM
Clock
4'd0
0
1
Red
Reset

Figure 10.2.8 Structural Design for pixel data control

Also, note that a clock was used by each ROM because this always results in Vivado synthesizing using BRAM to implement the memory, enabling less race conditions. If you use a purely combinational ROM with no clock, then the synthesizer will use LUT's to implement the memory unit instead of its dedicated high-speed memory in BRAM, which will create race conditions, resulting in an image that has a few distorted pixels. Knowing how to take advantage of the FPGA's dedicated memory is part of being an FPGA engineer. Ideally, you would be able to design assuming the parts are going to work like they should, but unfortunately that's not how the world works, which is why optimization methods like using clocks in ROMs are necessary.

The final step now is to modify the code where we replicated HSYNC and VSYNC signals by incorporating the structural design shown in Figure 10.2.8. If you're highly ambitious, you may want to attempt it yourself. Regardless, the final code and explanation is shown next.

Final VGA Code

```
`timescale 1ns / 1ps

module VGA(Clock,HSYNC,VSYNC,red,green,blue);
   input Clock;
   output [3:0] red,green,blue;
   output reg HSYNC,VSYNC;

   wire Pixel_Clock;
   reg [9:0] hs = 0;
   reg [9:0] vs = 0;
   reg [19:0] Pixle_Count = 0;
   reg Reset = 0;
   reg [3:0] hs_Interval = 0; // register for simulation purposes
   reg [3:0] vs_Interval = 0; // register for simulation purposes
   wire [3:0] green_ROM,blue_ROM,red_ROM;

   // Structural Design for Pixel data Control //

   CLK100MHZ_divider IN0(Clock, Pixel_Clock);

   ROM0 IN00(Pixle_Count, Pixel_Clock, green_ROM);
   assign green = Reset ? 4’b0000 : green_ROM;

   ROM1 IN01(Pixle_Count, Pixel_Clock, blue_ROM);
   assign blue = Reset ? 4’b0000 : blue_ROM;

   ROM2 IN02(Pixle_Count, Pixel_Clock, red_ROM);
   assign red = Reset ? 4’b0000 : red_ROM;

   // Reset signal for memory units
   always@(*) begin
      if(hs_Interval != 4’hD || vs_Interval != 4’hD) Reset = 1; // Sets Reset during blanking periods
      else Reset = 0;
   end

   always @(posedge Pixel_Clock) begin
      if(hs_Interval == 4’hD && vs_Interval == 4’hD) Pixle_Count <= Pixle_Count + 1;
      if(Pixle_Count == 307199) Pixle_Count <= 0;
      if(hs < 799) hs <= hs + 1; // incriment horizontal count
      if(hs == 799) begin // the end of a line
         if(vs < 524) vs <= vs + 1; // incriment vertical count
         if(vs == 524) vs <= 0; // reset vertical count
         hs <= 0; // reset horizontal count
      end
   end

   // This sets HSYNC low during hs_Interval = B, and high every other time
   always @(*) begin
      if(hs_Interval == 4’hB) HSYNC = 0;
```

```
      else HSYNC = 1;
   end

   // This sets VSYNC low during vs_Interval = B, and high every other time
   always @(*) begin
      if(vs_Interval == 4'hB) VSYNC = 0;
      else VSYNC = 1;
   end

   // This combinational always block updates hs_Interval for simulation purposes
   always @(*) begin
      if(hs < 16) hs_Interval <= 4'hA; // 16 clock cycles long
      if(hs > 15 && hs < 112) hs_Interval <= 4'hB; // 96 clock cycles long
      if(hs > 111 && hs < 160) hs_Interval <= 4'hC; // 48 clock cycles long
      if(hs > 159 && hs < 800) hs_Interval <= 4'hD; // 640 clock cycles long
   end

   // This combinational always block updates vs_Interval for simulation purposes
   always @(*) begin
      if(vs < 10) vs_Interval <= 4'hA; // 10 line cycles long
      if(vs > 9 && vs < 12) vs_Interval <= 4'hB; // 2 line cycles long
      if(vs > 11 && vs < 45) vs_Interval <= 4'hC; // 33 line cycles long
      if(vs > 44 && vs < 525) vs_Interval <= 4'hD; // 480 line cycles long
   end

endmodule

module CLK100MHZ_divider(CLK100MHZ, New_Clock);
   input wire CLK100MHZ;      // Input clock signal
   output reg New_Clock;

   // Initialize Clock to 0 for simulation purposes
   initial begin
      New_Clock = 1'b0;
   end

   // Divided clock output
   reg [31:0] count = 0; // [31:0] is large enough to hold any value
   always @(posedge CLK100MHZ) begin
      count <= count + 1;  // Increment count
      if (count == 32'd1) begin
         New_Clock <= ~New_Clock; // Toggle New Clock
         count <= 32'b0;         // Reset count
      end
   end
endmodule

(* rom_style = "block" *)

module ROM0(Address, Clock, Data);
   input wire [19:0] Address; // 20-bit address for addressing up to 2^20 = 1048576 locations
```

```
  input wire Clock; // VGA Pixle Clock
  output reg [3:0] Data; // 4-bit data from each location

  reg [3:0] memory[0:307199];

  initial begin
    $readmemb("green.mem", memory); // Load binary data from "green.mem" into memory
  end

  always@(posedge Clock) begin
    Data <= memory[Address]; // Retrieve data based on the Address input
  end
endmodule

(* rom_style = "block" *)

module ROM1(Address, Clock, Data);
  input wire [19:0] Address; // 20-bit address for addressing up to 2^20 = 1048576 locations
  input wire Clock; // VGA Pixle Clock
  output reg [3:0] Data; // 4-bit data from each location

  reg [3:0] memory[0:307199];

  initial begin
    $readmemb("blue.mem", memory); // Load binary data from "blue.mem" into memory
  end

  always@(posedge Clock) begin
    Data <= memory[Address]; // Retrieve data based on the Address input
  end
endmodule

(* rom_style = "block" *)

module ROM2(Address, Clock, Data);
  input wire [19:0] Address; // 20-bit address for addressing up to 2^20 = 1048576 locations
  input wire Clock; // VGA Pixle Clock
  output reg [3:0] Data; // 4-bit data from each location

  reg [3:0] memory[0:307199];

  initial begin
    $readmemb("red.mem", memory); // Load binary data from "red.mem" into memory
  end

  always@(posedge Clock) begin
    Data <= memory[Address]; // Retrieve data based on the Address input
  end
endmodule
```

To begin, the three ROMs were created in lines 97-149 using the memory file method discussed in section 4.4. This approach was chosen because manually typing out 307,200 values for each color is impractical. Instead, the memory files were automatically generated by uploading an image into a computer program that converted it into three text files, each containing 307,200 values for red, green, and blue. The line "(* rom_style = "block" *)" was placed above each ROM module to suggest to the synthesizer that BRAM should be used.

Lines 21, 24, and 27 implement the ROMs, and lines 22, 25, and 28 implement the multiplexers shown in Figure 10.2.8. To ensure the "Reset" signal from Figure 10.2.8 was correctly generated, lines 31-34 set the reset signal high during blanking periods and low during display periods. This results in the RGB values from the ROMs being output only during the display time and zero at all other times.

To correctly generate the "Pixel_Address" signal from Figure 10.2.8, line 37 increments it only during the display time, and line 38 resets it to zero once the final pixel of the frame has been updated. Finally, line 19 generates the "Pixel_Clock" by dividing the 100MHz clock into a 25MHz clock.

To simulate the code above to see for yourself that we have indeed flawlessly implemented a VGA controller that manually generates any image, use the following QR code, download the files, and upload them to your board. The QR code includes not only the source and constraint files, but also the test bench, memory files, and the MATLAB program used. It is highly recommended to upload the project to your board and simulate it to further understand what is going on.

10.3 – Final Remarks & Tips

Now that you have been given a very precise and thorough demonstration of how to generate an image using a VGA display, you will need to apply what you have learned to make a Verilog program that alternates between red, green, and blue on a VGA screen indefinitely. To do this, you must have the RGB values alternate between {Green, Red, Blue} = {15, 0, 0}, {0, 15, 0}, and {0, 0, 15} for a controlled amount of time to make the VGA screen change colors.

If you choose to do it structurally, you may encounter some complexities. For example, simply having the first frame be green, the next frame red, and the one after blue may not be sufficient, as the display operates at 60 frames per second, causing the changes to occur too quickly to be noticeable. You might need to intentionally display each color for 60 frames before switching to make the changes visible.

A behavioral approach is recommended, where you use a case statement to alternate between the three colors on the rising edge of a slow clock. This method simplifies the process, as it allows you to avoid the intricate details required in structural approaches.

Final Message

Now that you have completely read through all the chapters, you should have a very good idea now on how to use Verilog. If you were able to complete all the labs, then you should be very proud. I say this because as a practicing engineer who uses Verilog to solve real problems, the topics in the labs are really all you need to implement SPI interfaces, frequency counters, clock recovery programs, state machines, and more. Obviously, there are more advanced topics that are beyond the scope of this book, but if you understood the labs, then you can already implement the projects I stated in the previous sentence. Before you go move on from this book and put it on the shelf, I would like to say a few things.

To start off, I encourage you to have an attitude of service in your engineering career and for any career you may choose. Make it your mission in life to have the best impact on the world that you can. As engineers, we all have the **potential** to have a huge impact in people's lives. Note how I must emphasize "potential". The truth is, not all people who graduate with a bachelor's in engineering go on to change the world, yet alone get a job that even requires using their degree. I strongly encourage you to do your very best to be the best engineer you can be. Don't shoot for barely passing. Shoot for an A always. Shoot for fully understanding everything you can, even if it means waking up early every time to go to office hours. The truth is, to learn engineering well, you need to spend way more time than is needed to barely pass your classes and get a degree. When your classmates only study for 15 hours a week, I encourage you to study 40. When your classmates only spend a few hours getting a homework assignment done without completely understanding it, I encourage you to spend as long as needed to understand everything, even if it means spending three as much time or even waking up early to go to office hours.

The truth is that on average, the only people in the world who have the power to do something that matters, that is, something that can have a positive impact on many people's lives, are people who have the position or skills to do so. You might be thinking it's impossible to have a meaningful impact without being born some superhuman or a millionaire, but that's just not at all true. When you're a student, do your best to learn the content, try your absolute hardest, even if it means working weekends. Be the person who your peers are inspired and motivated by.

I encourage you to make it your mission to have the greatest mark on the world you can. Work hard. Be kind to people. If you truly make this your goal, everything should fall into place, both for you, and for those around you. As far as we know, you only get **one shot** at life, so **make it count**.

Made in the USA
Columbia, SC
10 August 2024

39782841R00163